Mysticism and Intellect in Medieval Christianity and Buddhism

Mysticism and Intellect in Medieval Christianity and Buddhism

Ascent and Awakening
Bonaventure and Chinul

Yongho Francis Lee

LEXINGTON BOOKS
Lanham • Boulder • New York • London

Published by Lexington Books
An imprint of The Rowman & Littlefield Publishing Group, Inc.
4501 Forbes Boulevard, Suite 200, Lanham, Maryland 20706
www.rowman.com

6 Tinworth Street, London SE11 5AL, United Kingdom

Chapters 2, 4
Chinul, Pojo. *Numinous Awareness Is Never Dark: The Korean Buddhist Master Chinul's Excerpts on Zen Practice*. Translated with introduction and annotations by Robert E. Buswell Jr. Honolulu: University of Hawaii Press, 2016.

Chinul, Pojo. *Selected Works*. Translated with introduction and annotations by Robert E. Buswell Jr. Vol. 2 of *Collected Works of Korean Buddhism* (Seoul: Jogye Order of Korean Buddhism, 2012)

Chapter 3
Bonaventure. *Itinerarium Mentis in Deum*. Translated by Zachary Hayes. Introduction and "Notes & Commentary" by Philotheus Boehner. Vol. 2 of *Works of St. Bonaventure*. Rev. ed. St. Bonaventure, NY: Franciscan Institute, 2002.

British Library Cataloguing in Publication Information Available

Library of Congress Control Number: 2020900547

ISBN: 978-1-7936-0070-7 (cloth : alk. paper)
ISBN: 978-1-7936-0072-1 (pbk : alk. paper)
ISBN: 978-1-7936-0071-4 (electronic)

♾️™ The paper used in this publication meets the minimum requirements of American National Standard for Information Sciences—Permanence of Paper for Printed Library Materials, ANSI/NISO Z39.48-1992.

To Kenan B. Osborne, OFM

Contents

Acknowledgments

This book is the fruit of a long period of learning and reflection. There are many who have inspired and prepared me for this task, without whom I would not have been able to start or complete this book. Some people have provided me with necessary in-depth or broad knowledge, some with profound insights, and others with moral and emotional support. Thanks to all of these individuals, I was able to balance my own intellectual life and spiritual life in the course of writing this book.

First, I should express my gratitude to Sr. Ilia Delio. I had my first serious encounter with Bonaventure a decade ago in her seminar class on Bonaventure. She introduced me to the world of Bonaventure, a person of mind and heart and at the core of whose intellectual works was always charity. The seed of this book was planted in that year in the classroom with her.

I also want to thank Sr. Margaret Guider, OFS, with the Boston College School of Theology and Ministry. Her support and encouragement as my academic adviser at Boston College did not end after two years of graduate studies, but continued through my doctoral studies and even afterward. She always showed her support in my interest in comparative studies between East and West. Among many professors at BC, I should also express my gratitude to Prof. John Makransky in the Theology Department. His classes on Buddhism provided me with a good foundation for further study. I am also indebted to Fr. Francis Clooney, SJ, also from my time in Boston, who inspired my interest in and pursuit of comparative studies. I always remember his advice that I should develop my own way of doing comparative theology as an Asian scholar rooted in the Asian context.

This book comes out of my doctoral dissertation at the University of Notre Dame. For the six years there, I was guided and accompanied by many professors and colleagues in the World Religions and World Church program in the Department of Theology. I remember the heartfelt words of encouragement from Matthew Kuiper, Alison Fitchett-Climenhaga, and Fr. Enno Dango, CP. I also want to extend my gratitude to Sr. Ann Astell and Prof. David A. Clairmont, who, respectively, guided my research with their expertise in medieval theology and profound knowledge of Buddhism. This book could never have happened without the intellectual and moral support of Prof. Robert M. Gimello, my academic adviser at Notre Dame. From the start of my doctoral studies, he guided me in reading Buddhist texts in Classical Chinese. These sessions helped me understand the importance of reading original texts in developing an intimate understanding of a religion. All of his patient explanations, plus our debates and casual conversations about textual materials, expanded my knowledge of Buddhism and, more importantly, helped me develop my own approach to the comparative study of Buddhism and Christianity. He is an exemplary model of a scholar who manages to balance the spiritual and intellectual life.

I could not have begun or completed this project without the permission, moral support, encouragement, and patience of my Franciscan brothers in Korea. I also received the constant support of my family, which sustained me throughout a long period of study abroad. I cannot fully express my gratitude to all of them. I should also mention the religious communities that kindly allowed me to stay with them—the Franciscan brothers of Holy Name College in Silver Spring, Maryland; the Discalced Carmelite brothers in Brighton, Massachusetts; the Conventual Franciscan brothers in Mishawaka, Indiana; and the Holy Cross brothers and fathers at Notre Dame. Their fraternal love and care nourished not only my body but also my spiritual and intellectual life. Although my beloved mother and father are no longer present on Earth, I feel their unceasing love and support. They planted and nurtured the seeds of whatever I achieve in this life.

I would like to extend my gratitude to Lexington Books for publishing this book. I especially thank Michael Gibson and Mikayla Mislak, who were interested in the project, kindly provided me with guidance in publication, and patiently waited for the manuscript. I feel fortunate that they are my publication editors. I also want to thank Gregory Black, who provided editorial assistance at the beginning of the process of publication. His help made this book more readable.

I am saddened that Fr. Kenan B. Osborne, OFM, did not live to see this book published. Fr. Kenan, who passed away on April 19, 2019, enriched my research not only with his expertise on Bonaventure and the Franciscan intellectual and spiritual tradition, but also with his constant support, expressed through his genuine smile, encouraging words, and fraternal love.

He was very interested in learning about other religions and cultures and valued my comparative work. He had more confidence in me than I did. He was a role model for me by demonstrating how a Franciscan friar who is also a scholar should live. I dedicate this book to him, my teacher, my friend, and my brother.

Introduction

Most would agree that prayer, ritual, charity, and scriptural and doctrinal study are all essential parts of religious life, but there have been debates among adherents of religious traditions as to which of these should take precedence. Should the intellectual endeavors of scriptural and doctrinal study or experiential practices like meditation and contemplation be emphasized? Those who emphasize learning and study argue that without a proper intellectual understanding of a religion's fundamental teachings, not only might practitioners fall prey to errors and heresies, but their practice might not be fruitful because it would be directed toward an improper end far from salvation and liberation. On the other hand, advocates of contemplative or mystical experience and practice often insist that any attempts to comprehend the ultimate truth of a religion by intellectual effort alone are insufficient, and perhaps even harmful. Intellectualism, they insist, hinders a sincere practitioner from having a direct encounter with the absolute reality. The tension between those who advocate intellectual study and those who advocate meditative practice is associated with different views about the role of language and intellect and even how to understand the nature of the religious ultimate. Is it to be attained by a process of negation, for which apophatic or negative discourse, which relates more to what God is rather than what God presumably is, and practices of denial are required and the transcendence of the religious ultimate is stressed. Or is it to be attained by processes of affirmation, for which cataphatic or affirmative discourse and affirmative modes of piety and practice are required, as part of which the immanence of the religious ultimate is emphasized?

This book deals with these fundamental issues by exploring how they have been grappled with by two major world religions, Christianity and Buddhism.

1

Christianity, historically the dominant religion in the West, has attracted a large number of followers from every region of the world. It is a theistic religion that distinguishes the creator (or God) from the created. The unbridgeable gulf between God and the human being is addressed in various ways in theistic world religions, and differentiated degrees of emphasis on that gulf entail different approaches to various challenges facing these religions, including striking a proper balance between the intellectual and spiritual life. Buddhism, which has been the dominant religion in the East, is extending its intellectual and spiritual influence in the West. This nontheistic religion rejects the idea of an absolute being like God—although its cosmology includes heavenly deities, these celestial beings are not considered to be much different from human beings; they are certainly not seen as absolute beings in the way that Christians understand God. Despite denying the existence of God, Buddhism too is challenged by a tension between different understandings of the ultimate reality of the world, a tension that is arguably analogous to the Christian tension between the transcendence and immanence of God. This tension is at the root of varying approaches to study and meditation in Buddhism.

It is the intention of the author that this comparative investigation of Christianity and Buddhism will promote a better understanding of these religions generally. This is accomplished through a close study of two particular religious masters, one Christian and one Buddhist, against the broader backdrop of the religious reality pertaining to each religion and of the religious dynamics within their religious orders. Moreover, it is hoped that this focused study of the tensions embedded in the theoretical and practical realms of religious life of these two world religions—one theistic and the other nontheistic—will lead committed religious practitioners in both to acknowledge the complexity of religious life as it manifests itself in the course of pursuing seemingly unattainable religious goals. It will also invite scholars and practitioners to a further and ongoing conversation with other religions, in which they may gain new insights for deepening their understanding of their own religious tradition.

By focusing on Christianity and Buddhism, it is hoped that this study will also facilitate connections between East and West, not only of a cultural, religious, and social nature, but also connections within the personal experience of individuals. Numerous Easterners and Westerners have had meaningful encounters with both religions in the course of their religious practices or intellectual pursuits; for example, Asian Christians who grew up in a Buddhist society or Western scholars of Buddhism whose cultural and religious identity has been formed in the Christian environment of the West.

The tensions between different modes of religious discourse, practice, and doctrine can first be noted in relation to Buddhism. For Buddhists, the ultimate goal of religious practice is to come to know the true nature of reality, for Buddhists believe that in this quest craving is eliminated, and that with the elimination of craving comes the cessation of suffering. Although every religious activity in Buddhism is essentially directed toward this end, most Buddhists insist that true reality is ineffable and inconceivable, beyond the reach of language and conceptual thought, and therefore accessible only to highly advanced practitioners. Some Buddhists argue that there exist two kinds or levels of truth—absolute or ultimate and relative or conventional— and that mere learning and study through the medium of language and the function of intellect leads a practitioner only to the second. Some go so far as to warn that any reliance on language in the pursuit of the ultimate (or at least reliance on affirmative language) may actually lead one to mistake relative truth for absolute truth and turn the pragmatic value of relative truth into an object of attachment and thus into an impediment to liberation. From these considerations arise pressing questions; for example, what use can be made of scriptural reading and speculative study in the religious life of a Buddhist practitioner, or, for that matter, of a practitioner of any religion? And if use of language as is required in scriptural study and doctrinal argument is to be dispensed with or devalued, how can Buddhism or any religion communicate its essential teachings to the whole of humanity, not to mention its own followers? If the inefficacy of verbal and intellectual comprehension of the ultimate or infinite should be overemphasized, neither Buddhism nor any other religion would be able to sustain itself. Religion would lose a necessary tool to develop and spread its teachings, and for Buddhists in particular, would in the end fail to attain its soteriological goal of enlightenment and saving humanity from the incessant cycle of suffering.

Among the various Buddhist traditions, questions about the relationship between language and reality and between intellectual study and spiritual advancement were especially urgent and subject to controversy in Chan Buddhism (the Chinese term for Sŏn in Korean and Zen in Japanese). Whereas some Chan traditions were quite forceful in their denigration of learning and doctrinal theorizing as paths to enlightenment, others recognized their practical utility as propaedeutics, and rather than discarding them, advocated for their incorporation into meditative practice. One of the two focuses of this book, the medieval Korean Sŏn monk Pojo Chinul (1158–1210), chose the latter route and urged the reconciliation of learned Buddhism with Chan practice. By Chinul's time in the twelfth century, Korean Buddhism had grown weary of the long-standing conflict between Sŏn, the meditative school, and the various schools of learned Buddhism, collectively known as Kyo, especially Hwaŏm (C. Huayan).

Chinul devoted much of his career to effecting a reconciliation of these two competing groups. He saw the conflict between them as futile and wasteful, and argued that, despite their seeming differences, it was possible to bring them into harmony with each other. Specifically, he strove to show that the Sŏn emphasis on contemplative practice and the Kyo emphasis on doctrinal and scriptural study were not really antithetical, but were, instead, actually complementary insofar as study was a necessary foundation for Sŏn practice.

This complicated relationship between scriptural and theoretical study and meditative practice in Buddhism has an analog in Christianity in the tension related to different levels of emphasis on intellectual and spiritual life. Implicit in this tension are two deeper ones. The first involves an understanding of the divine as immanent versus an understanding that it is transcendent, and the second relates to the differences between positive and negative modes of discourse about the divine. Whereas an emphasis on the immanence of God would seem to support the use of affirmative or cataphatic discourses, an emphasis on His transcendence would seem to demand the privileging of apophatic discourse and negative theology.

In reality, the Christian tradition has always found value in both positive and negative theological discourse. After all, Christians believe that God, transcendent though he surely is, made Himself manifest in Christ and *spoke*, His speech having been recorded in scripture, in which He told human beings both what He is and what He is not. No one saw this more clearly than the great fifth/sixth-century Syrian theologian known as Pseudo-Dionysius, renowned as the father of "negative theology," as exemplified in his work *The Mystical Theology*. Pseudo-Dionysius is also revered for his cataphatic theology as developed in two other surviving works, *The Divine Names* and *The Celestial Hierarchy*.

These two strains of theology, both explicated by Pseudo-Dionysius, have, with varying degrees of emphasis on each, greatly contributed to the development of Christian theological and practical traditions. While both cataphatic and apophatic theologies are employed in the speculative theology and spiritual practice of Christianity, it may be said that spirituality, and especially what is commonly called "mysticism," tends to have an affinity with apophatic theology, while cataphatic theology is usually seen in connection with more speculative, constructive, and systematic modes of theology. The relationship between speculative theology and spirituality may be said to be analogous to the relationship between cataphasis and apophasis (though not completely so). For this reason, the tension between theology and spirituality resonates with the tension between cataphasis and apophasis.

Buddhism somewhat resembles Christianity in this regard, for it harbors a similar historical tension, that between its emphasis on scriptural, doctrinal study on the one hand and on meditative practice on the other. As briefly mentioned, Chinul, the Sŏn master, strove to resolve this tension, and Bonaventure of Bagnoregio (ca. 1217–1274), the thirteenth-century Franciscan master, could be considered his Christian counterpart. Bonaventure exerted himself toward reconciling two contending groups within his own Franciscan Order (the Order of Friars Minor): one group, holding to the ideal of poverty and simplicity, insisted on a life full of spiritual zeal, whereas the other, mindful of the church's need to preach and minister, was engaged in learning and in the intellectual training of friars. As both a talented theologian who was educated and taught at a prestigious university in Europe and a man of deep mysticism who was inspired by the life of St. Francis of Assisi (1181/1182–1226), it was Bonaventure's task to show that theology and spirituality can be integrated in the service of the one soteriological goal of union with God.

This book is a comparative study of Christian and Buddhist attempts to reconcile the two competing models of religious life. It demonstrates that, for both Bonaventure and Chinul, respectable masters well versed in religious knowledge who emphasized meditative and spiritual practice, scriptural and theological study do not impede such practice, but rather can be an aid to it by providing necessary theoretical grounding. Both men demonstrated that a contemplative life does not preclude a life of learning. These integrative endeavors are explored in relation to doctrinal tensions and different modes of discourse within each religion.

Chapters 1 and 2 explore the ways in which these two figures applied learned teachings to spiritual practice: Bonaventure's synthesis of theology and spirituality in chapter 1, and Chinul's incorporation of Kyo into Sŏn practice in chapter 2. In their investigation of the integrative efforts of the two masters, these chapters analyze the tensions between and the complementarity of study and spiritual life, understood as the two essential dimensions of the religious life.

Chapter 3 proceeds by investigating the analogous underlying tension between cataphatic and apophatic religious discourses, showing its relationship to the tension between study and practice. After surveying the historical development of the Dionysian distinction between cataphasis and apophasis, this chapter further analyzes Bonaventure's articulation of the spiritual exercises set forth in the *Itinerarium*, examining how his emphasis on cataphasis and apophasis changes throughout the successive stages of the spiritual journey described in that work.

Chapter 4 examines the Buddhist analog of the Christian distinction between cataphasis and apophasis, and the relationship between various doctrinal understandings of ultimate reality in Buddhism, most importantly the differences between the doctrines of "buddha-nature" and "emptiness." This chapter also explores the correlations and relationships between the different modes of discourse and different styles of meditative practice in Buddhism.

The relationship among various religious elements—textual and theoretical study, meditation, modes of discourse, and doctrines—will be discussed from the general perspective of the historical development of Chan, and also from the particular perspective of Chinul's Sŏn theory and practice.

Following from these four chapters, the conclusion, after summarizing what has been discussed, shows how Buddhism and Christianity, specifically the representative figures of Chinul and Bonaventure, have negotiated three different tensions within their respective traditions: first, between intellectual and spiritual practice; second, between cataphasis and apophasis; and third, between the doctrines of immanence and transcendence, examining also how these three tensions relate to each other in both traditions.

Chapter One

Bonaventure's Integration of the Intellectual and Spiritual Life

Few observers perceive St. Francis of Assisi, one of the most beloved of all Christian saints, to have been an intellectual man. Some of the epithets most frequently attributed to the saint are *il poverello*—the little poor man—or the lover of creatures, images which do not seem to fit with a person having a sophisticated mind. Though he was not a learned scholar, his followers the Franciscans have established one of the three major intellectual traditions in the history of the Western Catholic Church—along with the Dominicans and Augustinians.[1] The catalogue of eminent Franciscan scholars includes Alexander of Hales (ca. 1185–1245), St. Bonaventure of Bagnoregio (ca. 1217–1274), Roger Bacon (ca. 1210–1292), John Duns Scotus (ca. 1266–1308), and William of Ockham (ca. 1285–1347), to name but a few.[2] Even though most of these medieval scholars, like previous Christian intellectuals, were engaged in "philosophical and theological interpretations of the Catholic Faith,"[3] their way of "doing theology" was different because they employed the methods of "Scholasticism," a highly speculative and systematic intellectual enterprise. Modern readers who encounter their writings can be easily intimidated by their speculative and meticulous reasoning and debates, and may find little that kindles their spiritual zeal.

Our impression of the Scholastic theologians seems to be the opposite of the typical picture of Francis, who was a simple man. Francis might have been short on intellectual sophistication, but he abounded in spiritual zeal. In Franciscan history, Bonaventure of Bagnoregio is one of the main thinkers who was able to bridge these two seemingly disparate aspects of the Franciscan heritage, the intellectual and the spiritual, using his intellectual prowess to present the profound spiritual experiences of Francis in a systematic manner.

7

This chapter explores the integration of intellectual and spiritual life as found in Bonaventure's writings. The first part of the chapter surveys the drastic transformation of the Franciscan movement from a band of simple men inspired by the charism of Francis to a well-organized order (the Order of Friars Minor, also known as the Franciscan Order) governed by educated priests. The second and third parts will investigate Bonaventure's efforts in detail.

HISTORICAL BACKGROUND: THE QUESTION OF EDUCATION IN THE EARLY FRANCISCAN MOVEMENT

St. Francis of Assisi and His Attitude toward Education of the Friars

The Early Development of the Franciscan Intellectual Environment

In 1209, Francis of Assisi received papal approval to form a religious group with a small band of laymen gathered around him in the region of Umbria, Italy. They wanted to live the evangelical life as the Gospels depict it. Francis could not have imagined that the Franciscan movement would grow into one of the most influential religious orders in Christian history.[4] By 1221, the friars numbered somewhere between three and five thousand, and they came from all corners of Europe. The members of the order were no longer solely humble laymen, for by this time, clerics and well-educated theologians were included among their number as well.[5] This rapid growth of a charismatic movement entailed a process of institutionalization as the friars took on an active participation in the task of evangelization. Church authorities had requested that the friars actively engage themselves in evangelization, and this request required the intellectual training of friars.

Watching over the rapid development as well as the clericalization and intellectualization of the order, some of the thirteenth-century friars criticized these changes as an abandonment of their founder's ideal. Even some modern scholars have spoken dismissively of the institutionalization of the order when discussing early Franciscan history.[6] In his general survey of the history of the Franciscan Order, John Moorman identifies four serious problems during its early development involving the observance of poverty, papal grants of privilege, an overemphasis on the priesthood (clericalization), and the friars engaging in higher-level studies (intellectualization).[7] While the four problems identified by Moorman are obviously interconnected, Paul Sabatier explains that Francis saw the potential problems associated with learning as being more serious than the temptation of wealth.[8] The pages to come will investigate how the spread of learning contributed to the intensification of other problems by investigating the friars' embrace of learning as an essential part of Franciscan identity and criticisms of the changes within the order.

Francis's Attitude toward the Pursuit of Learning

Moorman's criticisms of the changes in the order, in particular in regard to learning, were drawn from the author's understanding of Francis's ideal of Christian life and his attitude toward learning. Therefore, it is necessary to examine what Francis himself thought about studies and learning.

Unlike Bonaventure, who was highly intellectual and learned, so much so that he became a master at the University of Paris, Francis of Assisi presents himself as a simple and unlearned man: "And we [Francis and his early companions] were simple and subject to all," and "I have offended the Lord in many ways by my serious faults especially in not observing the Rule that I have promised Him and in not saying the Office as the Rule prescribes either out of negligence or by reason of my weakness or because I am ignorant and [unlearned]."[9] Oktavian Schmucki questions Francis's self-deprecating statement, arguing that he was neither "unlearned" nor stupid. In fact, Francis attended primary school (*schola minor*) at the family's parish church of San Giorgio in Assisi, where he learned to read and write Latin. His Latin was defective in grammar, vocabulary, and spelling, and he might have needed aid from other well-educated friars to grasp the proper understanding of what he read and to polish his writings. Nevertheless, considering the educational situation of his time, in which most lay people were illiterate, his modest education was adequate enough so that he should not be considered "unlearned." Therefore, rather than taking literally the Latin word "idiota," it may be more accurate to keep in mind that Francis is recalling the simple character of the brotherhood as seen in the *The Testament of St. Francis*; he stresses in *A Letter to the Entire Order* the spirit of minority (a humble life) to his order, which began to be characterized by a lax lifestyle because of the pretentious expression of intellectual knowledge and privileges.[10]

In fact, despite his basic level of education, Francis was able to understand the essential meaning of biblical texts. Moreover, taking into consideration his educational level and absence of any formal scriptural or theological training, his knowledge of the scriptures was extraordinary. He developed this knowledge through deep contemplation of the scriptures, arduous prayer, and the continuous exercise of virtues, as Bonaventure describes.[11] Francis, the humble man, was indeed "the gifted *idiota*."[12]

Since Francis himself had received a basic level of education and his spiritual life was centered on humility and poverty, it is important to ask about his attitude toward the pursuit of learning. Paul Sabatier, in his *Vie de*

Saint François d'Assise (the Life of St. Francis of Assisi), published in 1894, represented Francis as "*il poverello*" (the little poor man) who had striven to reform the institutional church and had resisted the process of clericalization in his order.[13]

There is a gap between Sabatier's representation of Francis and the traditional portrayal of the saint presented by the Franciscan Order, the one that is most widely known among Catholics. Sabatier's portrayal of Francis was drawn from his interpretation of hagiographical materials ascribed to Francis's early companions.[14] In these sources, Francis's theological insights and biblical understanding, so the authors deduced, had been inspired by the Holy Spirit and were not the result of his education. On the other hand, the authors depicted learned friars in a negative way. In this portrayal, the learned friars did not understand Francis's ideal, but rather had taken the order in a wrong direction. The older hagiographies did not say explicitly that Francis disliked or denounced the study of the scriptures and theology, but in general Francis was depicted as being worried that an excessive concern for learning would ruin the order.[15]

For Sabatier and like-minded scholars, study and learning were not essential to the life of the early Franciscans. On the other hand, a number of other scholars have argued that intellectual pursuit and training were an integral part of Franciscan life from the beginning, claiming that Francis was not against study as long as it did not hinder a life of prayer and simplicity. In support of their claim, these scholars highlight Francis's own writings, such as the *Later Rule* (*The Rule of 1223*), the *Admonitions,* and the *Letter to Anthony of Padua*. The *Letter to Anthony* in particular is considered to support Francis's approval of learning and teaching theology.[16] Michael W. Blastic, interpreting the texts of the *Earlier Rule* (*The Rule of 1221*) and the *Later Rule* within their historical and textual context, concludes that "the *Letter to Anthony* would seemingly open the way to the study of theology, at least for those who were literate."[17]

By the time of the approval of the *Later Rule*, the early brotherhood, which consisted primarily of laymen and sustained itself with manual labor and mendicancy, had been transformed into an influential religious order that included clerics and scholars, and its significant activities ranged from penitential exhortations to clerical ministries. Francis had witnessed these changes and more or less accepted them; nevertheless, he would not encourage his brothers to pursue learning since he did not intend that the members of his order become a group of learned scholars. Francis admonished "illiterate" brothers "not to be anxious to learn."[18]

What, then, is the stance of the *Later Rule* concerning the pursuit of learning? To this question, Neslihan Şenocak answers that it neither supports nor rejects it.[19] However, Şenocak points out that it is almost impossible to pursue formal education while faithfully observing the *Later Rule* since it prohibits holding a permanent residence or receiving money for the purchase of books.[20] Therefore, rather than investigating Francis's written texts to understand whether Francis was totally opposed to the pursuit of learning, it would be better, as Bert Roest suggests, to try to discern how Francis strove to "square the need for studies with his desire for evangelical poverty and humility."[21] Francis bluntly admonishes friars not to pursue studies for selfish reasons, nor to fall prey to pride and abandon humility and simplicity. Instead, the founder encourages his disciples to strive to put into practice what they learn.[22]

Early Franciscans and the Issue of Education

Developing from its humble origins as an evangelical movement founded by a band of laymen in the early thirteenth century, the Franciscan Order drastically expanded in its number and geographical extent. Because of this, the order could not avoid transformations in its internal and external structures, nor in its members' spiritual lives, all of which caused unease and conflicts. These transformations, which occurred from the time of Francis until 1260, have been termed "clericalization" by Laurentio C. Landini.[23] He defines "clericalization" as "the development whereby a greater number of friars became priests within the order."[24] Within four decades after the death of Francis, the nature and purpose of the order had changed, primarily with respect to the life and ministry of Franciscan priests.

Before the brotherhood had grown to become a well-organized religious order, the early brothers had wandered village to village preaching penance and the kingdom of God, striving to live a life of poverty and simplicity. As the brotherhood expanded rapidly, it became very difficult for Francis himself to manage it and to address its problems, and the difficulties inherent in governing a large community led to Francis resigning his position as general minister. Landini suggests that Francis himself was well aware that control of the growing order was beyond his abilities so he handed leadership responsibilities to Peter Catanii in about 1217 and later to Elias as vicar in 1221.[25] Despite Francis's renunciation of his administrative role in the order, Rosalind Brooke shows that he continued to have a significant influence over the friars, not only spiritually but also sometimes in matters of administration.[26]

Whether Francis wanted to be or not, he was necessarily involved in the rapidly advancing process of institutionalization.[27] Pope Honorius III (r. 1216–1227) introduced the religious novitiate into the order in 1220 and also commanded the superiors to keep in check those friars who strayed from the

path of obedience.[28] The church's engagement in organizing and stabilizing
the order was reflected in the order's legislation, in particular the *Earlier Rule*
(1221) and *Later Rule* (1223). Landini shows that the concerns about recruit-
ing new friars and an emphasis on obedience, as manifested in the Rule,[29]
began to bear fruit in the greater stability and discipline of the order. While
the Rule restrained the wandering character of the friars' lives, the friars in
leadership were concerned about the preaching apostolate. The wandering
friars' preaching had raised unease and worries about possible intrusion into
the authority of bishops and the danger of heresy. The Rule took these worries into consideration, and was intended to check the apostolate of preaching: chapter 17 of the *Earlier Rule* admonishes preacher-friars to follow the
practice and teachings of the church and suggests that ministers be cautious
when granting friars permission to preach. Similarly, chapter 9 of the *Later
Rule* commands preachers to submit to bishops.[30]

From the inception of the early brotherhood, the simple preaching of peni-
tence and the kingdom of God had been an essential part of the Franciscan
life. However, as the brotherhood developed into an organized religious order, the apostolate of preaching began to require that preachers be qualified
and supervised, which tended to favor learned clerics over laymen. Landini
argues that the clericalization of the order should be seen in the context of the
clericalization of the wider church that had been developing from the twelfth
century onward. With the development of canon law, the church began to
recognize a sharp distinction between clerics and laymen in their juridical and
ministerial rights and responsibilities, restricting the care of souls to clerics.
The Order of Friars Minor was deeply immersed in the church and it was almost impossible for it to avoid the progress of clericalization.[31] Landini asks:

> Would the Friars Minor, rooted as they were in such an apostolate which went to
> the very heart of their way of life, forego this apostolate? Or would they become
> an Order of clerics and continue this apostolate as well as the *cura animarum*,
> thereby finding the needed means of support for stabilizing institutions, e.g.,
> their novitiates, convents and training centers?[32]

The process of clericalization was accelerated with the increased number
of clerics within the order and the consequent granting of clerical and pastoral
privileges by popes. The papacy considered the bishops and the friars minor
to be collaborators, with the friars preaching against heresies and providing
ing pastoral care to the faithful, tasks which had formerly been restricted to
priests. The papacy even helped the order train new friars for these purposes.[33]

Various privileges of a clerical and pastoral nature granted by the papacy
were welcomed and even sought after by the learned clerics of the order.[34]
The learned clerics favored the liberal interpretations of the Rule that they

saw as being for the benefit of the order and the more efficacious care of the faithful, and advocated for the papal privileges.[35] Redefining the purpose of the order as caring for souls, the learned friars, who valued learning over manual labor, had changed the nature and life of the order, and this change had further downgraded the position of laymen and solidified the order's clericalization.[36] Based on the *Chronicle* of Thomas of Eccleston (1258–1259), Landini presents the case of the English province. When the first nine friars landed in England on September 10, 1225, four of them were clerics, and from the start, it was obvious that the English province favored the recruitment of learned clerics as new members of the order. The early English friars were fervent about pursuing theological studies, and consequently very quickly developed one of the best educational networks within the order.[37] Landini argues that since the ultramontane provinces, including the English province, had been clerically oriented from the beginning, which made them different from the Italian provinces, they had not had to deal with hostility or friction between laymen and clerics.[38]

After the forced resignation of Elias from the generalate in 1239, the position of minister general was handed to Albert of Pisa (d. 1240), and after the sudden death of Albert, to the Englishman Haymo of Faversham in 1240 (d. 1244).[39] Both Albert and Haymo were highly educated clerics from the English province. During Haymo's tenure as minister general from 1240 to 1244, the clericalization of the order was solidified by legislation confining positions of leadership to clerics and restricting the entrance of laymen into the order. It seemed that the internal struggle for minority (a humble life) and fraternity (equality among friars) ended when the learned clerics had become victorious.[40] In fact, the conflict among the friars was to unfold more violently in the decades to come. To a certain extent, the seeds of tension between various groups of friars was already present at the beginning of the order in light of the fact that it was composed of members from different social, economic, and educational backgrounds. Indeed, the vision of the order was so diverse that even Francis struggled to hold it together.

Development of an Educational System and the Incorporation of Learning into Franciscan Identity: Clericalization and Literacy

In his aforementioned study of the early development of the Order of Friars Minor, Landini focused on the clericalization or "sacerdotalization" of the order.[41] However, as his investigation of the implications of the term "cleric" in medieval times shows, it had two different meanings: in the common meaning, a cleric could mean a person having basic literacy, and in the ecclesiastical or canonical sense, a cleric could refer to a person on whom holy orders in the church had been conferred.[42] Although a literate person is not necessarily educated to be ordained to a holy order, a priest must be a literate man, perhaps even well educated. Moreover, when the church needed the friars to be involved in pastoral and preaching ministry, they were required to be equipped with more than basic literacy—it was also demanded that they attain doctrinal and theological knowledge so that they could debate against heresies. Therefore, the "sacerdotalization" or clericalization of the Order of Friars Minor in the ecclesiastical sense inevitably involved the "intellectualization" of friars beyond what was required by the common meaning of "cleric." Francis himself was aware of the need for friars who were deeply engaged in missionary endeavors to receive theological tranining. Roest infers that despite his reservations, Francis did not fully condemn the pursuit of studies,[43] and has been described as both an "idealist" and a "realist."[44]

The process of clericalization culminated in the abdication of the lay brother Elias (d. 1253) and the ensuing marginalization of lay brothers with respect to leadership positions afterward. Most of the available written records witness to Elias's tyrannical administrative style. Nevertheless, he is considered to have resisted the total clericalization, if not institutionalization, of the order and strove to preserve the equality among lay brothers and clerical brothers.[45] Through these efforts, he might have defied the clericalization of the order in the canonical sense, but he and all the early minister generals, all of who were learned men whether they were laymen or priests, actively promoted learning within the order. As early as 1219–1220, Franciscans established a study house in Bologna. Moreover, Roest argues convincingly that from the 1220s onward, individual friaries requested lectors and Franciscans established the network of *studia generalia* in which friars from different provinces would be educated to become lectors. From the early stage of their spread throughout Europe, Franciscans settled in towns with prestigious theological schools and universities, including Paris (1217) and Oxford (1224). Once the presence of friars had been established, learned laymen, clerics, and students joined the order. Eventually, Franciscans began to create their own schools for advanced theological studies.[46]

Landini views the clericalization of the order within the broader context of the church, which had seen an increasingly sharp distinction between laity and clergy and was characterized by rising concerns about heresies. Neslihan Şenocak also situates the rise of Franciscan learning and the organization of a Franciscan educational system within the general environment of thirteenth-century Europe, in which learning began to be associated with a person's sanctity. In addition, she also looks at the phenomena in terms of power, in that those who attained knowledge, in particular theological knowledge, were given authority to interpret and impose religious, social, and even cultural values on society.[47]

As early as the 1230s, there appeared a conviction that learning, in particular the study of the scriptures, was not only a help to better preaching but also to making friars better Christians by helping them cultivate virtues and curb vices. Anthony of Padua (1195–1231) was presented as a model who combined learning with virtues such as poverty and humility.[48] Even Francis was depicted as simple and at the same time learned, not taught by human teachers, but divinely illuminated.[49] However, Bonaventure argues that the case of Francis was rare in human history, and that other people must be taught by human teachers, which justifies the educational pursuits of friars.[50] Moreover, learned Franciscans claimed that the Franciscan life was the most suitable for the pursuit of learning because of its emphasis on poverty. Şenocak writes:

> Along with making the pursuit of learning into an element of the saintly life, Franciscan discourse introduced the claim that the Franciscan life was the ideal state in which learning could be pursued. Therefore, if anyone wished to dedicate themselves to the study of sacred scripture, it was best for them to study it while living the Franciscan life, at the heart of which lay the ideal of apostolic poverty.[51]

Şenocak argues that, despite Francis's consistent claim regarding the virtue of poverty, he had not prioritized that virtue over other primary virtues such as wisdom, simplicity, humility, charity, and obedience. She suggests that the rise of absolute poverty to preeminent status was spurred by the "learned" brothers who claimed a connection between poverty and learning. Although the theoretical development of Franciscan poverty was achieved during the century-long debates between secular scholars and mendicant friars in the thirteenth and fourteenth centuries, certain justifications of poverty appeared as early as the 1230s. From the early stages of the order's expansion, Franciscan poverty, which distinguished the Franciscans from other religious orders and secular priests, strongly appealed to students and scholars,[52] and these intellectual brothers began to establish learning as an essential part of the Franciscan life, along with poverty and humility. John of Parma, the minister general from 1247 to 1257, reportedly said that the Franciscan Order was constructed on two columns: a good life and learning.[53]

It is true that the rise of learning within the order was not what Francis himself intended and that the idea of sanctity associated with learning is distant from simplicity and humility. However, Şenocak defends the masters and superiors for their endeavors to incorporate learning as an essential element of Franciscan identity. She argues that those who had entered the order after Francis's death were not sufficiently informed about Francis and the life of the early friars and that it was natural for them to establish their Franciscan identity in accordance with what they already did and knew.[54] The observance of Franciscan poverty—communal, voluntary, and absolute—would seem to impede intellectual undertakings, but as Şenocak points out, it is ironic that "the same apostolic poverty of the friars evolved from being an impediment to becoming a substantial justification for the friars' involvement in studies, as Franciscan scholars claimed to be better teachers in comparison with those who did not live in apostolic poverty."[55]

Resistance to Learning and Study

In reading hagiographical texts of the thirteenth century and later writings on the early period of the development of the order—particularly ones by observant friars—it is easy to get the impression that there were contending factions and serious conflicts among friars with regard to alleged laxness in observing the founder's ideal. Nobody would deny the fact that the order had changed from a primitive brotherhood to a well-organized religious order administered by competent and well-educated priests. Şenocak and David Burr argue that this was an inevitable development closely associated with various social, cultural, and ecclesiastical factors. They also agree that there were no severe conflicts or explicitly contending groups in the order until at least the late 1270s.[56]

There might not have been explicitly contending groups with regard to the direction of the order, but it is undeniable that there were concerns about the state of the order and the life of the friars. Witnessing deviations from the early simple life of the brotherhood—inequality between friars based on learning and socioeconomic status, laxness in lifestyles, excessive privileges granted by the papacy, and abuses by learned friars—some friars expressed their concerns.[57] The "Leonine corpus," or *Scripta Leonis*, and *The Remembrance of the Desire of a Soul* by Thomas of Celano from 1247 (*Second Celano*)[58] reflected these concerns about the allegedly wrong direction of the order.[59]

According to the *Second Celano*, Francis said that when a learned man joins the order, he should abandon even his learning because a wealthy man abandons his possessions as being possible obstacles to following Christ.[60] Celano also takes the position that the simplicity of the friars should be "the driving spirit"[61] of the order. Even if they lack intellectual training, friars can be truthful witnesses to living the gospel through their exemplary lives. Like Francis, Celano did not disapprove of learning itself, nor of the learned friars. However, it is clear that he esteemed the simple friars more than the erudite ones and that what concerned him most was the unity of the order. Celano writes: "He [Francis] wanted to unite the greater to the lesser, to join the wise to the simple in brotherly affection and to hold together those far from each other with the glue of love."[62]

The *Assisi Compilation* (1244–1260) adopted an even more suspicious stance regarding the penetration of studies into the life and structure of the order: "He [Francis] could smell in the air that a time was coming, and not too far away, when he knew learning would be an occasion of ruin."[63] As Roest points out, although this text claimed to express the mind of Francis himself, the critical view of learning expressed therein had much to do with events that had affected the order and the general situation of the order from the 1240s.[64] The *Assisi Compilation* stated that learning would distract friars from prayer, threaten poverty, and make them vulnerable to pride and to the pursuit of vainglory, all of which actually happened in the friaries and deeply concerned even the learned friars in leadership.[65]

In light of all this, Şenocak raises a question: "The learned and the simple could live together if only the learned could renounce their learning, but could the Order promote simplicity and the pursuit of learning at the same time?"[66] The *Second Celano* and the Leonine corpus clearly see the tension as almost impossible to resolve, and Francis's reverence for theologians[67] but at the same time his discouragement of ignorant friars from studying seem ambiguous. Şenocak argues that this seeming contradiction can be resolved in the light of the Leonine corpus, explaining that "precisely because he saw theologians as objects of reverence and honor, he did not want his own friars to become theologians or respectable men in general."[68]

It should come as no surprise that when the ministers decided to encourage recruitment of the learned while at the same time imposing restrictions on the reception of laypeople into the order,[69] many friars who were acquainted with Francis and his ideal viewed the changes with dismay. Burr characterized this change as one of clericalization, something Francis himself did not intend for his brotherhood, and Şenocak describes the dynamics this way:

> When the learned friars introduced the systematic study of theology into the Order's mission, they thus rendered the Order's extraordinary fabric of equal brotherhood vulnerable and prone to transformation into a socially hierarchical structure. . . . It was intellectual prowess that came to decide the function of a friar within the Order. Ultimately, therefore, it was the pursuit of learning that shaped the nature of the institution rather than the other way around.[70]

She even argues that the favorable relationship between Franciscans and the papacy and the church's requests that the order engage in pastoral care of the faithful were preceded by the order's readiness to supply trained personnel for the task.[71]

Thus, it is obvious that there had been tension and some amount of resistance from the friars to the intellectualization and clericalization of the order. However, the learned friars defended themselves and continued implementing the already-begun changes, taking advantage of their administrative and legislative authority and papal support. They also provided a justification of learning itself by associating it with sanctity, arguing, together with certain theologians, that study and learning do not impede, but rather facilitate, sanctity.

The integration of learning and sanctity should be understood within the broader context of thirteenth-century Europe, in which the intellectual domain was transitioning from traditional monastic intellectualism to the rapidly developing Scholasticism, which would become a highly sophisticated, speculative, systematic, and theoretical enterprise. Despite this development, the early Franciscan scholars, who advocated learning and connected it with Franciscan ideals, seemed still to be following partly, if not fully, the monastic tradition that integrated intellectual enterprise into the ascetic, virtuous, and spiritual life.[72]

St. Bonaventure of Bagnoregio is one of those medieval intellectuals who embraced the values and usefulness of the monastic intellectual tradition in the context of the new Scholastic knowledge and system. He was a Franciscan mystic who was aware of the dangers of learning and scholarship, and he tried to articulate and incorporate Francis's profound spirituality into his intellectual enterprise. The following section will explore the various aspects of Bonaventure's synthetic position: his transition from a master of theology at the University of Paris to the general minister of the Franciscan Order, a reconciler of conflicting parties within the order and between the order and the secular clerics, and most importantly a writer about a spiritual journey that led the mind of an intellectual to the flaming ecstasy of the heart.

BONAVENTURE OF BAGNOREGIO: HIS LIFE AND WORKS

The Life of Bonaventure

Through his life and works, Bonaventure left indelible marks on medieval Latin Christendom. He stood out as one of the most brilliant intellects teaching at the University of Paris, at the time the most prominent intellectual center in the West, and he assumed responsibility for the administrative and spiritual care of the large Franciscan family through his election as minister general of the Order of Friars Minor. In the half century after its founding, the order had grown into one of the most influential religious orders in Europe. His influence over religious matters was not limited to the Franciscan family but also reached to the wider church in his role as cardinal and advisor to popes. As a learned scholar, Bonaventure synthesized the philosophical, theological, and spiritual traditions of his day. Guy Bougerol views Bonaventure's writings as "the summit of achievement of Franciscan Scholasticism."[73] His successors in the order would draw from Bonaventure both theological inspiration and a powerful intellectual structure in which further scholarly developments could be framed. As a leader of the Franciscan family, which had been experiencing tensions and conflicts engendered by the order's rapid expansion, he strove to steer it in the right direction with administrative competence and spiritual wisdom. For his contributions, he has been recognized as the order's second founder and the chief architect of its spirituality.[74]

Bonaventure was born in the town of Bagnoregio in central Italy in 1217 or 1221.[75] He was baptized with the name of Giovanni after his father, Giovanni di Fidanza, who was reportedly a physician. His mother's name was Maria Ritella. It is possible that he received the name Bonaventure when he entered the Order of Friars Minor.

Even before embracing the religious life, Bonaventure's life had been touched by the Franciscans. In the prologue to the *Major Legend of Saint Francis*, he presents two reasons he took up the task of writing. In addition to a request by the general chapter of the order that he do so, he was obliged to write in praise of Francis's virtues, actions, and words out of gratitude, for in his youth he was healed from a serious illness thanks to his mother's plea to the saint.[76] When the young Giovanni was growing up, there had been Franciscan friars present in his hometown, and a papal document states that Giovanni received his early education from these friars.[77]

Bonaventure's higher education began at the University of Paris in 1234–1235. When he arrived in Paris in 1230s, the city had been undergoing multiple transformations with royal support and with the influx of "Europe's best and brightest."[78] Christopher Cullen describes three historical movements swirling around Paris at the time, and notes that these movements were interacting with each other and stirring up conflicts.[79] These movements were the twin intellectual strains of Aristotelianism and Scholasticism, the development of University of Paris, and the rapid influx of the mendicant orders—the Dominicans and Franciscans. As a university student, Bonaventure would have immersed himself in these great medieval movements. In fact, in just two decades, he would come to be a highly esteemed master of theology and an adept scholar of Aristotelian philosophy,[80] a Franciscan friar, and eventually minister general of the Order of Friars Minor. With his intellectual brilliance and ecclesiastical authority, he would play a central role in the development of each of these three movements.

Upon becoming a master of arts, Bonaventure joined the Order of Friars Minor and began his novitiate at the friary in Paris in 1238 or 1243.[81] It is obvious from the two legends of Francis—major and minor—written by

Bonaventure himself, that Francis himself had played an important role in Bonaventure's Franciscan vocation. Besides the draw of devotional piety toward the saint, Bonaventure was also attracted to the Franciscan way of evangelical life. The inspiring and highly intellectual religious community of Franciscans in Paris, which consisted of masters of high esteem and many students known for their virtue and humility, inflamed a religious zeal in the heart of young Giovanni.[82] This can be seen in his *Letter in Response to Three Questions of an Unknown Master* (*Epistola de tribus quaestionibus ad magistrum innominatum*),[83] written sometime in the period 1254–1255 when he was teaching at the University of Paris after acquiring a master's degree there. It was Bonaventure's intention in this letter to allay a master's suspicions of some abuses by friars so as to persuade him to join the order.

> For I confess before God that what made me love St. Francis's way of life so much was that it is exactly like the origin and the perfection of the Church itself, which began first with simple fishermen and afterwards developed to include the most illustrious and learned doctors. You find the same thing in the Order of St. Francis; in this way God reveals that it did not come about through human calculations but through Christ. For since the works of Christ do not diminish but ceaselessly grow, this undertaking was proved to be God's doing when wise men did not disdain to join the company of simple folk.[84]

One of "the most illustrious and learned doctors" who joined the order and inspired the young Giovanni would be Alexander of Hales (ca. 1186–1245).[85] Alexander and Bonaventure developed such a strong relationship of mutual respect and intimacy that Bonaventure spoke of Alexander as his father and master.[86] The master's fraternal affection toward young Bonaventure and his admiration for Bonaventure's life is revealed in his comment that "it seemed that Adam had not sinned in him [Bonaventure]."[87]

Alexander of Hales was one of the most distinguished theologians of his time and paved the way for the further blossoming of medieval Scholasticism.[88] Bougerol considers Alexander the founder of the "Franciscan School" of theology.[89] He joined the Franciscan Order in 1236, abandoning his wealth, status, and reputation for the sake of the evangelical life, following in Francis's footsteps. This event must have inspired Bonaventure to consider his own religious vocation. When he entered the order, Alexander brought with him the Chair of Theology he already held at the University of Paris. This chair was later filled by other brilliant Franciscans like Jean de La Rochelle (d. 1245), Eudes Rigaud (d. 1275), and William of Meliton (d. 1257), all of who had a significant impact on Bonaventure's intellectual and spiritual formation.[90]

After completing one year of his novitiate in 1239 (or 1244), Bonaventure continued to study theology under Alexander's guidance. According to the chronology of Bonaventure's studies presented by Jay M. Hammond, he first studied the scriptures and the *Sentences* of Peter Lombard at the university from 1244 to 1248 and was subsequently licensed by then minister general John of Parma to lecture to Franciscan students from the private chair of the Franciscan school in Paris. While teaching Franciscans at the University of Paris, he commented on the scriptures as a bachelor of the Bible (*baccalaures biblicus*) (1248–1251) and expounded on the text of Peter Lombard as a bachelor of the *Sentences* (*baccalaures sententiarum*) (1252–1253). Upon completing these requirements, he received the status of formed bachelor (*baccalaures formatus*). In this role, he was required to preach to the public and participate in a series of public debates. After becoming a bachelor, it usually did not take a long time for a candidate to be accepted into the guild of masters of theology at the university.[91] However, a dispute between the secular and mendicant masters at Paris likely delayed Bonaventure's reception into the master's guild as a regent master of theology.[92]

Despite the ambiguities regarding the dating of the significant events of Bonaventure's life and formation, most scholars agree that he was elected to minister general of his order in 1257. This event shifted the focus of his life from intellectual tasks to administrative and pastoral responsibilities as the leader of the whole Franciscan family. Later, he became an important councilor to the papacy when he was appointed to the cardinalate with the title of Cardinal Bishop of Albano by Pope Gregory X (r. 1271–1276) in 1273. After living a life that had touched the minds and hearts of innumerable people, Bonaventure died unexpectedly at Lyon, France, on July 15, 1274, while attending the Second Council of Lyon. He was canonized by Pope Sixtus IV (r. 1471–1484) in 1482, and a century later, in 1588, was declared Doctor of the Church by Pope Sixtus V (r. 1585–1590), who conferred on him the title of "Seraphic Doctor."[93]

Bonaventure's Writings

As a brilliant mind and charismatic leader of his time, Bonaventure left an extensive corpus addressing a wide variety of concerns of an intellectual, spiritual, and administrative nature. As published by the Quaracchi editors, his writings comprise nine folio volumes amounting to several thousand pages printed in double columns.[94] They include commentaries on the *Sentences* and the scriptures, disputed questions, spiritual writings, letters, sermons, and lectures. They deal with philosophical and theological questions, spiritual guidance, devotions, administrative admonishment, and the controversial issues of his time.[95]

His early writings were composed while he was studying and teaching at the University of Paris. During those years, he composed the four volumes of commentaries on the *Sentences*. Around the time of his departure from the university and his election to a leadership position with the order, he composed another work of theological significance, the *Breviloquium* (*Brief Commentary*), for the purpose of helping his fellow Franciscans attain better knowledge of general theological topics. This work is a brief theological summa, and Bougerol subtitled it "a manual of theology."[96] Among other scholarly writings, there are scriptural commentaries on Luke, John, and Ecclesiastes, and also three sets of "disputed questions": *Disputed Questions on Evangelical Perfection, Disputed Questions on the Knowledge of Christ,* and *Disputed Questions on the Mystery of the Trinity*. For Bonaventure, all intellectual endeavors were meant to foster the knowledge of divine revelation, knowledge that he believed would ultimately lead to mystical union with God. This idea is explicated in *On the Reduction of the Arts to Theology* (*De reductione artium ad theologiam*), which was Bonaventure's inaugural sermon as regent master. In this brief document—a mere seven pages in the Quaracchi edition—Bonaventure insists that all human knowledge drawing on the studies of arts and sciences should serve the end of mystical union.[97]

The same idea is clearly embedded in *The Soul's Journey into God* (*Itinerarium mentis in Deum*), but with more obvious spiritual weight. While the text is one of the greatest and most popular works of Christian spirituality, it is also loaded with scriptural, philosophical, and psychological knowledge. Bonaventure composed this masterpiece after returning from a retreat to Mount Alverna in 1259 during the early years of his generalate. Inspired by the mystical event of Francis's receiving the stigmata of Christ on his body upon the visitation of a six-winged seraph, Bonaventure structured the *Itinerarium* in six steps. This work best manifests his lifelong project—the integration of intellectual and spiritual life.

Another important work of Bonaventure from the period of his early generalate is the *Major Legend of St. Francis* (*Legenda major sancti Francisci*). There were already a few well-written biographies of Francis, including those by Thomas of Celano (d. 1260) and Julian of Speyer (d. 1250), but Bonaventure was commissioned to write the biography of Francis by the general chapter of the Order of Friars Minor at Narbonne in 1260. In the *Major Legend*, Francis is presented as a person who had completed the spiritual journey described in the *Itinerarium*.

Although spirituality was never absent from his writings, even in his highly speculative works, such as the four volumes of commentaries on the *Sentences*, Bonaventure also produced works that were focused exclusively on spirituality and the virtues: *The Tree of Life* (*Lignum vitae*), *On the Threefold Way* (*De triplici via*), *Soliloquy* (*Soliloquium*), and *On the Five Feasts of the Child Jesus* (*De quinque festivitatibus pueri Jesu*), among others. Among many spiritual writings, the *Threefold Way* is noteworthy in that it provides a systematic structure to Bonaventure's spiritual journey—the spiritual journey develops through the threefold dynamics of purgation, illumination, and perfection.[98] The 381 extant sermons are also important resources for understanding Bonaventure's spirituality and biblical exegesis.

After leaving his teaching position at Paris in 1257 upon his election as minister general of the order, Bonaventure continued to involve himself in spiritual, political, and academic activities in the city with his sermons and collations[99] and by engaging in controversy with secular masters concerning the legitimacy of the mendicant lifestyle. Bonaventure's prodigious intellectual abilities and his active involvement in the academic setting of Paris is on full display in his collations. Three sets of collations, delivered between 1264 and 1274, have come down to us: the *Collations on the Ten Commandments* (*Collationes de decem praeceptis*), the *Collations on the Seven Gifts of the Holy Spirit* (*Collationes de septem donis Spiritus sancti*), and the *Collations on the Hexaemeron* (*the Six Days*) (*Collationes in hexaemeron*). As a philosopher and theologian trained at Paris, he did not discard the teachings of Aristotle, but he was worried about the Averroistic interpretation of Aristotelianism, whose fundamental errors, Bonaventure thought, subjected Christian theology and divine revelation to great danger. The three collations explicitly reveal his resistance to Averroistic Aristotelianism.[100]

The conflict between secular masters and mendicant masters over the Franciscan mode of life, and in particular evangelical poverty, that broke out around the time of Bonaventure's election to the generalate would stir up not only intellectuals in Paris, but also the newly rising mendicant orders—the Dominicans and Franciscans—and, for that matter, all of Western Europe. William of Saint-Amour (d. 1276), a secular master at the University of Paris, attacked the legitimacy of the mendicant lifestyle by publishing two treatises: the *Book of Antichrist* (*Liber de antichristo*) in 1254 and the *Treatise on the Dangers of Recent Times* (*Tractatus de periculis novissimorum temporum*) in 1256. Bonaventure became deeply involved in the controversy—he responded to the secular master's attack by defending the Franciscan ideal of poverty in one of his three books of "disputed questions," the *Disputed Questions on Evangelical Perfection*. The first stage of the controversy ended with Pope Alexander IV's condemnation of William in 1256. However, the polemic resumed when Gerard of Abbeville (d. 1271), a master of theology and disciple of William, published his *Against the Adversary of Christian Perfection* (*Contra adversarium perfectionis christianae*) in 1269. Against Abbeville's attack on the Franciscan life, Bonaventure wrote the *Apology of the Poor* (*Apologia pauperum*), defending Franciscan poverty as an authentic way to live evangelical perfection.[101]

The Generalate of Bonaventure (1257–1274)

Bonaventure was not present at the general chapter that elected him to the generalate. This general chapter was held at Rome on February 2, 1257, in the presence of Pope Alexander IV. John of Parma (g. 1247–1257[102]), then minister general, summoned the brothers with the intention of stepping down from his office. He was concerned that the allegation of his support for Joachimism (on which see below) would negatively impact the whole order, and he designated Bonaventure as his successor. Ironically, later Bonaventure had the repsonsibility of sitting in the judge's chair for John's trial for heresy.[103]

Many of the friars had been sympathetic to the prophecy of Joachim of Fiore (ca. 1135–1202). Joachim had developed a theory that there were three stages of world history corresponding to the three Persons of the Trinity: the stage of the Father, which coincided with the period of the Old Testament, the stage of the Son that began with the New Testament and had been governed by the church, and the third and last stage of the Holy Spirit, which would be ushered in with the emergence of two new religious orders filled with spiritual men characterized by their lifestyle of contemplation and poverty.[104] This apocalyptic vision of history was welcomed by both Franciscans and Dominicans, but it soon caused controversy. Gerard of Borgo San Donnino (d. 1276), a young Franciscan student in Paris and a zealous Joachimite, published the *Introduction to the Eternal Gospel* (*Introductorius in evangelium aeternum*) in 1254, which predicted the coming of the third age in 1260 and insisted that the Holy Spirit had entrusted the eternal gospel to the Franciscan Order. The church condemned Gerard's book and the Joachimist prophecy as being heretical in 1256, which led to the resignation of John of Parma.[105]

The publishing of *Eternal Gospel* provided the secular masters in Paris with a useful opportunity to attack the mendicant orders, especially their mixing of absolute poverty and higher learning, a combination that seemed contradictory to them. The charge that the friars had been following heretical Joachimism together with the Poverty Controversy revealed the tensions between the secular masters and clerics and the mendicants. The number of the latter had been growing rapidly, penetrating the realm of secular clerics, earning papal privileges, and encroaching on the interests of secular masters by establishing their own educational system, thus competing for school chairs and students.[106] The mendicants even claimed moral superiority over the seculars, which only exacerbated the seculars' antipathy toward them. As Şenocak suggests, "Had the friars kept a low and humble profile, mendicancy would probably not have become a target."[107]

Thus, when Bonaventure was elected to the generalate, the order was faced with attacks from outside the order. These conflicts would continue to occupy his and his successors' attention for several decades, but the problems Bonaventure was forced to struggle with were not only external. The rapidly growing religious movement, which at the time of Bonaventure's election to the generalate numbered roughly thirty thousand brothers[108] scattered throughout the vast territory of Christendom, also faced troubles caused by Franciscans themselves. Although he had been in the sheltered world of academia before his election to the office of general minister, he was well aware of the scandalous lifestyles of and abuses committed by some Franciscans. Right after his election in 1257, while he was still in Paris, he hastened to send his first encyclical to all the friars of the order through its provincials and custodians.

> Had I been at the general chapter I would have addressed them more freely and at greater length. But a number of reasons make it urgent that I write you at this point: the dangers still threatening our Order, the wounds being inflicted on the consciences of many brothers, not to mention the scandals being given to secular persons, for whom our Order, which ought to be a shining mirror of sanctity, has become in many parts of the world an object of loathing and contempt.[109]

In this letter, Bonaventure enumerates ten practices that are inappropriate for Franciscans including the improper handling of money, idleness, aimless wandering, abuse of begging, construction of lavish buildings, inappropriate interaction with women, inappropriate assignment of offices, abuses of ministries, frequent and inappropriate changes of residence, and excessive expenditures. He urges friars to correct their misconduct and encourages them to live in accordance with the Rule.[110]

Bonaventure declared in his first encyclical that he would confront the friars' troublesome behavior. Théophile Desbonnets lists three stages in which the resolute new general enacted his intentions for the order.[111] First, Bonaventure unified all of its previous legislation. Since the approval of the *Later Rule* in 1223, general chapters had promulgated statutes to supplement it, so at the time of Bonaventure a lack of regulations was not the problem. The problem was that the statutes were incoherent and had not been enforced by the ministers of province and custody, so Bonaventure set out to review all of them and reorganize them thematically. He presented this reorganization in 1260 at the first general chapter he presided over in person in Narbonne, France. The new codification of the existing legal regulations that had been approved by the chapter, known as the *Constitutions of Narbonne*, would establish the direction of the order for centuries to come. Dominic Monti points out that Bonaventure deserves great credit for his efforts to set forth "uniquely Franciscan" laws by reorganizing preexisting provisions around the themes of the order's most fundamental legislation—the Rule. In the new constitutions, he urged the brothers to live the values of the Rule.[112]

In order to encourage the brothers to observe the new constitutions, Bonaventure implemented the second stage of his plan, which was to appeal to the example of the life of Francis. He wrote the *Major Legend* with the *Constitutions of Narbonne* in mind so that friars might be inspired to abide by them.[113] Bonaventure's new biography of Francis was approved by the Chapter of Pisa in 1263 and was distributed to the provinces.

The third stage of Bonaventure's plan was to make the *Major Legend* the guidebook that would lead friars to a unified model of Franciscan life. Bonaventure, with the approval of the Paris Chapter of 1266, promulgated the destruction of other biographies and the distribution of the new book both inside and outside the order.[114] Thus, with these two writings—the *Constitutions of Narbonne* and the *Major Legend*—Bonaventure would "shape the ideals and life of the brotherhood for generations to come."[115] Because of this, he would be deemed the "second founder" of the Franciscan Order.[116]

Another significant issue that greatly concerned Bonaventure was the division of the brothers over the observance of poverty and of the Rule. Scholars agree that major splits among the friars, for instance into different groups such as Spirituals and Conventuals, only occurred after Bonaventure's death. Nevertheless, tensions had arisen among the friars already in the time of Bonaventure's generalate. Bonaventure sought to unite the whole order, balancing between zealous friars and more relaxed friars, as he strove to lead all the brothers to follow Francis. In order to achieve this goal, he had to take a middle way that might not have satisfied either extreme, but he embraced the majority of friars by providing concrete guidelines constraining them from straying from the spirit of the Rule.

Opinion on the generalate of Bonaventure is divided. Some, as has been noted, consider him the "second founder" of the Order of Friars Minor, whereas others see him as "a betrayer" of the ideal of Francis.[117] However, whatever their personal judgments might be, nobody would deny that Bonaventure solidified the direction of the order for many centuries. In addition, he put a great deal of effort into defending the ideals, lifestyle, and institutional foundation of the order from outside attacks. Most importantly, his actions and policies were both necessary and efficacious for sustaining the young, still-forming religious order. Desbonnets, who is critical of Bonaventure's role in the institutionalization and clericalization of the order, nevertheless acknowledges his contribution: "Even if we regret the overall disregard for the essential elements of Francis' intuition, we must recognize that Bonaventure's activity was beneficial. Flowing from a dynamic awareness of history, that [activity] was intended as a vital force in the Order."[118]

This section has surveyed, first, Bonaventure's life and academic journey; second, some of his works; and third, the tenure of his generalate. If this section dealt primarily with his reconciliatory efforts in academia, in the church, and within the order, the following section will explore in greater depth Bonaventure's endeavor of integrating the intellectual life of a scholar with the spiritual life of a Franciscan friar.

THE INTEGRATION OF INTELLECTUAL AND SPIRITUAL LIFE

Attaining Knowledge and Living Holiness for Bonaventure

Bonaventure's Attitude toward Learning and Teaching

By the time of Bonaventure's election to the generalate, a well-organized Franciscan educational system had been established and a culture that favored study and learning prevailed among those in leadership positions.[119] Moreover, in the course of defending their lifestyle—mendicancy combined with engagement in the intellectual arena—Franciscan intellectuals claimed superiority over the secular clerics and masters. On the other hand, there were also friars who were cautious about learning, considering it detrimental to the virtue of simplicity.[120] Thomas of Celano (d. 1260) is one of those who emphasized holy simplicity over learning. In his biographies of Francis (*First Celano* and *Second Celano*), written respectively in 1229 and in 1247, he depicted Francis as a simple man, praising Francis's wisdom, which had not been attained by intellectual studies but had been given by divine inspiration.[121] Celano was optimistic with regard to the possibility that friars, as long as they persevered in their penitential life with an arduous cultivation of virtues, could be open to and receive the divine wisdom that had been granted to Francis.[122]

Bonaventure too agreed on the divine origin of Francis's wisdom; however, he had a different opinion on the learning of friars. In a sermon on Francis, Bonaventure, after quoting St. Paul's confession that his teachings came through a revelation of Jesus Christ, likened Francis to the apostle, but argued that not everybody is meant to receive their learning directly from God.

> St. Francis learned his teaching in the same way. Indeed, one may well wonder at his teaching. How was he able to teach others what no man had taught him? Did he come by this knowledge of himself? Be assured he did not. The evidence of that is found in the account of his life. When he was instructed by another man or had to prepare something himself, he had absolutely nothing to say. In that, however, he is more to be praised and wondered at than imitated. Hence

it is not without reason that his sons attend the schools. To arrive at knowledge without a human teacher is not for everyone, but the privilege of a few. Though the Lord himself chose to teach St. Paul and St. Francis, it is his will that their disciples be taught by human teachers.[123]

Thus, Bonaventure commands his audience to learn the truth of God's revelation, if not by divine gift, then through the help of human teachers.

Bonaventure believed that learning would be necessary on the path of holiness. In this, his view was similar to other Franciscan intellectuals. Julian of Speyer, describing the life of Anthony of Padua, revealed his conviction that learning is not only useful for preaching but also beneficial to spiritual life because it encourages a person to live a virtuous life and avoid heresies.[124] In Anthony of Padua, Julian saw that the saint's erudition coexisted with simplicity. He was an ideal Franciscan who could combine his learning with a virtuous life of humility, simplicity, and poverty. Along the same lines, a Parisian master, John of Rupella (also known as John of la Rochelle, d. 1245), understood learning and teaching as a way to observe the Franciscan Rule, which commands the friars to live the gospel. Unless one is taught the gospel, how can one live it or preach it? Moreover, considering that Christ himself was a teacher of the scriptures, Franciscans, as His disciples, should follow in His footsteps by teaching.[125]

Bonaventure also finds an example of learning in the life of St. Francis. He wrote: "He [Francis] himself would have been a transgressor of the Rule, for though he was not very well educated as a youth, he later advanced in learning in the Order, not only by praying but also reading."[126] In addition, for Bonaventure the order's development from its humble beginnings with simple and uneducated people into a prominent religious order with illustrious and learned doctors was evidence of divine favor.[127] Thus, Bonaventure viewed learning as an integral part of the development of the order.

Incorporation of Scientific Knowledge into Theology

Bonaventure did not believe, however, that friars should engage in intellectual pursuits for the sake of learning itself. He condemned those who pursued learning out of curiosity, considering this a "petty and venial sin."[128] Although Bonaventure was aware of the dangers of philosophy, in particular one form of Aristotelianism that was introduced into and enthusiastically accepted in the European universities through the Latin translations of Arabic Aristotelian texts, he did not eschew the study of philosophy as a whole. He rather defended it, as can be seen in his response to a concerned master: "If the writings of the philosophers are sometimes of much value in understanding truth and refuting errors, we are not departing from the purity of faith if we at times study them, especially since there are many questions of faith which cannot be settled without recourse to them."[129] He appealed to St. Augustine: "Read Augustine's *On Christian Doctrine*, where he shows that Sacred Scripture cannot be understood without familiarity with the other sciences."[130]

For Bonaventure, philosophy and other sciences are not to be studied for their own sake, but are meant to facilitate theological and scriptural understanding.[131] As regards the relationship between philosophy, faith, and theology, Timothy Noone and R. E. Houser state that "without exception, every word of philosophy Bonaventure ever wrote is contained in works explicitly religious—in sermons, works of spiritual direction, and theology."[132] Noone and Houser explore how Bonaventure incorporated philosophical principles into his thought so as to present theology as a science, as he articulated, for instance, in his prologue to the *First Book of the Commentary on the Sentences* (hereafter *Commentary on the Sentences I*).[133]

Bonaventure uses the Aristotelian division of four causes: material, formal, final, and efficient. As for material cause, Bonaventure taught that theology studies the object of faith so as to make faith intelligible with the aid of reason. As for formal cause, he taught that theology proceeds by the method of reasoning and inquiry. For final cause, Bonaventure asserted that the end of theology is contemplation[134] and the holiness of persons. Finally, he noted that the efficient cause of theology is human beings, in particular theologians, who are made capable of this work by the primary cause, God. In this way, philosophical categories, methodology, and reasoning became an integral part of Bonaventure's theology.[135]

Perhaps the most important part of Bonaventure's systematic explication of theology's function as a science is his teaching regarding its end. Aristotle distinguished two kinds of science: speculative or theoretical science, which concerns contemplation of truth, and practical or moral science, which concerns human deeds and becoming good. Bonaventure argues for the superiority of theological knowledge, or wisdom, attained through the science of theology, over merely philosophical knowledge, for wisdom involves both theoretical knowledge and moral deeds. In this regard, theology can be said to have the dual aim of increasing people's faith and also of making them holy. But Bonaventure emphasizes that theology is "principally for the sake of our becoming good." He further shows how theological knowledge makes better Christians: "This knowledge aids faith, and faith resides in the intellect in such a way that, in accord with its very nature, it moves our affections. This is clear; for the knowledge that Christ died for us, and other such truths, move us to love, unless we are talking about a hardened sinner."[136]

For Bonaventure, not only philosophy but also all kinds of science must contribute to theology and eventually to one's union with God through love. He insists that all knowledge should serve theology so that one can contemplate the truth revealed in the scriptures, strengthen one's faith, and move toward love. In the brief text *On the Reduction of the Arts to Theology*, Bonaventure explains in detail how the various branches of knowledge, such as the mechanical arts, sense knowledge, rational philosophy, natural philosophy, moral philosophy, and sacred scripture, can lead one to the mystery of God. At the conclusion of this sermon, he once again emphasizes the end of all knowledge.

> And so it is evident how the *manifold wisdom* of God, which is clearly revealed in sacred Scripture, lies hidden in all knowledge and in all nature. It is clear also how all divisions of knowledge are servants of theology, and it is for this reason that theology makes use of illustrations and terms pertaining to every branch of knowledge. It is likewise clear how wide the illuminative way may be, and how the divine reality itself lies hidden within everything which is perceived or known. And this is the fruit of all sciences, that in all, faith may be strengthened, *God may be honored*, character may be formed, and consolation may be derived from union of the Spouse with the beloved, a union which takes place through charity: a charity in which the whole purpose of sacred Scripture, and thus of every illumination descending from above, comes to rest—a charity without which all knowledge is vain because no one comes to the Son except through the Holy Spirit who teaches us *all the truth, who is blessed forever. Amen.*[137]

Divine reality is hidden in everything in the universe, and all sciences and knowledge are to be an aid in elucidating this hidden mystery. Thus, Bonaventure affirms the positive function of the sciences, learning, and study. Rather than being an obstacle to holiness, he came to understand these things as part of an illuminative path to union with God. As Bougerol puts it, "Paris has not destroyed Assisi. Rather, Paris has become, through Bonaventure, the fullest flowering of Assisi in the field of thought."[138]

The Relationship between Theology and Spirituality

Bonaventure does not draw a bright line between theology and spirituality; in fact, for him, even though theology is in part an intellectual discipline, it serves primarily to facilitate one's union with God, which is essentially spiritual in nature rather than intellectual.[139]

Bonaventure studied, taught, and lived in an age when speculation and spirituality were not yet considered "strangers and rivals."[140] However, there were portents that this opposition would happen sooner or later. For one, the universities of thirteenth-century Europe were developing a relatively new form of theology. This new intellectual enterprise was known as Scholasticism, and was characterized by its scientific, systematic, and philosophical approach to theology. Logical reasoning and debate played significant roles in this methodology. The new way of doing theology had begun in cathedral schools in towns and later developed in the universities throughout the twelfth and thirteenth centuries.

Before the development of a system of higher education was formalized, intellectual and religious education had been provided mostly by monasteries. The theology practiced in monasteries was distinguishable from the later-developing Scholasticism in several ways. The former was contemplative, personal, and subjective, and was intended to foster monks' spiritual growth and ultimate union with God. Teaching in the monastic setting focused on spiritual experience rather than intellectual understanding and dealt with the mysteries of faith and the daily morality of ordinary Christians. Scholasticism, in contrast, was practiced in the schools and universities where the teachers (masters) were intellectuals who had devoted themselves primarily to learning and teaching, and theology tended to be speculative and theoretical.[141]

The separation between spirituality and theology developed in the High Middle Ages as theologians more and more began to engage primarily in scientific and systematic theology. In this transitional era, Bonaventure drew his spiritual sense and theological insights largely from the tradition of monastic theology—and patristic theology as well—including thinkers like Augustine, Pseudo-Dionysius, Bernard of Clairvaux,[142] and Richard and Hugh of St. Victor. At the same time, he was one of the most distinguished masters of theology at the University of Paris, where the Scholastic theology and method had developed and was practiced. In other words, Bonaventure, the master of Scholasticism, was also a mystic who greatly appreciated the experiential aspect of the religious life. He inherited from the monastic tradition the idea that the ultimate goal of the Christian is union with God.

As mentioned above, Bonaventure insists that the proper aim of theology is to make Christians more holy. This task cannot be accomplished only through theological pursuit as a mere intellectual work of reason: human reason should be elevated by faith and aided by the Holy Spirit.[143] Therefore, theology is not only a human work but also related to divine grace.[144] The theologian can become holy not through knowledge alone, but by joining the pursuit of knowledge with love; this combination is known as wisdom.[145] Wisdom allows the theologian to go beyond the speculative realm into the practical realm, motivated by love. Therefore, the goal of theology is to reach the Divine Wisdom,[146] which is possible only through contemplation aided by the gift of wisdom from the Holy Spirit.[147]

According to Bonaventure, while the gift of wisdom enables one to reach the highest Good through contemplation, the development of wisdom necessitates personal holiness since "without sanctity, a man cannot be wise."[148] In the pursuit of wisdom, therefore, one should endeavor to pass from the study of knowledge to the study of holiness, and again from the study of holiness to that of wisdom.[149] In such a way, inasmuch as theology aims at wisdom that eventually delivers one's soul into mystical union with God, the theological enterprise is by nature a spiritual exercise.

This integration of intellectual endeavor and spiritual life is evident in Bonaventure's writings. Nowhere is this more evident than in what is probably his most famous book, the *Itinerarium mentis in Deum* (*The Soul's Journey into God*). Ewert Cousins deems the work "an extraordinarily dense *summa* of medieval Christian spirituality."[150] In his spiritual writings, Bonaventure brought together the tradition of Christian spirituality and philosophical, theological speculation. As Cousins states, "In no other medieval Christian spiritual writer were such diverse elements present in such depth and abundance and within such an organic systematic structure."[151]

Bonaventure was most of all a faithful follower of Francis of Assisi. For Bonaventure, Francis was an inspiration for theological reflection and spiritual living. In order to unfold Bonaventure's spiritual summa, one must comprehend not only his intellectual milieu and spiritual insights, but also Francis's influence on him, which is the subject of the following section.

St. Francis of Assisi and St. Bonaventure

Nobody would deny that the life and words of Francis greatly influenced Bonaventure, not only in his following in the footprints of the the saint's life, but also in developing his theology and spirituality.[152] It is not easy to find explicit references to Francis in Bonaventure's writings prior to his election to the generalate.[153] Nevertheless, Bonaventure must have acquired a profound knowledge of the life of Francis and the Rule of the order, and he strove to live the evangelical life in accordance with them.[154]

However, for Bonaventure, Francis was not merely a virtuous saint. He also recognized the extraordinary depth of Francis's theological and spiritual insights, deeming them to have come from a divine origin:[155] Francis's understanding of God as the source of goodness, his appreciation and reverence of the creature as a manifestation of the divine, his understanding of Divine Love as fully revealed in the crucified Christ, and his zeal for conformity to the crucified One—which Francis eventually achieved with his reception of the stigmata. All of this had a great impact on Bonaventure, helping him develop his theological and spiritual approaches to questions concerning God, the world, redemption, and the development of the spiritual path. In this regard, Gregory F. LaNave considers Bonaventure to be "a commentator" on Francis.[156]

For Bonaventure, Francis was a theologian who had inspired, taught, and guided him in his intellectual and spiritual journey to God. Bonaventure was both master of Paris and disciple of Assisi. As a faithful disciple would, Bonaventure contemplated the experience of his master, and gave it philosophical and theological expression in a unique way that synthesized the long tradition of Christian spirituality and made use of the intellectual methods of his time.[157]

Zachary Hayes presents three distinctive elements of Francis's spirituality which would inspire and shape a theological tradition among Franciscan scholars, including Bonaventure: (1) a strong sense of God as a loving Father, (2) an understanding of creation as the mirror and image of God and God's relationship with the created world, and (3) a focus on Christ.[158]

With respect to the first of these elements, Francis's experience of God as a loving Father helped Bonaventure develop his own understanding of the nature of the Trinity, which synthesized the trinitarian thinking of Pseudo-Dionysius and of the Victorines. As to the second, Francis loved and revered God's creatures as visible manifestations of the Divine Goodness. This spiritual insight is embedded in Bonaventure's theology of creation: his acknowledgement of "the inherent goodness and sanctity"[159] of all created realities, his understanding of creation as an "emanation" of God's goodness, and his doctrine of "exemplarism," which articulates the relationship between the created world and its creator. Here, in Bonaventure's cosmology, as in his views on the trinitarian relationship, God's love and goodness is the essential cause of creation. Bonaventure sees that the love of God is not confined within the Trinity; rather, due to its self-diffusive nature it overflows outward to the creation of the universe.

As to the third element, Francis's love for and conformity to the crucified Christ shaped Bonaventure's Christology, a Christology that firmly places Christ at the center of everything. This Christocentrism is prominent in his theologies of the Trinity, Creation, and Salvation. Christ is the Incarnate Word, the visible form of the invisible principle of creation, and the Second Person of the Trinity, the eternal Word of God. Bonaventure's embrace of Francis's spiritual insights regarding Christ as the revealer of God was the basis for his development of a cosmic Christology.[160] Bonaventure also stressed that Christ is present at both the beginning and the end of each human being's spiritual journey toward God, as well as being the path to be followed on this journey.

Another notable element in Bonaventurian theology is the significant role of affection. The emphasis on *affectus* as an essential element in his theology was inspired by Francis's love and desire for God, which would be displayed externally through his reception of the stigmata. The crucial influence of

Francis's mystical experience of God on Bonaventure is also found in Bonaventure's heightened emphasis on experience over speculative efforts. As much as Francis was a mystic deeply immersed in the Divine Love, mystical elements are also noticeable in Bonaventure's writings, especially as Francis took a more central position in his theological quest.

Though Bonaventure praised Francis as a divinely inspired theologian and adopted many of his insights, in truth he did not learn of Francis through the saint's theological writings. Rather, Bonaventure's information about the saint came from some of Francis's spiritual writings, such as letters, the Rule of the order, and his life stories, which were full of significant spiritual experiences. It was Bonaventure's profound spiritual insights and theological capacities that allowed him to see the logic connecting Francis's experiences and to turn them into a metaphysical synthesis. One can find Francis's spirituality and Bonaventure's theology most closely interwoven in the *Itinerarium*. The following pages will explore this intellectual and spiritual summa in greater detail.

Itinerarium mentis in Deum (The Soul's Journey into God)

Bonaventure's writings, whether speculative or spiritual, are generally directed to the true wisdom to be found in a union with God. In *On the Reduction of Arts to Theology*, Bonaventure explains how all the sciences can and must contribute to this end.

> This is the fruit of all the sciences, that in all, faith may be strengthened, God may be honored, character may be formed, and consolation may be derived from a union of the Spouse with the beloved, a union which takes place through charity; a charity in which the whole purpose of sacred Scripture, and thus of every illumination descending from above, comes to rest—a charity without which all knowledge is vain because no one comes to the Son except through the Holy Spirit who teaches us all the truth, who is blessed forever.[161]

The *Itinerarium* is an elaborately constructed text that explicitly aims at this union with God. It uses the metaphor of a "journey," and speaks of the spiritual preparation one must undertake to accomplish this journey.[162] Despite its apparent spiritual goal, this remarkable synthesis is also a work of the mind, relying heavily on intellectual knowledge and the intellectual life.[163] Indeed, the book is hard to comprehend without a high-level education in philosophy, theology, and the scriptures. The integrative nature of the intellectual and spiritual in the book is evident in its prologue.

> Therefore, I first of all invite the reader to groans of prayer through Christ crucified, through whose blood we are purged from the stain of our sins. Do not

think that reading is sufficient without unction, speculation without devotion, investigation without admiration, circumspection without exultation, industry without piety, knowledge without divine grace, the mirror without the inspiration of divine wisdom.[164]

The intellectual reflections detailed in the *Itinerarium* are meant for those "who are already disposed by divine grace" and whose mind is "cleansed and polished."[165] Unless the reader is well prepared, he will be in danger of falling into darkness rather than being awakened to Divine Wisdom. There is no one who can be compared with Francis in terms of being prepared to set out on this intellectual/spiritual journey. Francis, through his example of a virtuous life, his spiritual insights, and his mystical experience inspired Bonaventure to follow this path. Philotheus Boehner notes that although Francis's influence was ubiquitous in all of Bonaventure's writings, "the fetters of scholastic method and tradition" often make it hard for those not familiar with it to feel Francis's presence when reading Bonaventure.[166] Not so in the *Itinerarium*—not only is the presence of Francis clearly tangible, but Bonaventure explicitly confesses that the saint's experience provided the framework of this spiritual masterpiece.

> It happened around the time of the thirty-third anniversary of the death of the saint that I was moved by divine inspiration and withdrew to Mount Alverna since it was a place of quiet. There I wished to satisfy the desire of my spirit for peace. And while I was there reflecting on certain ways in which the mind might ascend to God, I recalled, among other things, that miracle which the blessed Francis himself had experienced in this very place, namely the vision of the winged Seraph in the form of the Crucified. As I reflected on this, I saw immediately that this vision pointed not only to the uplifting of our father himself in contemplation but also to the road by which one might arrive at this experience.[167]

When Bonaventure visited Mount Alverna in September or October 1259, he had been leading the Order of Friars Minor for over two years. He had worked ardently and traveled through Europe attending to diverse administrative tasks, dealing with problems and conflicts both within and outside the order. Even before his taking this leadership position, he had been engaged in fierce debates with opponents of the mendicant orders. Living in such constant tension, he may have needed a retreat for rest and peace, and there would have been no better place than Mount Alverna for this purpose.[168] However, his need of rest might not have been the only reason he withdrew to this solitary place. He was responsible for the souls of his Franciscan brothers and sisters, and knew his need for spiritual resources from which he could feed his brothers. Mount Alverna was the best place for this, too. Francis had often withdrawn there for contemplation, and it was there that he saw the vision of the six-winged seraph in the form of the crucified One and received the stigmata.

It is not clear whether Bonaventure attained his "eagerly desired" peace during his retreat at Alverna.[169] However, while there and while meditating on Francis's mystical experience, Bonaventure conceived a map of the spiritual journey that would lead a contemplative to the ecstatic peace that Francis had achieved.[170] This peace that Bonaventure sought and toward which the spiritual journey would lead was not the mere dissolution of conflicts; rather, it was the perfection of wisdom which surpasses all intellectual understanding. It was this, in Bonaventure's understanding, that Francis proclaimed in his preaching.

As seen in the *Itinerarium,* Bonaventure's mystical journey does not exclude the intellect; in fact, it develops through intellectual investigation. In this regard, as Charles Carpenter suggests, Bonaventure's intellectual contemplation of the six-winged seraph and the stigmata of Francis shows that "not only was study not a hindrance to spiritual elevation, but now was seen to be the surest way for us to reach God."[171]

The Meaning of Itinerarium mentis in Deum

To better grasp the meaning and structure of this mystical and intellectual masterpiece, it is helpful to understand the deep meaning of its title, *Itinerarium mentis in Deum.* What follows relies on Boehner's informative annotations.[172] First, *itinerarium* means in general a journey, a plan for or a description of a journey. It also pertains in a medieval sense to a pilgrimage or a description of a pilgrimage to the Holy Land, or to a prayer for a safe journey to the Holy Land. Second, *mens,* that is mind or soul,[173] refers to the soul possessing three powers, memory, intellect, and will, and also connotes reason. Bonaventure, following Augustine, categorizes reason into two parts: inferior and superior. While inferior reason pertains to knowledge, superior reason directs us to wisdom, the journey to which involves three stages: purification, illumination, and perfection. Therefore, *mens* in the title refers to the image of God in man and to reason that yields to wisdom. Lastly, *in Deum,* translated as "into God," has a profound mystical dimension. Bonaventure deliberately chose the preposition "*in*" not "*ad*," indicating that this spiritual journey does not merely lead to (*ad*) God, but leads a soul "into" God where it would rest in a mystical union.[174]

Thus, the *Itinerarium,* while requiring the exercise of the intellect or speculation,[175] is a work which ultimately charts out a set of spiritual exercises, exercises that necessitate purification of the heart and the grace of the Holy Spirit. It is also a roadmap for the pilgrimage to the heavenly Jerusalem, the city of peace, in the innermost place of which God resides. Here, God's furnace would inflame, transform, and move a soul from this world to a mystical union with the Father. In the end, the pilgrim finds the peace for which he sets out the journey in the first place.[176]

The Structure of the Itinerarium

Francis's vision of the six-winged seraph kindled in the soul of Bonaventure the spiritual reflections of this book. It also provided a template for the layout of these reflections, with each wing symbolizing a certain stage or step in the ascent to God. Bonaventure writes: "The figure of the six wings of the Seraph, therefore, is a symbol of six stages of illumination which begin with creatures and lead to God to whom no one has access properly except through the Crucified."[177] These six stages are divided into three levels in accordance with the subject of speculation, each of which symbolically corresponds to one of three pairs of wings. The first level deals with the material world; the second with the soul; and the third with God.

> In order to arrive at that First Principle which is most spiritual and eternal, and above us, it is necessary that we move through the vestiges which are bodily and temporal and outside us. And this is to be led in the way of God. Next we must enter into our mind which is the image of God, an image which is everlasting, spiritual, and within us. And this is to enter into the truth of God. Finally we must pass beyond to that which is eternal, most spiritual, and above us by raising our eyes to the First Principle. And this will bring us to rejoice in the knowledge of God and to stand in awe before God's majesty.[178]

Each of these three levels contains two aspects, and the six-step journey in the ascent to God corresponds to the six chapters of the *Itinerarium*.[179] The soul sets out on its journey, following the guidance of the first two chapters, by contemplating on God as reflected in the vestiges of the created world that we perceive through our senses. Next, the soul's contemplation of God moves from the external to the internal. As articulated by Bonaventure in chapters 3 and 4, the soul meditates on the ways in which, as the image of God, it reflects God first in its natural powers and then as reformed by the gifts of grace. Then, at the final stage in chapters 5 and 6, the soul turns to God above the soul, contemplating Him first as Being and then as the Good. This contemplation will lead the soul into mystical union with God. Thus, the six chapters of the *Itinerarium* describe "the progress" that the soul makes in its ascent to God. A concluding seventh chapter deals with "the goal of the journey" itself.

The three main stages identified in the *Itinerarium*—meditation on nature, the soul, and God—constitute Bonaventure's own take on the long tradition of

Christian spirituality and theology since Augustine.[180] Ewert Cousins stresses
that Bonaventure's development of his three-stage (and finally six-stage) spiritual journey integrates earlier Christian thought, drawing its inspiration and
content from the insights of Francis on the contemplation of nature,[181] from
Augustine on the soul, and from Pseudo-Dionysius on God.[182]

As already noted, the six stages, each subject to a threefold division, frame
the structure of the *Itinerarium*. However, Bonaventure employed several
other structural principles in organizing his account of spiritual development,
which are explored in detail below. First, a more detailed summary of the
contents of the *Itinerarium* is presented.

Summary of the Itinerarium

The text consists of a prologue, six chapters articulating the six stages of the
soul's ascent to God, and a seventh chapter describing the final goal of the
journey. As has already been noted, in the prologue Bonaventure writes that
he conceived the idea for the structure and contents of the *Itinerarium* while
contemplating on Francis at Mount Alverna. He briefly mentions that the
soul in pursuit of peace will be uplifted by the six steps of illumination that
correspond to the six wings of the seraph and finally will pass over to true
peace through the burning love of the crucified Christ. Before setting out the
journey, he warns readers to prepare themselves with prayer and purification
of the mind.

Bonaventure titled chapter 1 "The Steps of the Ascent into God and
Speculation on God through the Vestiges in the Universe."[183] In the first part
of chapter 1 (1.1),[184] he describes the general framework of the journey in
a more detailed way, advises appropriate preparation of one's mind, heart,
and life for the journey, and emphasizes the need for God's grace. Chapter 1
details the process mentioned in the prologue, which begins "with creatures
and leads to God." The mind first directs its gaze outward to investigate the
material world that contains vestiges of God in bodily and temporal existence.
Then, it moves inward to meditate on the mind itself that is made in the image of God. Finally, the mind looks above itself to contemplate God Himself,
who is eternal and utterly spiritual (1.2). Bonaventure subdivides each of
these three steps into two: "through" and "in" the vestiges and "through" and
"in" the image, which altogether comprise the first four chapters, and the
consideration of God as the "alpha" and the "omega," which comprise the last
two chapters (1.5). At the beginning of creation, the human being was created with the capability of ascending to God by contemplating the universe.
However, because of original sin, the human mind was infected with ignorance and the flesh with concupiscence, which in turn disable the mind from
acknowledging God through and in the vestiges and the image of God. This

obstacle can be overcome only through Jesus Christ, who will bring wisdom and justice to the human mind (1.7). This can only happen with preparation and desire, prayer, a virtuous life, meditation, and contemplation (1.8).

Bonaventure next shows how sense-based knowledge leads the mind to God, whose supreme power, wisdom, and benevolence are apparent in created things (1.10). First, when the mind contemplates created things in themselves in terms of "weight, number, measure"; "mode, species, order"; and "substance, power, operation," it will be led to an understanding of the immense power, wisdom, and goodness of God (1.11). Second, seeing the universe through faith in terms of its origin, development, and end, the mind will come to consider the power, providence, and justice of God (1.12). Third, in carefully observing the created world, the mind will come to see, by means of reason, the created world's hierarchical order. It will come to see, for example, the distinction between beings that are merely corporal and those that are partly corporal and partly spiritual, a distinction that will give rise to the conclusion of the existence of the wholly spiritual. In a similar way, the mind will conclude that there must be a being both immutable and incorruptible. Thus, through sense-based knowledge of the created world, the mind comes to consider God in His power, wisdom, and goodness. (1.13). Bonaventure also briefly explains how considering the sevenfold properties of creatures— their origin, greatness, multitude, beauty, fullness, activity, and order—can lead one to realize the power, wisdom, and goodness of God (1.14), which are, he stresses, almost impossible not to notice in the universe (1.15).

While chapter 1 explores the ways in which the attributes of God are revealed "through" creatures, chapter 2 contemplates God "in" creatures by examining how God is present in them. Chapter 1 mostly deals with knowledge received through human senses, whereas chapter 2 focuses on the process by which the mind perceives this sense-based knowledge (2.1). Through three stages—appreciation, pleasure, and judgment—the sensible world or "macrocosm" enters the human soul (2.2). First, the mind comes to be aware of external sensible objects through the five senses. The mind appreciates these objects not in their substantial realties but by means of their likenesses generated in the sense medium (2.3). Once appreciated, sense experiences are to be enjoyed when the perceived likeness of the objects is proportionate to their form, power, and operation (2.4–2.5). Then, one moves to the intellectual activity that inquires into the cause of pleasure generated by sense experiences. This is the process of judgment, which depends on the proportion of harmony (2.6).[185] Bonaventure goes on to explain how each of these three stages are the vestiges of God. First, as a sensible thing generates a likeness of itself and we perceive it through the impressions made on our sense organs, we can see that the universe is the vestige of God generated by God's likeness, that is, the Word, the Image, or the Son (2.7). Likewise, the highest proportion of true delight and eternal truth with the greatest certainty of judgment are all found in God (2.8–2.9). In addition, Bonaventure develops his contemplation in chapter 2 by considering seven kinds of numbers. All things in the universe are considered beautiful and delightful in some way because of their proportionality, which can ultimately be seen in numbers. From this, it can be concluded that numbers are the principal exemplar in the mind of the creator and that creatures are meant to lead us to wisdom (2.10).

Chapter 3, entitled "The Speculation on God through the Image Imprinted on Our Natural Powers," brings the reader's gaze from things outside the soul to the inside of the soul in order to see the image of God as found in the soul's threefold powers (3.1). Investigating carefully the operations of the soul's three powers—memory, intellect, and will—leads one to eternity, truth, and the highest Good, all of which belong to God and flow into the soul from God (3.2–4). Furthermore, considering the order, origin, and relations of these powers will lead one to contemplate the Trinity by acknowledging the similarity between the operations and relations of the three faculties of the soul and the three Persons of the Trinity (3.5).

This reflection on the triune principle as revealed in the powers of the soul can be enhanced, according to Bonaventure, by analyzing the sciences. For instance, Bonaventure speaks of the division of philosophy into three parts, the natural, the rational, and the moral, each of which is again subdivided in a threefold way based on the triune principle (3.6). All sciences are subject to definite, infallible laws that are related to eternal laws. Thus, it is impossible for the wise not to reflect on the eternal laws and the eternal light while contemplating both the soul and the sciences (3.7).

Although God is close enough to be recognized by our soul, few are able to appreciate Him "through" and "in" the creature and the soul. In chapter 4, entitled "Speculation on God in the Image Reformed by the Gifts of Grace,"[186] Bonaventure explains that the human mind is so distracted by concerns, obscured by sense perceptions, and disordered by desires that it fails to properly contemplate God (4.1). Due to its sinful state, the soul cannot experience unhindered delight in God despite its ability to acquire knowledge. Only proper meditation on Christ, who is the ladder between God and humans, enables the soul to reenter into the enjoyment of God (4.2). Appreciation of Christ is made possible through the reformation of the soul by means of the three theological virtues of faith, hope, and love. These purify, illuminate, and perfect the soul when it believes in Christ as the uncreated Word, hopes to receive the inspired Word, and loves the Incarnate Word. This exercise of the three theological virtues restores the soul's spiritual senses and enables the soul to delight in God. This leads the soul to spiritual ecstasies (4.3). In this way, the soul—the image of God—is reformed and reordered hierarchically by grace so that it can ascend to the heavenly Jerusalem (4.4).

At this level of contemplation, the sacred scriptures are helpful in reforming the soul because they address faith, hope, and most especially love, the last of which is fully manifested in Jesus Christ, who purges, illumines, and perfects the church and each sanctified soul as the supreme hierarch (4.5). Thus, through the three theological virtues, the reformed spiritual senses, the spiritual ecstasies, and the three hierarchical acts of the mind, the soul returns to its interior where it sees God (4.6–4.8). In chapter 4, therefore, some crucial shifts in Bonaventure's account can be seen: from nature to grace, from rational to affective, and from philosophy to the scriptures, which add a further binary framework to the tripartite division of the spiritual journey.[187]

However, in chapter 5, "Speculation on the Divine Unity through God's Primary Name, Which Is Being,"[188] Bonaventure returns to his tripartite division, now contemplating God at a level above our souls. Bonaventure suggests contemplating God's invisible and eternal qualities in two ways: first, contemplating God as Being, and second, contemplating God as the Good, as described in the Old and New Testaments, respectively (5.1–5.2). By means of the philosophical categories of logic, Bonaventure shows that the intellect cannot help but recognize that Being itself must be the Divine Being, and that this Being, which is pure, simple, and absolute, is the first, the eternal, the simplest, the most actual, the most perfect, and the supremely one Being (5.3–5.6). Furthermore, the intellectual realization of the paradoxical attributes of this Being—such as its being both first and last, eternal and most present, simplest and greatest, most actual and unchangeable, most perfect and immense, supremely one and all-embracing—will lift the seeker in wonder (5.7–5.8).

After contemplating God as Being through the essential attributes of God, in chapter 6, "Speculation on the Most Blessed Trinity in its Name, Which is the Good,"[189] Bonaventure turns to the contemplation of God as the Good and also expounds his doctrine of emanation (6.1), which holds that the supreme Good must be self-diffusive, the quintessential example of which is found in the relationship between the Persons of the Trinity: the Father, the Son, and the Holy Spirit. The highest sort of love requires the Second and the Third Persons, or both a beloved and a co-beloved; God who is supremely diffusive consists of the Father, the Son, and the Holy Spirit. The Father gives the whole of Himself to the Son by way of generation, and the Father and the Son give the whole of Themselves to their co-beloved, the Holy Spirit, by way of spiration. Thus, the relationship among the three Persons of the blessed Trinity is characterized as one of supreme communicability, consubstantiality, conformability, coequality, coeternity, and mutual intimacy (6.2). However,

Bonaventure points out that there remain incomprehensible truths regarding the blessed Trinity in that each of these six characteristics are paired with paradoxical ones: the highest communicability with the property (or individuality) of each Person, the highest consubstantiality with the plurality of hypostases, the highest conformability with discrete personality, the highest coequality with order, the highest coeternity with emanation, and the highest intimacy with mission. Consideration of these paradoxes will lead one to awe and wonder (6.3).

After contemplating the essential attributes of God and the characteristics of the blessed Trinity, Bonaventure leads the reader's gaze toward the Mercy Seat that the two cherubim are facing. Here at the Mercy Seat, one sees Jesus Christ, in whom God and humanity are united. If one was amazed at the series of paradoxes derived from the contemplation of God as Being and God as the Good, he should be even more amazed at the marvelous paradoxes manifested in the union of God and humanity in the person of Christ (6.5–6.6). Through Jesus Christ, the contemplation of God in His Being and Goodness is made relevant to humanity because the mind sees humanity made in the image of God so marvelously exalted and humanity and God so ineffably united in Christ (6.7).

Now, when the mind comes to Jesus Christ, as described in chapter 7,[190] it finds mysteries that surpass the power of the human intellect. Seeing these mysteries, the mind must pass beyond the sensible world and the world of the soul, and this is possible only through the crucified Christ (7.1–7.2). This passing over into God in contemplation through the way of the crucified Christ had already been accomplished by Francis (7.3). In this passing over, affection must play a dominant role. Now the mind enters into the divine darkness through death with Christ by silencing all our cares, desires, and imaginations. Only in this darkness can the soul truly see God (7.4–7.6).

The Itinerarium *as an Integrative Text of Intellectual Knowledge and Spirituality: Analysis of the Structural Principles of the* Itinerarium

Bonaventure draws on and explicitly cites theologians, monastic authors, and philosophers in constructing the staircase of spiritual ascent. Whether seen in specific terms, philosophical categories, quotations from learned authors, or in the systematic organization of the text, the *Itinerarium* is an intellectual treasure reflecting Bonaventure's accumulated learning and life-long spiritual practices.

There are many ways one could show the intellectual character of the *Itinerarium*. One could enumerate and explicate all the philosophical, theological, psychological, and even mathematical terms in the text; one could highlight the citations from the scriptures and prominent authors; or one could analyze the systematic framework of the text itself. Each of these would display the vast store of Bonaventure's knowledge and his capacity for analytical, systematic, and integrative thinking.[191] Undertaking all these tasks is beyond the scope of this book. It is the intent of this section to explore Bonaventure's efforts to integrate and synthesize speculation and spirituality; the multiple structural principles of the *Itinerarium* will be analyzed in order to show how Bonaventure incorporated the depth and breadth of the Christian intellectual tradition into the framework of his spiritual masterpiece.[192] In order to better understand the structural principles of the work, it will be necessary to refer to some of Bonaventure's speculative works.

Like other theologians of his time, Bonaventure inherited the long and profound tradition of Christian spirituality, but his work can be distinguished by his efforts to synthesize this tradition in his own way. One can enumerate a long list of theologians, philosophers, mystics, and monks who influenced Bonaventure. Bonaventurian scholars mostly agree, however, about the profound influence of Augustine, with some deeming Bonaventure's theology and spirituality "the supreme example of medieval Augustinianism."[193] In fact, Bonaventure's Augustinianism is a synthesis of the Dionysian and Augustinian forms of Neoplatonism, a synthesis that is indebted to the works of Hugh of St. Victor.[194] Denys Turner examines carefully how the complex, integrated structure of the *Itinerarium* draws on these two Christian Neoplatonisms. Turner praises Bonaventure's ability to maintain these two traditions in equilibrium, comparing this task to that of a medieval architect: "Indeed, one might fairly say that in Bonaventure's *Itinerarium*, as in a medieval cathedral, the engineering of the structure does much of the work of the aesthetic."[195] But in any event, the spiritual masterpiece that is the *Itinerarium* is a building constructed through Bonaventure's arduous studies of the intellectual treasures handed down to him, which includes not only theology but also philosophy and various other sciences.

The first structural principle of the *Itinerarium* that must be considered is its tripartite division—outside the soul, within the soul, and above the soul, a scheme Bonaventure borrows from Augustine.[196] Not only the threefold framework, but also the idea of a spiritual ascent to God, was inspired by Augustine. Frederick Van Fleteren shows how Bonaventure inherited the idea of the ascent of the soul—an idea that was first expounded by Plato (ca. 429–347 BCE), developed by Plotinus (204/5–270) into an ascent from without to within and then above, further developed by Porphyry (ca. 234–ca. 305) in a more mystical way, and then later Christianized by Augustine. Van Fleteren explores in particular Augustine's influence on Bonaventure by comparing the categories, ideas, and biblical references in Bonaventure's *Itinerarium* to those in Augustine's works, such as the *De quantitate animae, De vera religione, De trinitate, De musica,* etc. He insists that the overall structural features of the *Itinerarium*, namely, its tripartite divisions, its notion of seven stages, and its idea of vestiges of God, constitute a concatenation of Augustinian texts and ideas. He argues further that because Augustine's philosophy and theology became an integral part of Bonaventure's, sometimes it is difficult to trace precise references to Augustine in Bonaventure's works.[197]

The second important structural principle is the vestige/image/likeness distinction Bonaventure describes in the general layout of his spiritual master plan in chapter 1. This second division is closely associated with Hugh of St. Victor's understanding of the universe as symbol, representation, and image (or simulacrum) of something invisible. Hugh compares nature to a book that is the only means by which the human mind may read its author. However, these *simulacra naturae* (simulacra of nature) can only signify God; they cannot provide us with any proper meaning regarding the divine author, a limitation that is further exacerbated by sin. Hugh suggests that originally humans possessed three "eyes" to see and understand the divine: with the "eye of the flesh" we can see the external world, with the "eye of reason" we can perceive the soul within, and with the "eye of contemplation" we can see God and understand divine things. However, due to sin, the eye of contemplation was made blind and the eye of reason became obscured. Although the eye of flesh is still intact so that humans can see the world and appreciate its beauty, they nevertheless cannot fully understand the divine meaning of what they see. According to Hugh, only the grace mediated by Christ transforms the nature of fallen humans: through grace nature regains its power to reveal divine signs, and the eyes are restored to their ability to read the *simulacra gratiae* (simulacra of grace). The simulacra of grace are distinguished from the simulacra of nature in that they do not just signify the Creator, but because they are sacraments—what is signified is present in them. Hugh extends this sacramentality of the universe to human history and the scriptures. Hugh understands that the visible book of nature and the perceivable book of the scriptures are sacraments of the invisible, and that these two books can only be read properly by means of the book of life, that is, Jesus Christ in his humanity.[198]

This understanding of the universe as a book is evident in Bonaventure's understanding of the created world as a ladder leading to God.[199] Before Bonaventure incorporated Hugh's ideas of three eyes, three books, and ascent into the *Itinerarium*, he had already done so in some of his philosophical and theological works. For instance, in the *Breviloquium* Bonaventure summarizes his long speculation on the created world as follows:

> From all we have said, we may gather that the created world is a kind of book reflecting, representing, and describing its Maker, the Trinity, at three different

levels of expression: as a vestige, as an image, and as a likeness. The aspect of vestige ("footprint") is found in every creature; the aspect of image, only in intellectual creatures or rational spirits; the aspect of likeness, only in those spirits that are God-conformed. Through these successive levels, comparable to steps, the human intellect is designed to ascend gradually to the supreme Principle, which is God.[200]

Furthermore, in his exploration of the threefold stages of the ascent, Bonaventure relates these three stages to Hugh's metaphor of the three eyes with which humans can see the external world (outside them), the interior of the soul (inside them), and God and divine things (above them).[201] Hugh's description of the three eyes, in particular the eye of reason, is also briefly referred to in chapter 3 of the *Itinerarium*.[202] Bonaventure took up in his own way the Hugonian analogy of the creature that explores the relationships between it and its Creator by employing the metaphor of the three eyes and the vestige/image/likeness distinction.[203]

The tripartite way of reaching God through vestige, image, and likeness, briefly mentioned in the *Breviloquium*, is further expounded in chapters 1, 3, and 4 of the *Itinerarium*. Here, it can be seen that Bonaventure had expounded the analogy between creatures and God previously in his more speculative works, including the commentaries on the *Sentences* and the *Breviloquium*.[204]

However, although the analogy of the creature with its threefold distinction of vestige, image, and likeness was explored in depth in the earlier Scholastic texts, in the *Itinerarium* Bonaventure does not arrange the structure of the spiritual ascent on this basis. Those who are already acquainted with the analogy would naturally expect chapters 5 and 6 to deal with contemplating creatures as "the likeness" of God. However, the third part of the *Itinerarium* actually explicates the ways to contemplate God in His Being and Goodness. In fact, Bonaventure uses the term *similitudo* (likeness or similitude) only once in the *Itinerarium*, where he refers to the similitudes of the divine characteristics.[205] Here, similitude has a different implication from the similitude (or likeness) described in Hugh's analogy between the created world and God. The latter describes the state of conformation to God.

Thus, the vestige/image/likeness distinction does not apply to the entire framework of the six chapters of the *Itinerarium*. It is a distinguishing principle in only the first four chapters: chapters 1 and 2 contemplate the created world as the vestige of God, chapter 3 contemplates the human mind as the image of God, and chapter 4 contemplates the human soul in its reformed state as the likeness of God. In addition to this distinction, Denys Turner suggests that a further distinction between image and likeness divides the entire six chapters into two.[206] Bonaventure himself clarifies the distinction between chapters 3 and 4 as follows.

We can come to understand that we are led to divine things through the powers of the rational soul itself which are implanted in the soul by nature, and through their operations, relations, and the habits of knowledge they possess. This becomes clear at the third step. We are also led by the reformed faculties of the soul itself; and this includes the gifts of the virtues, the spiritual senses, and the mental ecstasies. And this is clear at the fourth level.[207]

While at the third step of the spiritual journey the mind speculates on its natural powers, the fourth step expounds on the restoration of the soul that has become conformed to God by grace. As noted above, in his analogy of the creature as book or simulacra, Hugh suggested two kinds of simulacra (likenesses)—the simulacra of nature and the simulacra of grace. While the simulacra of nature only signify their creator as representation, image, or symbol, the simulacra of grace not only more powerfully reveal their creator but also help restore to humans the power to read all the simulacra.[208] Hugh's distinction between the simulacra of nature and the simulacra of grace is seen in Bonaventure's distinction between image and likeness, as he explains in the *Second Book of the Commentary on the Sentences.*

An image occurs in the order of nature and likeness in the order of grace; . . . for . . . an image . . . is exemplified in the case of the natural powers of the soul, namely memory, intellect and will; so it is that an image is something in the natural order. But because a likeness is an actual sharing, and is the common possession of a quality; and because the quality by which the soul is made like to God is grace; for this reason a likeness is said to be something in the order of grace.[209]

This image and likeness distinction articulated in the *Commentary on Sentences II* is clearly employed in chapter 4 of the *Itinerarium*, though Bonaventure does not explicitly use the term "likeness" there. Drawing on this distinction, Denys Turner divides the *Itinerarium* into two parts: first, natural contemplation, subdivided into contemplation through vestige, in vestige, and through image; and second, supernatural contemplation, subdivided into contemplation in image and two contemplations of the divine properties, Being and Goodness.[210]

While Bonaventure appropriates Hugh's idea of the two simulacra, he expands it into the six-stage ladder. Ian P. Wei identifies additional characteristic shifts found at the transition from the third to the fourth step.[211] Beginning with the fourth step, the ascent comes to concern more the experience of the affections than rational considerations. In addition, at that step the study of the divinely inspired scriptures become more helpful than philosophy in contemplating nature and the soul.[212] Thus, the nature/grace distinction implied in the image/likeness distinction is the third underlying structural principle of the *Itinerarium*.

Besides the three structural principles discussed so far—the Augustinian tripartite division of without, within, and above; another threefold distinction of vestige/image/likeness; and the Hugonian binary division of nature and grace—a fourth underlying structural principle of the *Itinerarium* is "the Dionysian epistemological hierarchy of affirmative theologies."[213] After contemplating God through vestige and image without and within the soul, the reader comes to contemplate God through God's primary properties or names—Being and Goodness—in the final two steps of the ascent. Turner relates chapters 5 and 6 to Pseudo-Dionysius's *Divine Names* by pointing out the similarities in their chapter titles: the titles of chapters 4 and 5 of the *Divine Names* correspond to chapters 6 and 5 of the *Itinerarium*.[214] Furthermore, Turner argues that the Dionysian threefold classification of affirmative theologies—symbolic, representational, and conceptual—corresponds to the tripartite structure of the *Itinerarium*.[215] On the other hand, Wei presents Bonaventure's three modes of theology—symbolic, proper, and mystical[216]—as the developed form of the Dionysian threefold categories of theology.[217]

The fifth structural principle of the work is the distinction between the prepositions "through" (*per*) and "in" (*in*). The first four chapters of the *Itinerarium* consist of contemplations through and in vestige and through and in image. Although the through/in distinction is a significant subdividing principle, the text of the *Itinerarium* does not provide a clear definition of it. As explored above, the image/likeness distinction, which reflected the Hugonian distinction of nature and grace, helped Bonaventure to clarify the meaning and distinctiveness of "through image" and "in image" in chapters 3 and 4. However, this distinction is not applicable to an understanding of the two contemplations described in chapters 1 and 2—through vestige and in vestige. A careful reading of those two chapters, however, helps the reader understand the meanings of the contemplation of God "through vestige" and "in vestige." In the former, one rises from visible realities to contemplation of the various properties of God; in the latter, by speculating on the mind's perception of sensible things, one comes to realize that all sensible and mental activities are made possible because of the presence and operation of their corresponding divine powers. This understanding of the distinction between "through" and "in" vestige, which the reader induces from reading the text, had been clearly defined previously in Bonaventure's *Commentary on Sentences I*.

It is one thing to know God in a creature, another [to know God] through creatures.[218] But to know God in a creature is to know his presence flowing into the creature. But to know God through a creature is to be raised up by the knowledge of the creature to the knowledge of God, as by means of a ladder between them.[219]

These definitions of "through" and "in" are also implied in chapters 3 and 4, which contemplate God "through" and "in" the soul as the image of God. Speculation on the triune powers of the soul leads one to the Blessed Trinity, while the reformation of the soul by the gifts of grace enables one to experience God intimately.[220]

This section has explored the various principles governing the organization of the complex structure of the *Itinerarium*. In general, as noted earlier in this section, the spiritual ascent to God is composed of six steps in three broad stages with a binary structure for each stage. Bonaventure makes it clear that his speculations are arranged according to the Augustinian threefold contemplation of God—without, within, and above—with binary subdivisions. Bonaventure draws on not only Augustine but also the works of Hugh of St. Victor and Pseudo-Dionysius, which helped him develop his six-step ascent to God. The analogy of the creature as a ladder to God dominates the first four chapters of the *Itinerarium*. These chapters contemplate the ways in which one can be led to God through the created things that represent their author. Furthermore, Bonaventure employed Hugh's distinction between created reality as being simulacra of nature or simulacra of grace in the image/likeness distinction that governs the development of the third and fourth chapters. The nature/grace distinction not only distinguishes chapters 3 and 4, but it also divides the reading of the text into two halves: chapters 1, 2, and 3, and chapters 4, 5, and 6. However, in the last two chapters, Bonaventure draws on Dionysian conceptual theology in his discussion of contemplation of God above the soul. The Dionysian categories of theology—symbolic, representational, and conceptual—can be considered as another threefold principle determining the hierarchical ascent of the soul to God.

Integration of Learning into the Itinerarium, a Work Written for Spiritual Purposes

Thus, the structure of the *Itinerarium* draws on a wide variety of theological and spiritual resources. Employing multiple resources and ingenious structural divisions, Bonaventure produced an organically synthesized, unified, and integrated text.[221] No matter how elegant, however, the text is not easy for ordinary readers without a proper education to comprehend. Knowledge of the works and theology discussed above is needed to facilitate a better understanding of the text, and it is necessary to consult Bonaventure's previous Scholastic works, such as the commentaries on the *Sentences* and the *Breviloquium*, because most of the structural principles of the *Itinerarium* mentioned are defined and explained in these works.

Obviously, the *Itinerarium* is full of explicit and implicit references to the scriptures and to the thought of many philosophers and theologians. Bonaventure sometimes paraphrases or does not bother to provide detailed explanations of his sources because he expects his readers to be familiar with these materials.[222] For modern readers, even those with a great deal of knowledge of medieval Scholasticism, it is difficult to grasp the full meanings of the text without commentaries that provide clarifying definitions of terms and analogies.[223]

The *Itinerarium* is concerned to help the reader make a spiritual ascent to God. However, it is without a doubt also a profound exercise of the mind and intellect. Bonaventure, rather than separating the two aspects of the spiritual and the intellectual, integrates them, intending to "demonstrate the coincidence of the hierarchy of theological knowledge with that of the soul's personal ascent into God."[224] Bonaventure employs the various sciences he had learned and taught at the University of Paris in the service of this goal. He does this beginning with the salvation history of humanity and the metaphysics of the properties of creatures (more specifically, natural philosophy or physics)[225] in chapter 1; enlists the aid of psychology in exploring the processes of the mental perception of sensible objects and mathematics for speculation on the seven kinds of numbers as principles of creation in chapter 2; again employs psychology to investigate the operations and relationships of the three mental powers as an analogy to the Trinity and various kinds of philosophy associated with the triune principle in chapter 3; uses Holy Scripture and theology to transform human beings in conformity to God in chapter 4; and finally, engages in metaphysical speculations on the two divine properties of Being and Goodness in chapters 5 and 6.[226]

Thus, the learned academic disciplines are incorporated into the articulation of a spiritual journey. In this respect, Turner considers the *Itinerarium* "a thirteenth-century rewriting of Augustine's *De Doctrina Christiana*, which was Augustine's survey of the breadth and divisions of the whole of Christian *learning* as serving the ends of Christian *charity*"[227] and "a compendious *Reductio Artium ad Theologiam*."[228] Bonaventure insists that the laws associated with sciences are all related to or governed by the Eternal Law and that the source of truths is Eternal Wisdom. Therefore, sciences will lead one to the reflection of God.

All these sciences are governed by certain and infallible laws that are like lights and beams coming down from that eternal law into our mind. Therefore, our mind, enlightened and filled with such splendors, can be guided to reflect on this eternal light through itself if it has not been blinded. The irradiation of this light and the reflection on it lifts up the wise in admiration.[229]

Through his studies and teaching at the University of Paris, Bonaventure attained to a profound knowledge of a wide variety of sciences. Inspired by Francis's mystical experience, Bonaventure built a ladder to God utilizing his intellect. Thus, the *Itinerarium* is not meant for all Christians, but for the learned who aspire to ascend to God by the ladder built by Bonaventure in the spirit of Francis.[230] Through the *Itinerarium*, the spirituality and mystical experience of Francis is made accessible to those with the proper education. Citing Bougerol's words again, "Paris has not destroyed Assisi. Rather, Paris has become, through Bonaventure, the fullest flowering of Assisi in the field of thought."[231]

SUMMARY

This chapter explored the historical development of learning and study in the Order of Friars Minor and the tension produced among the friars by the growing intellectualization of the order. The Franciscan Order, which began as a humble movement of simple laymen, rapidly expanded in its number and geographical extent, and grew into an influential religious order. The order also experienced a drastic transformation when large numbers of clerics and learned men joined its ranks, entailing a new emphasis on pastoral ministry and intellectual training. These changes greatly concerned friars who regarded poverty and simplicity as crucial to the Franciscan lifestyle, following the example of St. Francis of Assisi. Francis himself often warned of the dangers of the vain pursuit of knowledge but had great respect for theologians; he neither totally rejected nor approved of learning within the order.

Despite the concerns of some friars, study and learning came to be an essential part of the Franciscan life and was supported by friars in positions of leadership. These leaders encouraged the recruitment of learned scholars and students into the order and facilitated the establishment of a well-structured educational network throughout Europe. Franciscan theologians justified the pursuit of learning, claiming that even though Francis knew the Christian doctrines and mysteries through divine inspiration, those who had not received such inspiration should strive to be better Christians through human teachers. Furthermore, they contended that if one is not taught the gospel, one cannot live as a disciple of Jesus Christ.

At this time of growth and struggle, Bonaventure of Bagnoregio was elected as general minister of the Franciscan Order. In this role he assumed the heavy responsibility of guiding and governing his Franciscan brothers and sisters. He was obliged to protect the order from attacks coming from outside it and to resolve divisive tensions within it. As a follower of Francis, he regarded poverty, simplicity, and sanctity as being important to the Franciscan ideals and lifestyle, and he was in agreement with Francis that knowledge should not be pursued for its own sake, neither from motives of curiosity nor privilege. On the other hand, as a well-known master of theology at the University of Paris, he was convinced that intellectual enterprise was beneficial to the friars, for he believed that all forms of knowledge—including knowledge of the scriptures and of theology—could serve their spiritual growth. For this reason, Bonaventure did not believe that intellectual development should be separated from spiritual practice.

His integrative view of intellectual and spiritual practice was most evident in the *Itinerarium mentis in Deum*, his spiritual masterpiece. In this text, Bonaventure articulates in detail how the mind can reach God through intellectual contemplation of various subjects, and how it can finally be united with God in mystical ecstasy. The six steps of contemplation are set forth with a vast range of scientific knowledge and frequent references to eminent intellectuals and their writings, which Bonaventure had become familiar with as part of his education and teaching at the University of Paris. Bonaventure made full use of his intellectual capabilities in order to present a spiritual guidebook for those who are both learned and aspire to spiritual growth. The analysis presented of the multiple structural principles of the text showed that fully understanding the *Itinerarium* requires a good deal of intellectual knowledge.

Despite the prevalence of scientific knowledge and reasoning in its pages, the *Itinerarium* is a spiritual writing that attempts to represent the mystical experience of Francis's vision of the six-winged seraph. While the first six chapters deal with intellectual endeavors, Bonaventure makes it clear that this theoretical, analytical exercise must be accompanied by spiritual exercises like prayer, charity, and the cultivation of virtues, all of which must be aided by divine grace. The seventh chapter, which will be discussed more thoroughly in chapter 3 of this book, describes the state of mystical union with God, which is made possible not by intellect but through affection "directed to God and transformed in God."[232] Thus, the exercise of the intellect is not an end itself, but rather serves spiritual ends by becoming integrated into what is primarily a spiritual exercise.

NOTES

1. Kenan Osborne, *The Franciscan Intellectual Tradition: Tracing Its Origins and Identifying Its Central Components* (St. Bonaventure, NY: Franciscan Institute, 2003), 1.

2. For a brief survey of notable Franciscan scholars at the universities in Paris and Oxford, see Osborne, *The Franciscan Intellectual Tradition*, 42–52.

3. Osborne, *The Franciscan Intellectual Tradition*, 1.

4. "The first brotherhood was . . . socially heterogeneous. This very broad recruitment base continued during the thirteenth century and well beyond. Nevertheless, a predominance of the middle class remains evident, even from the upper level of the middle class, anyone from which would surely possess an inheritance to be disposed of for the benefit of the poor." Théophile Desbonnets, *From Intuition to Institution: The Franciscans*, trans. Paul Duggan and Jerry Du Charme (Chicago: Franciscan Herald, 1988), 19.

5. Desbonnets, *From Intuition to Institution*, 80.

6. Paul Sabatier (1858–1928) with the publication of the *Vie de S. François d'Assise* in 1894 prompted historical studies on the hagiographical sources, which resulted in vigorous debates about the life of Francis. These scholarly debates and studies are collectively known as the "Franciscan Question." Sabatier was a notable critic of the development of the Franciscan Order in the thirteenth century. For a brief survey of modern historical perspectives on thirteenth-century Franciscan history and the "Franciscan Question," see Neslihan Şenocak, *The Poor and the Perfect: The Rise of Learning in the Franciscan Order, 1209–1310* (Ithaca, NY: Cornell University Press, 2012), 9–16. For a brief introduction to the "Franciscan Question," see also Regis J. Armstrong, OFM Cap., J. Wayne Hellmann, OFM Conv., and William J. Short, OFM, eds., *Francis of Assisi—The Saint*, vol. 1 of *Francis of Assisi: Early Documents* (New York: New City Press, 1999), 22–24 (hereafter *FA:ED*, 1).

7. John Moorman, *A History of the Franciscan Order: From Its Origins to the Year 1517* (Oxford: Clarendon Press, 1968), 53.

8. Paul Sabatier, *The Life of St. Francis of Assisi*, trans. Louise S. Houghton (London: Hodder and Stoughton, 1902), 277; Şenocak, *The Poor and the Perfect*, 14.

9. "Et eramus *idiotae* et subditi omnibus." Francis, *The Testament* 19, in Enrico Menesto and Stefano Brufani, eds., *Fontes Franciscani* (Assisi: Edizioni Porziuncola, 1995), 229 (italics mine). "In multis offendi mea gravi culpa, specialiter quod regulam, quam Domino, promisi, non servavi, nec officium, sicut regula praecipit, dixi sive negligentia sive infirmitatis meae occasione sive quia ignorans sum et *idiota*." Francis, *Letter to the Entire Order* 39, in *Fontes Franciscani*, 102–3 (italics mine). English translations are taken from *FA:ED*, 1:125 (*Testament*), 119 (*Letter to the Entire Order*) (bracketed insertions mine). Francis used the Latin word *idiotae* in plural form in *The Testament* and *idiota* in singular form in *A Letter to the Entire Order*. Armstrong translates the former as "simple" and the latter as "stupid," but Paul Barrett, OFM Cap., translates *idiota* in *A Letter to the Entire Order* as "unlearned." See Oktavian Schmucki, OFM Cap., "St. Francis's Level of Education," trans. Paul Barrett, OFM, *Greyfriars Review* 10, no. 2 (1996): 153. I follow Barrett's translation.

10. Schmucki, "St. Francis's Level of Education," 153–70. For the life of "minority" (living a life identified with the poor and marginalized), see Giovanni Miccoli, "The Writings of Francis as Sources for the History of Franciscan Origins," trans. Edward Hagman, *Greyfriars Review* 18, no. 1 (2004): 20; Michael W. Blastic, OFM, Jay M. Hammond, and J. A. Wayne Hellmann, OFM Conv., eds., *The Writings of Francis of Assisi: Letters and Prayers*, vol. 1 of *Studies in Early Franciscan Sources* (St. Bonaventure, NY: Franciscan Institute, 2011), 132.

11. Bonaventure, *The Major Legend of Saint Francis* 11.1, in Regis J. Armstrong, OFM Cap., J. A. Wayne Hellmann, OFM Conv., and William J. Short, OFM, eds., *Francis of Assisi—The Founder*, vol. 2 of *Francis of Assisi: Early Documents* (New York: New City Press, 2000), 525–683 (hereafter *FA:ED*, 2). See Schmucki, "St. Francis's Level of Education," 167.

12. Bert Roest, *Franciscan Learning, Preaching and Mission c. 1220–1650*, vol. 10 of *The Medieval Franciscans* (Boston: Brill, 2014), 8. Francis's knowledge of the scriptures was understood as a gift to him from God. Thomas of Celano writes: "Although this blessed man was not educated in scholarly disciplines, still he learned from God wisdom from above." *The Remembrance of the Desire of a Soul* 102, in *FA:ED*, 2:314 (widely known as and hereafter cited as *Second Celano*). For more of Celano on Francis's understanding of the scriptures and related miracles, see *Second Celano* 102–7, in *FA:ED*, 2:314–18.

13. Sabatier, *The Life of St. Francis of Assisi.*

14. Sabatier and the scholars who followed his analysis gave great weight to these hagiographical sources, which reflected the voice of Francis and of direct witnesses, such as the *Anonymous of Perugia* (*Anonymus Perusinus*), the *Legend of the Three Companions* (*Legenda Trium Sociorum*), the *Assisi Compilation* (*Compilatio Assisiens*, also known as the *Legenda Perusina*), the *Deeds of Blessed Francis and His Companions* (*Actus Beati Francisci et Sociorum Eius*), and the *Mirror of Perfection* (*Speculum Perfectionis*). Roest provides informative references to the scholarly works discussing how Francis was depicted in the hagiographies. See Roest, *Franciscan Learning, Preaching and Mission*, 2n3.

15. Roest, *Franciscan Learning, Preaching and Mission*, 4–5.

16. Roest, *Franciscan Learning, Preaching and Mission*, 7.

17. Blastic, Hammond, and Hellmannn, *The Writings of Francis of Assisi: Letters and Prayers*, 127. In hagiographies and sermons, St. Anthony of Padua was depicted as "a friar whose wisdom and erudition were in perfect harmony with the mainstream Franciscan virtues of poverty and humility." Şenocak, *The Poor and the Perfect*, 113. For a detailed discussion of Anthony, see Şenocak, 109–17.

18. Francis, *The Later Rule* 10.7, in *FA:ED*, 1:105.

19. Şenocak, *The Poor and the Perfect*, 34–37.

20. Francis, *The Later Rule* 4, in *FA:ED*, 1:102–3. On the prohibitions against ownership of any dwelling and receiving books, *The Earlier Rule* is more explicit. See Francis, *The Earlier Rule* 7.13, 8.3, in *FA:ED*, 1:69–70.

21. Roest, *Franciscan Learning, Preaching and Mission*, 12.

22. Francis, *Admonitions* 5, 7, in *FA:ED*, 1:131–32.

23. Laurentio C. Landini, "The Causes of the Clericalization of the Order of Friars Minor: 1209–1260 in the Light of Early Franciscan Sources" (PhD diss., Pontificia Universitas Gregoriana, Facultas Historiae Ecclesiasticae, 1968). Landini states that the clericalization of the order was largely complete by 1260, the year in which the Constitutions of Narbonne were adopted.

24. Landini, "The Causes of the Clericalization," xxi.

25. See *Second Celano* 143, in *FA:ED*, 2:340; *Assisi Compilation* 11, 39, in *FA:ED*, 2:125–26, 142–43; Landini, "The Causes of the Clericalization," 36. The

exact year of Francis's resignation is uncertain. For more information, see Rosalind B. Brooke, *Early Franciscan Government: Elias to Bonaventure* (Cambridge: Cambridge University Press, 1959), 76–83.

26. For the ambivalent position of Francis in the order after his resignation in about 1217, see Brooke, *Early Franciscan Government*, 106–22.

27. In *From Intuition to Institution*, Théophile Desbonnets surveys the development of the Franciscan movement, which began as an "intuition" and solidified into an "institution." He also speaks in terms of the shift from a brotherhood to a religious order. Desbonnets, *From Intuition to Institution*.

28. *Cum secundum consilium*, September 22, 1220. See Landini, "The Causes of the Clericalization," 38.

29. Here and below "the Rule" refers to the *Earlier* and *Later Rules* taken together unless indicated otherwise.

30. See Landini, "The Causes of the Clericalization," 40.

31. See Landini, "The Causes of the Clericalization," 45. See also Landini, 3–23, for the development of clericalization in the church before the Franciscan movement. Landini points out that from the very beginning of the order and throughout his life, Francis tried to be faithful to church authority, seeking out both approval and advice. He suggests that Francis's veneration of priests as Eucharistic ministers and of theologians as ministers of God's words anticipated future developments within the order. See Landini, "The Causes of the Clericalization," 29, 49–55.

32. Landini, "The Causes of the Clericalization," 45. *Cura animarum* means "the care of souls."

33. For the papal bulls relating to and papal support for the clericalization of the order, see Landini, "The Causes of the Clericalization," 56–76.

34. See Landini, "The Causes of the Clericalization," 116.

35. Landini gives the example of the 1241 *Exposition of the Rule* by the four masters of Paris. Landini, "The Causes of the Clericalization," 77–81.

36. Landini, "The Causes of the Clericalization," 81–84. Landini summarizes this process, which had developed within the four decades since the order's founding.

At first, the popes introduced the Minors to the bishops as Catholic and orthodox men living a life approved by the Holy See. Because of the presence of priests and clerics in the Order, privileges of praying the Office in time of interdict, of using portable altars, of having services in their own oratories, and of burying their own dead, were granted to the friars. As the number and quality of priests grew, the papacy, during the 1230's, asked the prelates to permit the Minors to preach in their churches and hear confessions, and to accept them as co-workers in the vineyard of the Lord. In the 1240s and 1250s, more liberal privileges were granted regarding study, the advancement of friars of Holy Orders and the *cura animarum*. We have treated all of these developments in chapter 4, interpreting these privileges as a response conditioned by the growth of clerics within the Order and their involvement in the *cura animarum*. (Landini, 116)

37. Landini, "The Causes of the Clericalization," 85–93; Şenocak, *The Poor and the Perfect*, 29.

38. Landini, "The Causes of the Clericalization," 121.

39. Aware of some historians' criticism of these leaders, Şenocak defends them, suggesting that they did not believe themselves to have strayed from the ideals of the founder. Şenocak, *The Poor and the Perfect*, 21–22.

40. Drawing on the statistics of the number of German friars in the thirteenth century, Şenocak suggests that great numbers of laymen were accepted until 1239. See Şenocak, *The Poor and the Perfect*, 40. Roest asserts that the exclusive control of the order by learned clerics permanently skewed its direction.

> When highly educated clerical factions took control over the order in and after 1239, promptly began to issue constitutions that sanctioned the creation of strict hierarchies, and pursued policies that disqualified older ways of life, some companions of old reached for their pens to denounce the pursuit of learning. By then, theological scholarship had come to stand for everything that was undercutting older ideals of evangelical poverty, humility and fraternal equality: Paris had destroyed Assisi. (Roest, *Franciscan Learning, Preaching and Mission*, 18)

41. Landini, "The Causes of Clericalization," xxvi.

42. See Landini, "The Causes of Clericalization," xxi–xxvi, Şenocak, *The Poor and the Perfect*, 36.

43. Roest, *Franciscan Learning, Preaching and Mission*, 16. For a further reference to the significance of preaching as part of the Franciscan vision and its relation to learning within the order, see Bert Roest, "Preaching: Cornerstone of the Franciscan Education Project," chap. 7 in *A History of Franciscan Education c. 1210–1517* (Leiden: Brill, 2000), 272–324.

44. Brooke, *Early Franciscan Government*, 86.

45. For Elias, see Brooke, *Early Franciscan Government*, 83–105, 137–67.

46. Roest, *Franciscan Learning, Preaching and Mission*, 19–50.

47. Şenocak, *The Poor and the Perfect*, 24, 143. For a further exploration of the reasons for the development of advanced studies within the order, see Şenocak, "Beyond Preaching and Confession," chap. 3 in *The Poor and the Perfect*, 144–88. See also David Burr, *The Spiritual Franciscans: From Protest to Persecution in the Century after Saint Francis* (University Park, PA: Pennsylvania State University, 2001), 6–7. Roest and Şenocak offer excellent scholarly works on early Franciscan education. Roest's *A History of Franciscan Education (c. 1210–1517)* provides a comprehensive survey of the medieval development of the Franciscan educational system, whereas Şenocak's *The Poor and the Perfect* tells "a story of how and why learning became part of Franciscan way of life, and the consequences of this integration" (Şenocak, 2).

48. Şenocak, *The Poor and the Perfect*, 112–13.

49. Şenocak, *The Poor and the Perfect*, 109–11.

50. See Eric Doyle, *The Disciple and the Master: St. Bonaventure's Sermons on St. Francis of Assisi* (Chicago: Franciscan Herald Press, 1984), 64; Şenocak, *The Poor and the Perfect*, 110.

51. Şenocak, *The Poor and the Perfect*, 120.

52. Şenocak, *The Poor and the Perfect*, 117–28.

53. Thomas Eccleston records the words of John of Parma that "Cum ex duobus parietibus construatur aedificium Ordinis, scilicet moribus bonis et scientia" [Because the building of the order is constructed with the two walls of good life and learning]. The Latin text is found in Thomas of Eccleston, "De adventu minorum in angliam," in *Monumenta franciscana*, ed. J. S. Brewer (London: Longman, 1858), 1:50. For John's statement, see also Burr, *The Spiritual Franciscans*, 37; Şenocak, *The Poor and the Perfect*, 111.

54. Şenocak, *The Poor and the Perfect*, 142.

55. Şenocak, *The Poor and the Perfect*, 46.

56. Burr, *The Spiritual Franciscans*, 1–41; see also Şenocak, *The Poor and the Perfect*, 11–16.

57. The friars involved expressed their concerns by "borrowing" Francis's voice in the form of hagiography. See Burr, *The Spiritual Franciscans*, 16; Roest, *Franciscan Learning, Preaching and Mission*, 17.

58. Thomas Celano penned a previous hagiography in 1229 titled *The Life of St. Francis*, known as *First Celano.*

59. These materials attributed to the early companions of St. Francis were often referred to in the writings of late thirteenth- and early fourteenth-century spiritual writers such as Ubertino of Casale and Angelus Clarinus. For the significance of *Scripta Leonis* for the Spirituals, see Duncan Nimmo, *Reform and Division in the Franciscan Order: From Saint Francis to the Foundation of the Capuchins* (Rome: Capuchin Historical Institute, 1987), 78–95.

60. *Second Celano* 194, in *FA:ED*, 2:371.

61. Şenocak, *The Poor and the Perfect*, 86.

62. *Second Celano* 191, in *FA:ED*, 2:370. See Şenocak, *The Poor and the Perfect*, 91.

63. *Assisi Compilation* 47, in *FA:ED*, 2:147.

64. Roest, *Franciscan Learning, Preaching and Mission*, 17.

65. Masters and bachelors received special rooms and even servants. They were also exempted from convent mass, prayers, and communal meals and labors if necessary. Roest, *A History of Franciscan Education*, 236–37. However, Roest points out that those privileges were granted mostly to those who were engaged in advanced studies in school friaries, such as custodial schools and *studia generalia*. For a survey, see Şenocak, "Paradise Lost," chap. 4 in *The Poor and the Perfect*, 189–214.

66. Şenocak, *The Poor and the Perfect*, 91.

67. Francis, *The Testament* 13, in *FA:ED*, 1:125.

68. Şenocak, *The Poor and the Perfect*, 95.

69. *Constitutiones Prenarbonenses* 75 (1239) and *Constitutiones Narbonenses* 39 (1260). The content of these two documents may be found in Roest, *A History of Franciscan Education*, 239.

70. Şenocak, *The Poor and the Perfect*, 244.

71. Şenocak, *The Poor and the Perfect*, 244. See also Landini, "The Causes of the Clericalization," 116.

72. Philip Sheldrake briefly explains the monastic intellectual tradition as follows:

From the patristic period until the development of the "new theology" of scholasticism around the twelfth century theology was a single enterprise. To say that theology was a unified enterprise does not simply mean that the later distinctions between intellectual disciplines were not present. The unity of theology implied that intellectual reflection, prayer and living were, ideally speaking, a seamless whole. (Philip Sheldrake, *Spirituality and Theology: Christian Living and the Doctrine of God* [London: Darton, Longman & Todd, 1998], 36)

73. J. Guy Bougerol, *Introduction to the Works of Bonaventure*, trans. José de Vinck (Paterson, NJ: St. Anthony Guild, 1964), vii.

74. Ewert H. Cousins, introduction to *Bonaventure: The Soul's Journey into God·The Tree of Life·The Life of St. Francis*, trans. and ed., with introduction, Ewert H. Cousins (New York: Paulist Press, 1978), 1.

75. Few records documenting Bonaventure's early life have been preserved. Even concerning the periods of his life spent in Paris and as minister general, extant records often do not provide specific dates for significant events and writings. There are, however, two specific dates in the life of Bonaventure that are known with certainty: the date of his election as minister general of the Order of Friars Minor (1257) and the date of his death (1274). For brief introductions to Bonaventure's life, see J. Guy Bougerol, *Introduction to the Works of Bonaventure*, 3–10, 171–77; Cousins, introduction to *Bonaventure*, 2–11; Timothy Johnson, ed., *Bonaventure: Mystic of God's Word* (Hyde Park, NJ: New City Press, 1999), 10–28; Timothy Noone and R. E. Houser, "Saint Bonaventure," in *The Stanford Encyclopedia of Philosophy*, ed. Edward N. Zalta (Winter 2014), http://plato.stanford.edu/archives/win2014/entries/bonaventure/ (accessed February 12, 2019); Christopher M. Cullen, *Bonaventure* (Oxford: Oxford University Press, 2006), 3–22. For the debates on dating important events in Bonaventure's life, see John F. Quinn, "Chronology of St. Bonaventure (1217–1257)," *Franciscan Studies* 32 (1972): 168–86; Von Theodore Crowley, "St. Bonaventure Chronology Reappraisal," *Franziskanische Studien* 56, no. 2 (1974): 310–22; Jay M. Hammond, "Dating Bonaventure's Inception as Regent Master," *Franciscan Studies* 67 (2009): 179–226.

76. *Major Legend*, prol. 3, in *FA:ED*, 2:528; Bonaventure, *The Minor Legend of Saint Francis*, chap. 7, eighth lesson, in *FA:ED*, 2:717. Bonaventure composed *The Minor Legend* as an abbreviated version of the *Major Legend* for liturgical purposes.

77. This is mentioned in the bull issued by Pope Sixtus IV granting indulgence to the pilgrims to the Chapel of St. Bonaventure in the Church of St. Francis in Bagnoregio on October 14, 1482. See José M. Pou y Marti, ed., *Bullarium Franciscanum*, vol. 3 (1471–1484) (Ad Claras Aquas [Quaracchi]: Collegium S. Bonaventurae, 1949), 838.

78. Cullen, *Bonaventure*, 3.

79. Cullen, *Bonaventure*, 3–8.

80. Bonaventure would also become a cautious critic of erroneous interpretations of the ancient Greek philosopher—in particular of Averroist Aristotelianism.

81. There are debates as to the exact date of Bonaventure's entrance into the order. See Cullen, *Bonaventure*, 11.

82. Bougerol, *Introduction to the Works of Bonaventure*, 4–6.

83. Bonaventure, *A Letter in Response to Three Questions of an Unknown Master (1254–55),*" in *St. Bonaventure's Writings Concerning the Franciscan Order*, trans., with introduction, Dominic V. Monti, vol. 5 of *Works of St. Bonaventure* (St. Bonaventure, NY: Franciscan Institute, 1994), 39–56 (hereafter cited as *WSB*).

84. *A Letter in Response to an Unknown Master* 13, in *WSB*, 5:54.

85. See Maurice de Wulf, *The History of Medieval Philosophy*, trans. P. Coffey (London: Longmans, Green, and Company, 1909), 277–81; Joseph Sauer, "Alexander of Hales," in *The Catholic Encyclopedia*, vol. 5 (New York: Robert Appleton, 1909), http://www.newadvent.org/cathen/01298a.htm (accessed February 15, 2019).

86. See Bougerol, *Introduction to the Works of Bonaventure*, 4.

87. From the *Chronicle of the Twenty-Four Generals of the Order of Friars Minor*, written by Arnald of Sarrant from 1369 to 1374. An English translation can be found in Arnald of Sarrant, *Chronicle of the Twenty-Four Generals of the Order of Friars Minor*, trans. Noel Muscat, OFM (Malta: Tau Franciscan Communications, 2010). Two papal documents also record the close relationship between Alexander and Bonaventure. See *Superna caelestis*, Pope Sixtus IV's declaration of Bonaventure's canonization, an English translation of which may be found at http://www.franciscan -archive.org/bullarium/supern-e.html (accessed January 28, 2019), and *Triumphantis Hierusalem*, Pope Sixtus V's declaration of Bonaventure as a Doctor of the Church, at http://www.franciscan-archive.org/bullarium/triumphe.html (accessed February 15, 2019).

88. Alexander's teaching method involved answering questions in three steps: the *pro*, the *contra*, and the *resolutio*. He also introduced the practice of commenting on the *Sentences* of Peter Lombard and actively incorporated Aristotle's works in order to present Catholic doctrines in a systematic way.

89. Bougerol, *Introduction to the Works of Bonaventure*, 15.

90. Cullen, *Bonaventure*, 11; Bougerol, *Introduction to the Works of Bonaventure*, 13–21; Roest, *Franciscan Learning, Preaching and Mission*, 32.

91. On the process of earning a degree of theology at a medieval university, see Paul F. Grendler, *The Universities of the Italian Renaissance* (Baltimore: Johns Hopkins University, 2002), 360–61. The book describes the educational system of Italian universities, but Grendler makes the point that the Italian system followed that of the University of Paris.

92. For the debate on dating Bonaventure's ascent to the position of master of theology, see Hammond, "Dating Bonaventure's Inception as Regent Master," 206–23, and Cullen, *Bonaventure*, 11–12.

93. See *Superna caelestis* and *Triumphantis Hierusalem*.

94. *Doctoris seraphici S. Bonaventurae opera omnia*, 10 vols., ed. the Fathers of Collegium S. Bonaventurae (Quaracchi: Collegium S. Bonaventurae, 1882–1902). Volumes 1–4: commentaries on the four books of the *Sentences*; volume 5: theological treatises; volume 6: commentaries on the scriptures; volume 7: a commentary on the Gospel of Luke; volume 8: mystical works and writings concerning the Order of Friars Minor; volume 9: sermons; and volume 10: indices.

95. Ewert Cousins classifies Bonaventure's writings into three groups, the scholastic treatises, the spiritual writings, and the lecture series, which correspond to three

periods of his life: the first at the University of Paris, the second during the early and middle stages of his generalate from 1257 to 1267, and the third during the last stage of his generalate and cardinalate, from 1268 until his death in 1274. Cullen divides Bonaventure's corpus into only two groups: his writings during his years at Paris and his writings during his tenure as minister general. Cousins, introduction to *Bonaventure*, 8–11; Cullen, *Bonaventure*, 15.

96. Bougerol, *Introduction to the Works of Bonaventure*, 108.

97. Bonaventure, *On the Reduction of the Arts to Theology*, trans., with introduction, Zachary Hayes, vol. 1 of *WSB* (St. Bonaventure, NY: Franciscan Institute, 1996), 36–61. See also Joshua Benson, "Identifying the Literary Genre of the *De reductione artium ad theologiam*: Bonaventure's Inaugural Lecture at Paris," *Franciscan Studies* 69 (2009): 149–78; Joshua Benson, "Bonaventure's *De reductione artium ad theologiam* and Its Early Reception as an Inaugural Sermon," *American Catholic Philosophical Quarterly* 85 (2011): 7–24.

98. Cousins, introduction to *Bonaventure*, 15.

99. A collation is a form of public sermon derived from monastic tradition in which a preacher restates a biblical theme from that day's liturgical reading in the evening. Collations are typically delivered outside of the liturgical context and often contain scholarly content. This tradition was introduced into the university setting by a Dominican, Jordan of Saxony, in 1231. The simple delivery of collations developed over time into public conferences or university lectures in which theologians explained important exegetical and spiritual themes. Collations were held on Sundays and feast days and were attended by the students and masters of Paris. The lectures would be recorded and published after revision. For more information on the literary genre of the collation and Bonaventure's collations, see Bougerol, *Introduction to the Works of Bonaventure*, 125–34; Roest, *Franciscan Learning, Preaching and Mission*, 89n18; Cullen, *Bonaventure*, 17–18; Zachary Hayes, introduction to Bonaventure, *Collations on the Seven Gifts of the Holy Spirit*, trans., with introduction, Zachary Hayes, vol. 14 of *WSB* (St. Bonaventure, NY: Franciscan Institute, 2007), 7–25; Paul Spaeth, introduction to Bonaventure, *Collations on the Ten Commandments*, trans., with introduction, Paul Spaeth, vol. 6 of *WSB* (St. Bonaventure, NY: Franciscan Institute, 1995), 1–18.

100. Bonaventure presents six errors associated with the teachings of Averroistic Aristotelianism in his collations. Cullen summarizes them:

> (1) the denial of exemplarism (or the theory of forms in a transcendent cause, which Bonaventure explicitly associates with Plato); (2) the denial of divine knowledge of world; (3) the necessity of all things; (4) the denial of eternal life where reward or punishment is found; (5) the eternity of the world; and (6) the existence of a single intellect for all men. (Cullen, *Bonaventure*, 18)

For Bonaventure's critique of Aristotelianism see Bonaventure, *Collations on the Hexaemeron* (*Collations on the Six Days*) 6.2–5, in *Collations on the Hexaemeron*: *Conferences on the Six Days of Creation*, trans., with introduction and notes, Jay M. Hammond, vol. 18 of *WSB* (St. Bonaventure, NY: Franciscan Institute, 2018), 160–61; see also Bougerol, *Introduction to the Works of Bonaventure*, 125–34. There are differences between Bonaventure and his contemporary Thomas Aquinas respecting Aristotelianism; Aquinas took a moderate stance by insisting on correct interpretation in the effort to rescue Aristotle, whereas Bonaventure condemned the fundamental rationalism of Aristotelianism. For a brief summary, see Ian P. Wei, *Intellectual Culture in Medieval Paris: Theologians and the University c. 1100–1330* (Cambridge: Cambridge University, 2012), 161–69; Cullen, *Bonaventure*, 18.

101. The second phase of what came to be known as the "Poverty Controversy" dissipated in 1271 with the victory of the mendicant orders after receiving the support of newly elected Pope Gregory X (r. 1271–1276). Another, third phase would take place during the papacy of Pope John XXII (r. 1316–1334) in the 1320s. For the polemics surrounding Franciscan poverty from the mid-thirteenth to the early fourteenth century, see Virpi Mäkinen, *Poverty Rights in the Late Medieval Discussion on Franciscan Poverty* (Leuven: Peeters, 2001); Malcolm Lambert, *Franciscan Poverty* (St. Bonaventure, NY: Franciscan Institute, 1998).

102. "g." is the abbreviation for "generalate."

103. For the transition from John of Parma to Bonaventure and its relationship to the controversy over Joachimism, see Brooke, *Early Franciscan Government*, 270–71; Moorman, *A History of the Franciscan Order*, 112–16; Lambert, *Franciscan Poverty*, 112–15.

104. M. F. Laughlin, "Joachim of Fiore," in *New Catholic Encyclopedia*, vol. 7, second ed. (Detroit: Gale, 2003), 876–77, Gale Virtual Reference Library; Moorman, *A History of the Franciscan Order*, 114–15. For a further study of Joachim of Fiore and his influence on the medieval church, see Marjorie Reeves, *The Influence of Prophecy in the Later Middle Ages: A Study in Joachimism* (Oxford: Clarendon, 1969).

105. Prior to this condemnation, the church had been aware that the Joachimist prophecies had the potential to undermine its authority and was concerned about the the mendicants' excess zeal for them. See Moorman, *A History of the Franciscan Order*, 115. Some of Joachim's theological positions had previously been condemned, but the church had not condemned Joachim's prophecies as a whole prior to the publication of Gerard's work. Although Bonaventure was required to investigate whether his predecessor was a follower of Joachimism, and while he was well aware of the dangers of Joachim's historical schema and prophecies, he sympathized with the trinitarian division of history and the goal of spiritual illumination through the study of the scriptures. Marjorie Reeves writes about Joachimism's influence on Bonaventure that "whatever [Bonaventure] thought about Joachim's view of history, he does in fact envisage at the end of history a crisis and a stage beyond, which form a new *status*. In this he was a Joachite." Reeves, *The Influence of Prophecy in the Later Middle Ages*, 180.

106. Both inside and outside the University of Paris, the influence of the mendicants was increasing quickly with support from the papacy, a fact that irritated local bishops. The popes endowed the friars with privileges which gave them broad autonomy beyond the rights of local bishops to intervene, including the privileges of preaching, hearing confessions, celebrating Mass, officiating at burials, and performing other services. Consequently, the bishops and the clergy of France allied themselves with the secular masters in Paris against the friars. See Mäkinen, *Poverty Rights in the Late Medieval Discussion on Franciscan Poverty*, 25–27.

107. Şenocak, *The Poor and the Perfect*, 129.

108. Monti, introduction to *St. Bonaventure's Writings Concerning the Franciscan Order*, in *WSB*, 5:1.

109. Bonaventure, *First Encyclical Letter*, in *St. Bonaventure's Writings Concerning the Franciscan Order*, *WSB*, 5:59.

110. Bonaventure, *First Encyclical Letter*, in *WSB*, 5:58–62. Bonaventure would write a second encyclical letter in 1266 after the Chapter of Paris, and it is clear from that letter that ten years' time had not remedied the abuses. In this second letter the minister general once again exhorts his friars to comply with the order's legislation and urges ministers to implement stricter policies. See Bonaventure, *Second Encyclical Letter (1226)*, in *St. Bonaventure's Writings Concerning the Franciscan Order*, *WSB*, 5:225–29; Lambert, *Franciscan Poverty*, 130.

111. Desbonnets, *From Intuition to Institution*, 128–32.

112. Monti, introduction to *The Constitutions of Narbonne*, in *St. Bonaventure's Writings Concerning the Franciscan Order*, in *WSB*, 5:73.

113. While acknowledging the spiritual value of the *Major Legend*, Desbonnets criticizes Bonaventure's modifications of Francis's life story: "The *Legenda Major* was indeed a magnificent synthesis of spirituality. But the work also discloses the successful operation of exhuming, embalming, and reburial of a corpse that was not permitted to interfere with real Franciscan life as Bonaventure intended it to be." Desbonnets, *From Intuition to Institution*, 131.

114. Desbonnets, *From Intuition to Institution*, 132.

115. Monti, introduction to *The Constitutions of Narbonne*, in *St. Bonaventure's Writings Concerning the Franciscan Order*, in *WSB*, 5:71.

116. Desbonnets, *From Intuition to Institution*, 132; Noone and Houser, "Saint Bonaventure," in *The Stanford Encyclopedia of Philosophy*.

117. For a survey of different points of view on Bonaventure's generalship, see Lambert, *Franciscan Poverty*, 115–31; Monti, introduction to *St. Bonaventure's Writings Concerning the Franciscan Order*, in *WSB*, 5:1–36.

118. Desbonnets, *From Intuition to Institution*, 132 (bracketed insertion mine).

119. Şenocak, *The Poor and the Perfect*, 76.

120. Rosalind B. Brooke, trans. and ed., *Scripta Leonis, Rufini et Angeli Sociorum S. Francisci: The Writings of Leo, Rufino and Angelo, Companions of St. Francis* (Oxford: Oxford University Press, 1970), 211–13. For the relationship between holy simplicity and the pursuit of learning, and the incorporation of learning and teaching into the Franciscan identity, see Şenocak, *The Poor and the Perfect*, 82–143.

121. *Second Celano* 102, in *FA:ED*, 2:314–15.

122. Şenocak, *The Poor and the Perfect*, 109.

123. Bonaventure, *The Morning Sermon on Saint Francis, Preached at Paris, October 4, 1255*, in *FA:ED*, 2:511–12.

124. Julian of Speyer, "Officio ritmico e Vita secunda," in *Fonti agiografiche antoniane*, ed. Vergilio Gamboso (Padua: Edizioni Messaggero, 1985), 390–92, quoted in Şenocak, *The Poor and the Perfect*, 113.

125. Şenocak, *The Poor and the Perfect*, 115.

126. Bonaventure, *A Letter in Response to an Unknown Master* 10, in *WSB*, 5:51.

127. Bonaventure, *A Letter in Response to an Unknown Master* 13, in *WSB*, 5:54.

128. Bonaventure, *A Letter in Response to an Unknown Master* 12, in *WSB*, 5:52–53.

129. Bonaventure, *A Letter in Response to an Unknown Master* 12, in *WSB*, 5:53.

130. Bonaventure, *A Letter in Response to an Unknown Master* 12, in *WSB*, 5:53.

131. In the time of Bonaventure, philosophy began to take on relative autonomy with respect to theology. Bonaventure, while acknowledging the distinctiveness of the two intellectual disciplines, still subordinated philosophy to theology or Christian revelation because philosophy is subject to error and reason must be guided by faith. See Cullen, *Bonaventure*, 33.

132. Noone and Houser, "Saint Bonaventure," in *The Stanford Encyclopedia of Philosophy*.

133. *I Commentarius in quatuor libros Sententiarum Petri Lombardi*, Quaestiones Prooemii, in *Opera omnia*, 1:6a–15b; English translation in Bonaventure, *Commentary on the Sentences: Philosophy of God*, trans., with introduction and notes, R. E. Houser and Timothy B. Noone, vol. 16 of *WSB* (St. Bonaventure, NY: Franciscan Institute, 2013), 1–15.

134. Here "contemplation" means "speculative" or "theoretical" knowledge. See *Commentary on the Sentences: Philosophy of God*, in *WSB*, 16:21n39.

135. Noone and Houser show in "Saint Bonaventure," in *The Stanford Encyclopedia of Philosophy*, how philosophical reasoning plays a significant role in the organization of and argumentation contained in Bonaventure's theological treatises, in particular *Disputed Questions on the Mystery of the Trinity* and *On the Reduction of the Arts to Theology*.

136. *I Commentarius in quatuor libros Sententiarum Petri Lombardi*, Quaestiones Prooemii, q. 3, concl., resp., in *Opera omnia*, 1:13a–b; *Commentary on the Sentences: Philosophy of God*, in *WSB*, 16:12.

137. Bonaventure, *On the Reduction of the Arts to Theology* 26, in *WSB*, 1:61.

138. Bougerol, *Introduction to the Works of Bonaventure*, 168.

139. Charles Carpenter explores Bonaventure's integration of theological pursuits and the spiritual life in his book *Theology as the Road to Holiness in St. Bonaventure* (New York: Paulist Press, 1999).

140. Michael Downey, foreword to *Bonaventure: Mystic of God's Word*, ed. Timothy Johnson, 8.

141. For the distinct development and characteristics of the two theologies—monastic and Scholastic—see Jean Leclercq, "The Renewal of Theology," in *Renaissance and Renewal in the Twelfth Century*, ed. Robert Benson (Toronto: University of Toronto, 1991), 68–87; for a historical survey of the relationship between spirituality and theology, see Sheldrake, "The Divorce of Spirituality and Theology," in *Spirituality and Theology*, 33–64.

142. Bernard McGinn lists Bonaventure as one of "the two premier mystical teachers of the medieval West" along with Bernard of Clairvaux but recognizes that Bonaventure inherited his theology and spiritual sensibility from Bernard. McGinn is also well aware of differences between the two great mystics, which have been ascribed largely to Bonaventure's incorporation of scientific and rational Scholasticism.

Bernard McGinn, *The Flowering of Mysticism: Men and Women in the New Mysticism (1200–1350)*, vol. 3 of *The Presence of God: A History of Western Christian Mysticism* (New York: Crossroad, 1998), 87. See also Zachary Hayes, introduction to *On the Reduction of the Arts to Theology*, in *WSB*, 1:8–9.

143. Bonaventure, *Mystery of the Trinity* q. 1, a. 2, ad 3, in *Disputed Questions on the Mystery of the Trinity*, trans., with introduction, Zachary Hayes, vol. 3 of *WSB* (1979: repr., St. Bonaventure, NY: Franciscan Institute, 2000), 134.

144. Carpenter, *Theology as the Road to Holiness*, 26. For Bonaventure's theological method, see Gregory LaNave, "Bonaventure's Theological Method," in *A Companion to Bonaventure*, ed. Jay M. Hammond, J. A. Wayne Hellmann, and Jared Goff (Leiden: Brill, 2014), 81–120.

145. For Bonaventure's understanding of wisdom, see Cullen, *Bonaventure*, 23–35.

146. In the commentaries on the Sentences, wisdom is said to embrace both knowledge and affection. For example, in *Commentary on the Sentences I*, Bonaventure writes, "And this *habitus* is called wisdom, which means at the same time both knowledge and love." *I Commentarius in quatuor libros Sententiarum Petri Lombardi*, Quaestiones Prooemii, q. 3, concl., in *Opera omnia*, 1:13b; English translation in Carpenter, *Theology as the Road to Holiness*, 14. Also, in the *Collations of the Hexaemeron*, Bonaventure explicates three fruits of wisdom: "This descending light (*lux*) makes the intellective [power] (intellectivam) beautiful, the affective [power] (affectivam) delightful, and the operative [power] robust." (Bracketed insertions in original). *Collations on the Hexaemeron* 2.1, in *WSB*, 18:93. Here, this descending light refers to wisdom. Bonaventure emphasizes that affection for wisdom will empower one to be holy. *Collations on the Hexaemeron* 2.3–4, in *WSB*, 18:94–95. On the process by which one pursues wisdom, Bonaventure writes: "Now wisdom is above, as noble, but knowing (*scientia*) is below, yet it is seen by a person as beautiful, and so one wants to embrace it, and the soul (*anima*) is inclined to knowable (*scibilia*) and sensible (*sensibilia*) [things], and one wants (*vult*) to know (*cognoscere*) them and to test (*experiri*) what one knows (*cognita*), and consequently to be united to them." (Bracketed insertions in original). *Collations on the Hexaemeron* 19.3, in *WSB*, 18:328.

147. "We attain perfection by arriving at the highest good, which is the One; this is accomplished through the gift of wisdom. Hence, the hidden knowledge [*arcanum*] of contemplation ends at the top, as it were, in a single cubit." (Bracketed insertion in original). Bonaventure, *Breviloquium* 5.5.8, in *Breviloquium*, trans., with introduction and notes, Dominic V. Monti, vol. 9 of *WSB* (St. Bonaventure, NY: Franciscan Institute, 2005), 190. For the relationship between contemplation and wisdom, see also *Itinerarium mentis in Deum* (hereafter cited as *Itin.*) 1, 8, in Bonaventure, *Itinerarium Mentis in Deum*, trans. Zachary Hayes, introduction and "Notes & Commentary" by Philotheus Boehner, vol. 2 of *WSB*, rev. ed. (St. Bonaventure, NY: Franciscan Institute, 2002), 2:53; *Itin.* prol. 2, in *WSB*, 2:37.

148. *Collations on the Hexaemeron* 2.6, in *WSB*, 18:96.

149. *Collations on the Hexaemeron* 19.3, in *WSB*, 18:329.

150. Cousins, introduction to *Bonaventure*, 12. Zachary Hayes writes:

In the remarkable text of *The Journey of the Soul into God* we find the most synthetic statement of the Seraphic Doctor's program. It involves both the pursuit of the mind and the pursuit of the heart, both knowledge and wisdom, both the life of the intellect and the life of the mystic. It is not some sort of philosophical proof for the existence of God, since it clearly begins with a person of faith. (Zachary Hayes, *Bonaventure: Mystical Writings* [New York: Crossroad, 1999], 43)

151. Cousins, introduction to *Bonaventure*, 2.

152. See also Regis J. Armstrong, "Francis of Assisi and the Prisms of Theologizing," *Greyfriars Review* 10, no. 2 (1994): 179–206.

153. He speaks of Francis twice in his *Commentary on the Gospel of Luke*, twice in his commentaries on the *Sentences*, and once in *Disputed Questions on Evangelical Perfection*. See Bougerol, *Introduction to the Works of Bonaventure*, 6.

154. This is clearly manifested in his *A Letter in Response to an Unknown Master.* See Bougerol, *Introduction to the Works of Bonaventure*, 6–7.

155. See, e.g., *The Morning Sermon on Saint Francis, Preached at Paris, October 4, 1255*, in *FA:ED*, 2:511.

156. Regarding Francis as a theologian and the object of Bonaventure's theology, see Gregory F. LaNave, "The Place of Holiness in the Task of Theology according to Saint Bonaventure" (PhD diss., Catholic University of America, 2002), 160–72, the quotation at 172.

157. Paul Rout, *Francis and Bonaventure* (Liguori, MO: Triumph, 1996), 35–47.

158. Zachary Hayes, "Christ, Word of God and Exemplar of Humanity: The Roots of Franciscan Christocentrism and Its Implications for Today," *The Cord* 41, no. 1 (1996): 3–6.

159. Rout, *Francis and Bonaventure*, 42.

160. In the *Collations on the Hexaemeron* Bonaventure contemplates the threefold Word of God: "The uncreated Word by whom all things are brought forth; . . . the incarnate Word by whom all things are restored; and . . . the inspired Word by whom all things are revealed." *Collations on the Hexaemeron* 3.2, in *WSB*, 18:112. Bonaventure focused on each aspect of the threefold Word of God at different times in his life, beginning with the uncreated Word during his scholarly career, the Incarnate Word during his ministerial career, and the inspired Word in the later stages of his life. For Bonaventure's understanding of Christ as the Word of God, see Johnson, *Bonaventure: Mystic of God's Word*, 18–26.

161. *On the Reduction of the Arts to Theology*, in *WSB*, 1:61.

162. For Bonaventure, the mystical life involves three "ways"—the purgative, the illuminative, and the perfective. The six steps of the *Itinerarium* deal primarily with the illuminative way; nevertheless, as this chapter makes clear, the entirety of the threefold way is not absent from the text. See *Itin.* 1.8, in *WSB*, 2:53; Boehner, introduction to *Itinerarium*, in *WSB*, 2:22–27. The illuminative way of meditation and contemplation is also articulated in *De triplici via* [see p. 22]. However, the manner in which it is described is different in these two works: while *De triplici via* explains it in a way that is accessible to the relatively unlearned, the *Itinerarium* is directed at learned people. See Boehner, introduction to *Itinerarium*, in *WSB*, 2:26.

163. Hayes, *Bonaventure: Mystical Writings*, 42.

164. *Itin.* prol. 4, in *WSB,* 2:39.

165. *Itin.* prol. 4, in *WSB,* 2:39–41.

166. Boehner, introduction to *Itinerarium,* in *WSB,* 2:9.

167. *Itin.* prol. 2, in *WSB,* 2:37.

168. See Ewert Cousins, *Bonaventure and the Coincidence of Opposites* (Chicago: Franciscan Herald Press, 1978), 73–75.

169. *Itin.* prol. 1–2, in *WSB,* 2:36–37.

170. It is, however, not clear whether Bonaventure wrote the *Itinerarium* at Alverna or not.

171. Carpenter, *Theology as the Road to Holiness,* 71–72.

172. Boehner, "Notes and Commentary" on [see fn 191] *Itinerarium,* in *WSB,* 2:143–45.

173. The Latin term *mens* can be translated either as mind or soul. However, the modern English usage of "mind" has a largely intellectual meaning. Therefore "soul" may be a better English translation for *mens.* See Cousins, introduction to *Bonaventure,* 21.

174. Along with dynamic movement into the "interior" of God, vertical movement is also important in the *Itinerarium,* which employs the symbols of the six-winged seraph, the mountain, and the ladder, all of which relate to a soul ascending up to God. See Cousins, introduction to *Bonaventure,* 78–79.

175. Terms such as "speculation," "consideration," "contemplation," and even "meditation" are related to the illuminative way. Philotheus Boehner notes that these words have approximately the same meaning in the *Itinerarium.* "Speculation" is etymologically connected with *speculum,* which means mirror, and is therefore related to the mirroring function of the mind or soul. Through this function, the mind comes to be aware of God's reflection or presence in all creatures and in the soul. Similarly, as discussed by Bonaventure in the *Itinerarium,* perceiving an object, whether in the created world or the soul, or perceiving the highest ideas like "being" and "goodness" in relation to the creator has been called "contuition." This "contuition" involves both intellectual and mystical elements. See Boehner, introduction to *Itinerarium,* in *WSB,* 2:26–27, 148–49n12; for an explanation of the definition of Bonaventure's "contuition" and Francis's influence on the development of this concept, see Leonard J. Bowman, "Bonaventure's 'Contuition' and Heidegger's 'Thinking': Some Parallels," *Franciscan Studies* 37 (1977): 18–31, 24; Jay M. Hammond, "Order in the *Itinerarium,*" in *Divine and Created Order in Bonaventure's Theology,* J. A. Wayne Hellmann, trans. and ed., with an appendix by Jay M. Hammond (St. Bonaventure, NY: Franciscan Institute, 2001), 209–11; Ilia Delio, *Simply Bonaventure* (Hyde Park, NY: New City Press, 2001), 63; Lydia Schumacher, "Bonaventure's Journey of the Mind into God: A Traditional Augustinian Ascent?" *Medioevo: Rivista di Storia della Filosofia Medievale* 37 (2012): 217; Armstrong, "Francis of Assisi and the Prisms of Theologizing," 194–99.

176. See *Itin.* prol. and chap. 7, in *WSB,* vol 2. Another noteworthy work by Bonaventure about the spiritual journey to Jerusalem is the *Five Feasts of the Child Jesus.* See Bonaventure, *Bringing Forth Christ: Five Feasts of the Child Jesus,* trans. Eric Doyle (Oxford: Sisters of the Love God Press, 1988).

177. *Itin.* prol. 3, in *WSB,* 2:37–39.

178. *Itin.* 1.2, in *WSB*, 2:47.

179. *Itin.* 1.4, in *WSB*, 2:49.

180. Philotheus Boehner points out the resemblance between Bonaventure's and Richard of St. Victor's description of the six steps of contemplation (drawing on the image of the six-winged seraph). Nevertheless, he stresses the uniqueness of Bonaventure's scheme. See Boehner, introduction to *Itinerarium*, in *WSB*, 2:28. In Bonaventure's construction, one distinguishing element is that each step is not discrete but rather is smoothly connected to the next, making the ascent more achievable, in the manner of the ascent of "the cordonata capitolina," Michelangelo's wide-ramped staircase in Rome.

181. Francis's influence on the first two chapters of the *Itinerarium* is indisputable. However, Francis's simple and direct appreciation of God's goodness contrasts with Bonaventure's speculative reflection loaded with philosophical and theological elements. See Cousins's comparison between Francis's "Canticle of Brother Sun" and the *Itinerarium*. Cousins, introduction to *Bonaventure*, 27–30.

182. Cousins, introduction to *Bonaventure*, 20.

183. See *Itin.* 1, in *WSB*, 2:44–45. The Latin title of chapter 1 is "De gradibus ascensionis in et de speculatione ipsius per vestigia eius in universo." In the *Itinerarium*, Bonaventure uses speculation and contemplation interchangeably but mostly employs the term "contemplation"; however, he uses "speculation" for the chapter titles.

184. The numbers in parenthesis indicate chapter and section numbers of the *Itinerarium*.

185. *Proportio aequalitatis* in Latin.

186. *Itin.* 4, in *WSB*, 2:96–97.

187. Wei, *Intellectual Culture in Medieval Paris*, 137.

188. *Itin.* 5, in *WSB*, 2:110–11.

189. *Itin.* 6, in *WSB*, 2:122–23.

190. The title of chapter 7 is "The Mystical Transport of the Mind in Which Rest Is Given to the Intellect and through Ecstasy Our Affection Passes over Totally into God" ["De excessu mentali et mystico, in quo requies datur intellectui, affectu totaliter in Deum per excessum transeunte"].

191. The Quaracchi edition of the *Itinerarium* (5:293–316) provides detailed information about explicit and implicit references to the scriptures, other authors, and even Bonaventure's other writings. Most English translations of the *Itinerarium* draw on this edition. In addition, Philotheus Boehner's "Notes & Commentary" annexed to Zachary Hayes's English translation of the *Itinerarium* furnishes the reader with extensive information about specific terms, intellectual categories, and citations from Bonaventure's corpus. Boehner, "Notes & Commentary" on *Itinerarium*, in *WSB*, 2:143–225.

192. Jay M. Hammond calls the concurrent interplay between various theological ideas in Bonaventure's theology "combinatory logic." This combinatory logic is clearly present in the multilayered structure of the *Itinerarium*. Hammond, "Order in the *Itinerarirum*," 196.

193. Denys Turner, *The Darkness of God: Negativity in Christian Mysticism* (Cambridge: Cambridge University Press, 1995), 102.

194. Turner, *The Darkness of God*, 102–17. See also Grover Zinn, "Book and Word: The Victorine Background of Bonaventure's Use of Symbols," in *S. Bonaventura, 1274–1974*, vol. 2 (Roma, Grottaferrata: Collegio S. Bonaventura, 1973), 144.

195. Turner, *The Darkness of God*, 103.

196. The soul's movement of ascent from without to within and then above was originally articulated by Plotinus, well before Augustine. After Plotinus, this scheme became fundamental to Christian works describing spiritual development. See Frederick Van Fleteren, "The Ascent of the Soul in the Augustinian Tradition," in *Paradigms in Medieval Thought, Applications in Medieval Disciplines*, ed. Nancy van Deusen and Alvin E. Ford (Lewiston, NY: Edwin Mellen Press, 1990), 97.

197. Fleteren, "The Ascent of the Soul in the Augustinian Tradition," 93–110. Despite Bonaventure's great indebtedness to Augustine, Lydia Schumacher argues that Bonaventure's primary emphasis was on Franciscan values and spiritual insights, so much so that, in some crucial respects, Bonaventure freely departs from Augustine. In fact, Schumacher notes that "Bonaventure enlisted Augustine in promoting Franciscan thought." Her argument does not, however, negate the significant influence Augustine had on Bonaventurian theology and spirituality, in particular the tripartite divisions employed in the *Itinerarium*. Schumacher, "Bonaventure's Journey of the Mind into God: A Traditional Augustinian Ascent?" 201–29, 202.

198. Turner, *The Darkness of God*, 102–7. Grover Zinn, Greg LaNave, and Dale Coulter also expound the Victorine background of Bonaventure's use of various symbols. Zinn argues that Bonaventure inherited Augustinianism through the Dionysian fusion executed by Hugh of St. Victor. He also shows how Bonaventure was influenced by the Hugonian theology of symbols with its metaphysical and soteriological emphasis and by the Christocentric nature of Victorine thought, which employed the threefold "analogy of the creature" of Tree, Book, and Word and the threefold speculations of the creature in their immensity, beauty, and utility; these speculations are related to the reflection of the triune elements of power, wisdom, and goodness. This scheme is adopted in chapter 1. *Itin.* 1.13–14, in *WSB*, 2:57–59. Zinn argues that "Hugh framed perspectives, formulated approaches, and provided fundamental themes, definitions, and elements which Bonaventure incorporated into his systematic and mystical theology." See Zinn, "Book and Word," 144. While Zinn focuses on Hugh's influence on Bonaventure, LaNave investigates Richard of St. Victor's influences on Bonaventure, particularly with regard to "a similar emphasis on six levels of knowing connected to the soul's powers, the symbolic use of the cherubim and ark of the covenant at the final two steps of ascent (five and six), and a description of the soul's reformation through justice and knowledge." LaNave's summary of Richard's influence on Bonaventure is taken from Dale Coulter, "The Victorine Sub-Structure of Bonaventure's Thought," *Franciscan Studies* 70 (2012): 400; for LaNave's study on Richard's influence on Bonaventure, see Gregory LaNave, *Through Holiness to Wisdom: The Nature of Theology According to Bonaventure* (Rome: Istituto storico dei Cappuccini, 2005). Coulter further explores the Victorine influences on Bonaventure. He points out the two parallel symbolisms found in Richard's writings and in the *Itinerarium*: "First, Bonaventure's use of the six-winged Seraph, while taken from Francis's vision, no doubt also draws upon Richard's use of the same imagery. To

both, the six wings symbolize the six levels of active reflection. Secondly, Bonaventure describes the journey in terms of becoming 'true Hebrews' who cross over from Egypt to the promised land." Coulter, "The Victorine Sub-Structure of Bonaventure's Thought," 403–4. Furthermore, Coulter notes that the idea of death with the crucified Christ, which is crucial at the final stage of the spiritual ascent and for the associated idea of ecstasy, is common to both Richard and Bonaventure. See Coulter, "The Victorine Sub-Structure of Bonaventure's Thought," 399–410.

199. *Itin.* 1.2, in *WSB*, 2:47.

200. *Breviloquium* 2.12.1, in *WSB*, 9:96.

201. Bonaventure writes in the *Breviloquium*:

> For this triple vision, human beings were endowed with a triple eye, as explained by Hugh of St. Victor: the eye of flesh, the eye of reason, and the eye of contemplation; the eye of flesh, to see the world and what it contains; the eye of reason, to see the soul and what it contains; the eye of contemplation, to see God and those things that are within God. Thus with the eye of flesh, human beings see those things that are outside them; by the eye of reason, those things that are within them, by the eye of contemplation, the things that are above them. But the eye of contemplation does not function perfectly except through glory, which human beings have lost through sin, although they may recover this through grace and faith and the understanding of the Scripture. By these means, the human soul is cleansed, enlightened, and perfected for the contemplation of heavenly things. For fallen human beings cannot attain these things unless they first recognize their own insufficiency and blindness, and this they cannot do unless they consider and attend to the ruin of human nature. (*Breviloquium* 2.12.5, in *WSB*, 9:98)

202. *Itin.* 3.1, in *WSB*, 2:81.

203. The Bonaventurian adaptation of the Hugonian analogy of the creature is also found in the summary of Part Two "On the Creation of the World" in the *Breviloquium*, in which not only the threefold layout of vestige/image/likeness, but also the particular way of speculating about God through vestige, image, and likeness, is suggested in a concise manner.

> Now, a creature cannot have God as its origin without being configured to that principle in accordance with unity, truth, and goodness. Nor can it have God as its object if it does not grasp God through memory, understanding, and will. Finally, it cannot possess God within itself as an infused gift without being conformed to God through the three-fold dowry of faith, hope, and love. Since the first conformity is remote, the second proximate, and the third most intimate, that is why the first is said to be a "vestige" of the Trinity, the second an "image," and the third a "likeness." (*Breviloquium* 2.12.3, in *WSB*, 9:97)

Although Bonaventure inherits from Hugh the analogy of the book and the metaphor of three eyes, the threefold distinction of vestige, image, and likeness and its application to the ascent to God is Bonaventure's unique articulation. See Turner, *The Darkness of God*, 108.

204. *I Commentarius in quatuor libros Sententiarum Petri Lombardi*, d. 3, in *Opera omnia*, 1:66–94, and *II Commentarius in quatuor libros Sententiarum Petri Lombardi*, d. 16, in *Opera omnia*, 2:93–408; *Breviloquium* 2, in *WSB*, 9:59–98. For

textual references to the specific elements of the analogy of the creature, see also Ephrem Longpré, "Bonaventure (saint)," in *Dictionnaire de Spiritualité Ascétique et Mystique, Doctrine et Histoire*, vol. 1, ed. Marcel Viller (Paris: G. Beauchesne et Ses Fils, 1932–1995), cols. 1773–76.

205. "Our mind has contemplated God outside itself through and in the vestiges; within itself through and in the image; and above itself through the similitude of the divine light shining on us from above in as far as that is possible in our pilgrim state and by the exercise of our mind." *Itin.* 7.1, in *WSB*, 2:133. See Wei, *Intellectual Culture in Medieval Paris*, 127.

206. Turner, *The Darkness of God*, 110–12.

207. *Itin.* 4.7, *WSB*, 2:107.

208. Turner, *The Darkness of God*, 105–6.

209. *II Commentarius in quatuor libros Sententiarum Petri Lombardi*, d.16, a.2, q.3, resp., in *Opera Omnia*, 2:405. The English translation is quoted from Turner, *The Darkness of God*, 110.

210. Turner, *The Darkness of God*, 111–12

211. Wei, *Intellectual Culture in Medieval Paris*, 136–37.

212. *Itin.* 4.2, 4.5, in *WSB*, 2:97–99, 103–5.

213. Turner, *The Darkness of God*, 114.

214. Turner, *The Darkness of God*, 114.

215. In the *Mystical Theology*, Pseudo-Dionysius briefly summarizes his previous works: the *Symbolic Theology*, the *Theological Representations*, and the *Divine Names*. The Mystical Theology 3, in *Pseudo-Dionysius: The Complete Works*, trans. Colm Luibheid with introductions by Jaroslav Pelikan, Jean Leclercq, and Karlfried Froehlich (New York: Paulist Press, 1987), 139. See Turner, *The Darkness of God*, 114–16.

216. "He [Jesus] has taught the knowledge of truth according to three modes of theology, namely symbolic, proper, and mystical, so that through symbolic theology we might use sensible things correctly, through theology in the proper sense we might deal with intelligible things correctly, and through mystical theology we might be drawn up to ecstatic experience." *Itin.* 1.7, in *WSB*, 2:51.

217. Wei, *Intellectual Culture in Medieval Paris*, 127–28.

218. Turner translated *per creaturam* as "creatures" plural. Bracketed insertion in original.

219. *I Commentarius in quatuor libros Sententiarum Petri Lombardi*, d. 3, p. 1, a. 1, q. 3, in *Opera omnia*, 1:74. The English translation is quoted from Turner, *The Darkness of God*, 109.

220. LaNave argues that the through/in distinction is applicable not only to subdividing the first two of the three stages of the spiritual ascent, but that it also bifurcates the *Itinerarium* into two trajectories: seeing God "through" the visible world, the soul, and what is above the soul; and seeing God "in" the same realms. The knowing of God "through" (chapters 1, 3, and 5) considers what things are. As regards the second trajectory—knowing God "in"—LaNave suggests that this concerns our capacity to see God in things, employing Bonaventure's doctrine of sensation expounded in chapter 2. Bonaventure argues that the three activities of sensation—apprehension,

pleasure, and judgment—are vestiges in which we can see God. LaNave applies this idea as a way of interpreting chapters 4 and 6:

> The ramifications of the doctrine of sensation extend further, however, through the other stages of this trajectory. The considerations of God in his image reformed by grace (chap. 4) and in the name of the blessed Trinity, which is Good (chap. 6), are likewise marked by the qualities of sensation. They include a direct apprehension of God in the soul and in what is above the soul, a capacity to receive pleasure in that apprehension, and a formation of the soul in conformity to what it perceives (corresponding to *judgment*). (Gregory F. LaNave, "Knowing God through and in All Things: A Proposal for Reading Bonaventure's *Itinerarium mentis in Deum*," *Franciscan Studies* 67 [2009]: 282)

For LaNave's detailed argumentation see LaNave, "Knowing God through and in All Things," 267–99. For the first trajectory, LaNave relies on Bonaventure's works, in particular the commentaries on the *Sentences* and the *Disputed Questions on the Mystery of the Trinity*, whereas for the second, he applies the doctrine of sensation derived from chapter 2. Jay M. Hammond criticizes LaNave's argument, pointing out inconsistencies in the application of the criteria by which he bifurcates the structure of the *Itinerarium* into chapters 1, 3, and 5 and chapters 2, 4, and 6. Hammond also criticizes LaNave for ignoring the threefold structure that is clearly mentioned in the *Itinerarium*. See Jay M. Hammond, "Bonaventure's Itinerarium: A Respondeo," *Franciscan Studies* 67 (2009): 301–21.

221. J. Guy Bougerol briefly introduces the scholars who influenced Bonaventure. See Bougerol, *Introduction to the Works of Bonaventure*, 23–49.

222. See Etienne Gilson, *The Philosophy of St. Bonaventure*, trans. Dom Illtyd Trehowan and Frank J. Sheed (Paterson, NJ: St. Anthony Guild Press, 1965), 185; Turner, *The Darkness of God*, 103.

223. For such a commentary, see Boehner, "Notes & Commentary" on *Itinerarium*, in vol. 2, *WSB*; Cousins, introduction to *Bonaventure*, 24–34.

224. Turner, *The Darkness of God*, 115.

225. See *Itin.* 3.6, in *WSB*, 2:91–93.

226. Boehner, introduction to *Itinerarium*, in *WSB,* 2:28–31; Turner, *The Darkness of God*, 115–16.

227. Turner, *The Darkness of God*, 115.

228. Turner, *The Darkness of God*, 116.

229. *Itin.* 3.7, in *WSB*, 2:93.

230. Boehner, introduction to *Itinerarium*, in *WSB*, 2:10.

231. Bougerol, *Introduction to the Works of Bonaventure*, 168.

232. *Itin.* 7.4, in *WSB*, 2:137.

Chapter Two

Chinul's Integration of Buddhist Doctrinal Teachings and Sŏn Practices

There might not be any more apt Buddhist counterpart to Bonaventure than the Korean Buddhist thinker Pojo Chinul (1158–1210). Studying Chinul in conversation with Bonaventure will open up new avenues in the dialogue between Christianity and Buddhism, especially as concerns the integration of spiritual and intellectual life. Like Bonaventure, Chinul lived in a time of historical tension, which had a great influence on his spiritual and intellectual life, and in particular on the development of his reformative, reconciliatory, and integrative endeavors, an influence that is manifested in his writings. This chapter will explore Chinul's life, thought, and work, along with the general historical context of Korean Buddhism, an exploration that will facilitate an understanding of Chinul's efforts to integrate meditative practice and doctrinal study. It will also be shown how Chinul systematizes and theorizes the Sŏn practice in light of the scriptural and doctrinal teachings of the Hwaŏm school.

KOREAN BUDDHISM BEFORE THE TIME OF POJO CHINUL

Buddhism before the Koryŏ Dynasty (918–1392)

The Development of Buddhism and the Chan Tradition in China

Buddhism, a religion of Indian origin, was introduced into China during the Han 漢 dynasty (206 BC–AD 220), and from that time, Buddhist missionaries from India and central Asia as well as indigenous Chinese Buddhists strove to translate the religion's sacred texts into Chinese so as to communicate its foreign teachings to the Chinese people. After centuries of effort, Buddhism began to flourish during the Tang 唐 dynasty (618–907), and continued to prosper until the end of the thirteenth century under the Song 宋 dynasty (960–1279). Over time, Buddhism became an integral part of Chinese religious and cultural identity.[1] Maturing in their understanding of Buddhist traditions transmitted directly from India or via central Asia, and influenced by indigenous religions, Chinese Buddhists began to sinicize the foreign religion. This resulted in the emergence of the Tiantai 天台, Huayan 華嚴, Jingtu 淨土 ("Pure Land"), and Chan 禪 schools.

Among these sinicized Buddhist traditions, Chan 禪 (K. Sŏn, J. Zen)[2] in particular would take a prominent place in the history of Buddhism in Korea; it still remains among the most popular Buddhist traditions in modern Korea. The Chan (S. *Dhyāna*, meaning meditation) tradition was allegedly transmitted to China by the Indian (or central Asian) monk Bodhidharma 菩提達磨 during the fifth and sixth centuries, and all the Chan lineages trace back to him, the first Chan patriarch, or *zushi* 祖師 (K. *chosa*).[3] Bodhidharma passed the Chan tradition on to Huike 慧可 (c. 487–593), Sengcan 僧璨 (d. 606), Daoxin 道信 (580–651), and Hongren 弘忍 (601–674). After Hongren, the fifth patriarch, there was a split in the tradition between Shenxiu 神秀 (c. 605–706) and Huineng 惠能 (638–713). Shenxiu was the leading disciple of Hongren and later was highly respected by the imperial court. Shenxiu spread the dharma in the north and, together with his disciples, established what came to be known as "the northern school" (C. Bei zong 北宗). Huineng, by contrast—to whom most of the later Chan schools traced back their lineages—established what became known as "the southern school" (C. Nan zong 南宗). Heze Shenhui 荷澤神會 (684–758), the renowned leading disciple of Huineng, engaged the followers of the northern school in a polemical debate about the nature of enlightenment. Whereas the northern school held that enlightenment is a gradual process, the southern school insisted on the idea of sudden enlightenment.

Another noteworthy Chan master of the southern school during the early period of Chan development was Mazu Daoyi 馬祖道一 (709–88), who established the so-called Hongzhou 洪州 school. Most of the Korean monks during the Silla dynasty period in Korea (57 BC–AD 935) who transmitted Chan teachings from China to their home country studied under the Chan masters of the Mazu lineage. The other two prominent Chan schools during the Chinese Song dynasty, the Linji 臨濟 and Guiyang 潙仰 schools, also claimed that their lineage was connected to Mazu. During the Song dynasty, while the fortune of doctrinal schools declined, other Buddhist schools such as Chan and Pure Land Buddhism, which emphasized the meditative and devotional aspects of religious practice, prospered. Chan Buddhism during this period has been categorized into "five houses" and "seven schools" 五

家七宗: the five houses consisted of Guiyang 潙仰, Linji 臨濟, Caodong 曹洞, Yunmen 雲門, and Fayan 法眼, and later, two more—Huanglong 黃龍 and Yangqi 楊岐—were added to Linji, making altogether seven houses, or schools.[4]

The Development of Buddhism in Korea during the Period of Unified Silla and the Later Three Kingdoms

Buddhism was introduced into Korea through China during Korea's Three Kingdoms period (57 BC–AD 676). It was first introduced into the Kingdom of Koguryŏ 高句麗 in 372 and the Kingdom of Paekche 百濟 in 384. The third of the Three Kingdoms, the Silla Kingdom 新羅, accepted Buddhism as its official religion in 527. Though first introduced as a foreign religion, Buddhism would take deep root in Korean soil, and would throughout its history play a significant role in almost every aspect of the life of the Korean people. Buddhism thrived especially during the Unified Silla period (676–935),[5] the Later Three Kingdoms period 後三國 (892–936),[6] and the Koryŏ period 高麗 (918–1392). Buddhism was almost continuously suppressed during the Chosŏn 朝鮮 dynasty (1392–1910), but it survived and experienced a rebirth in the twentieth century, regaining its vitality and its influence on the social, cultural, and religious life of modern Koreans.[7]

During the Unified Silla period, the practice of Buddhism spread beyond the confines of the royal court and aristocracy to permeate the religious realm of ordinary people. Even before unification in 676, the influence of Buddhism in the Silla society was significant for its political implications—the ruling class adopted the foreign religion with the intention of enhancing royal authority by the development of an ideology that identified the monarch as a Buddha figure. However, Buddhism evolved during the Unified Silla period beyond its role as a political ideology and devotional practice into a sophisticated philosophical system. This included the establishment of various doctrinal schools by eminent scholar monks who journeyed on pilgrimage to China, central Asia, and India to learn about different Buddhist traditions and to bring back diverse philosophical systems and sacred texts. Eventually, five primary doctrinal schools were founded in Korea: Kyeyul chong 戒律宗 (C. Jielu zong) or the "Vinaya" school, Yŭlban chong 涅槃宗 (C. Niepan zong) or the "Nirvana" school, Hwaŏm chong 華嚴宗 (C. Huayan zong) or the "Avataṃsaka" (Flower Garland) school, Pŏpsŏng chong 法性宗 (C. Faxing zong) or the "Dharma-Nature" school, and Pŏpsang chong 法相宗 (C. Faxiang zong) or the "Dharmalakṣana" (Dharmic Characteristics, also known as Yogācāra or Yuga chong) school.[8]

Among many Silla-period scholar monks, Ŭisang 義湘 (625–702) and Wŏnhyo 元曉 (617–686) are the most notable. Ŭisang founded the Hwaŏm school during the Silla dynasty when he returned from China after studying under Zhiyan 智儼 (602–668), the second patriarch of the Chinese Huayan school. The Hwaŏm school flourished during the Unified Silla period as a prominent doctrinal school, and its teachings constituted the foundation of the Buddhist doctrines that would have a long-lasting influence on Korean Buddhism. Unlike Ŭisang, Wŏnhyo did not go to China to study Buddhism; nevertheless, his learning in various Buddhist schools and his insights into the Buddhist texts were so profound that he was respected in the broader Buddhist world of East Asia. Among the five doctrinal schools, Wŏnhyo established Pŏpsŏng chong, a genuinely Korean school.

Although these two eminent monks did not share the same doctrinal views, both contributed to integrating and harmonizing the state after unification. One of the primary teachings of the Hwaŏm school is the doctrine of *wŏnyung* 圓融 (C. *yuanrong*), meaning "consummate interfusion," which holds that everything in the universe is perfectly interfused. Principle is interfused into phenomena and phenomena into principle; individual phenomena are interfused into all other phenomena without being in conflict. This idea of interpenetration and harmony promoted the reconciliation, harmony, and integration the society greatly needed in order to overcome the conflicts between regions and classes that followed the unification of the three kingdoms. The political implications of the Hwaŏm teachings appealed to the ruling class of the Silla dynasty.[9]

While Ŭisang focused on the Hwaŏm texts and doctrines in his studies and teachings, Wŏnhyo did not limit his reading of Buddhist texts, or his studies of philosophical systems and devotional practices, to one particular school. He was erudite in diverse Buddhist texts, and his scriptural understanding and insights into various philosophical systems led him to write numerous treatises. Competent in the various Buddhist intellectual traditions, Wŏnhyo attempted to synthesize the teachings of the different schools and stressed the harmony that existed among them. As profound as his doctrinal expertise was, he also paid close attention to the practical elements of Buddhism. While Ŭisang and his school had a close connection to the royal families and aristocrats, Wŏnhyo distanced himself from the ruling class by criticizing the political adaptation of Buddhism and the excessive formality of its Buddhist practices. He eventually left a promising life in the capital and immersed himself in the life of the people, traveling from village to village throughout the country and promoting the devotional practices of Buddhism, such as the recitation of Amitābha Buddha. The integrative and practical approach of Wŏnhyo has repeatedly been adopted by eminent monks throughout the history of Korean Buddhism, including, as will be seen below, by Chinul, who worked to integrate Kyo 敎 (C. Jiao), that is, doctrinal teachings and scriptural studies, and Sŏn 禪 (C. Chan) during the middle period of Koryŏ (late twelfth and early thirteenth centuries).[10]

The Introduction and Development of Sŏn in the Unified Silla Period (676–935)

While doctrinal Buddhism flourished with the establishment of the five major doctrinal schools around the time of unification in the seventh century and afterward, in the later Unified Silla period, Sŏn Buddhism began to spread throughout the country. Chinese Chan Buddhism was first transmitted to Unified Silla Korea by Pŏmnang 法朗 (flourished [hereafter fl.] ca. 632–646) in the seventh century. However, it was in the ninth century that Chan 禪 (K. Sŏn) began to captivate the minds of the Buddhist masses. This occurred when Toŭi 道義 (d. 825) and subsequently other monks returned to Korea, bringing the Chan teachings of the Hongzhou school, which traces its patriarchal Sŏn transmission back to Mazu Daoyi 馬祖道一 (709–788).[11] These Sŏn monks committed themselves to ardent meditation and teaching in the monasteries located in the mountains, and these places became the centers from which Sŏn teachings spread. Among many others, nine monasteries especially flourished and comprised the Nine Mountains schools of Sŏn (Ku-san Sŏnmun 九山禪門) in the late Unified Silla and early Koryŏ periods (ca. ninth and tenth centuries).[12] In contrast to the five doctrinal schools (Ogyo 五敎), which were distinguishable from each other by their different philosophical systems, the Nine Mountains schools of Sŏn exhibited only slight differences in their practice and teachings because most of the founders of Sŏn schools studied Chan under the Chinese masters of the Mazu lineage.

After unification, the Silla dynasty enjoyed prosperity and stability. Society flourished and culture blossomed under their firm control. However, the fortunes of Silla began to wane from the mid-eighth century when the authority and power of the central government was weakened by power struggles in the capital and with the rise of regional powers in the countryside.

In this time of political instability, Sŏn appealed to many people, especially to the local gentry. While Kyo schools relied on studying particular scriptures—sūtras[13] and treatises—together with their sophisticated philosophical systems, Sŏn stressed the individual's vigorous practice of meditation in silence rather than reading sacred texts or engaging in verbal debates. Sŏn's antitextual and antischolastic attitude gave rise to tensions with the doctrinal schools, especially in the capital.

The tension with Kyo regarding religious practices, combined with the lack of interest from the royal court and their intense focus on meditation, resulted in the Sŏn monks distancing themselves from the capital and retreating into the mountains. For their part, the local gentry found the individualistic soteriology of the Sŏn monks and their rejection of external authority appealing, largely because they strove to be independent of the control of the central government in the capital. Thus, Sŏn Buddhism was welcomed by the local gentry and flourished from the mid-ninth century on, primarily through their support.[14]

By the late ninth century, the corruption among the Silla rulers had reached an intolerable level, and central government control was weakened by peasant and slave riots and serious conflicts with local power centers in the countryside. All of this led to the establishment of the Later Three Kingdoms (892–936). The divided country was eventually unified once again in 936 by the Koryŏ dynasty founded by Wang Kŏn 王 建 (877–943, with the royal name of T'aejo 太祖) in 918.

Buddhism in Korea in the Early Koryŏ Period

From the Ninth through the Eleventh Centuries

Buddhism, which had become an integral part of the social, cultural, and religious texture of Korea in the period from the fourth to the ninth century, continued to flourish under the Koryŏ 高麗 dynasty (918–1392). King T'aejo of Koryŏ promoted Buddhism because he considered it a factor that could help unify the country. At the same time, he advised his successors to keep vigilant in the face of the corruption of the Buddhist community and its interference in state affairs. In the mid-tenth century, King Kwangjong 光宗 (r. 949–975) instituted the clerical examination system or *sŭngkwa* 僧科, which was modeled on the civil service examination. *Sŭngkwa* purported to improve the overall quality of monks[15] and to control the Buddhist community in conjunction with the well-organized Buddhist bureaucratic system or *sŭngjŏng* 僧政.

The examination system was somewhat different for the two major schools of Kyo and Sŏn. There were six possible ranks granted to a successful examinee, four of which were shared by monks of both schools—from the lowest, *taedŏk* 大德 (great virtue), up to *taesa* 大師 (great master), *jung daesa* 重大師 (second-grade master), and finally *samjung daesa* 三重大師 (third-grade master). In addition to these four ranks in common, two higher and more exclusive ranks were granted for each school: for Sŏn, *sŏnsa* 禪師 (Sŏn master) and *taesŏnsa* 大禪師 (great Sŏn master), and for Kyo, *sujwa* 首座 (head seat) and *sŭngt'ong* 僧統 (sangha overseer).[16] The institutional link between the central government and the Buddhist community was further enhanced by special appointments to two honorary positions among the highly respected senior monks, *kuksa* 國師 ("the state preceptor") and *wangsa* 王師 ("the royal preceptor.")[17]

The Koryŏ kings and aristocrats had a deep respect for the monks and the Buddhist community and supported them by constructing temples and monasteries, patronizing various Buddhist ceremonies and festivals, and producing woodblock editions of the Buddhist texts. They also made gifts of land to temples and monks and the state exempted monks from taxes, tributes, and corvée. Thanks to these favors and subsidies, the Koryŏ Buddhist communities accumulated considerable wealth and played a significant role in the national economy.[18]

Although Buddhism continued to prosper in the Koryŏ society, early Koryŏ Buddhism did not witness any significant developments that distinguished it from the already-established Buddhism of the Silla period. The division of Ogyo and Kusan—the five doctrinal schools and nine Sŏn schools—continued to be the primary characteristic of the sangha (the Buddhist monastic community) in the early Koryŏ period, up to the time of Ŭich'ŏn 義天 (1055–1101), the fourth son of King Munjong 文宗 (r. 1046–1083), who founded Ch'ŏnt'ae chong 天台宗 (the Tiantai school) after returning from his studies in China. Ŭich'ŏn learned from renowned masters and from the sacred texts of various Buddhist traditions during his time in China, which deepened his understanding of Buddhist teachings. In addition to acquiring philosophical and scriptural competence, he was also deeply influenced by the integrative and comprehensive approaches to the various Buddhist teachings and practices prevalent in Song China.

Ŭich'ŏn's founding of Ch'ŏnt'ae chong upon his return to Korea was an attempt to integrate the contending schools of Kyo and Sŏn. He was optimistic that a balanced cultivation of meditation and doctrinal studies (*kyogwan kyŏmsu* 教觀兼修) would contribute to harmonizing the Kyo and Sŏn schools in Koryŏ Korea. For a while it seemed that these efforts had been successful—many Hwaŏm and Sŏn monks joined the new sect. However, with the early demise of its founder in 1101, the influence of the Ch'ŏnt'ae school wavered, negatively affecting the overall drive in favor of integration within the sangha.

The emergence of Ch'ŏnt'ae chong had one unexpected consequence: namely, that the Sŏn monks, who did not sympathize with Ŭich'ŏn and refused to join the new sect, began to promote a collective self-identity among Sŏn students. The rise of this collective identity led eventually, in the early eleventh century, to a consolidation of the Nine Mountains schools into another Sŏn school,[19] Chogye chong 曹溪宗, intended as a competitor to Ch'ŏnt'ae chong.[20]

The Political Situation of Twelfth-Century Korea and Beyond

Wang Kŏn, the founder of the Koryŏ dynasty, did not hold absolute power over the state because it was founded with the support of local centers of power, from whose ranks Wang Kŏn himself had emerged. He attempted to centralize the power of the new dynasty by incorporating local centers of power into the royal court by marriage. His efforts appeared to be success-ful, but these marriages meant the formation of a new aristocracy centered in the capital, Kaesŏng. Because of this, his attempt to absorb the local powers through marriage had planted the seeds of future power struggles. The aris-tocratic families who made close connections with the royal court through marriage enhanced their influence in the bureaucracy by ascending to high official positions through the civil service examination. In addition to estab-lishing a solid foothold in the capital, these powerful families also controlled their home provinces as de facto administrators. These powerful aristocrats eventually came to vie with one another to obtain control over the royal court and the state. In the early twelfth century, this competition for power gave rise to violent revolts, one led by Yi Cha-gyŏm 李資謙 in 1126 and another by the monk Myoch'ŏng 妙淸 in 1135.[21]

These conflicts entered a new phase in 1170 when certain military officers participated in a rebellion that involved the massacre of the king's officials and eventually led to his deposition. These officers had been excluded from decision making and been mistreated by the king's officials for a long time. The successful coup d'état, however, was followed by an internal clash among its prominent leaders, thrusting the country into violent chaos until Ch'oe Ch'ung-hŏn 崔忠獻 (1149–1219) seized power and restored order through the institution of a military regime in 1196. Ch'oe Ch'ung-hŏn and his heirs ruled the country de facto until 1258; during this period, kings did not exercise political power in Korea.[22]

Along with political upheavals led by military officers, various revolts of the lower classes also erupted throughout the country beginning in the late twelfth and continuing through the early thirteenth century. At the time, the life of the peasant populace was miserable, with unbearable burdens placed on their shoulders by the state, including various forms of taxation, tribute ex-actions, and forced corvée. They were exploited by officials in the provinces and by the aristocrats in the capital. This situation of uncertainty and instabil-ity lasted until the Ch'oe family subdued all the chaotic conflicts roiling the country and brought a measure of stability.[23]

However, the country soon began to experience severe difficulties caused by the repeated Mongol invasions that occurred throughout the thirteenth and fourteenth centuries. In 1270, the Koryŏ central government fell to the Mon-gol empire of the Yuan 元, whose dominion over the Korean peninsula lasted until the reform-minded King Kongmin 恭愍 (r. 1351–1374) wrested control from the Yuan empire in 1356. After the assassination of King Kongmin in 1374, the central government again became vulnerable to power struggles, and the rise of the military commander Yi Sŏng-gye 李成桂 (1335–1408) brought about the emergence of a new dynasty, the Chosŏn 朝鮮, in 1392. This new dynasty promoted neo-Confucianism as the main principle of the political, social, moral, and cultural life of its people and suppressed Buddhism, which in any case had become corrupt due to its affluence and abuses of political power, and had lost its spiritual vitality.[24]

It is within this context—right in the middle of the history of the Koryŏ dynasty (918–1302)—that one finds the life of Chinul (1158–1210), one of Korea's greatest Buddhist thinkers. The period of Chinul's life, the late twelfth century, was a turbulent era impacted by many conflicts and much violence. One conflict after another pushed the lives of the ordinary people into deeper poverty and insecurity.

Political Changes and the Vicissitudes of Sŏn and Kyo

During this turbulent period, Sŏn Buddhism was revived under the patronage of the military regime led by the Ch'oe family. Michael Seth states, "Perhaps the most important cultural legacy of this period [of the military dictatorship of Ch'eo family] was the promotion of Sŏn Buddhism."[25] Sŏn Buddhism had not always been favored by the central government: in the first hundred years after its introduction into Korea, it did not in general appeal to the royal court and the central aristocracy. The leaders of the Sŏn school maintained their political, material, and spiritual base in the provinces and mountains, supported by local officials and other centers of local power. Since the ninth century various Sŏn schools of different dharma lineages had begun to flourish on the Korean peninsula and had received official recognition and support from the central government. Nevertheless, it is undeniable that the iconoclastic, anti-intellectual, and individualistic ideology of Sŏn appealed to the local gentry and other centers of local power, which strove to be independent of the centralized control of the court. Not only its local political importance but also the spiritual vitality of Sŏn attracted lay benefactors and monks, leading to the development of Sŏn schools of various lineages.

The growth of Sŏn continued until the early period of the Koryŏ dynasty (tenth and eleventh centuries), with the allied local powers who had contributed to the rise of the new kingdom supporting Sŏn temples and monks. The new Koryŏ state was in need of Sŏn monks who could help calm a society that had just emerged from a period of many violent divisions and conflicts. However, once the divided kingdoms were fully unified, there came the need of an ideology that could help harmonize the society and strengthen the authority of the new dynasty. As happened in the Unified Silla period, now the Kyo schools, especially Hwaŏm chong and Yuga chong (also known as Pŏpsang chong), gradually rose to prominence, supported in the eleventh and twelfth centuries by the court and the aristocracy. The political and social upheavals and the ensuing power shift from the literati to the military officers in the late twelfth century also provided an opportune atmosphere for the Sŏn school to bolster its status in the society.

The revival of Sŏn Buddhism in the late twelfth century was not only attributable to the political and social situation. It was also attributable to the fact that it was a kind of reform movement based on a critical awareness of the reality of the sangha in Korea. The abundant wealth and privileges afforded to the temples and monasteries had led to the corruption of monks and a laxity in their life, as monks neglected both study and meditation. In the monks' pursuit of fame and wealth, the practice of Buddhism had become overly ritualized.[26] Meanwhile, the contentiousness between Sŏn and Kyo monks continued into the Koryŏ period. Ŭich'ŏn saw the constant and problematic discord between these two Buddhist schools and in the late eleventh century sought reconciliation by calling for a more balanced cultivation of doctrinal studies and meditative practices. Although Ch'ŏnt'ae chong, the ecumenical school Ŭich'ŏn established, was considered to be primarily a Sŏn order, this attempt at integration was generally based on strengthening doctrinal studies.

Ŭich'ŏn's short-lived effort to integrate Kyo and Sŏn would be resumed a century later by Chinul, now with an emphasis more on Sŏn theories and practices. When Chinul decided to commit himself to Buddhist practices as a monk, he was aware of the serious problems prevailing in the Koryŏ-era sangha—the corruption at both the individual and communal levels, the unresolved conflict between Kyo and Sŏn, and the laxity of the practices of both Kyo and Sŏn monks. Before looking into Chinul's ecumenical understanding of the relationship between Sŏn and Kyo, the following section will introduce his life and writings, which can be better understood within the political and religious context of his time.

POJO CHINUL: HIS LIFE AND WRITINGS

The Life of Chinul

A Brief Summary of Chinul's Life

By the twelfth century, the Koryŏ dynasty had begun to confront violent upheavals emanating from both the dissatisfied ruling class and the weary masses living in wretched conditions of exploitation and impoverishment. At this time of social and political disturbances that inflicted much suffering on the masses of people, corruption and lax practices prevailed in the Buddhist monastic community. It was in the midst of all this that Chinul was born. According to Chinul's funerary inscription,[27] he was born in 1158 in the Tongju 洞州 district (currently the Sŏhŭng 瑞興 district in Hwanghae 黃海 Province) to the west of Kaesŏng 開城, the Koryŏ capital. His lay surname was Chŏng 鄭; Chinul 知訥, which means "Knowing Reticence," was his dharma name given at his ordination. Later, he liked to refer to himself as Moguja 牧牛子, or "ox herder."[28] Chinul is also known by the honorific title posthumously granted him by King Hŭijong 熙宗 (r. 1204–1211) of Puril Pojo *Kuksa* (also known in the abbreviated form of Pojo *Kuksa*) 佛日普照國師: "State Precep-tor Sun of Buddha that Shines Universally."

Chinul's father was Chŏng Kwang-u 鄭光遇, who worked in the State Academy in a bureaucratic position corresponding to *chŏng kup'um* 正九品, the lowest government rank. Apparently, Chŏng Kwang-u did not enjoy a prominent social status, despite the fact that he seems to have been edu-cated.[29] According to the funerary inscription, the young Chinul was very weak and suffered from frequent illnesses. His parents could not find any remedy for their son, and his father made a vow that his son would become a monk if he were cured. Chinul miraculously regained his health, and as promised, his father sent Chinul to Kulsansa 崛山寺 at the age of eight[30] under the auspices of the Sŏn master Chonghwui (Chonghwui Sŏnsa 宗暉禪師) of the Mt. Sagul branch of Sŏn (Sagul sanmun 闍崛山門). Although the master gave him the name "Chinul," it does not appear that Chonghwui had a significant influence on Chinul's spiritual development.[31] Kim Kun-su writes as if Chinul was received into the monastery and simultaneously or-dained: "Under him [Chonghwui], he shaved his head and received the full set of precepts."[32] However, Robert Buswell, taking into consideration other language in the funerary inscription stating that Chinul had been a monk for thirty-six years at the time of his death at the age of fifty-three, argues that Chinul was ordained at the age of sixteen.[33] Keel Hee-sung also doubts the accuracy of Kim Kun-su's account of Chinul's early years. He suggests that Chinul might have left home on his own between the ages of fifteen and twenty, and argues that the story of his miraculous recovery is little more than hagiographical flourish.[34] Furthermore, Keel conjectures that the turbulent political and social conditions of his time may have prompted the delicate mind of the adolescent to ponder the disorder of the world and to leave the world in pursuit of liberation.[35]

After several years of monastic training, Chinul took and passed the clerical examination in 1182 at the age of twenty-five at Pojesa 普濟寺 in Kaesŏng. According to Kim Kun-su, not long after this examination, he left the capital to travel south to concentrate on meditation. The clerical examination was an essential gateway for entering the ecclesiastical bureaucracy, which guaran-teed promotion, fame, and wealth, but although he passed the examination, he left behind thoughts of worldly success and instead pursued the path of the Buddha. Chinul's thoughts about the degenerate state of the sangha are manifest in *Encouragement to Practice: The Compact of the Samādhi and Prajñā Society* (hereafter *Encouragement to Practice*).

> Nevertheless, when we examine the inclination of our conduct from dawn to dusk, [we see that] even while we have entrusted ourselves to the Buddhadharma, we have adorned ourselves with the signs of self and person. Infatuated with material welfare and immersed in secular concerns, we are not cultivating the Way and its virtue but just squandering food and clothing. Although we have left home [to become monks, S. *pravrajita*], what merit does it have? Alas! Now, we may want to leave far behind the three realms of existence [S. *traidhātuka* of sensuality, subtle-materiality, and immateriality], but we do not practice freeing ourselves from the dust [of sensory objects]. We use our male body in vain, for we lack the will of a real man. Above, we fail in propagating the path; below, we are negligent in benefiting living creatures; and in between, we turn our backs on our four benefactors. This is indeed shameful! I, Chinul, have lamented all of this since long ago.[36]

In short, Chinul was well aware of the reality of the Buddhist community and deplored the fact that monks who should earnestly work to free themselves from the dust of the world were actually drawn to its glories. He might have witnessed the disease of the sangha more clearly than ever at the time of his examination, but in any case, out of disenchantment and frustration, he decided not to join the ecclesiastical bureaucracy. Instead, he resolved to immerse himself in the cultivation of the mind through the balanced practice of *samādhi* (concentration) and *prajñā* (wisdom). He met some monks at the clerical examination who sympathized with his intentions, and they made a pact to dedicate themselves to this noble cause. Chinul records the occasion:

> One day I made a pact with more than ten fellow meditators, who said: "After the close of this convocation we will renounce fame and profit and remain in seclusion in the mountain forests. There, we will form a retreat society designated to foster constant training in samādhi balanced with prajñā. Through worship of the Buddha, recitation of sūtra, and even through our manual labor, we will each discharge the duties to which we are assigned and nourish the [self-]nature in all situation. [We vow to] pass our whole lives free of entanglements and to follow the higher pursuits of accomplished gentlemen and authentic adepts. Would this not be wonderful?"[37]

Confirmed in the objectives of the pact, the ten monks who attended the convocation of the examination formally decided to participate in it.

> All those venerables who heard these words agreed with what was said and vowed, "On another day we will consummate this agreement, live in seclusion

deep in the forest, and be bound together as a society that should be named for samādhi and prajñā." In this manner the pledge was put to writing, and everyone affirmed their decision.³⁸

The pact to form a society dedicated to the enthusiastic practice of meditation was made in 1182; however, several years passed before the monks were actually able to retreat to a mountain monastery to put their aspirations into practice. While Chinul was residing in Pomunsa 普門寺 on Haga Mountain 下柯山 in 1188,³⁹ the Sŏn monk Tŭkchae 得才 (date unknown, hereafter d.u.), who had made the pledge in 1188, invited him and the other monks to Kŏjosa 居祖寺 on Kong Mountain 公山.⁴⁰ Together with some new recruits, they formally set out for the retreat in 1190, but among the initial ten members of the group at Kaesŏng, only a few made it to Kŏjosa.⁴¹ They named the group the "Samādhi and Prajñā Society" (*Chŏnghye kyŏlsa* 定慧結社), and to commemorate its beginning, Chinul composed *Encouragement to Practice*, published later in 1200.

Chinul answers various questions regarding religious practices in *Encouragement to Practice*. On the one hand, based on a faith in the potentiality of every individual, he criticizes the idea of the degenerate age of the dharma (*malpŏp* 末法), an idea which discouraged the practice of self-reliance; and on the other, he expounds proper approaches to cultivating one's mind in order to persuade fellow practitioners.

The Society appealed to many more of the same mind who had been yearning for zealous cultivation in a dedicated community under the guidance of a sagacious master, and the number of monks joining the Society grew rapidly. By 1197, its increased numbers necessitated an expansion of the monastery, but the site of Kŏjosa was not desirable for the expansion, and so Chinul sent Suu 守愚 (d.u.), one of his disciples, to find a suitable place for the Society's new center. Suu found Kilsangsa 吉祥寺 on Songgwang Mountain 松廣山 fitting, and even though the site was initially too small to accommodate all the monks, Chinul believed that it was appropriate for the needs of the growing community. He immediately set out to repair the extant buildings and to construct new ones.

Chinul moved into the monastery in 1200, and the construction was completed in 1205. When Chinul and his community relocated to Kilsangsa, they continued to use Chŏnghyesa 定慧寺 as the name of the monastery (derived from Chŏnghye kyŏlsa 定慧結社), but this caused confusion with another temple of the same name, also located near Kilsangsa. To solve this problem, King Hŭijong ordered Chinul to change the name of the community to Susŏnsa 修禪社, "Cultivating Sŏn Society." The king also honored the community and Chinul by granting an autographed name plaque for the monastery and by a gift of a fully embroidered clerical robe to the master. He further changed the name of Songgwang Mountain to Chogye Mountain 曹溪山 (C. Caoqishan), where Huineng, the sixth patriarch of Chan had resided in China, as a token of symbolic recognition of the new Sŏn community as the center of Sŏn renewal in Korea.[42]

The reputation of Chinul and Susŏnsa attracted enthusiastic people from all walks of life and all corners of the nation. The revival promoted by Chinul set a new direction in the development of Sŏn in Korea by providing "a spiritual renewal, a new ideology and identity,"[43] which continues even to the present day to have a great influence on Korean Buddhism. At Kilsangsa, Chinul was persistent in cultivating his mind and guiding the growing community up to his death in 1210. To pay tribute to the great master, King Hŭijong conferred on him the posthumous title Puril Pojo *Kuksa* 佛日普照國師, "State Preceptor Sun of Buddha that Shines Universally," and named the pagoda erected to contain Chinul's relics Kamnot'ap 甘露塔, "Sweet Dew Pagoda."[44]

Chinul's Journey to Enlightenment

After the pact made by the retreat society at Pojesa in 1182, Chinul left the capital of Kaesŏng alone and traveled around the country to immerse himself in the ardent practice of meditation. Then, in 1188 he joined those who had made the pledge and some other like-minded monks in Kŏjosa, and later settled permanently in Susŏnsa beginning in 1200. As Chinul diligently devoted himself to the practice of *samādhi* and *prajñā*, along with other Buddhist practices, his mind became sharpened, his virtue cultivated, his wisdom deeper, and his understanding of the Buddhist teachings and scriptures clearer. Along the way, there were three important religious experiences that would determine the future course of his religious practices.

The first came when Chinul was residing at Ch'ŏngwŏnsa 清源寺 in Ch'angp'yŏng 昌平, located in Tamyang 潭陽 District, South Chŏlla Province 全羅南道. In the funerary inscription, Kim Kun-su records the event as follows:

> By chance one day in the dormitory (*hangnyo* 學寮) as he was looking through the *Platform Sūtra of the Sixth Patriarch*, he came across [the following passage]: "The self-nature of suchness generates thoughts. Although the six sense-faculties may see, hear, sense, and know, they do not taint the myriad sensory objects and the true nature remains constantly autonomous."[45]

Chinul was overjoyed at reading this passage, as it helped him realize that sensory objects are a function of the self-nature of suchness (*chinyŏ chasŏng* 眞如自性), and that neither thought nor the objects of thought are defiled.[46] This passage celebrates the positive aspect of thought. Traditionally, negative opinions of thought, that it arises from ignorance and desires, had prevailed among the sangha. However, as Chan asserts, if thought arises from such-ness, it must have legitimacy. You may misunderstand things and have false conceptions, but nevertheless there is a kind of inherent purity in your think-ing and in the objects of your thinking. Despite leading to mistakes, thought itself is not contaminated; errors and false conceptions are not essential, but accidental. They do not come from our own nature, and neither do they taint the purity of our mind. Even when we make mistakes, it is our intrinsic buddha-nature that makes them. Thoughts themselves are manifestations of one's inherent buddha-nature or the self-nature of suchness. For Chinul, the legitimacy of our thought, which arises from the self-nature of suchness or the instrinsic buddha-nature, was compatible with the Sŏn tenet of "seeing into nature and becoming a buddha" (*kyŏnsŏng sŏngbul* 見性成佛).[47] This initial awakening experience encouraged Chinul to continue making a full commit-ment to the cultivation of the mind.[48] It also played a crucial role in setting the direction of his further practices, and he would repeatedly stress the im-portance of an initial awakening to his students.[49] From this point onward, the *Platform Sūtra* became one of Chinul's favorite Buddhist texts, and he often referred to it when expounding Buddhist doctrines.[50]

After staying in Ch'ŏnwŏnsa for three years, Chinul moved to Pomunsa 普門寺 on Haga Mountain 下柯(鶴駕)山.[51] Following his first awakening expe-rience, Chinul came to acknowledge the merit of reading scriptures. Despite this acknowledgment, Chinul continued to focus on the Sŏn practice, that is, meditation on the primary Sŏn idea that the mind is buddha, which was considered to be the most expedient approach to enlightenment in the Sŏn tradition. Nevertheless, he was still interested in the soteriological approaches of the doctrinal—in particular the Huayan—school. Making an inquiry about this interest to a Hwaŏm scholar, he received the unexpected criticism that Sŏn focuses too much on the mind and introspective awareness and does not pay any attention to the external world.

It occurred to Chinul that if the mind is truly illuminated there would not be a dichotomous view of the mind and the world, because one would realize that the mind and all phenomena are interfused. Chinul wanted to vindicate the Sŏn view within the scriptures, and so he diligently surveyed the Buddhist texts for three years. Finally, he came across this passage in the "Manifestation of the Tathāgata" chapter (C. *Rulai chuxian pin* 如來出現品) of the *Avataṃsakasūtra* (C. *Huayan jing* 華嚴經), which led him to a second awakening experience: "The wisdom of the tathāgatas is also just like this: . . . it is fully present in the bodies of all sentient beings. It is merely all these ordinary, foolish people . . . who are not aware of it and do not recognize it."[52] Chinul also found this teaching further expounded in the *Xin Huayan jing lun*

新華嚴經論 (*Exposition of the Avataṃsakasūtra*) written by Li Tongxuan 李
通玄 (635–730) (hereafter *Exposition*) to the effect that the sublime nature of
any ordinary person's mind is identical to the wisdom of a buddha, and the
mind and the body are not differentiated from the *dharmadātu*[53] or "dharma
realm" (C. *fajie*, K. *pŏpgye* 法界). Li further explained that the initial act of
faith in the true nature of one's mind is crucial for further advancing in one's
religious path to enlightenment, and Chinul came to believe that this Huayan
claim truly corresponded to sudden enlightenment in Sŏn.

   Through his thorough studies of the *Avataṃsakasūtra* and Li's *Exposition*,
Chinul came to realize the unity and complementarity of Kyo and Sŏn and began warning of the futility of the disputes and conflicts among scholar monks
and Sŏn adepts.[54] This acknowledgment of the essential harmony between
Kyo and Sŏn resolved Chinul's own struggle over the way to harmonize the
two traditions, and afterward Chinul strove to establish a "synthetic" and
"all-inclusive"[55] soteriological approach, work that would have a long-lasting
impact on Buddhist practices in Korea. Thus, Chinul's second awakening
experience had laid a firm foundation for the direction of Korean Buddhism
for centuries to come.[56]

   Concerning Chinul's third awakening experience, it will be recalled that
Chinul's community relocated to their larger monastery around 1200. Chinul
himself left Kŏjosa with a few companions for Kilsangsa in 1197; however,
rather than heading to the new place right away, on the way they stopped
at Sangmujuam 上無住庵 on Chiri Mountain 智異山 in order to meditate.
The monks stayed there for three years until they finally headed in the direction of Kilsangsa. It was here at the small hermitage on Chiri Mountain that
Chinul had the third awakening experience. It happened while reading a text,
this time the *Records* of Sŏn Master Dahui Pujue 大慧普覺禪師語錄. In the
funerary inscription, Kim Kun-su records this event as if Chinul himself were
describing it.

> The Master said, "More than ten years had passed since I came from Pomunsa. Al-
> though I was satisfied that I had cultivated diligently and had not wasted my time,
> I had still not forsaken passions and views—it was as if something were blocking
> my chest, or as if I were dwelling together with an enemy. While sojourning on
> Mount Chiri, I obtained the *Records of* Sŏn Master Dahui Pujue, which said, 'Sŏn,
> does not consist in quietude; it does not consist in bustle. It does not consist in the
> activities of daily life; it does not consist in ratiocination. Nevertheless, it is of first
> importance not to investigate [Sŏn] while rejecting quietude or bustle, the activi-
> ties of daily life, or ratiocination. Unexpectedly, your eyes will open and you then
> will know that these are all things taking place inside your home.' I understood
> this [passage] and naturally nothing blocked my chest again and I never again
> dwelt together with an enemy. From then on I was at peace."[57]

The passage from Dahui's *Records* asserts that a practitioner should not attach to any single way of Sŏn practice, whether it be meditation in quietude, engagement with daily life, or intellectual activities, because whatever one does takes place in one's mind. The passage asserts the importance of mind cultivation and confirms what Chinul discovered through the *Platform Sūtra*. However, Keel Hee-sung suggests that the first two discoveries were intellectual and abstract in its nature, whereas this one involved a mystical experience, free from intellectual understanding. In this regard, he interprets the enemy blocking his chest as "the disease of intellectual understanding," which had prevented "the perfect spontaneity of mystical experience."[58]

Whether Chinul's third awakening experience was anti-intellectual or not, the encounter with Dahui's *Records* led Chinul to the discovery of the "short-cut" approach (*kyŏngjŏl mun* 徑截門) of *kanhwa* Sŏn 看話禪 (C. *kanhua Chan*, "Chan of observing the keyword"). Dahui's *kanhwa* Sŏn emphasizes a direct experience of awakening through meditating on illogical keywords or *hwadu* 話頭 (C. *huatou*). Whereas Chinul's practice for the previous two decades had been characterized by his attempts to incorporate intellectual understanding into meditative practice, the adoption of *kanhwa* Sŏn set his practice on an apophatic path. Thanks to Chinul's advocacy and to that of his successor, Hyesim 慧諶 (1178–1234), *hwadu* meditation would become an essential part of Sŏn meditation techniques in Korea afterward.[59]

There is therefore no doubt that Dahui's thought had a great impact on the alteration of Chinul's approach. Still, Keel's interpretation of the third awakening experience, which stresses Chinul's recognition of intellectual understanding as a major obstacle to one's spiritual development,[60] does not fully explain what happened in the mind of Chinul at that time. The change of Chinul's mental state from uneasiness to peace should be considered from the perspective of his personal awakening experience, that is, in light of the twofold category of awakening—*haeo* 解悟 (C. *jiewu*, "understanding-awakening") and *chŭngo* 證悟 (C. *zhengwu*, "realization-awakening").[61]

According to Chinul,[62] an ordinary man begins his cultivation of the mind with an initial sudden awakening or understanding-awakening through which he comes to comprehend that his true nature is identical with a buddha. Through this awakening one enters the level of the ten faiths, the early stage of the soteriological path to buddhahood. However, since even after this initial awakening the adept is not fully freed yet from defiled habits, he needs to continue to cultivate his mind and undertake other religious practices until his understanding of the true nature of suchness is realized. Realization-awakening (*chŭngo* 證悟), achieved as the result of subsequent cultivation following the initial understanding-awakening, enables this understanding to permeate one's being so that one's understanding is not obstructed by ignorance, delusion, and greed. Through realization-awakening, the cultivator of the mind finally begins to walk the bodhisattva path and to help ferry other sentient beings across to the shore of enlightenment.[63]

In light of this twofold distinction, Chinul's first two awakening experiences can be considered "understanding-awakening," because even after these experiences, the true nature of his mind was still obscured by his habits that were attached to intellectual understanding and inconsistent with his acts. On the other hand, his third awakening experience can be considered his "realization-awakening." Here, Chinul came to fully realize the buddha-nature prevalent in himself, in the universe, and in every act of human life. With the realization of the true nature of everything in the universe and the harmony existing between his acts and dharma, the wandering mind of Chinul finally reached peace.[64]

This section briefly introduced the life of Chinul and examined some important moments in his experience that played a pivotal role in the development of his thought and practice. To gain further insight into Chinul's philosophical and spiritual insights, it is now necessary to turn to his writings.

Chinul's Writings

Chinul, an adept of a Buddhist tradition generally distinguished by its hostile attitude toward scriptural study and scholastic speculation, composed a significant number of texts. Although some are lost, many are extant. As Chinul is revered as one of the most influential thinkers and teachers in Korean Buddhist history, his writings have long provided the Korean Buddhist community with normative guidance for the spiritual quest and theoretical foundations of Sŏn practice.

Chinul's writings are also valuable for understanding the intellectual currents in Buddhist East Asia in the medieval era. As noted by Buswell, "Chinul's writings cover the entire expanse of the Chinese and Korean traditions and are recognized as some of the finest examples of medieval scholastic composition."[65] Considering that his writings were primarily intended for Sŏn students who might or might not have been trained in scriptural and doctrinal studies, the vast array of scriptural quotations and profound knowledge of philosophical traditions employed surely challenged the readers of his time, not to mention modern readers.

What follows is a synopsis of Chinul's major works in roughly chronological order. This brief introduction to these writings will help outline the development of Chinul's thought, mark his major soteriological approaches, and note his attempts to integrate Kyo and Sŏn.[66]

Encouragement to Practice: The Compact of the Samādhi and Prajñā Society (*Kwŏnsu Chŏnghye kyŏlsa mun* 勸修定慧結社文)

Chinul's earliest work, *Encouragement to Practice*, was written in 1190 at Kŏjosa on Kong Mountain to commemorate the official establishment of the Samādhi and Prajñā Society. The text briefly describes the founding of the community from the moment the members vowed to form the Society to its actual gathering at Kŏjosa. As clearly stated in the title, the text aims at persuading people to participate in the practice of *samādhi* and *prajñā* and to abandon the vain pursuit of fame and wealth. The text contains Chinul's critical observations about the Buddhist community of his time—that the monks' lifestyle was corrupt and their religious practices lax—and also describes his intention to reform the sangha.

Chinul also criticizes in this work the prevalence of the Pure Land practice of reciting the Buddha's name (*yŏmbul* 念佛). The popularity of this practice was attributed to the concept of the degenerate age of the dharma (*malbŏp* 末法). The supporters of the practice insisted that people's spiritual faculties are so degenerate that they are not capable of engaging in advanced religious practices. Thus, the Pure Land tradition (C. Jingtu zong, K. Chŏngt'o chong 淨土宗) promoted the constant invocation of the name of the Amitābha Buddha as an effective means of Buddhist practice, which would lead to people being reborn in the pure land. In criticizing this practice, Chinul reminds people of the sublime nature of the mind (which is identical with the buddha-nature) and encourages people to investigate their minds. Chinul presents *samādhi* and *prajñā* as a concrete way of cultivation, divided into two kinds—the "*samādhi* and *prajñā* that adapt to signs" (*susang chŏnghye* 隨相定慧) and the "*samādhi* and *prajñā* of the self-nature" (*chasŏng chŏnghye* 自性定慧). For Chinul, these two kinds are "relative" and "absolute," respectively.[67] This twofold categorization of *samādhi* and *prajñā* is also expounded in *Moguja's Secrets on Cultivating the Mind* (*Moguja Susim gyŏl* 牧牛子修心訣).

Admonitions to Neophytes (*Kye Ch'osim hagin mun* 誡初心學人文)

Admonitions to Neophytes (hereafter *Admonitions*) was composed in 1205 at about the time the Samādhi and Prajñā Society was officially renamed the Society of Cultivating Sŏn (Susŏnsa 修禪社) in Kilsangsa. This is the earliest text composed in Korea setting forth proper monastic conduct for a Sŏn monastery. In writing this text, Chinul was greatly influenced by *Chanyuan qinggui* 禪苑清規 (*Rules of purity for the Chan monastery*), the antecedent Chinese text written by Changlu Zongze 長蘆宗賾 (fl. ca. late eleventh to early twelfth centuries). Chinul's text was adopted in the

Buddhist monasteries in Korea as an introductory text for the training of novices, and is used for this purpose even now. *Admonitions* reveals in its composition Chinul's emphasis on the balanced practice of the "threefold training" (*samhak* 三學, S. *triśikṣā*)—ethical restraint (*kye* 戒, S. *śīla*), meditative absorption (*chŏng* 定, S. *samādhi*), and gnoseological wisdom (*hye* 慧, S. *prajñā*).[68] The work is divided into three parts: admonitions to neophytes, admonitions to monks regarding proper living in a monastery, and admonitions to monks regarding propriety in the meditation hall.[69]

Moguja's Secrets on Cultivating the Mind (Moguja Susim kyŏl 牧牛子修心訣)

While *Encouragement to Practice* invites people to cultivate the mind and *Admonitions to Neophytes* regulates proper conduct and decorum among monks, *Moguja's Secrets on Cultivating the Mind* (hereafter *Moguja's Secrets*) expounds on soteriological approaches to enlightenment. It was probably written between 1203 and 1205 as "a seminal text of the Korean Sŏn tradition" presenting "accessible and cogent accounts of Sŏn training."[70] *Moguja's Secrets* is still one of the most popular Sŏn texts in Korea.[71]

In this work, Chinul first explains the foundational principle of Sŏn that seeing the mind is seeing the Buddha and seeing one's nature is seeing the buddha-nature. This Sŏn tenet urges the Buddhist to dedicate oneself to the cultivation of the mind. He further expounds the two soteriological approaches that prevail throughout all his writings—sudden enlightenment and gradual cultivation—and discusses the concurrent cultivation of *samādhi* and *prajñā*. As for the twofold approach of sudden enlightenment and gradual cultivation, Chinul stresses that it epitomizes all the paths of Buddhism, as all the great sages had experienced both initial awakening, or understanding-awakening (*haeo* 解悟), and subsequent cultivation, eventually leading to a realization-awakening (*chŭngo* 證悟).

Because *Moguja's Secrets* primarily concerns how to cultivate the mind, it is important to define "the mind." For Chinul, it is the mind of void, calm, numinous awareness (*kongjŏk yŏngji chi sim* 空寂靈知之心). He understands that the mind is void and calm in its essence (*ch'e* 體) and is mysteriously aware of things happening inside and outside it, which is the function (*yong* 用) of the mind. Chinul relates the twofold distinction of the mind to the twofold cultivation of *samādhi* and *prajñā*. He presents *samādhi* as the essence of the mind and *prajñā* as the function of the mind. Furthermore, he expounds two ways of cultivating *samādhi* and *prajñā*—the absolute cultivation of *samādhi* and *prajñā* of the self-nature and the relative cultivation of *samādhi* and *prajñā* that adapt to signs. Chinul relates the relative type of cultivation of *samādhi* and *prajñā* to the paths of the gradual school and the absolute type to the sudden school; however, he makes it clear that both the relative and absolute types should be cultivated even after initial sudden enlightenment.

Preface and Conclusion from the Condensation of the Exposition of the Avataṃsakasūtra (Hwaŏm non chŏryo 華嚴論節要)

Written in 1207, the *Condensation of the Exposition of the Avataṃsakasūtra* consists of three-roll extracts from Li Tongxuan's 李通玄 (635–730) forty-roll commentary to the new translation of the *Avataṃsakasūtra—Huayan lun* 華嚴論 (K. *Hwaŏm non, Exposition of the Avataṃsakasūtra*). Unlike the *Treatise on the Complete and Sudden Attainment of Buddhahood*, which is a kind of commentary on Li's *Exposition*, this text is a verbatim abridgement of Li's work without any commentary. In this brief excerpt from Li's *Exposition*, Chinul focuses on "soteriological materials that help to demonstrate the convergence between Kyo doctrine and Sŏn practice."[72] Chinul added a short preface and conclusion to this work. The preface contains an important autobiographical account explaining his important religious experience at Pomunsa in 1185. In the conclusion, Chinul stresses the efficacy of the sudden enlightenment teachings of the Sŏn school for understanding Hwaŏm teachings.

Treatise on the Complete and Sudden Attainment of Buddhahood (Wŏndon sŏngbullon 圓頓成佛論)

This treatise (hereafter *Complete and Sudden Attainment*) was found among Chinul's belongings after his death and published posthumously by his successor, Hyesim 慧諶 (1178–1234) in 1215. It is thought to have been composed between 1207 and his death in 1210 as a complementary work to his summary of the *Exposition of the Avataṃsakasūtra* (*Hwaŏm non chŏryo* 華嚴論節要).[73]

Expounding on the status of buddhahood and the process by which one attains buddhahood (*sŏngbul* 成佛), Chinul insists that ordinary people can reach the goal of buddhahood, and argues for the compatibility of Kyo and Sŏn. He first explains the Hwaŏm tenets that the minds of ordinary people are identical with the Unmoving Wisdom of buddhas, and that if one believes and understands this principle at the initial stage of the bodhisattva path he would suddenly achieve buddhahood. These tenets, Chinul shows, correspond to the Sŏn tenets "Mind is buddha" and "See the nature and achieve buddhahood."[74] Furthermore, Chinul insists that Sŏn experience is not only sudden 頓 (*don*) awakening to the essence of the nature of *dharmadhātu* or the world of dharma (C. *fajie*, K. *pŏpgye* 法界), but it also involves perfecting (or completing, 圓 *wŏn*) the functions of *dharmadhātu* or the spiritual qualities inherent in it, through which one interacts with the world. Thus, Chinul argues that Sŏn is not only concerned with the transcendental realm but also engaged in the phenomenal world for the sake of other sentient beings, and shows that Sŏn, which claims to be antithetical to theory and doctrine, is compatible with Hwaŏm, whose claim is to be the complete teaching (wŏn'gyo 圓教).[75]

Treatise on Resolving Doubts about Observing the Keyword (Kanhwa kyŏrŭiron 看話決疑論)

Like *Complete and Sudden Attainment*, this treatise (hereafter *Resolving Doubts*) on the *kanhwa* Sŏn (C. *kanhua Chan* 看話禪) practice was discovered after Chinul's death and published in 1215 by Hyesim 慧諶. *Kanhwa* Sŏn is a meditative technique that focuses intensely on a keyword or phrase. The systematic development and promotion of *kanhua chan* in China is attributed to Dahui Zonggao 大慧宗杲 (1089–1163) of the Song 宋 dynasty. It was first brought into Korean Buddhism by Chinul and promoted by his successor Hyesim, and has ever since been a primary meditation practice in Korea. *Resolving Doubts* aims at introducing this new technique to the Sŏn adepts in Korea, and is structured in the form of responses to questions by a person who doubts its validity. The goal of the *kanhwa* practice is to break through all knowledge and understanding to attain a complete realization of the perfect interfusion of the *dharmadhātu*. This meditative technique is antithetical to doctrine and verbal explanation and therefore predominantly apophatic.

The treatise also discusses the relationship between Sŏn and Kyo by referring to the fivefold Huayan taxonomy, in which Sŏn and Huayan teachings are identified as the fourth and fifth categories (the sudden and complete teachings, respectively). In the Huayan doctrinal classification, the sudden teaching is characterized by an abandonment of words and thoughts. However, the Sŏn practice—especially *kanhwa* Sŏn—rather than simply focusing on its anti-intellectual and antiverbal method, emphasizes its ultimate goal, the realization of the perfect interfusion of all phenomena. This goal is not different from the pinnacle to be reached with the Hwaŏm teachings of the complete school. According to Chinul, even though its methodological approach can be identified with the category of the sudden teaching, the soteriological goal of Sŏn corresponds to the complete teaching of Hwaŏm.

However, Chinul does not limit himself to placing Sŏn into the highest category, equal to the Hwaŏm teaching. He argues that Sŏn is in fact *superior* to the Hwaŏm teaching because of its soteriological efficiency in terms of the speed with which the goal can be achieved. According to Chinul, the *kanhwa* is a shortcut approach that is more effective than the Hwaŏm complete teaching, which greatly relies on doctrinal understanding and requires an endless investment of time.

It is apparent that *Resolving Doubts* advocates an apophatic approach to enlightenment, an approach that transcends words and concepts. Nevertheless, it does not discard textual and theoretical studies entirely; in fact, the treatise contains many scriptural references and scholastic explanations in advocating for Sŏn teachings.

Excerpts from the Dharma Collection and Special Practice Record with Personal Notes (Pŏpchip pyŏrhaengnok chŏryo pyŏngip sagi 法集別行錄節要並入私記)

Chinul's "magnum opus"[76] (hereafter *Excerpts*) was written in 1209 at the pinnacle of his thought and study, one year before his death.[77] Together with *Complete and Sudden Attainment*, this work manifests Chinul's integrative approach to Kyo—he composed it for Sŏn adepts who he believed could benefit from scriptural and doctrinal study.[78] Chinul first discusses the taxonomy of the four major medieval Chinese Chan schools, drawing on Zongmi's explanation and critique of these schools—the northern school (Beizong 北宗), the Niutou 牛頭 or Oxhead school, the Hongzhou 洪州 school, and the Heze 荷澤 school. Guifeng Zongmi 圭峰宗密 (780–841) was the putative fifth patriarch of both the Huayan school and the Heze school of Chan, and had a great influence on Chinul's efforts to integrate Sŏn and Kyo. Naturally, Zongmi was in favor of the soteriological approach of the Heze school and dismissed the approaches of other schools.[79] However, Chinul, even while similarly championing the Heze approach, acknowledges the practical value of the approaches of the other Chan schools.

After describing the four Chan schools, Chinul expands his discussion by engaging with other taxonomies outlined by prominent Buddhist masters like Chengguan 澄觀 (738–839) and Yongming Yanshou 永明延壽 (904–975) from the perspective of the sudden enlightenment/gradual cultivation approach. While investigating the twofold approach of sudden enlightenment/gradual cultivation expounded by various teachers, Chinul also discusses other characteristic approaches to Buddhist practice—concurrent cultivation of *samādhi* and *prajñā*, faith and understanding according to the complete and sudden teaching of the Hwaŏm school, and *kanhwa* Sŏn 看話禪 (investigating the keyword), which has been introduced but will be explored in detail later. *Excerpts*, Chinul's most comprehensive work, is the fruit of the mature stage of his philosophical development and "covers the full range of his Sŏn and Hwaŏm thought."[80]

Other Writings

In addition to these writings, there are two texts attributed to Chinul whose authorship is questionable. The first is *Straight Talk on the True Mind* (*Chinsim chiksŏl* 眞心直說) (hereafter *Straight Talk*). Ch'oe Yŏn-sik refutes Chinul's authorship of this work and suggests the twelfth-century Jurchen monk Zhengyan as its author.[81] *Straight Talk* first discusses the essence and function of the true mind, referring to various scriptural resources from both the Kyo and Sŏn traditions. It then expounds ten approaches to the practice of no-mind, which, according to the author, is an efficient method for realizing the true mind. The treatise primarily focuses on the true mind and the practice of no-mind without mentioning other major approaches to the Sŏn practice, such as *samādhi* and *prajña*.

The second of these texts whose authorship is questionable is *Essentials of Pure Land Practice* (*Yŏmbul yomun* 念佛要門),[82] a brief treatise on the proper ways in the Pure Land practice of reciting the name of Amitābha Buddha. In *Encouragement to Practice*, Chinul criticized the popular practice of reciting the name of Amitābha Buddha with the aspiration of being reborn in the Pure Land as a substitute for fervently cultivating the mind. In this short text, however, instead of merely criticizing the practice, he (or whoever the author is) offers a syncretic approach to the practice, associating it with the practice of no-thought in the Sŏn tradition and describing ten proper ways of recollecting the Buddha. The author also stresses the need for proper moral preparation for the practice and warns its practitioners that their practice should not be skewed by misguided understanding and unwholesome desires.

One last text worth mentioning is *Postface to a Recarving of the Platform Sūtra* (*Pŏppogi tan'gyŏng chunggan pal* 法寶記檀經重刊跋). This brief postface was written in 1207 at the request of one of Chinul's disciples in order to commemorate the reprinting of the *sūtra* that played such a significant role at the moment of his first awakening experience.[83] In addition to the extant texts discussed here, Kim Kun-su's funerary inscription also makes reference to *Sangdangnok* (Record of formal discourse), *Pŏbŏ* (Dharma discourses), and *Kasong* (Songs and verses), which are not extant.[84]

Despite its brevity, this survey of Chinul's writings shows that each of the texts was composed with different emphases and for different purposes about various aspects of Buddhist principles and various approaches to Buddhist practice. Taken together, they reveal the great depth of Chinul's thought. Building on the foregoing study of his life and writings, the discussion will now proceed to some of the ways Chinul's thought was embedded in East Asian Buddhist traditions and at the same time distinctively adapted to his personal experience and the Korean context.

Chinul's Thought

Thanks to the considerable number of Chinul's extant writings,[85] it is possible to construct an outline of his thought, in particular his understanding of various Buddhist doctrines, Sŏn principles, and approaches to religious practice. In *Excerpts*, which, as already noted, is considered to be his most comprehensive work, the master writes:

> The approach to dharma I have discussed so far has been designed for students who can generate the access to the understanding-awakening while relying on words; it has offered a detailed assessment of the two aspects of dharma—adaptability and immutability—and the two approaches concerning person—sudden awakening and gradual cultivation. Through these two aspects [of dharma], they will be able to understand that the most crucial points of all the sūtras and śāstras in the entire canon [*Tripiṭaka*][86] are the nature and characteristics of one's own mind. Through these two approaches [concerning person], they will see the tracks followed by all the sages and saints are the beginning and end of their own practice. This sort of detailed assessment of the fundamental and ancillary aspects [of the process of practice] will obviously help people free themselves from delusion, transition from the provisional toward the real, and realize bodhi quickly.[87]

As is clearly stated in this quotation, Chinul developed his thought and writings around two aspects of Sŏn: the source of Sŏn and the practice of Sŏn, or the objective and subjective sides of Sŏn,[88] or again, the ontology and soteriology of Sŏn.[89] As his cognomen "Moguja," meaning "oxherd," implies, Chinul's main concern as both a Sŏn student and a Sŏn master was enlightenment or attaining the buddhahood, which prioritizes the practical aspects of Buddhism.

However, he was also well aware of the necessity of the right understanding of the dharma or the mind,[90] which is the source and at the same time destiny of all paths to enlightenment. Chinul insisted that a practitioner should understand well both the aspects of dharma and person, as "these two approaches of cultivation and the nature are like the two wings of a bird: neither one can be missing."[91]

In his later life, Chinul would introduce and advocate for the shortcut approach of *kanhwa* Sŏn, which, as mentioned earlier, was developed during the Song dynasty after the decline of the Heze school. Although this particular Sŏn meditation practice was not originally discussed in connection with the two aspects of dharma and person, the shortcut approach could be included within the category of the person—specifically the approach of gradual cultivation.[92] Hence, the distinction between the two aspects of dharma and

person could be an appropriate summary of Chinul's thought in its "clarity
and comprehensiveness."[93]

Therefore, following Keel Hee-sung's analysis of Chinul's theory of Sŏn,
this section will discuss Chinul's thought, first in regard to the foundational
theory of Sŏn, in particular the nature of the mind. This will be followed by a
discussion of the soteriological aspect of Sŏn, which concerns the two paths
of sudden enlightenment and gradual cultivation. This discussion will be
broken down further by considering Chinul's three paths to practice (*sammun*
三門[94]): one, the path of the balanced maintenance of alertness and calmness
(*sŏngjŏk tŭngji mun* 惺寂等持門) (i.e., the path of the concurrent cultivation
of samādhi and prajñā [*chŏnghye ssangsu mun* 定慧雙修門]); two, the path
of faith and understanding according to the complete and sudden teaching
(*wŏndon sinhae mun* 圓頓信解門); and three, the shortcut path of *kanhwa*
Sŏn (*kyŏngjŏl mun* 徑截門).[95]

*The Mind of the Void, Calm, Numinous Awareness (kongjŏk yŏngji
chi sim 空寂靈知之心)*

Sŏn instructs its followers that the mind is the starting point and destination of the religious quest to become a buddha or an enlightened one. In his
earliest work, *Encouragement to Practice*, which elaborates the goal and
soteriological paths of his newly established society, Chinul proclaims the
mind as the focal point of the society's Sŏn practice. At the beginning of the
treatise, he writes:

> Sentient beings are those who, having become deluded to the one mind, give
> rise to boundless afflictions (*kleśa*). Buddhas are those who, having awakened to
> the one mind, give rise to boundless sublime functions. Although delusion and
> awakening may be different, both essentially derive from the one mind. Hence,
> to seek buddhahood apart from that mind also would be impossible.[96]

The nature of the mind is untainted and innately complete, the same as
the nature of the Buddha or the buddha-nature (*pulsŏng* 佛性).[97] Therefore,
when a practitioner is not obscured by the conditioned arising (or dependent
origination)[98] of delusion and looks into the true nature of his own mind in its
sublime purity, he will attain the buddhahood.[99]

As noted above, Chinul defines "mind" as the mind of void, calm, numinous
awareness (*kongjŏk yŏngji chi sim* 空寂靈知之心),[100] the same term used by
Zongmi and Chengguan,[101] and commonly employed within the Heze school.
Zongmi summarizes the understanding of mind in the Heze school as follows:

> The basic premise of the Heze school is as follows. All dharmas are like a
> dream; this is what all the saints have taught. Consequently, deluded thoughts

are originally quiescent and the sense-spheres are originally void. This void and quiescent mind: its numinous awareness is never dark. In fact, this void and quiescent mind is the pure mind that was previously transmitted by Bodhidharma. Whether deluded or awakened, the mind is fundamentally self-aware. It does not come into existence through dependence on conditions; it does not arise with sense-objects as its cause. When deluded, it is subject to the afflictions, but this awareness is actually not those defilements. When awakened, it can manifest magic and miracles, but this awareness is actually not that magic or those miracles.[102]

Here, the void and calm nature is the principle of the mind, whereas numinous awareness is the original function of the mind or the self-nature.[103] This mind of void, calm, numinous awareness is the original source of all sentient beings.[104]

There are a myriad of teachings regarding the mind or the dharma. However, according to Zongmi, the Sŏn school categorizes them into the two aspects of immutability (*pulbyŏn* 不變) and adaptability (*suyŏn* 隨緣).[105] While the void and calm nature of the mind is immutable, awareness is immutable and at the same time adaptable. The awareness of the mind is never interrupted, which means immutability, whereas the mind is aware of discriminations and even produces all phenomena, which means adaptability.[106] When the mind is deluded, numinous awareness produces discriminative thoughts and emotions responding to sense objects, but the essence of this awareness remains always nonobscured, tranquil, and calm. On the other hand, when the mind is awakened it is free of any arising of discriminative thoughts and emotions,[107] since the void and calm awareness is free of thought and form.[108]

Sudden Enlightenment and Gradual Cultivation (*tono chŏmsu* 頓悟漸修)

This void, calm, numinous awareness is also brilliant, and Chinul constantly encourages his students to trace back the radiance of this bright mind.[109] Reflecting the influence of the Heze school, Chinul writes, "Now, there are many approaches for accessing the path but if we focus on what is essential, they are all subsumed under the twofold approach of sudden awakening and gradual cultivation."[110] Although some Sŏn schools advocate for sudden awakening/sudden cultivation, Chinul argues that this path is meant for people with extraordinary faculties. Furthermore, the twofold process is the path that all the saints have followed to gain realization.[111] Paraphrasing Zongmi's words, Chinul explains the twofold path.

As for "sudden awakening," when the ordinary person is deluded, he assumes that the four great elements are his body and the deluded thoughts are his mind. He does not know that his own nature is the true dharma-body; he does not

know that his own numinous awareness is the true Buddha. . . . If in one moment of thought he then follows back the light [of his mind to its source] and
sees his own original nature, he will discover that the ground of this nature is
innately free of afflictions (kleśa), and that he himself is originally endowed
with the nature of wisdom that is free from contaminants (āsrava), which is not
a hair's breadth different from that of all the buddhas. Hence it is called sudden
awakening. As for "gradual cultivation," although he has awakened to the fact
that his original nature is no different from that of the buddhas, the beginning-
less proclivities of habit (vāsanā) are extremely difficult to remove suddenly.
Therefore he must continue to cultivate while relying on this awakening so that
the efficacy of gradual suffusion is perfected; he constantly nurtures the embryo
of sanctity, and after a long, long time he becomes a sage. Hence it is called
gradual cultivation.[112]

This cultivation relying on sudden awakening will eventually remove all defilements acquired through countless lifetimes and lead to the final attainment
of sanctity and buddhahood. Cultivation without sudden awakening with the
mind still deluded, however, delays the ultimate enlightenment; and also sudden awakening without subsequent cultivation does not lead to full realization.
    Though Chinul is convinced that awakening is sudden, he nevertheless
understands that there are two types of awakening distinguished by their soteriological efficacy and sequential order, understanding-awakening (haeo 解
悟) and realization-awakening (chŭngo 證悟), which were explained above.
Chinul sees that the initial understanding-awakening should be followed by
subsequent cultivation until one attains the ultimate realization-awakening,
in which the initial understanding is no longer obscured. Thus, these two
approaches of sudden awakening and gradual cultivation are both essential
and inseparable "like the two wheels of a cart: neither one can be missing."[113]
    The twofold process of sudden awakening and gradual cultivation is a
condensed scheme encompassing a broad spectrum of Buddhist practices.
According to Kim Kun-su, Chinul developed the three practical approaches
or the Three Paths (sammun 三門) as ways of cultivating the mind: "the path
of faith and understanding according to the complete and sudden teaching,"
"the path of the concurrent cultivation of samādhi and prajñā," and finally
"the path of the shortcut of kanhwa Sŏn."[114] These three practical approaches
fit into the twofold scheme of sudden awakening/gradual cultivation. The
first path deals with the initial sudden awakening and the second path is the
primary method of meditation advocated by the Heze school as a way of
gradual cultivation. Although the practice of kanhwa Sŏn seems associated
with sudden cultivation with its emphasis on immediate efficacy, it could be
categorized as a part of gradual cultivation, considering that those of superior
spiritual capacities, who are capable of this advanced meditation technique,
have already undergone long periods of cultivation in previous lifetimes.

Discussion of these three paths will provide a more thorough understanding of Chinul's theory and practice of Sŏn.

The Path of Faith and Understanding according to the Complete and Sudden Teaching (*wŏndon sinhae mun* 圓頓信解門)

For Chinul, the true cultivation of the mind does not begin until one's initial awakening to the true nature of the mind and to the fact that the mind of the ordinary man is not different from the mind of the Buddha. The path of faith and understanding according to the complete and sudden teaching is concerned with this moment of incipient awakening to the true reality. For the articulation of this path, Chinul was greatly influenced by the Huayan teachings, in particular Li Tongxuan's 李通玄 practical interpretation of *Huayan Jing* (華嚴經, S. *Avataṃsakasūtra*).[115]

Employing Li's thought, Chinul suggests that the boundless dharma realm (*pŏpgye* 法界) or the *dharmadhātu* is the manifestation of the fundamental Immovable Wisdom (*kŭnbon pudongji* 根本不動智) of buddhahood, which is the source of all phenomena. In this regard, the Immovable Wisdom and phenomena are never separate from each other, and the mind of the ordinary person and the mind of a buddha are not different because both originate from the same Immovable Wisdom. The faith in and understanding of this principle is attained through awakening to this truth, which results from inward investigation or tracing back the radiance of one's mind. This introspective investigation will eventually lead a cultivator to the realization of the true nature of the *dharmadhātu*.[116] In contrast to the traditional Huayan understanding that the fruition of buddhahood can be attained at the first level of the ten abidings after the practice of innumerable lifetimes, Li Tongxuan insists that it can be achieved at the incipient stage of the ten levels of faith in the present lifetime.[117]

Chinul's articulation and promotion of the path of faith and understanding according to the complete and sudden teaching were the result of his own spiritual experiences and studies.[118] The teaching of the path of faith and understanding was intended to induce a sudden awakening to "the reality of one's fundamental buddhahood."[119] Without an initial awakening to the sublime and pure nature of the mind and the voidness of phenomena arising from delusion, any religious cultivation would be of no avail.

The Path of the Concurrent Cultivation of Samādhi And Prajñā (*chŏnghye ssangsu mun* 定慧雙修門)

Once a cultivator gains a proper understanding of the essence and functions of the mind and the origin of all phenomena, he continues to cultivate so that his understanding-awakening will permeate his whole being and so that there is no obstruction to his doing and no doubt in his knowing. From the early period of his religious life, Chinul advocated the concurrent cultivation of *samādhi* and *prajñā* (*chŏnghye ssangsu* 定慧雙修), or the balanced maintenance of alertness and calmness (*sŏngjŏk tŭngji* 惺寂等持), as a primary way of cultivation.

All Buddhist traditions, regardless of their philosophical differences and temporal or regional distances from each other, have emphasized ethical restraint (S. *śīla*, K. *kye* 戒), meditative absorption (S. *samādhi*, K. *jŏng* 定), and wisdom (S. *prajñā*, K. *hye* 慧). This conventional threefold training scheme is considered to be a gradual process that begins with the control of physical reactions to sensory objects through compliance with all the lay and monastic precepts. Once the body is under control, the cultivator strives to achieve a mental state of absorptive meditation or concentration (*samādhi*) undisturbed by external or internal stimuli. This mental state of concentration enables the practitioner to focus on investigating the true nature of oneself and the world, which will entail the development of wisdom (*prajñā*), eventually leading to enlightenment.[120]

Sŏn Buddhism too adopted this traditional training process but not without adapting it to its own principles associated with the true nature of the mind. Adopting the three conventional aspects of training and Sŏn's new interpretation, Chinul distinguishes two types of the threefold training: the relative type, or the three aspects of training that adapt to signs (*susang samhak* 隨 相三學) and the absolute type, or the aspects that accord with the self-nature (*chasŏng samhak* 自性三學). The first type, as explained above, is meant for people of inferior spiritual capacity, whose understanding of the world is confined within the conditioned realm. This is the gradual path (*chŏm mun* 漸 門). The second type can be commended to people of superior spiritual capacity and belongs to the sudden path (*ton mun* 頓門). In the advanced training experienced from the perspective of the absolute realm, there is inherently no perception of "I" in any activities, no distraction in meditation, and no delusion in wisdom. All three aspects of the training are merely three different aspects of the one mind or self-nature, which is innately void and bright, and all three aspects will be completed simultaneously at the very moment of awakening to the self-nature. This understanding of the threefold training was expounded in the *Platform Sūtra of the Sixth Patriarch* (C. *Liuzu tan jing* 六 祖壇經), a collection of Huineng's sermons promoted by the Heze school.[121]

Among the three aspects of the training, Chinul mainly expounds on *samādhi* and *prajñā*, which are considered to be an abbreviation of the three aspects, and he discusses the two types of training of *samādhi* and *prajñā* discussed above, the relative type that adapts to signs and the absolute type that accords with the self-nature. Chinul quotes from an otherwise unknown

Sŏn text entitled *Yi zhen ji* 翼眞記: "The two words '*samādhi*' and '*prajñā*' are an abbreviation for the threefold training, which in their complete form are called *śīla, samādhi,* and *prajñā.*"[122] Kang Kŏn-gi comments that the omission of *śīla* in Sŏn implies an emphasis on cultivating the mind rather than a rejection of ethical restraint. *Samādhi* and *prajñā* should be properly cultivated on the basis of a disciplined life, and Chinul repeatedly admonishes his students not to neglect their observance of morality.[123]

For Chinul, the concurrent cultivation of *samādhi* and *prajñā* (*chŏnghye ssangsu* 定慧雙修) is identified with the balanced maintenance of alertness and calmness (*sŏngjŏk tŭngji* 惺寂等持). He explains the way one should reflect inwardly as follows: "First, subdue mental agitation with calmness [*chŏkjŏk* 寂寂]; next, bring torpor under control with alertness [*sŏngsŏng* 惺惺],"[124] and calmness and alertness must be cultivated simultaneously so that one can effectively reflect on one's mind.[125] Furthermore, the best way to cultivate the mind is just to let the mind manifest itself effortlessly without any involvement of thoughts and words, since the mind is innately calm and alert. For this reason, alertness and calmness are associated with both "relative cultivation" or "actual practice," and "absolute nature" or "the ineffable essence of mind."[126]

Chinul encourages his students to ardently cultivate *samādhi* and *prajñā* throughout their lives. Although he stresses the efficacy of "*samādhi* and *prajñā* that accord with the self-nature (*chasŏng chŏnghye* 自性定慧)," he also suggests cultivating "*samādhi* and *prajñā* that adapt to signs (*susang chŏnghye* 隨相定慧)," in accordance with one's capacities to develop individual practice.[127]

The Path of the Shortcut of Kanhwa Sŏn (kanhwa Sŏn kyŏngjŏl mun 看話禪徑截門)

The two paths discussed above—the path of faith and understanding according to the complete and sudden teaching and the path of the concurrent cultivation of *samādhi* and *prajñā*—constitute the conventional Sŏn approach to enlightenment. One should commit oneself to meditation practice with a foundational and proper understanding of the goal and process of religious practices, leading to actual realization (realization-awakening) of what one has come to understand (understanding-awakening). Chinul's earlier writings expound on and commend this approach, incorporating the doctrinal teachings of Kyo for Sŏn adepts, whereas in his later writings—especially *Resolving Doubts* and the last part of *Excerpts*—Chinul appears to emphasize more exclusively Sŏn practice over the conventional approach involving the provisional adaptation of words and concepts.

Concerned that meditative practices involving intellectual activities might hinder further advancement toward realization-awakening, Chinul presents the shortcut approach (*kyŏngjŏl mun* 徑截門) of *kanhwa* Sŏn (看話禪 "observing the keyword") as an expedient way of progressing toward enlightenment. The *kanhwa* Sŏn practice as a meditation technique was developed and popularized by Dahui Zonggao 大慧宗杲. This Song-dynasty Chan master was greatly influenced by his master Yuanwu Keqin 圜悟克勤 (1063–1135), who lectured on *cong'an* (K. *kongan* 公案) or "public cases," anecdotes of renowned Chan masters. Dahui further developed the analysis of *cong'an* to include the investigation of its keyword or phrase (C. *huatou*, K. *hwadu* 話頭). In this investigation, one moves from inquiring into the keyword's meaning or intention to investigating the keyword itself. While the former process involves intellectual understanding that will lead to puzzlement or doubt, the latter involves the meditator proceeding toward a cognitive experience of nonconceptualization that results from pushing doubt to its extreme conclusion.

In the later period of his life, Chinul seems to have focused on the shortcut approach of *kanhwa* Sŏn, expounding on and promoting the new meditation technique in his writings. However, his commitment to the *kanhwa* Sŏn meditation does not mean that he discarded the other two approaches to Sŏn practice—Chinul makes it clear that the shortcut approach is recommended only for advanced practitioners.[128]

As a philosopher Chinul was well-acquainted with the vast array of Buddhist scriptural and philosophical traditions. At the same time, he was also a Sŏn adept who was well aware of the importance of practice. The scheme of the two aspects of dharma and person described above was a suitable way to communicate Chinul's balanced emphasis on both theory and practice, while the discussion of the three approaches to practice offered a closer look at his soteriological blueprint. Based on this general understanding of Chinul's thought, next will be an exploration in greater detail of the integrative aspects of his thought and practice, which have already been glimpsed earlier in this chapter.

CHINUL'S INTEGRATION OF DOCTRINAL TEACHINGS AND MEDITATION

The Balanced Practice of Study and Meditation for Chinul

As the four principles of Sŏn—"separate transmission [of the dharma] outside of doctrinal teaching," "no establishment of words and letters," "direct pointing to the mind of man," and "seeing into nature and becoming a buddha"— imply, the attitude of Sŏn adepts tended to be hostile toward the scriptural and theoretical studies of the Kyo doctrinal schools.[129] However, Chinul, himself a Sŏn student and master, had a different opinion of Kyo. Drawing on a profound knowledge of doctrinal teachings attained through extensive studies of the Buddhist scriptures and philosophical debates, he came to have a balanced understanding of Kyo and incorporated it into his Sŏn practice, rather than blindly criticizing and ignoring it. He acknowledged the validity of its ontological and soteriological teachings and appreciated its efficacy in the Buddhist path to enlightenment.

While Chinul appreciated the ways in which doctrinal and scriptural studies could contribute to one's journey to awakening, he was also well aware of the limitations of words and concepts, which he believed could hinder the cultivator from reaching a realization of the truth beyond intellectual understanding. In addition, he was concerned that teaching people the absolute reality by using words would result in attachment to discriminative knowledge and the pursuit of fame and wealth. He warned:

> If one is a person who gives rise to views in accordance with words, develops understanding through the texts, pursues doctrine and deludes the mind, does not distinguish the finger from the moon, and does not renounce the aspirations for fame and profit, and yet still wants to be a person who ferries across people by expounding the dharma—[such a person] is like a filthy slug that befouls itself and others. This, then, is the worldly dharma master of letters. How can this be described as someone who is intent on samādhi and prajñā and is not seeking name and fame?[130]

Despite these risks, hearing and learning the dharma through the medium of words and letters "can," according to Chinul, lead to awakening as long as one is not obstructed by them.[131] Even while warning against the dangers inherent in the exclusive pursuit of texts and theoretical explanations,[132] Chinul suggests that Sŏn students should engage themselves in doctrinal studies along with meditation: "If, every now and then, you have time free from your contemplation practice, it does no harm to examine carefully the sacred teachings and the enlightenment stories of the worthy ones of old so that you can discern clearly the perverse and the proper and benefit both yourself and others."[133] This admonishment to Sŏn adepts is drawn from Chinul's own experience.

> I, Chinul, since my youth, have cast myself into the domain of the patriarchs and have visited meditation halls everywhere. I have investigated the teachings that the Buddha and the patriarchs so compassionately bestowed on beings, which are primarily intended to help us put to rest all conditioning, empty the mind, and remain centered there quietly, without seeking anything outside.[134]

This balance between the practice of meditation on the one hand and studies on the other led Chinul to understand that the sūtras and commentaries
were intended to facilitate an awakening to the mind and the associated practice of *samādhi* and *prajñā*.

Although meditation is a primary focus of the Sŏn school, Chinul points
out that the Kyo school also developed sophisticated theories of contemplative practice. For Chinul, the problem with Kyo monks was that they only
studied contemplation without putting it into practice, assuming that it is
meant for saints and that they are not worthy to practice it.[135] This lack of
confidence or self-demeaning (*chagul* 自屈), which was prevalent among
Kyo monks, is attributed to a lack of faith that their nature consists of the
pure and sublime mind identical to the buddha-mind. If the Kyo monks were
self-demeaning, Chinul repeatedly criticizes Sŏn students for being haughty
(*chasi* 自恃 or *chago* 自高). He observed that they were too confident of the
sublime nature of their minds so that they neglected cultivation.[136]

Even while constantly reminding monks of the obstacle presented by
words, Chinul needed to employ them to help both Sŏn and Kyo monks attain
awakening and commit themselves to cultivation. That is why he composed
a significant number of treatises and urged monks to listen to his words,[137]
an odd exhortation for a master of Sŏn who believed that there should be
"no establishment of words and letters." Chinul's promotion of scriptural
and doctrinal study is based on his conviction that sūtras and treatises are the
words and explanations of the Buddha.

> The dharma discourses I have just cited are sincere words spoken straight from
> the heart by the Buddha and bodhisattvas out of loving-kindness, compassion,
> and sympathy for those exceptional people who are cultivating the mind; they
> point out the essential factors in the process of cultivation. I, Chinul, feel deeply
> gratified to have encountered this dharma and will specially receive and keep
> these instructions for the rest of my life. I also encourage my fellow students to
> cultivate in accord with their injunctions.[138]

Chinul was well aware of the merit of learning from his study of Buddhist
writings, and he intended to benefit his Sŏn students through his own writings. He clarifies the purpose of writing *Excerpts*, which synthesizes Sŏn
and Kyo teachings: "Now, for the sake of those who can awaken to the mind
through the aid of the Teachings (Kyo/Jiao 教), I have abbreviated [the text's]
prolix verbiage and extracted its essentials so that it can serve as a vade mecum for contemplative practice."[139] Chinul employs words and letters to edify
his students so that they can "see the nature and achieve buddhahood."[140]

In order to incorporate Buddhist texts and doctrines into his Sŏn instruction, Chinul first had to become well versed in them, and second, he had to

demonstrate the compatibility of Sŏn and Kyo. The following pages will offer an exploration of the depth and breadth of Chinul's knowledge of the textual and doctrinal traditions of Buddhism. Then, there will be an examination of how Chinul demonstrates the compatibility of Sŏn and Kyo, influenced by and learning from the eminent masters of both schools, in particular Guifeng Zongmi 圭峰宗密 (780–841) and Li Tongxuan 李通玄 (635–730).

Chinul: A Synthesizer of Buddhist Textual Traditions

Chinul's accommodating attitude toward "words and letters" is not only manifested in his explicit promotion of the Buddhist scriptural and philosophical traditions, but can also be inferred from his profound knowledge of these traditions and of the Sŏn texts quoted or mentioned in his writings.

Im Yŏng-suk's thorough survey of references shows the range of Chinul's erudition in the Buddhist textual traditions.[141] Chinul quotes or cites sūtras (C. *jing*, K. *kyŏng* 經), treatises (C. *lun*, K. *lon*, S. *śāstra* 論), commentaries (*C. shu*, K. *so* 疏), and the words and anecdotes of Sŏn masters to explain Sŏn and Kyo teachings and bolster his arguments for the purpose of urging Buddhist practitioners to cultivation. Im Yŏng-suk's textual survey covers seven of Chinul's extant writings,[142] including *Straight Talk*. When *Straight Talk* is excluded, the result is that Chinul quoted or alluded to 93 Buddhist sources some 420 times. Among 20 categories of sūtra, *Huayan jing* 華嚴 經 (S. *Avataṃsakasūtra*, 15 times) was the most often quoted or mentioned, followed by *Prajñāpāramitāsūtras* 般若經 (C. *Bore jing*, 8), which includes *Diamond Sūtra* 金剛經 (C. *Jin'gang jing*, 1) and *Complete Enlightenment Sūtra* 圓覺經 (C. *Yuanjue jing*, 7). Besides scriptures, Chinul quoted or cited Li Tongxuan's *Exposition of the* New [*Translation of the*] *Avataṃsakasūtra* 新華嚴經論 (C. *Xin Huayan jing lun*, 57), the *Treatise on the Awakening of Faith According to Mahāyāna* 大乘起信論 (C. *Dasheng qixin lun*, 16), and the works of Guifeng Zongmi 圭峰宗密 (55), Qingliang Chengguan 清涼澄 觀 (30), Yongming Yanshou 永明延壽 (17), Heze Shenhui 荷澤神會 (18), Mazu Daoyi 馬祖道一 (16), Dahui Zonggao 大慧宗杲 (16), and Huineng 慧能 (14).

Chinul cited Li's *Exposition* primarily in *Complete and Sudden Attainment* (41 times out of a total of 57 references), while he quoted Zongmi and Chengguan primarily in *Excerpts* (47 times for Zongmi and 22 times for Chengguan). However, the proponent of *kanhua Chan* 看話禪 (K. *kanhwa Sŏn*), Dahui, was quoted or mentioned 14 times in *Excerpts* and *Resolving Doubts* (seven in each) out of a total of 17 references, while Chinul made reference to the Chan master only twice in *Moguja's Secrets*.[143] This may be taken to indicate the shift of emphasis to *kanhwa* Sŏn in his later life.

However, a count of citations and allusions by itself does not fully reveal the extent of each text's influence on Chinul's thought. For instance, as noted by Kim Kun-su, the *Platform Sūtra of the Sixth Patriarch* 六祖壇經 (C. *Liuzu tan jing*) played a significant role in Chinul's first awakening experience and subsequent development of the concurrent cultivation of *samādhi* and *prajñā*,[144] but Chinul only quoted the scripture once (concerning the Pure Land practice).[145] For this reason, it is necessary to closely examine the context of the various references in order to determine their significance.[146]

Despite its limitations, Im Yŏng-suk's brief survey reveals the breadth of Chinul's knowledge of the Buddhist literature of his time, and testifies to his comprehensive investigation of the teachings of the Buddha and the masters of the Sŏn and Kyo traditions. While Im Yŏng-suk provides data primarily concerned with textual influence, Ko Yŏng-sŏp's survey of Chinul's writings focuses on the influence the eminent Buddhists had on Chinul.[147] He lists all the names of eminent monks and laypersons, the texts pertaining to those monks, and the relevant sūtras referred to in each of Chinul's writings.[148] This data indicates that Chinul was indebted to many earlier writers.

With respect to Chinul's integrative approach to Sŏn and Kyo, he was greatly influenced by Zongmi, Chengguan, and Yongming, to name only three, who themselves had put a great deal of effort into the same cause.[149] The next section will explore the influence of Zongmi, whose writings are considered to have had the most influence on Chinul's integrative approach.

Zongmi and His Influence on Chinul's Integration of Kyo and Sŏn

Guifeng Zongmi and Pojo Chinul

Guifeng Zongmi 圭峰宗密 (780–841) and his writings might have not played as strong a catalytic role in Chinul's life-changing experiences of awakening as the important Buddhist texts the *Platform Sūtra* of *the Sixth Patriarch*, the *Exposition of Avataṃsakasūtra* of Li Tongxuan, and the *Records* of Dahui. Nevertheless, anyone who reads the writings of both Zongmi and Chinul recognizes Zongmi's immense influence on Chinul's development of Sŏn theory and practice, especially his soteriological scheme of sudden awakening/gradual cultivation, and his balanced development of *samādhi* and *prajñā*, which are prominent soteriological themes advocated by the Heze school of Chan.[150] Zongmi's influence on Chinul was also substantial with respect to the latter's effort to integrate doctrinal and textual study with meditative practice.[151]

Zongmi was the putative fifth patriarch of both the Heze 荷澤 school of Chan/Sŏn 禪 and the Huayan 華嚴 school of Jiao/Kyo 教, and his ecclesiastical position and reputation attest to the profundity of his meditative experience and knowledge of the vast array of Buddhist traditions. Besides the similarities in their Chan/Sŏn thought and their integrative approach to Chan/Sŏn and Jiao/Kyo, there are other notable parallels transcending the temporal and spatial distance between Zongmi and Chinul that relate to their historical contexts and personal experiences.

First, both Zongmi and Chinul were situated in ecclesiastical environments in which various Buddhist traditions and schools were contending with one another, each claiming the superiority of its own soteriological or philosophical stances. At the time of Zongmi, the Buddhist community in China was facing two kinds of fractious division: first, between scholarly monks and Chan monks, and second, between the various lineages of Chan schools. Tensions also existed during Chinul's life, chiefly between Kyo and Sŏn—represented respectively by the Hwaŏm school and the Chan lineages of the Hongju 洪州 (C. Hongzhou) school.[152]

Second, while both Zongmi and Chinul were called upon to respond to historical and ecclesiastical challenges that demanded synthesis and reconciliation, there is another important parallel factor related to the fact that they both experienced awakenings as a result of textual study. Zongmi belonged by birth to the local elite class and received a classical education with the intention of taking the Chinese civil service examination. His social and educational background would lead to his connections with prominent literary and political figures, and would result in many allusions to Chinese classics in his Buddhist treatises. Although he dabbled in the study of Buddhism in his youth, it was when he was twenty-four years old, in 804, that he encountered the Chan master Daoyuan of Suizhou 遂洲導圓 (d.u.). This caused him to leave home and fully immerse himself in Chan practice. Daoyuan must have had a great influence on Zongmi during his student phase when he was first learning the Chan tradition, in particular the Chan of the Heze lineage.

Not long after Zongmi committed himself to the pursuit of Buddhism, he had a major religious experience that would have a long-lasting impact on his spiritual and intellectual development. When he encountered for the first time the *Perfect Enlightenment Sūtra* 圓覺經 (C. *Yuanjue jing*), he had his first awakening experience after reading only a few pages of it, an experience that was so intense that he could not help but dance with joy. From this pivotal moment on, Zongmi would continue to study this apocryphal scripture of Chinese origin—it would provide a foundation for his lifelong task of synthesizing meditative practice and textual study, based on his conviction that "the scriptures provided a necessary counterbalance to Chan experience."[153]

After immersing himself in the intense practice of Chan for a period, he had a second major religious experience in 810, this time through an encounter with the texts of the Huayan school, specifically a copy of Chengguan's

澄觀 (738–839) commentary on *Huayan jing*. As with his earlier experience, Zongmi experienced overwhelming joy from this encounter. Afterward, he underwent an intense period of study of the Huayan texts, this time under the guidance of Chengguan, the author himself. Zongmi himself would later compose a corpus of exegetical works and treatises that would have a great impact on the development of Buddhism in East Asia, in particular in Korea through Chinul's enthusiastic appropriation of them.

Thus, as with Chinul's three major moments of awakening, Zongmi's significant religious experiences involved Buddhist texts. This parallel, together with Zongmi's prowess as a Chan practitioner and a Huayan exegete, undoubtedly gave Chinul a sense of affinity with Zongmi on the spiritual level. It appears that these parallel experiences predisposed the two masters toward undertaking the task of resolving tensions between those who supported doctrinal, textual study and those who supported meditative practice.

The Compatibility of Chan and Jiao for Zongmi

Convinced by his own experiences of awakening catalyzed by reading Buddhist texts, and also based on insights gained from vigorous Chan meditative practice, Zongmi propounded the compatibility of Chan and Jiao. Peter N. Gregory points out that Zongmi's claim of the compatibility of Chan and Jiao (C. *chanjiao yizhi* 禪教一致) should be considered in two discrete steps: first, the correspondence of Chan and the Buddhist scriptures (C. *chanjing yizhi* 禪經一致), and second, the correspondence of Chan traditions and doctrinal teachings (C. *zongjiao yizhi* 宗教一致).[154] Scriptures play a mediating role between doctrinal schools and Chan schools.

First, regarding the general compatibility between the Chan schools and the Buddhist scriptures, Zongmi, in his influential Chan writing, *Prolegomenon to the Collection of Expressions of the Chan Source* or *Chan Prolegomenon* (C. *Duxu*, K. *Tosŏ* 都序),[155] claims that since both Chan, which had been transmitted mind to mind through the patriarchs, and the Buddhist scriptures—sūtras and śāstras (treatises)—originated from the same source, Śākyamuni Buddha, the Chan transmissions and the teachings of the scriptures must ultimately agree with each other: "To say that there are [two sorts of] masters, the root and the branches, means that the first patriarch of all the [Chan] lineages is Śākyamuni. The sutras [經 C. *jing*] are buddha word [佛語 C. *foyu*], while Chan [禪] is the intention of the buddhas [佛意 C. *foyi*]. The mouth and mind of the buddhas cannot possibly be contradictory."[156] Zongmi's assertion of the compatibility of Chan and scripture is alluded to in Chinul's description of the integrative insight he attained through his second awakening experience, discussed earlier.[157]

Zongmi argues that although the disciples of the Buddha and their early followers continued to carry on the teachings of the Buddha at the same time as engaging in mind-to-mind Chan transmission, Buddhist monks gradually began to separate these two methods of dharma transmission, leading to an ever-greater rift between exegetical monks and Chan adepts. This was the situation when Bodhidharma, the putative founder of Chan, came to China. On the one hand, the meditative practices of the monks were performed at a superficial level without penetrating into principle. On the other, as explained by Zongmi, employing the simile offered by Bodhidharma that the moon does not lie in the finger pointing at the moon, Bodhidharma criticized the strong attachment of some monks to written words, and admonished them to understand that the dharma is their mind, which is similar to the well-known Chan principle of "mind-to-mind transmission without relying on written words" (C. *yixin chuanxin buli wenzi* 以心傳心 不立文字).

Despite its anti-intellectual implications, Zongmi points out that Bodhidharma's saying did not mean that words should be totally abandoned, but rather was intended as a warning against the danger of attachment. He further criticizes both Chan adepts and scholar monks for their misunderstanding of each other in not realizing that what the scriptures teach is identical to what Chan adepts must understand through meditative practice.[158] In light of his assertion of the compatibility between Chan transmission and scriptural teachings, Zongmi defends Chan against the scholar monks' criticism that Chan lacks a scriptural and philosophical foundation, while he also admonishes Chan adepts to acknowledge the efficacy of scriptures for the advancement of their meditative practice.[159]

Zongmi further demonstrates the complementarity of Chan and the scriptures through a discussion of the three sources of knowledge: inference (C. *biliang* 比量, S. *anumāna*), direct perception (C. *xianliang* 現量, S. *pratyakṣa*), and the word of the Buddha (C. *foyanliang* 佛言量, S. *buddhavacana*). These three sources of knowledge taken together, with one being the word of the Buddha, means that the knowledge one attains through intellectual and intuitive meditation must correspond to the teachings of the scriptures.[160]

This conviction regarding the compatibility of Chan and the scriptures leads Zongmi to a second step by which he attempts to connect Chan schools with different doctrinal teachings that are closely linked to the teachings of Buddhist texts. Zongmi first establishes two distinctive schemes: one to comprehensively organize various doctrinal teachings according to three primary teachings in the scriptures, and the other to categorize eight representative Chan schools into three axiomatic perspectives of Chan. Then, he proceeds to match doctrinal teachings with the Chan schools by identifying

the threefold classification of scriptural teachings with the threefold classification of Chan axioms.

Doctrinal classification (C. *panjiao*, K. *p'an'gyo* 判教) involved a unique
taxonomical system developed within the scholarly schools of Buddhism in
China. Over the centuries, a vast array of scriptures had been transmitted
from India and central Asia into China, but not necessarily in the chronological order according to when they were written. Chinese Buddhists were
confused by the substantial discrepancies and different philosophical ideas
contained in the Buddhist scriptures emanating from India. The development
of a doctrinal classification system was the result of a Chinese attempt to integrate a wide variety of Buddhist teachings into a single framework. It was
also intended to valorize the doctrinal teachings of particular schools.[161] Even
though he inherited the classifications of his predecessors, Zongmi developed
a distinctive scheme connecting Chan schools to doctrinal teachings. In *Chan
Prolegomenon*, Zongmi discusses the three axioms of Chan and the three
main teachings of scriptures that correlate with the three axioms.[162]

The first Chan axiom of "eliminating delusion and cultivating mind" (C.
xiwang xiuxin zong 息妄修心宗) claims that despite the identity of nature
between sentient beings and the Buddha, people do not see it because their
minds are obscured by beginning-less ignorance. When delusionary thoughts
are altogether extinguished, people will attain enlightenment. The northern
school (C. Bei zong 北宗) of Shenxiu 神秀 follows this axiom. The counterpart of this Chan axiom is "the teaching of cryptic meaning that relies on
[dharma] nature to speak of characteristics" (C. *miyi yixing shuoxiang jiao* 密
意依性説相教). It teaches that all existences and activities are characteristics
of the true nature without any inherent substance, and that they arise due to
a delusion about the nature. This type of teaching advocates a provisional
method that employs sense objects for people of inferior capacities, and can
be subdivided in three ways: the teaching of karmic cause and effect, the
teaching of cutting off delusions and extinguishing suffering, and the teaching that explains characteristics as unreal transformations of consciousness.
The Yogācāra sūtras and treatises belong to this first type of teaching, and
provide the Chan schools of the first axiom scriptural and theoretical support
for their Chan practices such as silent sitting and breath control meditation.

The second Chan axiom of "total abandonment" (C. *minjue wuji zong* 泯
絶無寄宗) states that everything is void and calm like a dream and therefore
there is no distinction between dharma and non-dharma, buddha and non-
buddha, which means there is no dharma to rely on and no buddha to become;
consequently there is nothing to do. The Oxhead school follows this Chan
axiom (C. Niutou zong 牛頭宗). Zongmi correlates the second Chan axiom
with the second "teaching of cryptic meaning that eradicates characteristics to

reveal the dharma nature" (C. *miyi poxiang xianxing jiao* 密意破相顯性教). This teaching claims that both mind and phenomena are mutually dependent and void in their nature. This teaching is expounded in scriptures like the *Perfection of Wisdom Sūtras* (S. *Prajñāpāramitā-sūtras*, C. *Bore jing*, K. *Panya kyŏng* 般若經) and the treatises of the Madhyamaka tradition.

The third Chan axiom of "directly revealing the mind-nature" (C. *zhixian xinxing zong* 直顯心性宗) teaches that although everything existent is void, it is at the same time the true nature. While the voidness of the mind-nature denies the possibility of any kind of discrimination, the mind, through its function, manifests itself in every form and characteristic. This axiom is advocated by two different Chan schools, the Hongzhou school 洪州宗 and the Heze school 荷澤宗, though their interpretations are distinguishable. The Hongzhou school claims that since the everyday activities of ordinary people are the manifestations of the buddha-nature, there is no cultivation of mind nor cutting off of thoughts required, but rather one must let the buddha-nature manifest itself. On the other hand, the Heze school propounds that one's true nature is the numinous awareness of the voidness and calm of all dharmas. Soteriologically, the Heze school teaches Chan adepts first to awaken to that void and calm awareness, then to cultivate the mind through the practice of no-thought 無念 (C. *wunian*). The third Chan axiom corresponds to the third "teaching of directly revealing that the mind is the nature" (C. *xianshi zhenxin jixing jiao* 顯示眞心即性教). This teaching holds that all sentient beings have the mind that is void, calm, intrinsically pure, and constantly aware. It also claims that although everyone possesses the mind of the Buddha, they do not see it due to ignorance and thereby the cycles of birth and death continue. Scriptures such as *Huayan jing*, *Perfect Enlightenment Sūtra*, and the *Awakening of Faith* expound this third teaching.

In addition, Zongmi presents two subdivisions of the third type of teaching: the approaches of radical rejection 全揀門 (C. *quanjian men*, K. *chŏn'gan mun*) and radical acceptance 全收門 (C. *quanshou men*, K. *chŏnsu mun*).[163] The former emphasizes the direct realization of the mind and adopts an apophatic approach in explaining the nature and process of enlightenment, whereas the latter sees all phenomena as manifestations of the true mind and therefore adopts a cataphatic approach. Zongmi further connects these two subdivisions to the other types of teaching: the approach of radical acceptance subsumes the first teaching of cryptic meaning that relies on (dharma) nature to speak of characteristics, and the approach of radical rejection subsumes the second teaching of cryptic meaning that eradicates characteristics to reveal the dharma-nature.

Thus, Zongmi presents a framework for synthesizing the vast array of Buddhist meditative, scriptural, and doctrinal traditions. However, although he endeavors to resolve various tensions within the larger Buddhist community in China, it is notable that his main concern is to unite all the contending Chan schools, convinced as he is that the teachings of each Chan school are right and conducive to the spiritual journey to enlightenment. Zongmi writes, "If one considers [the Chan houses] individually, then they are all wrong. If one brings them together, then they are all right."[164] In order to bringing together the various Chan points of view, he makes use of scriptures.

> I will use buddha word to illustrate the intention behind each of them, to select the strong points of each of them, to unify them into the three axioms, and to juxtapose these to the three canonical teachings. . . . (*What the buddhas have said shows variations and yet sameness, and so, if you condense the Buddha sutras, you bring the three [canonical teachings] into oneness.*)[165]

For Zongmi, with regard to the relationship between Chan and the scriptures, the Buddhist texts play the role of a measuring device. "The sutras are like an inked marking string which serves as a model by which to establish the false and the correct. The inked marking string is not the skill itself; a skillful craftsman must use the string as a standard."[166] It is obvious that scriptures are not Chan, but Chan adepts must use them as a norm.

Though Zongmi attempted to organize the various Chan schools into a comprehensive framework and to resolve the rifts among them, he nevertheless implicitly asserts the superiority of his own Chan school, the Heze school. In this regard, Zongmi's classification of Chan is characterized by the same ambivalence inherent in other doctrinal classifications, that is to say, "its simultaneously ecumenical and sectarian character."[167]

Zongmi's Influence on Chinul's Discussion of the Compatibility of Sŏn and Kyo

Zongmi's integrative approach had a great influence on Chinul. While he agrees with Zongmi about the compatibility of Chan and Jiao, Chinul adapted Zongmi's discussion to his own historical context. First, since in Chinul's time there was only one dominant doctrinal school, the Hwaŏm school, there was no need to develop or discuss a doctrinal classification scheme like Zongmi did. Second, since the Hongju school (C. Hongzhou zong) was the prominent Sŏn school and the Heze school promoted by Zongmi had disappeared long before, there was no need to establish a hierarchy of schools. Chinul was called on to develop a more inclusive and nonhistorical interpretation of the various Sŏn schools and to adapt Zongmi's heavily contextualized Chan classification.

Although Chinul does not adapt Zongmi's doctrinal classification, he still discusses Zongmi's Chan critique in detail. While agreeing with Zongmi's evaluations of the different Chan schools, Chinul's discussion can be differentiated from that of the Chinese master by his much more inclusive approach. Unlike Zongmi, who esteemed his own Heze school over all the other schools, the Korean master emphasizes the compatibility of and equality among the three major Sŏn schools—Niutou, Hongzhou, and Heze.[168] Chinul's synthesis of the Sŏn schools led him into a discussion of the complementarity between the doctrinal and the meditative tendencies within Buddhism.

In order to examine the compatibility between Sŏn and Hwaŏm, Chinul employs Zongmi's two approaches of radical rejection 全揀門 (C. *quanjian men*, K. *chŏn'gan mun*) and radical acceptance 全收門 (C. *quanshou men*, K. *chŏnsu mun*). Chinul adapts Zongmi's use of these approaches in order to demonstrate the compatibility of Sŏn and Hwaŏm (the complete teaching 圓教, K. *wŏn'gyo*), showing that both schools employ both approaches. As for Sŏn, Chinul argues that "the faculty of radical rejection as it is interpreted in the Sŏn school merely exposes the essence and points directly to the mind-nature that is originally ever quiescent and free from all relativity. If there is no clinging or rejection, this is then a radical rejection that remains centered in radical acceptance."[169] In order to demonstrate that Hwaŏm employs both approaches, Chinul brings in the example of Ŭisang's 義湘 *Dharma-Nature Gāthā* (a poetic verse) 法性偈,[170] which explains, "first, that the true nature is distinct from names and free of signs and, next, that the conditioned origination of the true nature is unimpeded."[171] The ineffability of the dharma-nature corresponds to the aspect of radical rejection, whereas the unimpeded conditioned arising corresponds to the aspect of radical acceptance. Chinul further clarifies that the description of the conditioned arising in Hwaŏm can be said to be associated with radical acceptance when it is considered from the perspective of nature origination, which claims that all conditioned arising reveals the dharma-nature.[172]

While Chinul shows that both Sŏn and Hwaŏm involve both the approaches of radical rejection and radical acceptance, he also acknowledges their different emphases—the doctrinal school Hwaŏm elaborates in detail the unimpeded interfusion of all phenomena, and thus emphasizes the approach of radical acceptance, whereas the pedagogy of the Sŏn patriarchs, intended to help their students cut off all meanings and words so as to directly point to the mind, emphasizes the approach of radical rejection. Chinul explains these different emphases as mere differences in the means employed by each tradition to accord with the abilities of its students, but uses these differences in the adaptation of various tools for the purpose of asserting the superiority of Sŏn over Hwaŏm, claiming that Sŏn practice is meant for students with superior faculties.[173]

Zongmi's influence on Chinul's efforts at integration was prominent, but the writings of another figure, Li Tongxuan 李通玄 (635–730), also helped Chinul confirm his conviction regarding the compatibility of Sŏn and Hwaŏm. Li's writings also provided scriptural and doctrinal resources that enabled Chinul to theorize about Sŏn practice in light of the Hwaŏm teachings. The following section will explore how Chinul actually demonstrated the complementarity of Hwaŏm and Sŏn by adapting Li Tongxuan's interpretation of the Hwaŏm scriptures and doctrines.

Li Tongxuan and His Influence on Chinul

Li Tongxuan was not deemed an authoritative master in the mainstream Huayan school until centuries after his death. His Huayan exegetical works, especially his forty-roll commentary to the new translation of the *Avataṃsakasūtra* by Śikṣānanda (*The Exposition of Huayan jing*), drew the attention of various Chan masters during the Song period and were eventually transmitted to Korea and Japan. In Korea, his *Exposition* had a profound impact on Chinul.

What most attracted Chinul's attention to Li Tongxuan's *Exposition* was the Huayan exegete's focus on the practical aspects of *Huayan jing*, which was different from the philosophical focus of the mainstream Huayan monks. For example, Fazang 法藏 (643–712), who was one of the most influential Huayan patriarchs and who systematized Huayan teachings, was especially concerned with understanding the ultimate state of the dharma realm (法界) or *dharmadhātu*.[174] In contrast, Li's practical reading of *Huayan jing* concentrates on the "path" to this *dharmadhātu*, with particular attention given to the lad Sudhana's journey to its realization.[175]

Another element of Li Tongxuan's thought that appealed to Chinul was his claim that buddhahood can be attained in one lifetime, at the first level of the ten faiths. This view contrasts with Fazang's suggestion that the process of reaching the final goal of buddhahood gradually occurs over three lifetimes.[176] Chinul quotes the *Exposition*:

> Although we propose a progressive course of advancement through the ten levels of faith and the five levels [of the bodhisattva path], and ultimately perfect thereby the practices of Samantabhadra, which are the final results produced by the fulfillment of such causes, still time also is motionless and the Wisdom of Universal Radiance is unchanged. One who brings this contemplation practice to perfection comprehends that the mind of faith means the simultaneous,

comprehensive understanding that exists from the ten levels of faith up through one's achievement of the fruition of buddhahood and the fulfillment of the practices of Samantabhadra. This is the initial arousal of the mind of faith in sentient beings of great aspiration nowadays, in which cause [the arising of faith] and result [right enlightenment] are simultaneous.[177]

Li justifies his radical claim that buddhahood can be attained in the present lifetime by the theory of nature origination (K. *sŏnggi*, C. *xingqi* 性起), in preference to the theory of conditioned origination (K. *yŏn'gi*, C. *yuanqi* 緣起). The doctrine of nature origination, also preferred by Chinul, emphasizes the ontological relationship between phenomena and principle, claiming that all phenomena have originated from the true nature of the mind, and therefore both phenomena and the mind share a common nature and are fundamentally identical. In contrast, the doctrine of conditioned origination focuses on the relationships among phenomena, stating that each phenomenon is defined by and at the same time defines all other phenomena individually, as well as the whole *dharmadhātu*, through the principle of unimpeded interpenetration or interdependence. This view of the interdependence of the whole *dharmadhātu* ultimately leads to an acknowledgment of the interfusion of buddhahood between buddhas and all sentient beings, which corresponds to the tenets of the nature origination theory, or the identity between all sentient beings and buddhas.[178] Li's advocacy of nature origination and its associated soteriology was preferred by Sŏn masters and also by Chinul because of its compatibility with Sŏn tenets. For example, the identity of sentient beings and buddhas corresponds to the Sŏn principle that views the mind of ordinary people as identical with the mind of the Buddha, and consequently emphasizes the cultivation of the mind. The simultaneity of cause and effect, moreover, parallels the subitist soteriology of Sŏn.

In the preface to his abridgement of Li's *Exposition*, the *Condensation of the Exposition of the Avataṃsakasūtra* (*Hwaŏm non chŏryo* 華嚴論節要), Chinul writes about how he came to immerse himself in the study of the Buddhist scriptures while still committing himself to contemplative practice, as was briefly mentioned above in the description of Chinul's second awakening experience. In the course of inquiring about the compatibility between Hwaŏm and Sŏn, a Hwaŏm monk urged Chinul to contemplate the *dharmadhātu* of the unimpeded interpenetration between phenomenon and phenomena (C. *shishi wu'ai fajie* 事事無礙法界), the most important principle of the four principles of the *dharmadhātu*,[179] instead of merely contemplating the mind. With regard to the Hwaŏm monk's suggestion, Chinul thought to himself:

If you contemplate phenomena with the mind, those phenomena will become impediments and needlessly disturb your own mind; when then would there be any resolution? But if just the mind is illuminated and your wisdom purified, then a single strand of hair and the entire universe will be interfused, for there perforce will be nothing that is an external object.[180]

As a Sŏn adept, Chinul finds the contemplation of phenomena detrimental to the cultivation of the mind, which the Sŏn school considers the most effective path to enlightenment.

Opposed to the hierarchy of the traditional Huayan scheme of the *dharmadhātu* principles, Chinul preferred the third category of the *dharmadhātu*—"the *dharmadhātu* of the unimpeded interpenetration between phenomena and principle" (C. *lishi wu'ai fajie* 理事無礙法界). He was convinced that once one awakens to the principle or mind he would simultaneously come to awaken to "the *dharmadhātu* of the unimpeded interpenetration between phenomenon and phenomena" (C. *shishi wu'ai fajie* 事事無礙法界), the realization of which is considered the ultimate goal of the Huayan teachings.

To confirm this preference, he resolved to go on retreat in order to study the scriptures. Confirmation came from his reading of passages from the *Avataṃsakasūtra* (C. *Huayan jing*).

I then retired into the mountains and sat reading through the canon in search of a passage that would confirm the mind doctrine of the Sŏn school. Three winters and summers passed [1185–1188] before I came across the simile about one dust mote containing rolls of scripture as numerous as the world systems of the trichiliocosm from the "Manifestation [of the Tathāgata]" chapter of the *Avataṃsakasūtra*. Later in the same passage, the summation said, "The wisdom of the tathāgatas is also just like this: . . . it is fully present in the bodies of all sentient beings. It is merely all these ordinary, foolish people . . . who are not aware of it and do not recognize it." I put the roll of scripture on my head in reverence and, unwittingly, began to weep.[181]

Although Chinul was overjoyed with this confirmation that the teachings of Sŏn and Kyo concur with regard to the identity of sentient beings and buddhas, he still had doubts as to whether the Hwaŏm teachings advocate immediate awakening in this lifetime. This doubt was resolved upon his reading Li's explanation of the first level of the ten faiths in the *Exposition*.

Chief of Enlightenment (Jueshou 覺首) Bodhisattva has three [enlightenments]. First, he is enlightened to the fact that his own body and mind are originally the *dharmadhātu* because they are immaculate, pure, and untainted. Second, he is enlightened to the fact that his nature, which is differentiated into his own body and mind, is originally free from the subject-object dichotomy and is originally the Buddha of Immovable Wisdom. Third, he is enlightened to the fact that his own mind's sublime wisdom, which readily distinguishes the genuine from the distorted, is Mañjuśrī. He becomes enlightened to these three things at the first level of faith and comes to be known as Chief of Enlightenment.[182]

While these three ontological aspects of enlightenment had already been confirmed with his reading of *Huayan jing*, Chinul was now convinced that Sŏn and Kyo concur even with regard to the immediate attainment of buddhahood in this lifetime. He came to this conclusion after reading Li's claim that enlightenment to the three truths occurs at the very first level of faith with no need to cultivate it during innumerable lifetimes in order to complete all ten levels of faith. Thus, for both Li Tongxuan and Chinul, faith plays a pivotal role in attaining buddhahood.

Chinul's account of his retreat describes the compatibility of Sŏn and Kyo.

> Thereupon, I set down the volume and, breathing a long sigh, said: "What the World-Honored One said with his mouth is Kyo. What the patriarchs transmitted with their minds is Sŏn. The mouth of the Buddha and the minds of the patriarchs can certainly not be in contradiction to one another. How can [students of both the Sŏn and Kyo schools] not plumb the fundamental source but instead, complacent in their own training, wrongly foment disputes and squander all their time?" From that point on, I have continued to build my mind of faith and have cultivated diligently without indolence; a number of years have already passed since then.[183]

To put it succinctly, Huayan doctrines, including the interfusion of sentient beings and buddhas, the simultaneity of cause and effect, and the immediate attainment of buddhahood at the very first level of faith, assured Chinul of the complementarity between the teaching of the scriptures and what was transmitted through the minds of the patriarchs. Chinul would systematically expound all of this in *Complete and Sudden Attainment*.

Treatise on the Complete and Sudden Attainment of Buddhahood

According to Buswell, *Complete and Sudden Attainment* is "one of Chinul's most important contributions to East Asian Buddhist thought" because it undertook to provide the doctrinal foundations of Sŏn soteriology.[184] In the following pages, this treatise will be carefully examined, drawing out Chinul's claim of the compatibility between Sŏn and Hwaŏm.

In the beginning of this exposition on the nature and process of attaining buddhahood, Chinul presents his thesis from the lips of a questioner.

> Someone asked Moguja 牧牛子: We have heard you have proposed that people who are cultivating the mind nowadays should first transform the seeds of their own [discriminative] states of mind, which they employ every day, into the

Immovable Wisdom (*avicalabuddhi, pudong chi* 不動智) of all the buddhas; subsequently, their Sŏn cultivation, which is based on the nature, will then become sublime. From this [perspective], is Immovable Wisdom the fruition of buddhahood, the ideal buddha of original enlightenment, or a phenomenal buddha that is produced anew?[185]

Chinul presents the core of his Sŏn theory in the form of a question. First, a pursuer of the dharma should awaken to the ontological truth of the identity between the mind of an ordinary person and the mind of buddhas. This awakening, in turn, leads the pursuer to cultivation. By bringing in the concept of the Immovable Wisdom of all the buddhas (a symbolic epithet associated with one of the ten tathāgatas discussed in *Huayan jing*)[186] instead of referring to the mind of buddhas, Chinul implies that he will discuss Sŏn theory and practice in light of Huayan doctrines, terms, and concepts.[187] The treatise consists of five questions and responses regarding the attainment of buddhahood.[188]

[1] Faith in the identity of the mind of ordinary people and the mind of buddhas

The first question (quoted above) is whether the Immovable Wisdom, or the fruition of buddhahood, is the ideal buddha of original enlightenment (*pon'gak ibul* 本覺理佛 or the *dharmakāya buddha*) or a phenomenal buddha that is produced anew (*sinsŏng sabul* 新成事佛). This question concerns the sameness of the mind of ordinary people with the mind of buddhas; that is to say, that the buddhahood is not something to be obtained anew, but is innate in one's nature.

For the answer to this question, Chinul relies on Li's *Exposition*. He first presents Li's primary concern in composing his commentary on *Huayan jing*: that ordinary persons of great aspiration (*taesim pŏmbu* 大心凡夫)[189] "would have a sudden awakening to the Immovable Wisdom of all the buddhas right here in this realm of birth and death; [this Immovable Wisdom would thus] serve as the source for arousing the bodhicitta[190] at the moment of the initial awakening."[191]

For Li Tongxuan, the crucial element of the initial awakening to the Immovable Wisdom is faith. Li understood that the initial awakening also simultaneously perfects the fruition of buddhahood, which occurs at the first level of ten faiths. Chinul summarizes Li's explanation regarding the attainment of buddhahood as follows:

> If we examine the [soteriological] explanations offered in this *Exposition*, the fruition of buddhahood in the three-vehicle [teachings] occurs after the ten *bhūmis*, while the fruition of buddhahood in the one vehicle occurs at the initial

stage of mind of the ten faiths. If we discuss this [issue] from the standpoint of accessing the five levels[192] [of the bodhisattva path], then [the fruition of buddhahood] occurs at the abiding stage of the initial arousal of the thought of enlightenment (*bodhicittotpāda*). If one accesses the initial stage of mind involving the ten faiths, then effortlessly one reaches the first state of mind involving the ten abidings; and if one accesses that first abiding stage, one then effortlessly reaches the ultimate stage (*kugyŏng chi* 究竟地) [of buddhahood]. In this wise, then, for bound, ordinary beings (*kubak pŏmbu* 具縛凡夫), the initial arousal of the thought of right faith is of crucial importance.[193]

The Kyo schools teach that buddhahood is attained at the first abiding stage (of arousing the aspiration for enlightenment, or bodhicitta). For these schools, tens of thousands of *kalpas*[194] of training are required to reach this stage beginning from the first stage of the ten faiths.[195] However, according to Li Tongxuan, the attainment of buddhahood can occur in the present lifetime at the very first stage of the ten faiths. Because faith is essential to the path to enlightenment, it is crucial to arouse faith in the mind of a cultivator, and, according to Chinul's understanding, that is the purpose for which Li incorporates scriptural and doctrinal studies.

I have found that the doctrine of the mutual interfusion between living beings and buddhas as presented by the commentator is essentially intended to induce those who contemplate the mind in order to access the path constantly to have faith that their own bodies, speech, and minds, as well as the characteristics of their sensory realms, all arise from the body, speech, mind and sensory realms of the tathāgatas.[196]

To emphasize the significance of faith, Chinul further cites Li's symbolic interpretation of the Golden World of the East 東方金色世界,[197] which Li used to help a practitioner "have faith in the principle of their own pure and immaculate *dharmakāya*."[198] In his analysis of *Huayan jing*, Li adapted the scheme of ten sites, ten assemblies, and forty chapters, each of which involves respective buddhas and bodhisattvas. Among those many symbolic narratives and associated elements, the second assembly is of great interest to Li with regard to having faith in one's own nature, a nature that is ultimately identical with the buddhas. The second assembly was held at the Hall of the Wisdom of Universal Radiance in the Golden World of the East, where the roles of the Buddha of Immovable Wisdom and Mañjuśri bodhisattva are prominent. Chinul further elaborates Li Tongxuan's symbolic interpretation.

That the buddha who is served originally is the Buddha of Immovable Wisdom prompts them toward direct faith in the fact that their own seed of ignorant discrimination is originally the Immovable Wisdom of all the buddhas. That

the chief bodhisattva is Mañjuśri prompts them toward direct faith in the fact
that their own fundamental wisdom (*mūlajñāna*) contains the signless, sublime
wisdom that involves skillful discernment.[199]

Drawing from Li's interpretations of Huayan cosmology, Chinul reas-
serts that the discriminative mind of ordinary people is identical with the
Immovable Wisdom of all the buddhas and innately contains the qualities of
the fruition of buddhahood,[200] while emphasizing the essential role of faith
in attaining buddhahood. This discussion implies the Sŏn principle that the
buddha-nature is innate in the minds of ordinary people, and Li Tongxuan's
claim that the immediate efficacy of faith supports the Sŏn approach of sudden awakening.

[2] Sudden awakening from the perspective of nature origination and gradual cultivation from the perspective of conditioned origination

Despite Chinul's explanation, the interlocutor raises a second question, this
time, specifically about the identity of sentient beings and a buddha who has
perfected the wisdom of the fruition (of buddhahood). He asks: "If [this explanation is given] from the standpoint of a progressive approach [involving a
sequential series of practices], then how can Vairocana Buddha, [the embodiment of] the fruition wisdom that is already perfected, be haphazardly corre-
lated with sentient beings at the bound stage who have not yet cultivated?"[201]

Seen from the standpoint of consummate interfusion, one's own fruition of
buddhahood attained at the moment of awakening is the same as that of the
buddhas, since the fruition of buddhahood of buddhas is universally pervasive
through space and time. However, seen from the perspective of a progressive
approach in which a person who has awakened to the fundamental wisdom
needed to develop the bodhisattva practices,[202] the fruition of buddhahood, or
the phenomenal qualities of the ordinary person, is barely perfected.[203]

To resolve this discrepancy created by two different perspectives on the
fruition of buddhahood, Chinul again turns to Li Tongxuan, who defines Immovable Wisdom as follows:

> If we examine the explanation offered in the *Exposition*, [we find that] this
> so-called Immovable Wisdom is also the fundamental Wisdom of Universal
> Radiance. It is exactly this fundamental wisdom that is called the fruition of all
> the buddhas. This fundamental wisdom is the essential nature of principle and
> phenomena, nature and characteristics, sentient beings and buddhas, oneself and
> others, tainted and pure, cause and fruition.[204]

In short, Immovable Wisdom, which is also the fundamental Wisdom of
Universal Radiance (*kŭnbon pokwangmyŏng chi* 根本普光明智), is the es-

sential nature of both principle and phenomena, sentient beings and buddhas, and cause and fruition. Therefore, awakening to the principle of the fundamental Wisdom of Universal Radiance by tracing back the radiance of the one's mind also involves the phenomenal fruition of buddhahood.[205]

According to Li, the unabiding wisdom and mysterious qualities of all the buddhas pervade the whole *dharmadhātu*, and all sentient beings, both in body and mind, are identical with all the buddhas. They are all devoid of their own substantive essence or nature since they are all conditionally originated from the nature of the *dharmadhātu*,[206] which is the doctrine of nature origination (*sŏnggi mun* 性起門), while distinctions exist between the forms and functions of sentient beings and buddhas.[207] Li assures the reader that "one who has this sort of faith and understanding is certain to attain buddhahood,"[208] and urges him to investigate his mind in accordance with these teachings, relying on the power of *samādhi* and *prajñā*. Once he attains full understanding for himself, then he should benefit all sentient beings with discriminating wisdom, adapting to each person's respective spiritual faculties while being aware of the immutability of the wisdom.[209] At the moment of awakening to the identity of sentient beings and buddhas, and the sameness of the deluded thoughts of his mind and the minds of awakened ones, one simultaneously perfects all the qualities of buddhahood. Nevertheless, he still needs to cultivate over many lifetimes so as to perfect his abilities to lead sentient beings to enlightenment in accordance with their respective faculties.[210]

The perfection of the fruition of buddhahood can be explained also through the unimpeded interpenetration and interfusion of all phenomena from the standpoint of the conditioned origination of the *dharmadhātu* (*yŏn'gi mun* 緣起門). According to this perspective, while sentient beings and buddhas are different in their essence, they affect all others and are simultaneously affected by all others. Therefore, the perfect fruition of Vairocana Buddha[211] interpenetrates the fruition of buddhahood attained by ordinary sentient beings and perfects their fruition.[212] Here, it can be seen that both the doctrines of nature origination and of unimpeded conditioned origination explain the simultaneity of cause and result.

Nevertheless, Chinul considers the doctrine of nature origination to be more suitable to contemplation practice and the attainment of buddhahood.[213] Chinul does not offer an explicit reason for his preference for nature origination. However, it can be inferred that he saw that the doctrine of nature origination, which focuses on principle rather than phenomena, is compatible with the Sŏn emphasis on the mind itself rather than thoughts that arise from the mind.[214]

Since the mind is fundamental in the Sŏn tradition, it is natural that Chinul pays close attention to the passages from Li's *Exposition* advocating cultivation of the mind. For example:

In the "Manifestation of the Tathāgata" chapter of this sūtra it is said, "Bodhisattva-mahāsattvas should know that each and every thought in their minds is invested with the right enlightenment achieved by the buddhas." This [statement] clarifies that all the buddhas, the tathāgatas, do not achieve right enlightenment apart from the mind. It also says, "The minds of all sentient beings are also the same. They are all invested with the right enlightenment achieved by the tathāgatas." This [statement] clarifies that the self-essence of the minds of both ordinary persons and sages are pure and indistinguishable; even though one may be deluded and the other awakened, there is not a hair's breadth of difference between them.[215]

Li's explanations of the two statements from *Huayan jing* clearly correspond to the Sŏn tenets' "direct pointing to the mind of man," and "seeing into nature and becoming a buddha." Chinul also quotes a poem attributed to Li: "The Buddha is the buddha in the minds of sentient beings, / in terms of personal capacities, [buddhas and sentient beings] are not different things. / If you want to know the source of all the buddhas, / awaken to the fact that your own ignorance originally is buddha."[216]

As buddhas and their fundamental wisdom are innate in the minds of ordinary people, and all the phenomena and the characteristics of buddhas originate from the Immovable Wisdom or the fundamental Wisdom of Universal Radiance, one should cultivate the mind, tracing back the radiance emitting from the Wisdom of Universal Radiance in one's own mind.[217] This claim once again supports the primacy of cultivating the mind in Chinul's conception of Sŏn soteriology.

[3] The importance of cultivating the mind

In the third question and response, Chinul further stresses the importance of cultivating the mind. To the repeated inquiry about the identity of sentient beings and the buddhas, Chinul admonishes the questioner to stop arguing and instead reflect inwardly. Nevertheless, Chinul continues to explain further and to cite the scriptures and other writings of eminent masters to the effect that all dharmas and teachings of scriptures are found within the mind, in which the fundamental wisdom of buddhahood is innate. In this way, Chinul tries to steer the interest of the questioner or any reader toward tracing back the radiance of their own minds.[218]

[4] The compatibility of Hwaŏm Scholasticism and Sŏn experience, and Sŏn as a complete and sudden approach

The fourth question concerns the limitations of Sŏn practice, which, the questioner argues, leads one only to a realization of the essence of the nature or the calm and pure mind, without a full realization of the forms or functions of the nature or of phenomena manifested in the *dharmadhātu*. This question implies criticism of Sŏn's unbalanced focus on the principle without paying attention to the phenomena. In response to this critique, Chinul quotes enlightenment poems recited by Sŏn masters who had awakened to their original minds and described their awakening experiences, such as Yongjia Zhenjue 永嘉眞覺 (665–713), Hongying Shaowu 洪英邵武 (1012–1070), and Dahui Zonggao 大慧宗杲 (1089–1163). Chinul explains that the Sŏn masters' awakening experiences correspond to the soteriological goal of the Hwaŏm teaching: "In this wise, [Sŏn practice] generates an awakening to the original minds, which produces, in the mirror of one's mind, a vision of the inexhaustible *dharmadhātu*, the multivalent net of Indra. Such experiences are so common in the biographies and records of the Sŏn school that they are uncountable."[219] For Buswell, this summarizes Chinul's view of the relationship between Sŏn and Hwaŏm, and he clarifies Chinul's attempt to reconcile the Scholastic explication of Hwaŏm with Sŏn experiences.

> Since the inexhaustible *dharmadhātu* is innate within the mind of every individual, by awakening to that mind, one perfects the *dharmadhātu*, thereby satisfying the goals of both Sŏn and Hwaŏm practice. "Buddhahood of the nature's purity": this concept of buddhahood refers to that found in the sudden teaching, where buddhahood means only the realization of principle. This realization does not involve the mastery of both principle and phenomena and is therefore an incomplete awakening. Chinul stresses here that in the Sŏn teachings, the unimpeded *dharmadhātu* within one's own mind is directly realized; Sŏn enlightenment therefore implies the mastery of the consummate interfusion of both principle and phenomena as well as phenomenon and phenomena, and the accomplishment of all the spiritual qualities inherent in the ideal buddha-nature.[220]

Chinul highlights the imprudent criticism of Sŏn by Kyo monks who, without having made a thorough investigation of Sŏn texts and Li Tongxuan's *Exposition*, hastily judge Sŏn as an insufficient teaching, insisting that it concerns only the principle without an understanding of the true reality of the *dharmadhātu*. Chinul then criticizes Kyo monks for a stagnation in their spiritual progress, which he judges to be the result of their attachment to mere verbal teachings and their neglect of mind cultivation. He criticizes Kyo monks' pursuit of mere verbal or intellectual understanding throughout this treatise. For example, in responding to the third question, Chinul rebukes the questioner for his persistent inquiry into the identity of sentient beings and buddhas: "This has been already discussed above. Just put your mind to rest and stop arguing; empty your heart and reflect inwardly. The essential thing is to produce the sublime function; why must you ask further questions?"[221]

Chinul demonstrates the correspondence between Sŏn experience and the
Hwaŏm description of the ultimate reality of *dharmadhātu*, and goes on to
argue that Sŏn is actually superior to Hwaŏm, showing that Sŏn is the best
form of the sudden and at the same time complete approach to enlightenment.
First, Chinul advocates for the soteriological methods of Sŏn over Kyo because of its mind-to-mind transmission of the dharma and its refraining from
prolix indoctrination:

> Because the dharma is one's own mind, he [Bodhidharma] did not establish
> words and letters [C. *buli wenzi*, K. *pullip munja* 不立文字] but only transmit-
> ted the mind with the mind [C. *yixin chuanxin*, K. *isim chŏnsim* 以心傳心].
> For this reason, the Sŏn approach values only the breaking of grasping and the
> manifestation of the true source; it has no use for a profusion of words or the
> positing of dogmas.[222]

The Hwaŏm explanation of the *dharmadhātu* might be the best Scholastic
articulation of the ultimate reality, the realization of which is the goal of all
the Buddhist traditions. However, attachment to verbal teachings hinders one
from leaving words and conceptual understandings behind in order to realize
the ineffable *dharmadhātu*.[223]

For Chinul, Sŏn is a perfect "complete and sudden approach to Buddhism."
It utilizes the strengths of both of the complete and sudden approaches while
overcoming the insufficiencies and dangers of other approaches. Sŏn accepts
Hwaŏm doctrines related to the *dharmadhātu* and aims at their full realization, since they are the ultimate goal of the complete teaching of the Hwaŏm
school. At the same time, Sŏn avoids the dangers of clinging to intellectual
understanding and verbal discussion.[224]

Chinul supports his advocacy of Sŏn by employing its threefold soteriological scheme, the three mysterious gates (*samhyŏn mun* 三玄門): one, the
mystery in the essence (*ch'ejung hyŏn* 體中玄); two, the mystery in the word
(*kujung hyŏn* 句中玄); and three, the mystery in the mystery (*hyŏnjung hyŏn*
玄中玄). Each of these three gates employs, respectively, textual and theoretical studies, terse phrases that break one's grasping for words and dogmas,
and nonverbal methods.[225] The first mysterious gate involves the Hwaŏm
Scholasticism that is considered the complete teaching, and the second and
third gates are associated with the sudden approach that transcends words and
concepts. Thus, this practical scheme of Sŏn incorporates the positive aspects
of the complete and the sudden approaches and develops discrete methods
that provide access to enlightenment.

To repeat: Chinul does not entirely deny the efficacy of verbal teachings
that facilitate an understanding of Sŏn principles. For example, the teaching that "there is a sublime mind, pure in its nature, that flows along with

the streams of falsity and pollution" helps a practitioner of inferior capacity understand and have faith in his true nature, even though eventually he must leave his intellectual understanding behind to achieve full realization.[226] Despite its relatively inferior status in the soteriological process—whether propounded in various kinds of scripture or in the records of Sŏn masters—all kinds of teaching "point out how to return to the one mind" in accordance with one's individual faculties,[227] thus serving the soteriological goal of Buddhism. However, as long as a student's understanding remains in the intellectual realm only, relying on words, he will be caught up in incessant doubts and questions with regard to the identity of ignorance and fundamental wisdom and the identity of sentient beings and buddhas. This can only be resolved by tracing back the radiance of one's own mind, abandoning words and thoughts.[228]

Thus, Chinul demonstrates how the teachings of Hwaŏm correspond to what Sŏn adepts ultimately realize in their experience. He advocates for the superiority of Sŏn by locating nonverbal, nonconceptual meditation practices at an advanced stage in the path to enlightenment, while at the same time acknowledging the need for scriptural and doctrinal learning in the early stage of religious practice for those with inferior abilities.

[5] Sudden awakening and gradual cultivation in the Hwaŏm soteriology

Up to this point Chinul, in responding to various questions regarding the attainment of buddhahood, has maintained that Sŏn awakening is compatible with the Hwaŏm explanation of an awakening that can be achieved at the first level of the ten faiths. Chinul's presentation has focused generally on the sudden awakening, the first aspect of the twofold soteriological path of the Heze school, which Chinul promotes as being the principal approach of the Sŏn practice. The fifth question, however, primarily concerns the role of gradual cultivation following sudden awakening.

The question is as follows: "If these days there are ordinary persons who awaken to the mind and achieve buddhahood, then is this the ultimate stage, or not?"[229] The questioner is confused about why, if awakening entails right enlightenment or the ultimate stage, it is called the initial arousal of the bodhicitta, as if there is an intermediate process that must occur between the initial stage and the ultimate stage. This question has to do with the necessity of subsequent cultivation; in other words, after one achieves the ultimate stage of buddhahood, why should he or she undertake further cultivation of the mind?

Drawing on Li's *Exposition*, Chinul explains that although an ordinary person, under the right conditions, can come to a realization of his or her own mind's fundamental Wisdom of Universal Radiance, he or she continues to be bound to the proclivities of habit (*sŭpki* 習氣) accumulated throughout countless lifetimes. This is called cognitive obstruction (*haeae* 解礙, S. *jñeyāvaraṇa*), which necessitates subsequent cultivation by the practitioner.[230]

To explain the seemingly contradictory approaches of the sudden and complete awakening and the need for subsequent cultivation, Chinul adapts Li's interpretation of the bodhisattva path in light of the six aspects of consummate interfusion 六相圓融 (C. *liuxian yuanrong*, K. *yuksang wŏnyung*) through which the Huayan school views all conditioned phenomena: universality (C. *zongxiang*, K. *ch'ongsang* 摠相), particularity (C. *biexiang*, K. *pyŏlsang* 別相), identity (C. *tongxiang*, K. *tongsang* 同相), difference (C. *yixiang*, K. *isang* 異相), formation (C. *chenxiang*, K. *sŏngsang* 成相), and dissolution (C. *huaixiang*, K. *koesang* 壞相).[231]

Li Tongxuan's explanation is as follows:

> That all five levels [of the bodhisattva path] are encompassed within a single [moment of] wisdom is called the aspect of universality. That there is progressive advancement in practice and understanding is called the aspect of particularity. The fact that fundamental wisdom is the same in all buddhas is called the aspect of identity. The cultivation of the discriminating wisdom is called the aspect of difference. The accomplishment of great Bodhi and the master of the practice of Samantabhadra are called the aspect of formation. The fact that the essence of wisdom abides nowhere and its functioning is nonmanifestative is called the aspect of dissolution.[232]

Based on Li's interpretation of the bodhisattva path, Chinul argues with respect to the tension between sudden awakening and gradual cultivation that those who advocate only one approach—either sudden awakening or gradual cultivation—and disregard the other are viewing the Buddhist path to enlightenment from only one aspect, either universality or particularity. This is because they are attached to their own views and their wisdom has not been perfected.[233] Chinul insists that when both universality and particularity are considered, the approaches of sudden awakening and gradual cultivation can be understood not as contradictory but complementary.[234]

This integrative understanding of sudden awakening and gradual cultivation can also be explained from the perspective of nature origination, according to which one's gradual progress in practice is understood as "the fundamental wisdom's aspect of responsive functioning and its perpetual impulses that accord with conditions."[235] Thus, the dual sudden awakening/gradual cultivation approach can be explained from both the perspective of nature origination and conditioned origination. Nevertheless, Chinul believes that nature origination fits better with sudden awakening that perfects the fruition of buddhahood, whereas the two aspects of consummate interfusion (*wŏnyung* 圓融) and progressive practice (*haengp'o* 行布) associated with conditioned origination provide a better theoretical explanation of gradual cultivation following sudden awakening.

Chinul's endeavors to explain the Sŏn approach to sudden awakening and gradual cultivation in light of the scriptural and doctrinal teachings of Hwaŏm are another step in his attempt to correlate the twofold Sŏn approach with the Hwaŏm scheme of the bodhisattva path.[236] After explaining the sudden awakening to the fundamental wisdom in one's own mind and the need for subsequent cultivation to extinguish long-accumulated proclivities of habit, he describes the process of cultivation in light of the five levels of the bodhisattva path.

> From the standpoint of gradual cultivation in the approach involving conditioned origination, after the initial [understanding-]awakening on the first level of the ten faiths, students diligently cultivate śamatha and *vipaśyanā*[237] until all the containments of materiality and mentality are utterly extinguished. They then reach the initial abiding stage where the power of samādhi is perfected and all the cognitive obstructions completely vanish.[238] Accessing the [remaining five] levels [of the bodhisattva path][239] through the realization-awakening, they then pass sequentially through the cultivation of the ten abidings, ten practices, ten dedications, and ten *bhūmis* until they reach the level of impartial enlightenment [the first of the two stages of buddhahood]. This cultivation is their own action, which is revealed in their true essence and made manifest in their own causes and effects of the three time-periods, as well as in the realm of the saṃbhogakāya buddha, and so forth; it all appears as if right before their eyes.[240]

This description of the soteriological process involves a convergence of two distinguished soteriological schemes, the first from the Sŏn tradition, the second from the Hwaŏm tradition: initial understanding-awakening/ the first level of ten faiths → gradual cultivation/the ten levels of faiths → realization-awakening/the first level of ten abidings → gradual cultivation/ the five levels of the bodhisattva path → ultimate enlightenment/ultimate stage of buddhahood.[241]

Here, the Hwaŏm scheme can be divided broadly into two paths before and after access to the first stage of ten abidings: the path of an ordinary person who just awakened to the true nature of dharma, and the path of bodhisattva.[242]

This practical process of enlightenment not only demonstrates the compatibility of the two soteriological schemes, but also explicitly and implicitly encompasses the three paths presented by Kim Kun-su as the primary Sŏn approaches developed by Chinul.[243] The path of faith and understanding according to the complete and sudden approach is related to access to the sudden and complete awakening at the initial level of the ten faiths. The path of concurrent cultivation of *samādhi* and *prajñā* is associated with subsequent cultivation following a sudden awakening; this is the primary practice that helps a cultivator extinguish his cognitive obstructions and improve compassion and wisdom so that he can finally attain the qualities of sainthood.[244]

It is not explicitly explained here, but the shortcut path of *kanhwa* Sŏn is also implicated in this step-by-step scheme of religious practice. Both the concurrent cultivation of *samādhi* and *prajñā* and the *kanhwa* Sŏn practice have the intention of achieving the realization-awakening.[245] Chŏng Hŭi-kyŏng asserts that *Resolving Doubts*, in which Chinul explains and advocates *kanhwa* Sŏn, primarily focuses on the way to realization-awakening rather than discussing the entire process of religious practice like Chinul's other treatises.[246]

The difference between the cultivation of *samādhi* and *prajñā* and the *kanhwa* practice with respect to attaining realization-awakening is their relative expediency, with the shortcut path of *kanhwa* Sŏn being a faster way to achieve the goal, since it skips the process of learning and conceptualization necessary for those students with inferior faculties, a process that must be abandoned as they progress in their cultivation. Chinul writes, "Those in the Sŏn school who have gained access through the shortcut remain unaffected from the beginning by acquired understanding in regard to both dharmas and their attributes."[247]

The *Treatise on the Complete and Sudden Attainment of Buddhahood* contains Chinul's demonstration of the concurrence of Sŏn and Hwaŏm. He achieved this by discussing the ontological and soteriological aspects of attaining buddhahood primarily from the perspective of the Hwaŏm scriptural and doctrinal teachings and explicitly and implicitly correlating them with the theoretical and practical teachings of Sŏn. The treatise is considered to be a summary of Li Tongxuan's *Exposition*; Li's words and his interpretation of *Huayan jing* inspired Chinul's integrative endeavor and provided him with a theoretical foundation for the systematization of Sŏn soteriology.

Chinul underwent profound experiences and had deep insights into Sŏn meditation practice, but at the same time was highly learned in the Sŏn theories and Kyo doctrines set forth in a vast array of textual and experiential traditions. Chinul demonstrated the compatibility of Sŏn and Kyo and urged his contemporaries to integrate study and meditation and to eschew futile conflicts with rival schools.

SUMMARY

Since it was first introduced into Korea in the later part of the fourth century through China, Buddhism put down its roots deep into the religious, cultural, and political soil of the country. Various forms of religious practice, different lineages of Buddhist schools, and diverse branches of philosophical systems were brought into Korea by Korean monks who had studied in China. However, the range of Buddhist schools was much narrower than in China, and as time passed, a few schools became dominant in Korea, which resulted in the organization of Buddhist communities, together with their theoretical and practical stances, into two broad parties: the schools of Kyo and Sŏn. The former is mainly represented by the Hwaŏm school (C. Huayan school) and the latter by the various lineages of the Hongju school (C. Hongzhou school).

At the time of Pojo Chinul in the twelfth century, the two major Buddhist schools had been contending against each other and disregarding the other's soteriological approaches. The Kyo monks criticized the Sŏn monks for their lack of scriptural and doctrinal learning, whereas the Sŏn meditation adepts looked down on their counterparts, pointing out their attachment to mere words and letters. The futile and destructive conflicts among Kyo and Sŏn were the subject of Chinul's attention, along with other serious problems, for example, the material and spiritual corruption of the sangha.

In this context, Chinul, a Sŏn adept, immersed himself in the vigorous practice of meditation, attained a great deal of insight into the Sŏn teachings, and had profound religious experiences. In addition, his unique endeavor of exploring the compatibility between Kyo and Sŏn entailed his acquisition of comprehensive knowledge of the vast array of Buddhist scriptures and philosophical systems. His study convinced him of the compatibility of Kyo and Sŏn. Based on this view, he wrote several treatises to demonstrate that scriptural teaching corresponds to the mind-to-mind transmission of the Sŏn patriarchs. He composed treatises in part to systematize Sŏn theories in light of Kyo doctrines. Nevertheless, while acknowledging that the contents and ultimate purposes of study and meditation are the same, and that theoretical learning and intellectual studies are necessary on the path to enlightenment, Chinul still valorizes Sŏn theory and practice above all.

This chapter has been primarily concerned with Chinul's integrative attitude toward Kyo and Sŏn and his theoretical approaches to demonstrating their compatibility. However, it is clear that Chinul valued the Sŏn practice over the Kyo study. Indeed, his advocacy of *kanhwa* Sŏn, which stresses the apophatic aspect of meditation practice, became increasingly prominent in his later writings. Keeping in mind these two aspects, the compatibility of Kyo and Sŏn and Chinul's advocacy of *kanhwa* Sŏn, the fourth chapter will examine the tension between cataphasis and apophasis for Chinul and explore his effort to integrate or reconcile these two seemingly contradictory modes of religious practice.

NOTES

1. The fortunes of Buddhism in China have been subject to various vicissitudes throughout Chinese history. One of the most significant of these was the nationwide persecution of Buddhism in 845, which had a seriously deleterious impact on the Buddhist community, so much so that the intellectual vitality of the Buddhist schools and the social and economic prosperity of the sangha (the Buddhist community) did not fully recover afterward. Kenneth K. S. Ch'en, *Buddhism in China* (Princeton, NJ: Princeton University Press, 1964), 232. Ch'en's work is a comprehensive general history of Buddhism in China.

2. Hereafter, "C." is the abbreviation for Chinese; "K." Korean; "J." Japanese; and "S." Sanskrit. Unless otherwise indicated, the pronunciation of a Classical Chinese term within round brackets is Korean.

3. For a brief survey of the Chinese and Korean Buddhist monks and explanations of Buddhist terms presented in this book, see Robert E. Buswell Jr. and Donald S. Lopez Jr., *The Princeton Dictionary of Buddhism* (Princeton, NJ: Princeton University Press, 2013), Kindle edition.

4. For the history of Chan Buddhism in China, see Heinrich Dumoulin, *Zen Buddhism: A History—India and China*, trans. James W. Heisig and Paul Knitter (New York: Macmillan Publishing, 1994). Also, for a brief survey of Chan lineage, see Buswell and Lopez, *The Princeton Dictionary of Buddhism*, s.v. "Chan."

5. Silla unified the southern and middle regions of the Korean Peninsula in 676.

6. At the end of the ninth century, the Korean Peninsula was divided into three kingdoms again until the Koryŏ dynasty unified them in 936.

7. For a general introduction to the history of Korea, see Jinwung Kim, *A History of Korea: From "Land of the Morning Calm" to States in Conflict* (Bloomington, IN: Indiana University Press, 2012); Michael J. Seth, *A History of Korea: From Antiquity to the Present* (Lanham, MD: Rowman & Littlefield Publishers, 2011). For a general history of religion and particularly of Buddhism in Korea, see James Huntley Grayson, *Korea—A Religious History*, rev. ed. (New York: Routledge Curzon, 2002); Byung-jo Chung, *History of Korean Buddhism* (Seoul: Jimoondang, 2007); Yong-tae Kim, *Global History of Korean Buddhism* (Seoul: Dongguk University Press, 2014).

8. For a brief introduction to these five schools and their origins in China, their introduction into Silla, and their distinctive doctrinal positions, see Grayson, *Korea—A Religious History*, 59–63.

9. Jinwung Kim, *A History of Korea*, 102.

10. For a brief introduction to Wŏnhyo's life and thought, see Yong-tae Kim, *Global History of Korean Buddhism*, 69–73.

11. One of the important tenets of Sŏn is that enlightenment is transmitted from a master to a student. The Sŏn monks claim that this Sŏn or Chan was transmitted from Bodhidharma (ca. late fourth to early fifth centuries), the putative founder of Chan Buddhism in China, and they even established the Chan transmission lineage tracing back to Śakyamuni Buddha himself. This patriarchal transmission consists of a continuous succession of enlightened masters who approve their disciples' enlightenment. Therefore, in *zushi Chan* 祖師禪 (K. *chosa Sŏn*), the patriarchal Chan

transmission tradition and the dharma lineage (the traceable genealogy of successive patriarchs) is essential to claims of a school's orthodoxy. See Sem Vermeersch, *The Power of the Buddhas: The Politics of Buddhism During the Koryŏ Dynasty (918–1392)* (Cambridge, MA: Harvard University Asia Center, 2008), 50–51. For the establishment of the patriarchal Sŏn transmission for the southern Sŏn school, which traces its origin to Bodhidharma through Huineng 慧能 (638–713), see Dumoulin, *Zen Buddhism: A History*, 155–59.

12. The term "Nine Mountains" or Kusan is commonly used by scholars to designate the Sŏn schools in the late Silla and early Koryŏ periods. However, there are different opinions as to the precise organization of the Sŏn schools. For a detailed discussion of this issue, see Vermeersch, *The Power of the Buddhas*, 51–62. See also Ik-chin Ko, *Han'guk kodae Pulgyo sasangsa* (Seoul: Tongguktae ch'lp'anbu, 1989), 503–9. Hŏ Hŭng-sik criticizes not only the making of a distinction between Sŏn schools but also between Kyo schools during the the late Silla and early Koryŏ periods. Instead, he suggests the greater importance of the differences between four primary orders—Hwaŏm, Chogye (or Sŏnjŏk), Yuga, and Ch'ŏnt'ae. See Hŭng-sik Hŏ, *Koryŏ Pulgyosa Yŏn'gu* (Seoul: Iljogak, 1986), 104–78.

13. A sūtra is a collection of the Buddha's discourses.

14. See Jinwung Kim, *A History of Korea*, 104. While acknowledging that Sŏn ideology played a role in undermining the established order of the central government in the late Unified Silla dynasty, Sem Vermeersch rejects the simple dichotomy between the central aristocracy and Kyo on the one hand and the local centers of power and Sŏn on the other. He argues that while the mountain Sŏn schools enjoyed a strong local base, they also took advantage of the official patronage of the court and some support of the central aristocracy. See Vermeersch, *The Power of the Buddhas*, 49–70. For the political and social background of the spread of Sŏn in the late Silla period, see also Ik-chin Ko, *Han'guk kodae Pulgyo sasangsa*, 523–32. James Huntley Grayson sees a parallel between the political and social characteristics of the rise of Sŏn in the late Silla period and those of the final phase of the Tang dynasty (618–907) in China: "In an epoch when traditional values were crumbling, old certainties disappearing, and the whole social and political order coming unhinged, it is no wonder that thoughtful men turned to a quietistic, meditative form of religion which put one beyond the hurly-burly of the times." Grayson, *Korea—A Religious History*, 72.

15. Jinwung Kim, *A History of Korea*, 149.

16. For a brief introduction to *sŭngkwa*, see Yong-tae Kim, *Global History of Korean Buddhism*, 82–83; Buswell and Lopez, *The Princeton Dictionary of Buddhism*, s.v. "sŭngkwa." For the development and functioning of the examination system in Koryŏ, see Hŭng-sik Hŏ, "Koryŏ sidae ŭi sŭngkwa chedo wa kŭ kinŭng," *Yŏksa kyoyuk* 19 (1976): 103–38.

17. For the distinction between *kuksa* and *wangsa*, see Buswell and Lopez, *The Princeton Dictionary of Buddhism*, s.v. "guoshi." For further studies of the *wangsa* and *kuksa* system in Korea, see Hŭng-sik Hŏ, "Koryŏ sidae ŭi kuksa·wangsa chedo wa kŭ kinŭng," *Yŏksa hakpo* 67 (1975): 1–44; Yun-jin Park, "Koryŏ Chŏn'gi wangsa kuksa ŭi immyŏng kwa kŭ kinŭng," *Han'guk hakpo* 116 (2004): 139–74; Yun-jin Park, "Koryŏ hugi wangsa·kuksa ŭi sare wa kinŭng ŭi pyŏnhwa," *Han'guk chungsesa*

yŏn'gu 19 (2005): 63–116; and Yun-jin Park, "Koryŏ sidae wansa·kuksa e taehan taeu," *Yŏksa hakpo* 190 (2006): 1–32. Also, Sem Vermeersch explores in detail the development of the monastic bureaucracy and its implications for the relationship between the state and the Buddhist community in the Koryŏ period. Vermeersch's research also compares the Koryŏ dynasty with the dynasties of China and Japan. Vermeersch, *The Power of the Buddhas*, 151–268. Hŏ Hŭng-sik argues that the history of *wangsa* and *kuksa* appointments reflected the alternative rise to prominence of the Kyo and Sŏn schools. After the unification and up to the accession of King Hŏn'an 憲安 (r. 857–861) in the late Silla period, most of the *kuksa*s were appointed from the Kyo schools. Then, between King Hŏn'an of Silla and the ninth year of King Kwangjong 光宗 (r. 949–975) of Koryŏ, the majority of both *wangsa*s and *kuksa*s were appointed from the Sŏn school. Afterward, until the time of King Yejong 睿宗 (r. 1105–1122), more *wangsa*s and *kuksa*s came out of the rising Kyo schools. Then, the wheel turned again and the Sŏn schools regained their dominance in the period between King Injong 仁宗 (r. 1122–1146) and King Kangjong 康宗 (r. 1211–1213). After King Kangjong, the appointments of *wangsa* and *kuksa* were not confined to a single school but given to various orders of both schools. For a division of Buddhist history in Korea according to the appointments of *wangsa* and *kuksa*, see Hŭng-sik Hŏ, "Koryŏ sidae ŭi kuksa·wangsa chaedo wa kŭ kinŭng," 43–44. For a list of *wangsa*s and *kuksa*s and their schools in the late Silla and Koryŏ periods, see Hŭng-sik Hŏ, *Koryŏ Pulgyosa Yŏn'gu*, 394, 428–34.

18. For a detailed study of the financial status of the Buddhist community in the early Koryŏ dynasty, see Vermeersch, *The Power of the Buddhas*, 271–372.

19. Hee-Sung Keel, *Chinul: The Founder of the Korean Sŏn Tradition* (1984; repr., Fremont, CA: Jain Publishing, 2012), 4. Ch'ŏnt'ae chong was officially categorized as a Sŏn order during the time of King Sejong 世宗 (r. 1418–1450) of the Chosŏn dynasty. There are different opinions among scholars about whether Ch'ŏnt'ae chong belonged to Kyo or Sŏn during the Koryŏ period. For the various arguments about the identity of Ch'ŏnt'ae chong, see Yun-jin Park, "Koryŏ Ch'ŏnt'ae chong ŭi chongpa munjae—Chosŏn ch'o Ch'ŏnt'ae chong ŭi Sŏn chong kwuisok ŭi yŏksajŏk paegyŭng," *Han'guksa hakpo* 40 (2010): 413–45.

20. The name Chogye 曹溪 refers to the mountain Caoxishan (C.) 曹溪山 in China where Huineng 慧能, the sixth patriarch of Chinese Chan tradition, resided. By adopting the name of Chogye, the Koryŏ Sŏn monks were asserting their connection to Huineng and the orthodoxy of their school. On the historical adaptation of the name Chogye chong 曹溪宗 as a designation of the Sŏn tradition in general, see Yŏng-ho Lee (Jin Wol), "Sip-i segi ch'ogi ŭi Han'guk Sŏn chong kwa Chogye chong sŏngnip sigi sogo," *Pulgyo hakpo* 59 (2011): 143–48. In modern Korea, Chogye chong is the largest Buddhist order and was reorganized during the Japanese colonial period (1910–1945). It traces its origin back to Toŭi (d. 825), the founder of the Kajisan 迦智山 school of Sŏn. The monks of modern Chogye chong also consider Pojo Chinul 普照知訥 (1158–1210) and T'aego Pou 太古普愚 (1301–1382) to have been restorers of the Sŏn tradition in Korea in the twelfth and fourteenth centuries. See Buswell and Lopez, *The Princeton Dictionary of Buddhism*, s.v. "Chogye chong." For the history of Korean Buddhism written from the perspective of the development of the Chogye

order, see Taehan Pulgyo Chogye chong p'ogyowŏn, *Han'guk Pulgyosa: Chogye chong sa rŭl chungsim ŭro* (Seoul: Chogye chong Press, 2011).

21. See Seth, *A History of Korea*, 77–85, 88–90. For details about these two revolts, see also Jinwung Kim, *A History of Korea*, 155–57.

22. For information on the conflicts described here and the ensuing rule of the Ch'oe family, see Seth, *A History of Korea*, 103–7; Jinwung Kim, *A History of Korea*, 157–61.

23. Jinwung Kim, *A History of Korea*, 162–63.

24. For a brief summary of the political, social, and cultural history of the late Koryŏ period, see Jinwung Kim, *A History of Korea*, 165–71, 181–85; Seth, *A History of Korea*, 110–25.

25. Seth, *A History of Korea*, 107.

26. Byung-jo Chung, *History of Korean Buddhism*, 86. For information about the Buddhist rituals especially favored by the state, see Vermeersch, *The Power of the Buddhas*, 313–64.

27. Chinul's funerary inscription was composed in 1211 by Kim Kun-su 金君綏 (fl. 1216–1220), a year after Chinul's death. It was commissioned by King Hŭijong 熙宗 (r. 1204–1211), who had respected Chinul and commanded that a memorial stele be erected for him. For the text in Classical Chinese and English, see *Funerary Inscription and Epitaph for the State Preceptor Puril Pojo of the Society for Cultivating Sŏn on Chogye Mountain*, in *Chinul: Selected Works*, trans., with introduction and annotations, Robert E. Buswell Jr., vol. 2 of *Collected Works of Korean Buddhism* (Seoul: Jogye Order of Korean Buddhism, 2012), 367–86 (hereafter cited as *CSW*). Besides the funerary inscription, there are three other important sources that provide information about Chinul's early life: the *Taesŭng Sŏnjong Chogyesan Susŏnsa chungch'anggi* [Record of the reconstruction of Susŏnsa of the Mahāyāna Sŏn order in Chogye Mountain] composed by Ch'oe Sŏn in 1207 when Chinul was still alive; *Kwŏnsu chŏnghye Kyŏlsamun*, published in English as *Encouragement to Practice: The Compact of the Samādhi and Prajñā Society*, in *CSW*, 115–94, and written by Chinul himself in 1190 when he was thirty-three; and the preface and conclusion from *Hwaŏm non chŏryo*, published in English as *Preface and Conclusion from the Condensation of the Exposition of the Avataṃsakasūtra*, in *CSW*, 355–66, also written by Chinul and published in 1207 (hereafter cited as either *Preface from Condensation of the Exposition* or *Conclusion from Condensation of the Exposition*). The preface of this work contains an autobiographical account of Chinul's spiritual experience. On the four primary sources from which the life of Chinul is reconstructed, see Hee-Sung Keel, *Chinul*, 8–10. The summary of Chinul's life offered here is greatly indebted to Hee-Sung Keel, *Chinul*, 1–55, and Buswell, introduction to *CSW*, 6–39.

28. The self-chosen name "Moguja" refers to Chinul's emphasis on cultivating the mind, which was the focal point of his religious practice. In the Sŏn tradition "herding ox" symbolizes the act of cultivating the mind. See Hee-Sung Keel, *Chinul*, 11n18. In *Moguja's Secrets on Cultivating the Mind*, in *CSW*, 205–46, Chinul explains "herding ox" as gradual cultivation following initial awakening: "After awakening, you must be constantly on your guard. If deluded thoughts suddenly arise, do not chase after them: reduce them and reduce them again until you reach the unconditioned.

Then and only then will [your practice reach] completion. This is what is meant by the practice of ox herding (*mogu haeng* 牧牛行) that follows awakening, [which is performed by] all the wise advisors under heaven." *Moguja's Secrets*, in *CSW*, 226 (bracketed insertions in original).

29. See Hee-Sung Keel, *Chinul*, 11–12.

30. Seven according to the Western method of reckoning ages.

31. Kim Kun-su writes: "In his studies, he had no permanent teacher, but was just a follower of the path." *Funerary Inscription*, in *CSW*, 370.

32. *Funerary Inscription*, in *CSW*, 370.

33. Buswell, annotation to *Funerary Inscription*, in *CSW*, 370n6.

34. About the early period of his monastic life, Chinul said, "I, Chinul, since my youth, have cast myself into the domain of the patriarchs and have visited meditation halls everywhere." *Encouragement to Practice*, in *CSW*, 116–17: Here, myonyŏn 妙年, translated as "youth" in English, refers to a young man around twenty. See Hee-sung Keel, *Chinul*, 14, and also Kŏn-gi Kang, *Chŏnghye kyŏlsamun kangŭi* (Seoul: Puril ch'ulpansa, 2006), 20–22.

35. See Hee-Sung Keel, *Chinul*, 13–14.

36. *Encouragement to Practice*, in *CSW*, 117–18: 然返觀我輩 朝暮所行之迹 則憑依佛法 裝飾我人 區區於利養之途 汩沒於風塵之際 道德未修 衣食斯費 雖復出家 何德之有? 噫! 夫欲出離三界 而未有絶塵之行 徒爲男子之身 而無丈夫之志。上乖弘道 下闕利生 中負四恩 誠以爲恥。知訥 以是長歎 其來久矣。 Bracketed insertions in original.

37. *Encouragement to Practice*, in *CSW*, 118–19: (歲在壬寅正月 赴上都普濟寺談禪法會) 一日與同學十餘人 約曰。「罷會後 當捨名利 隱遁山林 結爲同社。常以習定均慧爲務 禮佛轉經 以至於執榮運力 各隨所任而經營之。隨緣養性 放曠平生 遠追達士眞人之高行 則豈不快哉.」 Bracketed insertions in original.

38. *Encouragement to Practice*, in *CSW*, 190. 諸公聞語 咸以爲然曰 〈他日 能成此約 隱居林下 結爲同社 則宜以定慧名之。〉 因成盟文而結意焉。

39. Pomunsa is located in Yech'ŏn-kun 醴泉郡, North Kyŏngsang Province 慶尙北道. See Buswell, annotation to *Encouragement to Practice*, in *CSW*, 191n110.

40. Kong Mountain is also known as P'algong Mountain 八公山 and is located in Yŏngch'ŏn-si 永川市, North Kyŏngsang Province 慶尙北道. See Buswell, annotations to *CSW*, 373n15, 191n110. Tŭkchae's invitation and the founding of the retreat society are mentioned in *Encouragement to Practice*, in *CSW*, 117–18, and *Funerary Inscription*, in *CSW*, 373.

41. Besides the assumption that some could not join because of illness, death, or a decision to pursue fame and wealth, there may have been some other factors. In the late twelfth century, the Koryŏ-era countryside was engulfed in the successive military coups and violent revolts described above. These circumstances might have hindered some of the monks from traveling to and settling in an isolated monastery that may have been vulnerable to violence. Moreover, the purpose of the retreat society, which was antithetical to the goals of the hierarchical and degenerate sangha, might also have made it difficult to find an appropriate site. See Buswell, introduction to *CSW*, 15.

42. *Funerary Inscription*, in *CSW*, 377.

43. Hee-Sung Keel, *Chinul*, 42.

44. *Funerary Inscription*, in *CSW*, 381.

45. *Funerary Inscription*, in *CSW*, 371–72: 偶一日 於學寮 閱六祖壇經至曰 「眞如自性起念 六根雖見聞覺知 不染萬境 而眞性常自在。」 Bracketed insertion in original.

46. For a better understanding of the quoted passage, refer to additional passages from the *Platform Sūtra*. For example:

> Good friends, what is negated by the "non" (wu)? What kind of thing is "thought"? "Non" means to be without the characteristic of duality, to be without the mind of the enervating defilements. "Thought" is to think of the fundamental nature of suchness. Suchness is the essence of thought, thought is the function of suchness. Thought is activated in the self-nature of suchness—it is not the case that the eyes, ears, nose, and tongue are able to think, it is because of the self-nature of suchness that thoughts are activated. If suchness were nonexistent, then eyes and ears, forms and sounds would be simultaneously destroyed. (John R. McRae, trans., *The Platform Sutra of the Sixth Patriarch*, BDK English Tripiṭaka Series [Berkeley, CA: Numata Center for Buddhist Translation and Research, 2000], 44)

47. See Hee-sung Keel, *Chinul*, 26.

48. *Funerary Inscription*, in *CSW*, 372.

49. Buswell, introduction to *CSW*, 17.

50. *Funerary Inscription*, in *CSW*, 376.

51. *Funerary Inscription*, in *CSW*, 372.

52. *Preface from Condensation of the Exposition*, in *CSW*, 356.

53. In Sankrit, *dharmadhātu* means "dharma realm," or "realm of reality." In the Mahāyāna tradition, the term is used to indicate "the infinite in which the activity of all dharmas takes place—that is, the universe." It is also an alternative term for the ultimate reality. In East Asian Mahāyāna Buddhism, the *dharmadhātu* is divided into ten *dharmadhātus* that include the traditional six realms of rebirth and four additional realms of enlightened beings. The Huayan school developed another set of sophisticated categories of *dharmadhātu*: (1) the *dharmadhātu* of phenomena; (2) the *dharmadhātu* of principle; (3) the *dharmadhātu* of the unimpeded interpenetration between phenomena and principle; and (4) the *dharmadhātu* of unimpeded interpenetration of phenomenon and phenomena. This cosmological but at the same time ontological term is essential to understanding Chinul's thought and it plays a bridging role between Huayan doctrines and Sŏn practice. For a brief introduction to *dharmadhātu*, see Buswell and Lopez, *The Princeton Dictionary of Buddhism*, s.v. "dharmadhātu."

54. *Preface from Condensation of the Exposition*, in *CSW*, 358.

55. Buswell, introduction to *CSW*, 19.

56. Hee-sung Keel, *Chinul*, 31.

57. *Funerary Inscription*, in *CSW*, 374–75: 師嘗言。 「予自普門已來 十餘年矣。 雖得意勤修 無虛廢時 情見未忘 有物礙膺 如讎所。 至居智異 得大慧普覺禪師語錄云 <禪不在靜處 不在鬧處 不在日用應緣處 不在思量分別處。 然第一不得 捨却靜處鬧處 日用應緣處 思量分別處叅 忽然眼開 方知皆是屋裏事。> 予於此契會 自然物不礙膺 讎不同所 當下安樂耳。」 由是 慧解增高 衆所宗師。 Bracketed insertions in original.

58. Hee-sung Keel, *Chinul*, 39.

59. Buswell, introduction to *CSW*, 26.

60. Hee-sung Keel, *Chinul*, 39–40.

61. See Hee-sung Keel, *Chinul*, 94, 110; Buswell and Lopez, *The Princeton Dictionary of Buddhism*, s.v. "jiewu."; Buswell, introduction to *CSW*, 56–57, 95.

62. Chinul refers to Chengguan's distinction between the two kinds of awakening: "If we explain the characteristics of awakening, they are of only two kinds. The first is the understanding-awakening (*haeo/jiewu* 解悟), which is the clear comprehension of nature and characteristics. The second is the realization-awakening (*chŭngo/zhengwu* 證悟), which is the mind that reaches the arcane ultimate." *Excerpts from the Dharma Collection and Special Practice Record with Personal Notes*, in Chinul, *Numinous Awareness Is Never Dark: The Korean Buddhist Master Chinul's Excerpts on Zen Practice*, trans. with introduction and annotations, Robert E. Buswell Jr. (Honolulu: University of Hawaii Press, 2016), 128: 疏云 <若明悟相 不出二種 一者解悟謂明 了性相 二者證悟 謂心造玄極。 *Han'guk Pulgyo chŏnsŏ* 韓國佛教全書 [*Complete Books of Korean Buddhism*] 4:749a10–11 (hereafter cited as "H").

63. For a brief explanation of the two types of awakening, see Buswell, introduction to *The Korean Approach to Zen*, 58; Buswell, introduction to *CSW*, 56–57. See also *Excerpts*, in *Numinous Awareness*, 291.

64. In an article that reexamines Chinul's efforts to integrate Sŏn and Kyo, Chŏng Hŭi-kyŏng argues that Chinul's awakening experience inspired by reading Dahui's *Records* was a realization-awakening, as expounded in the *Treatise on the Complete and Sudden Attainment of Buddhahood*, in *CSW*, 247–314. See also Hŭi-kyŏng Chŏng, "Pojo Chinul ŭi Sŏn Kyo ilch'i e taehan chaegoch'al," *Pojo sasang* 39 (2013): 127. For Chinul, realization-awakening does not mean the end of cultivation but rather its "continuation." See Hŭi-kyŏng Chŏng, "Pojo Chinul ŭi Sŏn Kyo ilch'i e taehan chaegocha'l," 127–28. Regarding the obstruction experienced between understanding-awakening and realization-awakening, Chinul explains: "Nevertheless, although the ideal wisdom may have appeared, since the proclivities of habit from many lifetimes ago continue to invade thought-moment by thought-moment, one remains involved in conditioned fabrications, and neither materiality nor mentality are yet extinguished. This is what is called the locus of cognitive obstruction (*haeae* 解 礙, cf. *jñeyāvaraṇa*) for an ordinary person [who is still cultivating] the ten faiths." *Complete and Sudden Attainment*, in *CSW*, 298 (bracketed insertion in original).

65. Buswell, preface to *The Korean Approach to Zen: The Collected Works of Chinul*, trans. with preface and introduction, Robert E. Buswell Jr. (Honolulu: University of Hawaii Press, 1983), x.

66. This introduction to and abridgement of each of Chinul's works is indebted to *CSW* (2012), *The Korean Approach to Zen* (1983), and *Numinous Awareness Is Never Dark* (2016). *The Korean Approach to Zen* and *CSW* include most of Chinul's writings. *The Korean Approach to Zen* includes only English translations, whereas *CSW* includes both English translations and Classical Chinese. *The Korean Approach to Zen* included *Straight Talk on the True Mind* (*Chinsim chiksŏl* 眞心直說) and *Excerpts from the Dharma Collection and Special Practice Record with Personal Notes* (*Pŏpchip pyŏrhaengnok chŏryo pyŏngip sagi* 法集別行錄節要並入私記). These latter two works were omitted from *CSW*, but this volume included *Preface and*

Conclusion from Condensation of the Exposition (*Hwaŏm non chŏryo* 華嚴論節要).
Numinous Awareness Is Never Dark (2016) is a reworking of the *Excerpts* from the
1983 translation. For the Classical Chinese version of Chinul's writings with Korean
translations, see Chinul, *Pojo pŏbŏ* 普照法語, ed. Han-am Pang, trans. T'an-hŏ Kim,
rev. ed. (Seoul: T'anhŏ Pulgyo munhwa chaedan, 2006); Chinul, *Chŏngsŏn Chinul*,
vol. 2 of *Han'guk chŏnt'ong sasang ch'ongsŏ Pulgyo p'yŏn* (Seoul: Taehan Pulgyo
Chogyejong Han'guk chŏnt'ong sasangsŏ kanhaeng wuiwŏnhwoi ch'ulp'anbu,
2009). For a brief introduction to Chinul's writings, see also Hee-sung Keel, *Chinul*,
33–34, 43–44, 47–53.

67. Buswell, introduction to *CSW*, 69. Chinul understands that there are various
kinds of intellectual studies and meditative practices beneficial to monks with various
degrees of spiritual ability. Rather than despising inferior approaches, he acknowledges the validity of all approaches that are suitable to people's individual capacities.

68. For the threefold training, see Buswell, introduction to *CSW*, 67–69. Also for
Chinul's reference to the threefold training, see *Encouragement to Practice*, in *CSW*,
136, 188–89.

69. See *Admonitions*, in *CSW*, 195–203. For detailed studies on this text, see Ki-
jong Kwŏn, "*Kye Ch'osim hagin mun* ŭi yŏn'gu," *Pojo sasang* 12 (1999): 55–70. For
comments on the structure of the text, see Ki-jong Kwŏn, "*Kye Ch'osim hagin mun*
ŭi yŏn'gu," 58–61.

70. Buswell, introduction to *CSW*, 94.

71. Buswell, introduction to *CSW*, 95. For detailed studies and commentary on
Moguja's Secrets, see Kŏn-gi Kang, "*Susim kyŏl* ŭi ch'egye wa sasang," in *Moguja
Chinul yŏn'gu* (Chŏnju, Korea: Puch'ŏnim sesang, 2001), 155–91; Kŏn-gi Kang,
"*Susim kyŏl* ŭi ch'egye wa sasang," *Pojo sasang* 12 (1999): 9–47; Kŏn-ki Kang,
Maŭm tangnŭn kil: Susim kyŏl kangŭi, second ed. (Seoul: Puril ch'ulpansa, 2008).

72. Buswell, introduction to *CSW*, 107.

73. Buswell, introduction to *CSW*, 96–102. For a summary of the treatise in Korean, see Sŏng-nyŏl Ch'oe, "Pojo Chinul ŭi *Wŏndon sŏngbullon* punsŏk," *Pŏmhan
ch'ŏrhak* 24 (Autumn 2001): 131–45.

74. Robert E. Buswell Jr., *Tracing Back the Radiance: Chinul's Korean Way of
Zen* (Honolulu: University of Hawaii Press, 1991), 54.

75. Buswell, *Tracing Back the Radiance*, 55. The Huayan tradition categorizes the
Buddhist teachings into five groups. To the first group belong the Hīnayāna or Lesser
Vehicle teachings, and then there are four categories of Mahāyāna teachings. The
second group consists of the Mahāyāna inception (or elementary) teachings (*sigyo*
始教) that emphasize the doctrine of emptiness (S. *śūnyatā*)—Madhyamaka and
Yogācāra schools belong to this category. The third group, called the final teachings
of Mahāyāna (*chonggyo* 終教), pertains to the doctrine of *tathāgatagarbha*, "embryo of the *tathāgatas*" (meaning "the one who has thus come," *yŏrae* 如來), which
claims that all sentient beings are endowed with the buddha-nature (*pulsŏng* 佛性).
The fourth group is called the sudden teaching (*ton'gyo* 頓教), which is meant for
those advanced in their cultivation. It dismisses practices involving the use of words
or concepts. Due to its anti-intellectual approach, Sŏn teaching is categorized in this
fourth group, which is still inferior to the fifth—the complete teaching (*wŏn'gyo* 圓

教). The Huayan school belongs to this highest category. For the fivefold Huayan taxonomy of Buddhist teachings, see Buswell, introduction to *CSW*, 97; Buswell and Lopez, *The Princeton Dictionary of Buddhism*, s.v. "Huayan wujiao."

76. Buswell, introduction to *Excerpts*, in *The Korean Approach to Zen*, 262. For studies of Chinul's thought in this text, see Kŏn-gi Kang, "*Pŏpchip pyŏrhaengnok chŏryo pyŏngip sagi* rŭl t'onghaesŏ pon Chinul ŭi sasang," in *Moguja Chinul yŏn'gu*, 117–53. Chinul's text consists of excerpts of *Pŏpchip pyŏrhaengnok* with his own commentary. It has been claimed that *Pŏpchip pyŏrhaengnok* was written by Zongmi, but the text is not extant, which has led to scholarly debates about its provenance. See Robert E. Buswell Jr., "The Identity of the *Popchip pyŏrhaeng nok* [*Dharma Collection and Special Practice Record*]," *Korean Studies* 6 (1982): 1–16.

77. For an introduction to this text, see Buswell, introduction to *Excerpts*, in *The Korean Approach to Zen*, 262–63; Buswell, part 1 of translator's introduction to *Numinous Awareness*, 1–92; and Buswell and Lopez, *The Princeton Dictionary of Buddhism*, s.v. "Pŏpchip pyŏrhaengnok chŏryo pyŏngip sagi." For English translations of the text, see *The Korean Approach to Zen*, 263–340 and *Numinous Awareness*, 93–194. Hereafter, English translations of *Excerpts* will be quoted from *Numinous Awareness*.

78. "Now, for the sake of those who can awaken to the mind through the aid of the Teachings (Kyo/Jiao 教), I have abbreviated [the text's] prolix verbiage and extracted its essentials so that it can serve as a vade mecum for contemplative practice." *Excerpts*, in *Numinous Awareness*, 97 (bracketed insertion in original).

79. For a brief introduction to Zongmi and his influence on Chinul, see Buswell, introduction to *CSW*, 41–47.

80. Buswell, preface to *The Korean Approach to Zen*, xii. On the comprehensiveness of *Excerpts*, see also Hee-sung Keel, "*Pŏpchip pyŏrhaengnok chŏryo pyŏngip sagi* wa Chinul Sŏn sasang ŭi kusŏng [*Pŏpchip pyŏrhaengnok chŏryo pyŏngip sagi* and the Structure of Chinul's Sŏn thought]," *Pojo sasang* 17 (2002): 379–98. Keel points out that although *Excerpts* is a comprehensive work covering most of Chinul's thought, it is not systematically composed.

81. See Yŏn-sik Ch'oe (Yeonshik Choe), "*Chinsim chiksŏl* ŭi chŏja e taehan saeroun ihae," *Chindan hakpo* 94 (2002): 77–101. For a brief summary of Ch'oe's argument, see Buswell, introduction to *CSW*, 89–90. Yi Pyŏng-uk supports Ch'oe Yŏn-sik's argument based on his studies of Chinul's claims about the consistency between Sŏn and Kyo, noting that the language in *Straight Talk* concerning Sŏn-Kyo compatibility can be distinguished from Chinul's other texts. For a detailed discussion, see Pyŏng-uk Yi, "Pojo Chinul ŭi Sŏn Kyo t'onghap ŭi yŏrŏ yuhyŏng," *Pojo sasang* 14 (2000): 120–23. On the other hand, Kim Pang-nyong advocates for Chinul's authorship based on bibliographical research, textual comparison with other writings, and analysis of the consistency of Chinul's thought with the content of *Straight Talk*. See Pang-nyong Kim, "*Chinsim chiksŏl* ŭi chŏja e taehan koch'al," *Pojo sasang* 15 (2001): 73–118. For detailed studies of *Straight Talk*, see Kŏn-ki Kang, "*Chinsim chiksŏl* ŭi ch'egye wa sasang," in *Moguja Chinul yŏn'gu*, 193–227, and Kŏn-ki Kang, *Ch'ammaŭm iyagi: Chinsim chiksŏl kangŭi* (Seoul: Puril ch'ulpansa, 2004).

82. The authenticity of Chinul's authorship of this text has not been confirmed. See Yŏng-sŏp Ko, "Pojo Chinul ŭi sasang hyŏngsŏng e yŏnghyang ŭl kkich'in kosŭng—*Pojo chŏnsŏ* anp'ak ŭi kosŭngdŭl ŭl chungsim ŭro," *Pojo sasang* 42 (2014): 25–26; Jae-ryong Shim, "The Philosophical Foundation of Korean Zen Buddhism: The Integration of Sŏn and Kyo by Chinul (1158–1210)" (PhD diss., University of Hawaii, 1979), 160. See also Jae-ryong Shim, *Tongyang ŭi chihye wa Sŏn* (Seoul: Segyesa, 2005), 36–38. Shim Jae-ryong argues that, in light of his critical attitude toward the Pure Land practice in *Encouragement to Practice*, it is unlikely that Chinul wrote this text.

83. There is no English translation of this text available. For a brief introduction to *Postface*, see Jae-ryong Shim, "The Philosophical Foundation of Korean Zen Buddhism," 158. The Classical Chinese text is found in Chinul, *Pojo chŏnsŏ* (Seoul: Pojo sasang yŏn'guwŏn, 1989), 171–72; the Korean translation of the text can be found in *Pojo Kuksa chip* (Seoul: Tongguk yŏkkyŏngwŏn, 1995), 464–67.

84. *Funerary Inscription*, in *CSW*, 381.

85. According to Im Yŏng-suk, among the extant texts composed by Koryŏ Sŏn monks—twenty-one texts written by eleven Sŏn masters—Chinul authored the largest number, seven. Yŏng-suk Im, "Chinul ŭi ch'ansul Sŏnsŏ wa kŭ soŭikyŏngjŏn e kwanhan yŏn'gu," *Sŏjihak yŏn'gu* 1 (1986): 251.

86. Here, the Sanskrit term "*tripiṭaka*," which means literally "three baskets," corresponds to the English word "canon." *Tripiṭaka* consists of *sūtra-piṭaka* (the basket of the Buddha's discourses), *vinaya-piṭaka* (the basket of disciplinary texts), and *abhidharma-piṭaka* or *śāstra-piṭaka* (the basket of "higher dharma" or "scholastic treatises"). For detailed information, see Buswell and Lopez, *The Princeton Dictionary of Buddhism*, s.v. "tripiṭaka."

87. *Excerpts*, in *Numinous Awareness*, 186: 然上來所擧法門 並是爲依言生解悟入者 委辨法有隨緣不變二義 人有頓悟漸修兩門 以二義 知一藏經論之指歸 是自心之性相。 以兩門見一切賢聖之軌轍 是自行之始終如是揀辨本末了然 令人不迷 遷權就實 速證菩提。 H 4:764a3–9 (bracketed insertions in original). This general summary was given by Zongmi and quoted by Chinul earlier in *Excerpts*, at 107.

88. See Hee-sung Keel, *Chinul*, 65.

89. In addition to the popular twofold distinction of Chinul's thought between ontology and soteriology, Kim Chong-myŏng adds the phenomenological aspect of Sŏn, which primarily deals with a deluded perception of the dharma realm, presenting a threefold classification of Chinul's thought. See Chong-myŏng Kim, "Chinul ŭi *Pŏpchip pyŏrhaeng nok chŏryo pyŏngip sagi* e mich'in ch'ogi Sŏnjongsŏ ŭi sasangjŏk yŏnghyang: Kyubong Chongmil ŭi chŏsul ŭl chungsim ŭro," *Pojo sasang* 11 (1998): 159–61.

90. Chinul quotes Aśvaghoṣa, who interprets "dharma" as "the mind of a sentient being." *Excerpts*, in *Numinous Awareness*, 98: 馬鳴祖師云 所言法者 謂衆生心 H 4:741b6–7.

91. *Encouragement to Practice*, in *CSW*, 162: 此修性二門 如鳥兩翼 闕一不可。

92. Chŏng Hŭi-kyŏng shows that the shortcut approach of *kanhwa* Sŏn is a part of gradual cultivation, arguing also that this seemingly anti-intellectual path can be interpreted from the perspective of Chinul's understanding of the compatibility

between Sŏn and Kyo. For a detailed discussion, see Hŭi-kyŏng Chŏng, "Pojo Chinul ŭi Sŏn Kyo ilch'i e taehan chaegoch'al," 114–47. See also Chong-myŏng Kim, "Chinul ŭi *Pyŏngjip pyŏnrhaeng nok chŏryo pyŏngip sagi* e mich'in ch'ogi Sŏnjongsŏ ŭi sasangjŏk yŏnghyang," 165–68.

93. Buswell, introduction to *CSW*, 75.

94. The three approaches to practice (termed the Three Paths 三門) were devised by Kim Kun-su, the composer of Chinul's funerary inscription.

95. *Funerary Inscription*, in *CSW*, 376–77: 開門有三種 曰惺寂等持門 曰圓頓信解門 曰徑截門 依而修行信入者多焉。 These three approaches to Sŏn practice are well expounded by Chinul as expedient paths to enlightenment: the first two are discussed throughout his writings, and the third, the shortcut path, was introduced and promoted mainly in the treatises composed in the later period of his life. Shim Jae-ryong criticizes Kim Kun-su's summary in the funerary inscription, which he sees as a distortion of Chinul's thought by Confucianism. He instead advocates as a systematic summary of Chinul's practical approaches the Three Mysterious Gates (*samhyŏn mun* 三玄門), presented as a threefold approach to enlightenment by Chinul himself in three of his later writings. Shim Jae-ryong insists that the Three Mysterious Gates is the authentic summary of Chinul's soteriological approach. Jae-ryong Shim, *Tongyang ŭi chihye wa Sŏn*, 31–35. However, Ch'oe Yŏn-sik counters that Kim Kun-su must have consulted with Chinul's disciples with regard to the contents of the inscription and that they would not have distorted their master's thought. Yŏn-sik Ch'oe (Yeonshi Choe), "*Pŏpchip pyŏrhaeng nok chŏryo pyŏngip sagi* rŭl t'onghae pon Pojo sammun ŭi sŏnggyŏk," *Pojo sasang* 12 (1999): 115n2. In addition, Ko Yŏng-sŏp argues that Chinul's shortcut approach was influenced by Yongming Yanshou's approach to Sŏn practice, and that the development of the distinctive Sŏn practice of the Three Paths was inspired by the Three Mysterious Gates. Yŏng-sŏp Ko, "Pojo Chinul ŭi sasang hyŏngsŏng e yŏnghyang ŭl kkich'in kosŭng," 35–42; see also *Excerpts*, in *Numinous Awareness*, 126–27. It is the author's view that the Three Mysterious Gates 三玄門 reflects the shift of Chinul's approach to Sŏn practice in his later life, putting more weight on the path of *kanhwa* Sŏn, whereas the Three Paths 三門 articulated by Kim Kun-su shows the development of Chinul's theory of Sŏn practice throughout his life. For the Three Mysterious Gates of Chinul, see Buswell, introduction to *CSW*, 84–88, and for the historical development of the threefold taxonomy devised by Linji Yixuan 臨濟義玄 (d. 867), developed by Jianfu Chenggu 薦福承古 (d. 1045) and adopted by Chinul, see Yŏng-sik Chŏng, "Ch'ŏnbok Sŭnggo, Kakpŏm Hyehong kŭrigo Pojo Chinul ŭi samhyŏn mun haesŏk," *Han'guk Pulgyohak* 54 (2009): 5–34.

96. *Encouragement to Practice*, in *CSW*, 115–16: (恭聞「人因地而倒者 因地而起 離地求起 無有是處也。」) 迷一心 而起無邊煩惱者 眾生也 悟一心 而起無邊妙用者 諸佛也。 迷悟雖殊 而要由一心 則離心求佛者 亦無有是處也。 Also at the beginning of *Moguja's Secrets*, Chinul emphasizes that there is no other way to attain buddhahood except through cultivating the mind: "If you want to become a buddha—understand that the buddha is the mind, so how can you search for the mind in the far distance?" *Moguja's Secrets*, in *CSW*, 205. See also *Moguja's Secrets*, 207.

97. Cultivation of the mind, relying on awakening to the principle that the mind-nature (*simsŏng* 心性) is originally pure like the buddha-mind and that all deluded thoughts are originally void, is called Supreme-Vehicle Sŏn (*ch'oesang sŭng Sŏn* 最上乘禪) or the pure Sŏn of the tathāgatas (*yŏrae ch'ŏngjŏng Sŏn* 如來清淨禪). This is the highest category in Zongmi's fivefold taxonomy of Sŏn. See *Encouragement to Practice*, in *CSW*, 137–38; also *Moguja's Secrets*, in *CSW*, 224–29.

98. Conditioned arising or dependent origination is an important Buddhist teaching holding that all phenomena arise in connection with previous conditions.

99. *Moguja's Secrets*, in *CSW*, 207.

100. For a discussion of the mind of void, calm, numinous awareness in the Heze School and in Chinul, see Buswell, introduction to *CSW*, 41–47, 62–67. Keel Hee-sung also discusses the nature and function of the mind, greatly relying on *Straight Talk* and *Excerpts*. Buswell excludes *Straight Talk* because of the uncertainty about its authorship. See Hee-sung Keel, *Chinul*, 66–90.

101. Buswell, introduction to *CSW*, 64n101. For a brief summary of Zongmi's understanding of "awareness," see Peter N. Gregory, *Tsung-mi and the Sinification of Buddhism* (1991; paperback ed., Honolulu: University of Hawaii Press, 2002), 216–18.

102. Quoted in *Excerpts*, in *Numinous Awareness*, 99: 荷澤意者 謂諸法如夢 諸聖同說故妄念本寂 塵境本空 空寂之心 靈知不昧 即此空寂之心 是前達摩所傳清淨心也 任迷任悟 心本自知 不籍緣生 不因境起 迷時煩惱 知非悟時神變 知非神變 H 4:741b22–c3. See also *Excerpts*, 112–13, where Chinul further quotes Zongmi:

Heze was able to refer to various terms like unconditioned, unabiding, even ineffable, and so forth, by simply referring to them all as the void and quiescent awareness in which everything is subsumed. Voidness (śūnyatā) means that it is devoid of all signs; it is still an apophatic term. Quiescence (śānti) is the immutable attribute of the real nature; it is not the same as empty nothingness. Awareness refers to the attribute that exposes the thing itself; it is not the same as conceptual discrimination (*vikalpa*).

103. *Excerpts*, in *Numinous Awareness*, 105.

104. *Moguja's Secrets*, in *CSW*, 223.

105. *Excerpts*, in *Numinous Awareness*, 107–9.

106. *Excerpts*, in *Numinous Awareness*, 107–8. Throughout *Excerpts*, Chinul employs Zongmi's explanation of the various aspects of the mind-nature that uses the simile of a jewel that is "perfectly round, pure, lustrous, and untarnished by any shade of color." *Excerpts*, 107. The dynamic aspect of the mind or numinous awareness is distinguished in two ways: as the innate function of the self-nature and the function which adapts to conditions. Awareness is originally thoughtless and formless, but when it adapts to conditions, it produces all phenomena and activities. See *Excerpts*, 114–15.

107. *Excerpts*, in *Numinous Awareness*, 161

108. *Excerpts*, in *Numinous Awareness*, 100.

109. See Buswell, introduction to *CSW*, 63.

110. *Moguja's Secrets*, in *CSW*, 213.

111. *Moguja's Secrets*, in *CSW*, 213.

112. *Moguja's Secrets*, in *CSW*, 216–17: 答。頓悟者 凡夫迷時 四大爲身 妄想爲心 不知自性是眞法身 不知自己靈知是眞佛 ... 一念廻光 見自本性。而此性地 元無煩惱 無漏智性 本自具足 卽與諸佛 分毫不殊 故云頓悟也。漸修者 雖悟本性 與佛無殊 無始習氣 難卒頓除。故依悟而修 漸熏功成 長養聖胎 久久成聖 故云漸修也。(比如孩子 初生之日 諸根具足 與他無異 然其力未充 頗經歲月方始成人。) Bracketed insertions in original. For Zongmi's explanation of sudden awakening and gradual cultivation as quoted by Chinul, see *Excerpts*, in *Numinous Awareness*, 116–20.

113. *Moguja's Secrets*, in *CSW*, 227.

114. According to Kim Kun-su's record of the life of Chinul, the development of the Three Paths is closely related with Chinul's three awakening experiences, each of which is associated with a different Buddhist text. *Funerary Inscription*, in *CSW*, 370–74, 376. Ch'oe Yŏn-sik also sees the relationship among the three approaches as a sequential development and thus sees the development of the Three Paths as the outline of the development of Chinul's thought. See Yŏn-sik Ch'oe (Yeonshik Choe), "Chinul Sŏn sasang ŭi sasangsajŏk kŏmt'o," *Tongbang hakchi* 144 (2008): 146–47.

115. For Li Tongxuan's influence on Chinul, see Buswell, introduction to *CSW*, 47–55, and Jae-ryong Shim, *Korean Buddhism: Tradition and Transformation* (Seoul: Jimoondang, 1999), 59–76. This section is indebted to Buswell, introduction to *CSW*, 71–75, and Hee-sung Keel, *Chinul*, 90–110.

116. *Encouragement to Practice*, in *CSW*, 157–60. For the process of "tracing back the radiance" employed in the path of faith and understanding, see Buswell, introduction to *CSW*, 62–67.

117. *Huayan Jing* explains the fifty-two stages (五十二位) to enlightenment, which consists of ten stages of faith 十信, ten abidings (or abodes) 十住, ten practices 十行, ten dedications of merits 十廻向, ten grounds 十地, and two stages of buddhahood: virtual (or impartial) enlightenment 等覺 and marvelous (or sublime) enlightenment 妙覺. See Buswell and Lopez, *The Princeton Dictionary of Buddhism*, s.v. "*Avataṃsakasūtra*"; and also *Digital Dictionary of Buddhism*, s.v. "五十二位."

118. The definitions of both the "sudden" and "complete" teachings are based on the fivefold Huayan taxonomy of Buddhist teachings. See Buswell, introduction to *CSW*, 97–98.

119. Buswell, introduction to *CSW*, 71.

120. Buswell, introduction to *CSW*, 67–68.

121. See *Encouragement to Practice*, in *CSW*, 137.

122. *Encouragement to Practice*, in *CSW*, 136.

123. Kŏn-gi Kang, *Chŏnghye kyŏlsa mun kangŭi*, 130.

124. *Encouragement to Practice*, in *CSW*, 143 (bracketed insertions mine).

125. *Encouragement to Practice*, in *CSW*, 143.

126. *Encouragement to Practice*, in *CSW*, 149.

127. This introduction to Chinul's path of the concurrent cultivation of *samādhi* and *prajñā* is greatly indebted to Buswell, introduction to *CSW*, 67–71; Hee-sung Keel, *Chinul*, 110–43; Kŏn-gi Kang, *Chŏnghye kyŏlsa mun kangŭi*, 151–208.

128. See *Excerpts*, in *Numinous Awareness*, 186; *Resolving Doubts*, in *CSW*, 318–19. This brief explanation of the shortcut path of the *kanhwa* Sŏn is indebted to

Buswell, introduction to *CSW*, 75–88; see also Hee-sung Keel, *Chinul*, 144–59. For a brief explanation of *kanhua Chan*, see Buswell and Lopez, *The Princeton Dictionary of Buddhism*, s.v. "kanhua Chan." For detailed studies of Dahui and the development of *huatou* meditation, see Morten Schlütter, *How Zen Became Zen: The Dispute over Enlightenment and the Formation of Chan Buddhism in Song-Dynasty China* (Honolulu: University of Hawaii Press, 2008), 107–16.

129. Although Sŏn adepts distinguish themselves from Kyo monks by scorning scriptural and doctrinal studies, it is ironic that the Sŏn school is indebted to its counterpart for the development of its principles, which greatly draw on the sūtras, including *Laṅkatāra Sūtra* (C. *Lengjia jing* 楞伽經) and *Diamond Sūtra*. The essential concepts of "mind" and "nature" had been developed in philosophical systems like Dilun 地論, Sanlun 三論, Tiantai 天台, Faxing 法相, and Huayan 華嚴. The Sŏn school therefore cannot deny its debt to the Kyo school. In addition, even though a nearly exclusive emphasis on meditation would seem to have been unique to the Sŏn school, even before the development of Sŏn as a separate Buddhist school, there had been efforts to incorporate the practical act of contemplation into the doctrinal teachings, for example by the Tiantai and Huayan schools. For this reason, "Chan Buddhism, both in its thought and practice, was the culmination of the Chinese Buddhist spirit rather than a novelty in Chinese Buddhism." See Hee-sung Keel, *Chinul*, 57–58. Heinrich Dumoulin too acknowledges the significant role of scriptures and doctrine by attributing the flowering of Chan primarily to two major factors: "The Mahāyāna sūtras, which provides its religious-metaphysical roots, and the Chinese spirit, which provides its distinctive dynamics." Dumoulin, *Zen Buddhism*, 41.

130. *Encouragement to Practice*, in *CSW*, 164: 若隨語生見 齊文作解 逐敎迷心 指月不分 未忘名聞利養之心 而欲說法度人者 如穢蝸螺 自穢穢他。是乃世間文字法師 何名專精定慧 不求名聞者乎。 Bracketed insertion in original.

131. *Encouragement to Practice*, in *CSW*, 164.

132. *Encouragement to Practice*, in *CSW*, 165.

133. *Encouragement to Practice*, in *CSW*, 166: 但時中觀行餘暇 不妨披詳聖敎 及古德入道因緣 決擇邪正 利他利己而已。

134. *Encouragement to Practice*, in *CSW*, 116–17: 知訥 自妙年 投身祖域 遍參禪肆 詳其佛祖垂慈爲物之門。要令我輩 休息諸緣 虛心冥契 不外馳求。

135. *Encouragement to Practice*, in *CSW*, 130.

136. *Encouragement to Practice*, in *CSW*, 133–35, 161–62.

137. *Moguja's Secrets*, in *CSW*, 219, 220; see also 225: "But since your doubts persist, it seems that I will have to explain it again. You should clear your minds and listen carefully."

138. *Excerpts*, in *Numinous Awareness*, 165: 是諸佛菩薩 慈悲痛切 爲修心出世人 傾割肝膽 發誠實語 指出修行徑要之處 知訥感遇慶懷 特以此法 盡命受持 亦勸同學人 依而行之。 H 4.758b21–c1.

139. *Excerpts*, in *Numinous Awareness*, 97: 今爲因敎悟心之者 除去繁詞 鈔出綱要 以爲觀行龜鑑。 H 4.741a6–8 (bracketed insertion in original).

140. See *Excerpts*, in *Numinous Awareness*, 148.

141. Yŏng-suk Im, "Chinul ch'ansul sŏnsŏ wa kŭ soŭikyŏngjŏn e kwanhan yŏn'gu," 251–67. The numerical results of the survey can be found on pp. 262–66 of

the article. The methodology of the survey was as follows: (1) counting the number of quotations or citations for each category of text or author; (2) categorizing mentions of only the name of a Sŏn master without quotation of the Sŏn master; (3) categorizing references to *kongan* according to the associated Sŏn master; (4) categorizing references to a school according to the founder of that school; (5) categorizing ambiguous references, such as those to "sūtra," "Sŏn master," or "ancient sage," according to the text or author if its attribution can be determined; otherwise, categorizing them according to the terms used by Chinul; and (6) listing the results according to the number of references to a category of sūtra, a treatise or commentary, a Sŏn text, etc.

142. The seven texts are as follows: *Encouragement to Practice: The Compact of the Samādhi and Prajñā Society, Moguja's Secrets on Cultivating the Mind, Admonitions to Neophytes, Straight Talk on the True Mind, Treatises on Resolving Doubts about Observing the Keyword, Excerpts from the Dharma Collection and Special Practice Record with Personal Notes,* and *Treatise on the Complete and Sudden Attainment of Buddhahood.*

143. Chinul refers to Dahui once in *Complete and Sudden Attainment.*

144. *Funerary Inscription,* in *CSW,* 371.

145. See *Encouragement to Practice,* in *CSW,* 173. It should also be noted that the criteria used in the survey should arguably be reconsidered to include implicit references to texts or masters. For example, Im Yŏng-suk recognizes three references to Zongmi's writings in *Encouragement to Practice.* However, according to Buswell, Chinul made other references that can be linked to Zongmi, whether a disciple's commentary on Zongmi's writings that may have been influenced by Zongmi, or a comparison between two things originally made by Zongmi. See Buswell, annotations to *Encouragement to Practice,* 147n49, 135n24.

146. There is also the question of whether Chinul drew all his quotations directly from original sources or from encyclopedic anthologies or epitomes. For example, Yongming Yanshou's *Zongjing lu* 宗經錄 [*Records of the Mirror of the Source*] comprises hundreds of scriptures and sayings of eminent Chan masters, which, in addition to other similar encyclopedic texts, could have been the source of particular citations by Chinul. Also, since Chinul sometimes seems to assume that his readers are already familiar with cited texts, he does not provide proper references to them. See Buswell and Lopez, *The Princeton Dictionary of Buddhism,* s.v. "Zongjing lu"; Yŏng-sŏp Ko, "Pojo Chinul ŭi sasang hyŏngsŏng e yŏnghyang ŭl kkich'in kosŭng," 25. Ko Yŏng-sŏp does not deny the possibility that Chinul might have drawn many of his citations from *Zongjing lu,* but he assumes that Chinul might actually have read a significant number of the scriptures he refers to.

147. Yŏng-sŏp Ko, "Pojo Chinul ŭi sasang hyŏngsŏng e yŏnghyang ŭl kkich'in kosŭng," 13–53.

148. Yŏng-sŏp Ko, "Pojo Chinul ŭi sasang hyŏngsŏng e yŏnghyang ŭl kkich'in kosŭng," 26–30.

149. Yŏng-sŏp Ko, "Pojo Chinul ŭi sasang hyŏngsŏng e yŏnghyang ŭl kkich'in kosŭng," 33. See also Hee-sung Keel, *Chinul,* 59–61.

150. Buswell, introduction to *CSW,* 47. Peter N. Gregory shows that while advocating the balanced cultivation of *samādhi* and *prajñā,* Zongmi also correlates

samādhi with meditative practice and *prajñā* with textual studies. Chinul too promotes both the balanced cultivation of *samādhi* and *prajñā* and acknowledges the need of both textual study and meditation; nevertheless, he does not explicate the correlations between *samādhi*/meditation and *prajñā*/textual study as Zongmi did. Gregory also discusses the close relationship between the soteriological schemes of the sudden awakening/gradual cultivation and the practical approach of the balanced cultivation of *samādhi* and *prajñā*. See Peter N. Gregory, "Bridging the Gap: Zongmi's Strategies for Reconciling Textual Study and Meditative Practice," *Journal of Chinese Buddhist Studies* 30 (2017): 89–124. See also Peter N. Gregory, "The Integration of Ch'an/Sŏn and The Teachings (*Chiao/Kyo*) in Tsung-mi and Chinul," *The Journal of the International Association of Buddhist Studies* 12, no. 2 (1989): 12–13.

151. For a brief summary of Zongmi's influence on Chinul, see Buswell, introduction to *CSW*, 41–47.

152. Gregory, "The Integration of Ch'an/Sŏn and The Teachings (*Chiao/Kyo*) in Tsung-mi and Chinul," 9, 17. For a biographical introduction to Zongmi, see Gregory, *Tsung-mi and the Sinification of Buddhism*, 27–90; Jeffrey Lyle Broughton, *Zongmi on Chan* (New York: Columbia University Press, 2009), 1–9.

153. Gregory, *Sinification of Buddhism*, 53.

154. Gregory, "The Integration of Ch'an/Sŏn and The Teachings (*Chiao/Kyo*) in Tsung-mi and Chinul," 7–19. Gregory attributes the twofold scheme that demonstrates the compatibility of Chan and Jiao to Yoshizu Yoshihide, *Kegonzen no shiōshi-teki kenkyū* (Tokyo: Daitō shuppansha, 1985).

155. This text is a preface to *The Collection of Expressions of the Chan Source* (C. *Chanyuan zhuquanji duxu* 禪源諸詮集都序), *Taishō shinshū daizōkyō* 大正新修大藏經 2015:48.397–414 (hereafter cited as "T") which provides a comprehensive overview of the extensive, one-hundred-roll collection of Chan prose and verse. For an introduction to *Chan Prolegomenon*, see Broughton, *Zongmi on Chan*, 26–59; Buswell and Lopez, *The Princeton Dictionary of Buddhism*, s.v. "Chanyuan zhuquanji duxu."

156. *Chan Prolegomenon*, in *Zongmi on Chan*, 109: 初言師有本末者 謂諸宗始祖即是釋迦。經是佛語 禪是佛意 諸佛心口必不相違。T 2015:48.0400b10–11. Bracked insertions of the Chinese terms mine.

157. *Preface from Condensation of the Exposition*, in *CSW*, 358.

158. *Chan Prolegomenon*, in *Zongmi on Chan*, 109–10; T 2015:48.0400b10–28.

159. Gregory, "The Integration of Ch'an/Sŏn and The Teachings (*Chiao/Kyo*) in Tsung-mi and Chinul," 11–12.

160. *Chan Prolegomenon*, in *Zongmi on Chan*, 113; T 2015:48.0401a08–21.

161. For the historical development of doctrinal classification in general and in the Huayan tradition specifically, see Broughton, *Zongmi*, 93–135.

162. *Chan Prolegomenon*, in *Zongmi on Chan*, 120–41; T 2015:48.0402b15–405c29.

163. Buswell's English translation of the two terms 全揀 (C. *quanjian*, K. *chŏn'gan*) and 全收 (C. *quanshou*, K. *chŏnsu*) in his latest translation of *Excerpts* is acceptable. See *Numinous Awareness*, 167. In the English translation of Chinul's corpus published in 1983, Buswell translates the two terms as "radical analysis" and "comprehensive association," respectively. See *The Korean Approach to Zen*, 318.

164. *Chan Prolegomenon*, in *Zongmi on Chan*, 111: 局之則皆非。會之則皆是。
T 2015:48.0400c21–22. Bracketed insertion in original.

165. *Chan Prolegomenon*, in *Zongmi on Chan*, 111–12: 若不以佛語各示其意
各收其長。統爲三宗對於三教。(則何以會爲一代善巧俱成要妙法門。各忘其
情同歸智海) 唯佛所説即異而同。故約佛經會三爲一。 T 2015:48.0400c22–25.
Bracketed insertion in original.

166. *Chan Prolegomenon*, in *Zongmi on Chan*, 112: 三經如繩墨揩定邪正者。繩
墨非巧。工巧者必以繩墨爲憑。T 2015:48.0400c25–26.

167. Gregory, "The Integration of Ch'an/Sŏn and The Teachings (*Chiao/Kyo*) in
Tsung-mi and Chinul," 16.

168. Although Chinul treats the schools in a more inclusive way than did Zongmi,
like Zongmi he discounts the value of the northern school.

169. *Excerpts*, in *Numinous Awareness*, 171: 禪宗全揀門者 但剗體 直指心性 本
來常寂 絶諸待對爾。 非爲取捨 是乃全收中全揀也。H 4.760a12–14.

170. *Dharma Master* Ŭisang's 義湘/相 (625–702) *Gāthā* [Chart of the one-vehicle
Dharmadhātu of Hwaŏm (*Hwaŏm ilsŭng pŏpkye to*)] states: "The dharma-nature is
perfectly interfused and free from any sign of duality. / All dharmas are unmoving
and originally quiescent. / Nameless, signless, it [the dharma-nature] eradicates everything; / It is what the realization-wisdom knows, nothing else. / The true nature is
extremely deep and exceedingly sublime. / By not guarding any nature of its own, it
can freely adapt according to conditions. / In one is everything, in many is one. / One
is precisely everything, many are precisely one." *Excerpts*, in *Numinous Awareness*,
169–70: 如義湘法師偈云 「法性圓明無二相 諸法不動本來寂 離名離相絶一切
證智所知非餘境 眞性甚深極微妙 不守自性隨緣成 一中一切多中一 一即一切多
即一等」。 H 4.759b14–19.

171. *Excerpts*, in *Numinous Awareness*, 170: 此則先明眞性 離名絶相 次明眞性
緣起無碍。H 4.759b19–20.

172. *Excerpts*, in *Numinous Awareness*, 170; H 4.759b14–c1. For a discussion of
Chinul's synthesis of Sŏn and Hwaŏm employing the approaches of radical rejection ("radical analysis") and radical acceptance ("comprehensive assimilation"), see
Pyŏng-uk Yi, "Chongmil kwa Pojo ŭi sŏn'gyogwan pigyo," *Pojo sasang* 12 (1999):
102–8.

173. *Excerpts*, in *Numinous Awareness*, 171.

174. For a comparison between Fazang and Li Tongxuan, as well as Fazang's
influence on Li, see Jae-ryong Shim, *Korean Buddhism: Tradition and Transformation*, 59–74.

175. Sudhana (C. Shancai, K. Sŏnjae 善財) was a young pilgrim whose spiritual
journey is described in the final chapter of *Huayan jing* or *Avataṃsakasūtra*. See
Buswell and Lopez, *The Princeton Dictionary of Buddhism*, s.v. "Sudhana."

176. On the attainment of buddhahood over three lifetimes, see Buswell, annotation to *Resolving Doubts*, in *CSW*, 337n40.

177. *Complete and Sudden Attainment*, in *CSW*, 279: (又如出現品偈云 「佛智亦
如是 遍在衆生心 妄想之所纏 不覺亦不知。諸佛大慈悲 令其除妄想 如是乃出現
饒益諸菩薩。」 此是一一衆生心中 生佛互融恒然之義也。又論云) 「雖然安立
十信及五位次第 畢竟成普賢行 因滿果終 時亦不移 普光明智亦不異。此觀行及

者 了知此十種信心 直至佛果普賢行滿以來 一時摠解 名爲信心也。此是今日大心衆生 初發信心 因果同時也。」 Bracketed insertions in original. This passage is attributed to Li Tongxuan by Chinul, but has not been traced back to a specific source. See Buswell, annotation to *Complete and Sudden Attainment*, in *CSW*, 279n50.

178. For a brief explanation of the doctrines of nature origination and conditioned origination, see Buswell and Lopez, *The Princeton Dictionary of Buddhism*, s.vv. "xingqi," "fajie yuanqi"; for the historical development of causation theories in Chinese Buddhism, see Whalen Lai, "Chinese Buddhist Causation Theories: An Analysis of the Sinitic Mahayana Understanding of Pratityasamutpada," *Philosophy East and West* 27, no. 3 (July 1977): 241–64.

179. On the superiority of *shishi wu'ai fajie* over *lishi wu'ai fajie*, see Lai, "Chinese Buddhist Causation Theories," 256.

180. The conversation with the Hwaŏm scholar is in *Preface from Condensation of the Exposition*, in *CSW*, 356. The entire conversation is as follows: 然終疑 '華嚴教中悟入之門 果如何' 耳。遂往問講者 對曰 「當觀事事無碍。」 隨而誠之曰 「汝徒但觀自心 不觀事事無碍卽失佛果圓德。」 余不對 默自念言 「將心觀事事卽有碍 徒擾自心 何有了時? 但心明智淨 則毛刹容融必 非外境。」 See also *Complete and Sudden Attainment*, in *CSW*, 267–68.

181. *Preface from Condensation of the Exposition*, in *CSW*, 356–57: 退歸山中 坐閱大藏 求佛語之契心宗者 凡三周寒暑。至閱華嚴經出現品 舉一塵含大千經卷之喻 後合云 「如來智慧 亦復如是 具足在於衆生身中 但諸凡愚 不知不覺。」 予頂戴經卷 不覺殞涕。 Bracketed insertions in original.

182. *Preface from Condensation of the Exposition*, in *CSW*, 357–58: 覺首菩薩者有三。一覺自身心 本是法界 白淨無染故。二覺自身心分別之性 本無能所 本來是不動智佛。三覺自心 善簡擇正邪妙慧 是文殊師利。於信心之初 覺此三法 名爲覺首。」 Bracketed insertion in original.

183. *Preface from Condensation of the Exposition*, in *CSW*, 358: (「身爲智影 國土亦然 智淨影明 大小相入 如因陁羅網境界也。」) 於是 置卷長歎曰 「世尊說之於口卽爲敎 祖師傳之於心卽爲禪。佛祖心口 必不相違 豈可不窮根源 而各安所習 妄興諍論 虛喪天日耶?」 從此益加信心 勤修匪懈 于兹積歲矣。 Bracketed insertion in original

184. Buswell, introduction to *CSW*, 96.

185. *Complete and Sudden Attainment*, in *CSW*, 247–48: 或問牧牛子曰。聞汝所立 <今時修心人 先以自心日用之種 便爲諸佛不動智然後 依性修禪 方爲妙爾。> 此中不動智佛果 是本覺理佛耶 是新成事佛耶。 Bracketed insertions in original. Ch'oe Sŏng-nyŏl argues that the statement in this quotation that precedes the question summarizes Chinul's Sŏn theory and that the remainder of the treatise expounds on the compatibility of Sŏn and Hwaŏm in the literary form of question and response. Sŏng-nyŏl Ch'oe, "Pojo Chinul ŭi *Wondon Sŏngbullon* punsŏk," 132.

186. Buswell, annotation to *Complete and Sudden Attainment*, in *CSW*, 247–48n2. "Tathāgata" itself is one of the most common epithets of the Buddha and means "one who has thus come/gone."

187. Chŏng Hŭi-kyŏng examines how Chinul verifies the Sŏn approach of sudden awakening/gradual cultivation by employing both the doctrines of nature origination and conditioned origination. She further shows the compatibility of

Sŏn and Hwaŏm by demonstrating that both Hwaŏm and Sŏn advocate the same soteriological process—understanding-awakening→gradual cultivation→realization-awakening→gradual cultivation. See Hŭi-kyŏng Chŏng, "Pojo Chinul ŭi Sŏn-Kyo ilch'I e taehan chaegoch'al," 118–28.

188. There are five questions/responses in *Complete and Sudden Attainment*, which are set forth in the five subsections with a bracketed number below.

189. According to Li Tongxuan, the phrase "ordinary persons of great aspiration," refers to those who are capable of attaining the understanding-awakening. Chinul's various soteriological expositions are intended for these people, not for ordinary people with inferior faculties. About "ordinary persons of great aspiration," see Buswell, annotation to *Complete and Sudden Attainment*, in *CSW*, 253n15.

190. "Bodhicitta" means the thought or resolve to attain enlightenment.

191. *Complete and Sudden Attainment*, in *CSW*, 253–56: 詳夫論主旨趣 要以分析華嚴大義 令末世大心凡夫 於生死地面上 頓悟諸佛不動智 以爲初悟發心之源也。 Bracketed insertion in original.

192. According to Hwaŏm teachings, Mahāyāna soteriology or the bodhisattva path consists of fifty-two stages as described above in n. 117. In Chinul's text, the "five levels" (*owi* 五位) refer to the five stages from ten abidings to virtual enlightenment, considering the ten faiths as a preliminary stage of the path. See Buswell, annotation to *Conclusion from Condensation of the Exposition*, in *CSW*, 361n13; Buswell, annotation to *Encouragement to Practice*, in *CSW*, 152n58. See also *Digital Dictionary of Buddhism*, s.vv. "osibi wi," "五十二位." Shim Jae-ryong explains that the soteriological scheme of fifty-two stages was established by Fazang with the ten stages of faith added to the established forty-one stages (which do not include the ultimate stage of enlightenment) as initial or preparatory stages on the whole path to enlightenment. See Jae-ryong Shim, *Korean Buddhism: Tradition and Transformation*, 59–60.

193. *Conclusion from Condensation of the Exposition*, in *CSW*, 361–62: 牧牛子曰。審此論所明 三乘佛果 在十地之後 一乘佛果 在十信初心。若約入位言之 在初發心住。若入十信初心 任運至十住初心 若入住初 任運至究竟位。如是則具縛凡夫初發正信之心 最爲要門。 Bracketed insertions in original.

194. In English, "eon." A *kalpa* is the longest time period in the Indian cosmology. See *Digital Dictionary of Buddhism*, s.vv. "jie," "劫."

195. See *Complete and Sudden Attainment*, in *CSW*, 250.

196. *Complete and Sudden Attainment*, in *CSW*, 265–66: 此論主所示 生佛互融之義 要令觀心入道之者 常須自信自己身語意 及境界之相 皆從如來身語意境界中生。

197. The Golden World of the East is one of ten colored worlds where different wisdom buddhas and chief bodhisattvas reside. Buswell explains: "The Golden World of the East symbolizes the fact that the mind-ground of sentient beings is the pure and undefiled *dharmadhātu* of the self-nature. This world itself represents the pure and undefiled ideal essence of the fundamental nature of sentient beings." Buswell, annotation to *Complete and Sudden Attainment*, in *CSW*, 255n18. The Buddha of Immovable Wisdom and Mañjuśri bodhisattva reside in this world. For more detailed information, see Buswell, annotations to *Complete and Sudden Attainment*, 253–56nn16–20.

198. *Complete and Sudden Attainment*, in *CSW*, 254. *Dharmakāya* or dharma-body (C. *fashen*, K. *pŏpsin*, 法身) is one of three bodies or three aspects of a buddha (S. *trikāya*): *dharmakāya*, the dharma-body or truth-body; *saṃbhogakāya*, the enjoyment-body or reward-body; and *nirmāṇakāya*, the emanation-body or transformation-body. *Dharmakāya* is the true body of reality or absolute existence. It is also identified with *tathāgatagarbha* or "buddha-nature" and the one mind (C. *yixin*, K. *ilsim* 一心). See *Digital Dictionary of Buddhism*, s.vv. "fashen," "pŏpsin," "法身"; Buswell and Lopez, *The Princeton Dictionary of Buddhism*, s.v. "trikāya."

199. *Complete and Sudden Attainment*, in *CSW*, 254–56: (又擧十色世界 十智如來 十首菩薩 表法示之 令其易解。 先擧東方金色世界 令發心者 信是自己白淨無垢法身之理也) 本所事佛 是不動智佛 直信自己無明分別之種 本是諸佛不動智也 上首菩薩 是文殊師利 直信自己根本智中 善揀擇無相妙慧也。

200. See Buswell, annotation to *Complete and Sudden Attainment*, in *CSW*, 255n18.

201. *Complete and Sudden Attainment*, in *CSW*, 257–58: 若約行布門則已成果智盧舍那佛 與縛地位中不修衆生 云何混濫耶? Bracketed insertions in original.

202. The sequential fifty-two stages of the bodhisattva to enlightenment.

203. See Buswell, annotation to *Complete and Sudden Attainment*, in *CSW*, 257–58n23.

204. *Complete and Sudden Attainment*, in *CSW*, 258–60: 然審論文所示之義 所言不動智 亦是根本普光明智 當此根本智 名之爲諸佛果智也。 此根本智 是理事性相生佛自他染淨因果之體性故。 Bracketed insertion in original.

205. See Buswell, annotation to *Complete and Sudden Attainment*, in *CSW*, 259n25.

206. *Complete and Sudden Attainment*, in *CSW*, 260–62, 265–66.

207. *Complete and Sudden Attainment*, in *CSW*, 266.

208. *Complete and Sudden Attainment*, in *CSW*, 261.

209. *Complete and Sudden Attainment*, in *CSW*, 262–63.

210. See Buswell, annotation to *Complete and Sudden Attainment*, in *CSW*, 264n33.

211. Vairocana Buddha is considered to be the personification of the wisdom of Buddhahood and is also identified with the *dharmakāya* Buddha. See Buswell and Lopez, *The Princeton Dictionary of Buddhism*, s.v. "Vairocana."

212. *Complete and Sudden Attainment*, in *CSW*, 273–74.

213. *Complete and Sudden Attainment*, in *CSW*, 267.

214. In his comprehensive study of Buddhist causation theories, Whalen Lai notes that "[*Xingqi* or nature origination] can imply the awakening of the buddha-essence in man, and it would correspond to the concept of the arousal of the *bodhicitta*, the mind of enlightenment." Since the buddha-nature is the source that generates the phenomenal realm, once one awakens to the buddha-nature, he will also simultaneously and instantaneously awaken to the *dharmadhātu* of unobstructed interpenetration among phenomena. See Lai, "Chinese Buddhist Causation Theories," 259 (bracketed insertion mine).

215. *Complete and Sudden Attainment*, in *CSW*, 263–64: 此經如來出現品云 <菩薩摩訶薩 應知自心念念常有佛成正覺> 爲明諸佛如來 不離此心 成正覺故。 又

云 <一切眾生 心亦如是 悉有如來成正覺。> 此明凡聖心 自體清淨無異 但有迷悟 不隔分毫 . . . 」Bracketed insertions in original.

216. *Complete and Sudden Attainment*, in *CSW*, 270: 又論主頌云 「佛是眾生心裏佛 隨自根堪無異物。欲知一切諸佛源 悟自無明本是佛。」Bracketed insertion in original. This passage is quoted from Yongming Yanshou's *Mirror of the Source Record* (C. *Zongjing lu*), but the authorship of Li is not confirmed. Buswell, annotation to *Complete and Sudden Attainment*, in *CSW*, 270n42.

217. *Complete and Sudden Attainment*, in *CSW*, 271.

218. *Complete and Sudden Attainment*, in *CSW*, 273–80.

219. *Complete and Sudden Attainment*, in *CSW*, 283–84: 如是等開悟本心 得見自心鏡內 帝網重重無盡法界者 禪門傳記中 不可勝數。 Bracketed insertion in original.

220. Buswell, annotation to *Complete and Sudden Attainment*, in *CSW*, 283–84n55.

221. *Complete and Sudden Attainment*, in *CSW*, 274: 答。前已論之 但息心無諍虛懷內照 成辦妙果爲要 何更問耶?

222. *Complete and Sudden Attainment*, in *CSW*, 284–85: (非謂華嚴敎門說理未盡 但學者 滯在言敎義理分際 未能忘義了心 速證菩提。所以達摩西來 欲令知月不在指) 法是我心故 不立文字 以心傳心耳。是以禪門 只貴破執現宗 不貴繁辭義理施設。 Bracketed insertions mine.

223. *Complete and Sudden Attainment*, in *CSW*, 284–85.

224. *Complete and Sudden Attainment*, in *CSW*, 285–86; Buswell, annotation to *Complete and Sudden Attainment,* in *CSW*, 286n60.

225. *Complete and Sudden Attainment*, in *CSW*, 286–87.

226. *Complete and Sudden Attainment*, in *CSW*, 288.

227. *Complete and Sudden Attainment*, in *CSW*, 293, 287–93.

228. *Complete and Sudden Attainment*, in *CSW*, 294–95.

229. *Complete and Sudden Attainment*, in *CSW*, 296: 問。今日凡夫悟心成佛者 是究竟耶 未究竟耶? (若是究竟 何名初心 若未究竟 何名正覺?)

230. *Complete and Sudden Attainment*, in *CSW*, 298.

231. For the six aspects, see Li's explanation quoted by Chinul in *Complete and Sudden Attainment*, in *CSW*, 300–302, and Buswell and Lopez, *The Princeton Dictionary of Buddhism*, s.v. "liuxiang."

232. *Complete and Sudden Attainment*, in *CSW*, 302: 又以一智慧 該收五位 名爲摠相 行解昇進 名爲別相 同佛根本智 名爲同相 修差別智 名爲異相 成大菩提 具普賢行 名爲成相 智體無依用而不作 名爲壞相。 Bracketed insertions in original.

233. *Complete and Sudden Attainment*, in *CSW*, 300.

234. Chŏng Hŭi-kyŏng connects the two distinctive aspects of consummate interfusion 圓融 (*wŏnyung*) and progressive practice 行布 (*haengp'o*) associated with the doctrine of conditioned origination with the two aspects of universality and particularity. Hŭi-kyŏng Chŏng, "Pojo Chinul ŭi Sŏn Kyo ilch'i e taehan chaegoch'al," 121.

235. *Complete and Sudden Attainment*, in *CSW*, 306.

236. Yi Pyŏng-uk argues that the primary claim of *Complete and Sudden Attainment* is that the approach of sudden awakening and gradual cultivation is the perfect principle of Buddhist practice and that it corresponds to the Hwaŏm school. Pyŏng-uk

Yi, "Pojo Chinul ŭi Sŏn-Kyo t'onghap ŭi yŏrŏ yuhyŏng," 120. See also Hŭi-kyŏng Chŏng, "Pojo Chinul ŭi Sŏn Kyo ilch'i e taehan chaegoch'al," 118–33.

237. Śamatha, or "concentration meditation" (C. *zhi*, K. *chi* 止), is a meditative practice whose intention is the cessation of thoughts, and *vipaśyanā,* "investigation meditation" (C. *guan*, K. *kwan* 觀), is a meditative practice that investigates the principle of things with the aid of concentration.

238. In *Pŏpchip pyŏrhaeng nok* (*Excerpts*), quoted by Chinul in *Encouragement to Practice*, the difference between śamatha-vipaśyanā and *samādhi* and *prajñā* is briefly explained.

> When one first arouses the *bodhicitta* and begins to cultivate, they are called śamatha-vipaśyanā. (Śamatha brings external conditioning to rest and hence conforms with calmness; *vipaśyanā* illuminates nature and characteristics and hence corresponds to awareness.) When the practice continues naturally in all situations, they are called samādhi and prajñā. (Because it fuses the mind in concentration through its efficacy in stopping all conditioning, samādhi is calm and immutable. Because it generates wisdom through its efficacy of illuminating insight, prajñā is aware and undiscriminative.) When the afflictions have been completely extinguished, meritorious practices completely fulfilled, and buddhahood attained, they are called bodhi and nirvana. (Bodhi is a Sanskrit word meaning enlightenment; it is awareness. Nirvāna is a Sanskrit word meaning calm-extinction; it is calmness.) Hence, you should know that from the time of the first arousal of the *bodhicitta* until the ultimate [achievement of buddhahood], there is only calmness and only awareness. (Here, when we refer to "only calmness and only awareness," this means alertness and calmness.) (*Encouragement to Practice*, in *CSW*, 154–55. Bracketed insertion in original.)

239. In the English version, Buswell translates 證悟入位 as "accessing the [remaining four] levels [of the bodhisattva path] through the realization-awakening." However, the phrase literally means "entering the levels through the realization-awakening," and it should be translated as "the remaining *five* levels," taking into consideration the phrase that follows it, which enlists five levels: ten abidings, ten practices, ten dedications, ten *bhūmis*, and the level of impartial enlightenment. See Buswell, annotation to *Encouragement to Practice*, in *CSW*, 152n58; Hŭi-kyŏng Chŏng, "Pojo Chinul ŭi Sŏn Kyo ilch'i e taehan chaegoch'al," 125n20.

240. *Complete and Sudden Attainment*, in *CSW*, 312–13: 若約漸修緣起門 則十信初心先悟之後 勤修止觀 色心有漏摠盡 至住初定力已成 解礙摠亡 證悟入位 歷修十住十行十廻向十地 至等覺位 是修自業所見眞體中 所現自己三世因果 及報佛境界等 如對目前。Bracketed insertions in original. See also *Complete and Sudden Attainment*, 298–99.

241. There is a twofold division of cultivation in the path to enlightenment in the Hwaŏm school: (1) cultivation after sudden awakening throughout the ten levels of faith for an ordinary person still affected by the proclivities of habit; and (2) cultivation of discriminating wisdom as a bodhisattva after the attainment of the perfect wisdom of a buddha for the sake of all sentient beings until reaching the ultimate stage of buddhahood. This twofold division of cultivation is also present in the Heze school. By showing that Chinul too divided gradual cultivation into two levels by adapting Heze teaching, Chŏng Hŭi-kyŏng demonstrates Chinul's claim of the compatibility

between Sŏn and Kyo. See Hŭi-kyŏng Chŏng, "Pojo Chinul ŭi Sŏn Kyo ilch'i e taehan chaegoch'al," 128–33.

242. See also *Complete and Sudden Attainment*, in *CSW*, 262, 298–99.

243. Hŭi-kyŏng Chŏng, "Pojo Chinul ŭi Sŏn Kyo ilch'i e taehan chaegoch'al,"
138–40.

244. See *Excerpts*, in *Numinous Awareness*, 290–92.

245. Chŏng Hŭi-kyŏng argues that Chinul's understanding of realization-awakening as a stage that grants access to the first level of ten abidings is a reflection of his
own awakening experience, and that this insight occurred to him in his encounter with
the *Records* of Dahui. As described above, in this incident, according to Kim Kun-su,
Chinul experienced a sudden disappearance of something that had been blocking his
chest. *Funeral Inscription*, in *CSW*, 374. Chŏng Hŭi-kyŏng considers this experience
to have been the dissolution of his cognitive obstructions, and argues that he incorporated realization-awakening into the stage of access to the bodhisattva path, in which
all cognitive obstructions completely vanish. See Hŭi-kyŏng Chŏng, "Pojo Chinul ŭi
Sŏn Kyo ilch'i e taehan chaegoch'al," 127. However, taking into consideration that
the connection between *kanhwa* Sŏn and realization-awakening is also mentioned in
Chinul's discussion of Chengguan and Zongmi, neither of whom had anything to do
with *kanhwa* Sŏn, Chŏng Hŭi-kyŏng's view may be too simplistic. See *Excerpts*, in
Numinous Awareness, 292.

246. Hŭi-kyŏng Chŏng, "Pojo Chinul ŭi Sŏn Kyo ilch'i e taehan chaegoch'al,"
138.

247. *Resolving Doubts*, in *CSW*, 346: 禪門徑截得入者 初無法義聞解當情 (直以
無滋味話頭 但提撕舉覺而已)。

Chapter Three

The Spiral Dialectics of Cataphasis and Apophasis in Bonaventure

The final section of chapter 1 investigated the *Itinerarium* and addressed Bonaventure's integration of Franciscan spirituality and the powers of the intellect. The section examined Bonaventure's six steps of contemplation, which begins with meditation on the material world, proceeds to an exploration of the soul, and finally comes to contemplate God in His Being and Goodness. This speculation moves from the things of the external world, through the mental activities of the soul, to the conceptual summit of the divine attributes. As Bonaventure describes it, the pilgrim encounters Jesus Christ at the end of this intellectual and spiritual pilgrimage. At this stage, the mind of the pilgrim reaches the perfection of intellectual illumination that has been inspired by the divine light. While Jesus Christ is the pinnacle of the intellectual pilgrimage, he is at the same time "the way and the door"[1] enabling the soul to pass over to the divine from the perceptible and conceptual world. Chapter 7 of the *Itinerarium*, the focus of this chapter, articulates this final stage and its apophatic, mystical nature.

Bonaventure insists that at the mystical and secret passage that comes at the final stage, the soul should abandon all intellectual activities, and instead should direct all devotions and affections toward God.[2] This articulation of the mystical stage of the journey, in particular the total renunciation of intellect, clearly reflects the apophatic theology of Pseudo-Dionysius the Areopagite, a Syrian writer of the late fifth and early sixth centuries, known pseudonymously as Dionysius the Areopagite after the Athenian who was converted to Christianity by Paul as described in Acts 17:34.[3] The Dionysian corpus,[4] which merged Neoplatonism and Christian theology in a distinctive way, had a great influence on medieval theology and spirituality—its significant contribution to the development of Christian mysticism both in the speculative and spiritual realms is undeniable.

Therefore, prior to exploring the final stage of the *Itinerarium*, it is necessary to survey the thought of Dionysius, including his apophatic and cataphatic theology as well as his understanding of the mystical journey. This will enable the reader to see clearly the influence of Dionysius on medieval intellectuals and Bonaventure's distinctive adaptation of Dionysian Neoplatonism. These preliminary matters will be followed by a close investigation of chapter 7 of the *Itinerarium*, focusing on Bonaventure's adaptation of Dionysian apophaticism and unique understanding of the divine union. Among other things, this investigation will provide insight into the confusion many readers of the *Itinerarium* experience when encountering the seventh chapter's drastic transition to an apophatic and affective discourse, abandoning all the previous steps.

DIONYSIAN DIALECTICS OF CATAPHATICISM AND APOPHATICISM

Mystical theology in the West—including that of Bonaventure—cannot be understood without taking into consideration the thoughts and writings of Dionysius. The Dionysian distinction between cataphatic and apophatic theological discourse has played an especially significant role in the development of this mystical theology.[5] The cataphatic theology engages primarily in affirmative discourse employing conceptual names or perceptual images of God and draws on the divine manifestation in creation, biblical revelation, and the sacraments. On the other hand, apophatic theology employs negative discourse that rejects affirmative words or concepts about God. This latter discourse is closely related to the transcendence or ineffability of God and emphasizes the limitations of language and concepts in understanding and speaking about God. Apophatic theology holds that no words can describe God properly and no intellectual activity is adequate to understand God; therefore, cataphatic theology involving concepts and analogies is "defective," as viewed from the divine perspective.[6]

The Purpose of Cataphatic Theology

The inadequacy of an intellectual and linguistic approach to knowing and speaking about God begs an inevitable question: If the human mind cannot ever reach a full understanding of God, what is the purpose of cataphatic discourse? Dionysius's *Divine Names* may provide an answer to this question. In this text, Dionysius enumerates various names of the divine based on the perceptible and conceptual. However, even in this apparently affirmative discourse of the divine names, he reminds the reader of the inexpressibility of the divine: "Indeed the inscrutable One is out of the reach of every rational process. Nor can any words come up to the inexpressible Good, this One, this Source of all unity, this supra-existent Being. Mind beyond mind and word beyond speech are gathered up by no discourse, by no intuition, by no name."[7] Nevertheless, Dionysius leaves room for an intellectual pursuit of union with God, denying absolute incommunicability: "By itself it [the Good] generously reveals a firm, transcendent beam, granting enlightenments proportionate to each being, and thereby draws sacred minds upward to its permitted contemplation, to participation and to the state of becoming like it."[8]

Dionysius draws on the scriptures for the intelligible names of the divinity; we can rely only on the Holy Spirit who truly comprehends the divine and has the power to grant glimpses of it through the scriptural writers.[9] For Dionysius, the scriptures communicate "the immeasurable and infinite in limited measures," and are the only means of such communication proportionate to our human capacities.[10] Yet it remains obvious to Dionysius that, however hard one strives, it is impossible to reach the transcendent one, who is "unsearchable and inscrutable."[11] The treatise on divine names does not aim at comprehending God or aspire to an unimpeded encounter with Him. Its purpose is rather to direct one's mind upward to God. Dionysius writes of those who make intellectual efforts to trace back to the Divine Truth through contemplating the divine names:

> They do not venture toward an impossibly daring sight of God, one beyond what is duly granted them. Nor do they go tumbling downward where their own natural inclinations would take them. No. Instead they are raised firmly and unswervingly upward in the direction of the ray which enlightens them, they take flight, reverently, wisely, in all holiness.[12]

Through the contemplation of the divine in its names, one's mind is made "prudent and holy," able to offer proper worship to the One who is beyond thoughts and words.[13] Even denial, the reverse of affirmation, is a way to "praise the Transcendent One in a transcending way."[14] In the *Mystical Theology*, Dionysius employs the analogy of a sculptor who reveals hidden beauty by "clearing aside" every inessential part of the original rock.[15] Therefore, although the ultimate form of praise would be made after the total cessation of all intellectual activities and at the moment of union with the divine, until then, the contemplative should use symbols and concepts related to God, while at the same time striving to distinguish these symbols and concepts from God by use of negations. This will allow an appreciation of the beauty of God in the most direct way possible.[16]

Praising God both affirmatively and negatively—though it seems para-doxical—is based on another of Dionysius's paradoxical claims regarding the doctrine of God: God is manifested in creation and is at the same time the divine transcendence above creation. On the one hand, the premise that God created all beings in the universe enables the positing of affirmative descriptions of the Cause of these beings that manifests itself in the created world. On the other hand, the transcendence of the Cause necessitates negation of all affirmations due to the inadequacy of human language and intelligence.[17]

While the doctrine of creation allows affirmations and the doctrine of transcendence demands negations, Dionysian apophaticism goes beyond both affirmation and negation. The ultimate goal of apophaticism is reached in understanding the inadequacy of both affirmation and negation,[18] and the final stage of Dionysian apophaticism is to enter into silence through the negation of all conceptual and perceptible things. Although the affirmative approach may not directly lead the contemplative to a transcendant union with God, it is nevertheless "a necessary, even penultimate stage" in the ascent toward God.[19] Thus, the contemplative praises God in his affirmative discourse about God, who reveals Himself in created beings, and at the same time he walks "the path to a deeper knowledge of God," who will reveal Himself in His hiddenness at the end of the road.[20]

The Nature of Mystical Union with the Divine

In the *Mystical Theology*, Dionysius presents Moses's ascent to Mount Sinai as an allegory of the journey to God, which involves moral preparation and the use of affirmative and negative discourses about God until there comes a point where total silence is demanded.[21]

> It is not for nothing that the blessed Moses is commanded to submit first to puri-fication and then to depart from those who have not undergone this. When every purification is complete, he hears the many-voiced trumpets. He sees the many lights, pure and streaming abundantly. Then, standing apart from the crowds and accompanied by chosen priests, he pushes ahead to the summit of the divine ascents. And yet he does not meet God himself, but contemplates, not him who is invisible, but rather where he dwells.[22]

Becoming holy through purification, Moses sets out to journey to the source of light, and the higher he climbs, the purer and brighter is the light he sees. However, even at the summit of the mountain he does not see God, but only encounters His dwelling place, surrounded by the cloud of unknowing. At this point, Moses plunges into this unknown darkness and leaves the summit. The contemplative must abandon all his knowledge about God that he has acquired through sensible and intelligible activities: "Here, renouncing all that the mind may conceive, wrapped entirely in the intangible and the invisible, he belongs completely to him who is beyond everything."[23] Dionysius further articulates the final state that will be reached by plunging into the darkness: "Here, being neither oneself nor someone else, one is supremely united to the completely unknown by an inactivity of all knowledge, and knows beyond the mind by knowing nothing."[24]

The final stage of this ultimate destination of mysterious union with the divine can be conceived of as either intellectual in an extraordinary way, for God is beyond any knowledge, or experiential and affective, characterized by an indescribable affection (or love) for this personal union.[25] Denys Turner supports the former,[26] refuting the tendency of some to understand the mysterious encounter in darkness as "a certain kind of experience—of 'inwardness,' 'ascent,' and 'union,'" which, he argues, is derived from a modern misunderstanding of medieval Christian Neoplatonism.[27] Although Dionysius's articulations of ascent are full of "traditional metaphors of affectivity, touch, taste and smell," Turner insists that the governing principle of the process is intellectual.[28]

In fact, however, Turner does not entirely deny the significant role of the affective element. Rather, he emphasizes the role of "eros" in the Dionysian concept of creation. The divine Cause of the universe outpours itself from the Divine Goodness, Divine Love, and Divine Yearning into creatures, and continues to do so.[29] For Dionysius, this love and yearning must be mutual, for it is these that motivate and facilitate the creature's return to its Cause.[30] Turner writes:

> One of the most powerful effects of Platonic allegory on the mysticism of Denys is to be found in its resolute "intellectualism." Even were more emphasis to have been given than I have allowed for the presence in Denys' theology of a richly erotic imagery . . . the conclusion would be the same: it is the ascent of the *mind* up the scale of negations which draws it into the cloud of unknowing, where, led by its own *eros* of knowing, it passes through to the darkness of union with the light. It is therefore the *eros* of knowing, the passion and yearning for the vision of the One, which projects the mind up the scale.[31]

For Turner, eros implies an affective motivation to aspire to "know," and the final status of the divine union is definitely intellectual, which is to know "beyond the mind by knowing nothing."[32]

In his explication of eros in the *Divine Names*,[33] Dionysius writes: "What is signified [by *eros*] is a capacity to effect a unity, an alliance, and a particular commingling in the Beautiful and the Good."[34] Thus, eros makes both the soul and God yearn for each other and enables the soul to be united with God.[35] In this regard, Andrew Louth views eros as "ecstatic," which means "taken wholly outside oneself."[36]

While Louth understands *ekstasis* in the *Mystical Theology* as the ecstasy of love despite the absence of any explicit mention of either eros or agape in the text,[37] Paul Rorem, consistent with Turner's understanding of the nature of divine union, does not relate *ekstasis* with affectivity. He interprets the process of negation or abandonment, in which one leaves behind all perceptible and conceptual knowledge and finally even leaves oneself, as ecstasy itself.[38] Rorem insists that Dionysius did not understand the term *ekstasis* to be "a private, emotional, and supra-rational experience,"[39] and he sees Louth's understanding of ecstasy in the *Mystical Theology* as a misinterpretation fostered by his reliance on later medieval mysticism, not on Dionysius's own understanding.[40]

Turner agrees with Rorem's analysis that medieval mystics tended to misinterpret Dionysius in anti-intellectual and antimystical[41] ways. He argues that the later medieval Dionysians like Thomas Gallus (d. 1246) and the author of *The Cloud of Unknowing* (written in the late fourteenth century) were biased toward affectivity and thus replaced intellectual enlightenment with ecstatic union of the soul with God.[42] They applied this view, according to Turner, if not to the whole process of ascent, at least to the ultimate stage. However, it seems incorrect to imply that every medieval intellectual and mystic shared this view of Dionysius's works. Rorem suggests that there have been two distinct narratives of the ascent to the divine union—affective and intellectual. He names representative theologians and mystics who have advocated these respective approaches throughout history. With respect to the thirteenth and fourteenth centuries, Rorem describes Albert the Great and Meister Eckhart as heirs of the intellectual interpretation and Bonaventure and the author of *The Cloud of Unknowing* as advocates of the affective interpretation.[43] Whether Bonaventure had mistaken Dionysius's original intention or not, there is no doubt that Dionysian apophaticism had a great influence on Bonaventure, as can be seen especially in the seventh chapter of the *Itinerarium*, which will be investigated below. Before looking into the *Itinerarium* in light of Dionysian apophaticism, there will first be a discussion of Dionysius's influence on the development of medieval spirituality and theology. Special attention will be given to Bonaventure and his unique adaptation of Dionysius within the broader context of the medieval appropriations of Dionysius.

THE DIONYSIAN INFLUENCE IN THE MIDDLE AGES

The Medieval Adaptations of Dionysianism

The sixth-century articulation of mystical theology by Dionysius laid the foundation for the unfolding of the speculative discourses and spiritual practices of Christian mysticism, both in the East and in the West. The Dionysian corpus appealed to many medieval Christian thinkers and mystics for its spiritual and theological profundity, combined with the fact that the pseudonym of Dionysius endowed it with apostolic authority.

Despite some evidence that Christians—such as St. Gregory the Great (d. 604)—read and referred to the Dionysian corpus as early as the late sixth century, it was only in the ninth century that the West began to give close attention to Dionysius with the production of Latin translations of his corpus. First, Hilduin, abbot of the monastery of Saint-Denis near Paris, undertook the task of translating Dionysius's *Corpus Areopagiticum* from Greek into Latin between 835 and 840.[44] However, because of the unsatisfactory nature of this translation, a new translation was in demand, which John Scotus Eriugena (ca. 810–ca. 877) produced in 862. This was revised by Anastasius, a papal librarian, in 875. Other attempts at translating the Dionysian corpus were undertaken in the twelfth century by John the Saracen (Sarracenus) and Robert Grosseteste (ca. 1175–1253). With his corpus made accessible through these Latin translations, the influence of Dionysius was enhanced, a process given further impetus by the production of commentaries by influential theologians, including Eriugena, Hugh of Saint Victor (d. 1142), Thomas Gallus, Albert the Great (ca. 1200–1280), and Thomas Aquinas (1225–1274), to mention but a few.[45]

Because of linguistic obstacles, most Western theologians in the Middle Ages relied on the Latin translations, paraphrases, and commentaries that together constituted "the Latin Dionysian corpus."[46] This Latin corpus was a multilayered product that had evolved over time, which, according to some scholars, was "bent" from original or "pure" Dionysianism.[47] In his investigation of the medieval understanding of Dionysianism, Paul Rorem summarizes six distinct "bends" from original Dionysianism.[48] Nevertheless, as Rorem emphasizes, there is no doubt that the influence of Dionysius was "long, broad, and occasionally deep"[49] among medieval thinkers, and that Dionysianism, despite the criticism that it has been misunderstood and deformed, has contributed to the development of various aspects of Christian life, including the speculative, spiritual, liturgical, ecclesiastical, and aesthetical. The Dionysian corpus inspired and provided medieval theologians with apostolic authority for their adaptation of the idea of hierarchies of angels and ecclesiastical structure, the discourses on the divine names, the triple ways of purification, illumination, and perfection, and the significance of light as a divine symbol.[50] However, the most significant contribution of the Dionysian corpus, which also closely pertains to the topic of this chapter, mystical theology, is that it provided the keystone for the medieval development of anagogical (literally translated, "uplifting") theology, spirituality, and aesthetics,[51] drawing on the Neoplatonist and Christianized concept of procession and return.[52]

While scholars agree on the details of the medieval development of Dionysianism, they differ in their approach to it. Some are rather critical and others are more appreciative of this development. For example, Paul Rorem tends to emphasize that medieval appropriations skewed Dionysianism, whereas Bernard McGinn argues that this was unavoidable. "From the start his [Dionysius's] writings were treated much like the Bible itself as a divine message filled with inner life and mysterious meaning which could never be exhausted, but which needed to be reread in each generation and reinterpreted in the light of new issues."[53] McGinn also stresses the positive contribution of Dionysian mystical theology to the development of Christian mysticism in the medieval period. "He [Dionysius] created the categories (including 'mystical theology' itself) that enabled later Christian mystics to relate their consciousness of God's presence and the mystery of his absence to the tradition of the apostolic teaching represented by 'Dionysius.'"[54] The Dionysian corpus has never remained static like some ancient manuscript preserved in a glass box in a museum. Rather, it is a living set of texts, the meaning of which has been adjusted for different theological and ecclesiastical contexts from generation to generation.

Bonaventure's adaptation of Dionysian mysticism is no exception in this regard. While the apophatic description of the final stage of the spiritual ascent in the *Itinerarium* is indisputably Dionysian, his emphasis on the role of affectivity and on Jesus Christ is definitely something of a departure from the prevalent intellectualism and Neoplatonism of early Dionysianism.[55]

Pseudo-Dionysius and the Victorines

Dionysian mysticism, with its distinctive dialectic of knowing and unknowing, was transmitted first through early Eastern Christians, including John Scythopolis (d. ca. 548), Maximus the Confessor (ca. 580–662), and John of Damascus (ca. 675–ca. 749). It then made its way to John Scotus Eriugena (ca. 810–ca. 877) who introduced it into the intellectual and spiritual thought and practice of the medieval West. Paul Rorem argues that in the twelfth century, intellectual Dionysian mysticism began to merge with Western monastic spirituality, which was marked by an emphasis on emotion and the central role of Christ. This affective and Christocentric tradition was developed in the West by great Christians like Augustine (354–430), Gregory the Great (pope, r. 590–604), and Bernard of Clairvaux (1090–1153).

The canons of the Abbey of St. Victor in Paris played a pivotal role in combining Dionysianism with Western monastic traditions. Two regular canons of the abbey—Hugh of St. Victor (d. 1141) and Richard of St. Victor (d. 1173)—were eminent leaders who contributed greatly to the development of Christian spirituality during the innovative era of the twelfth and thirteenth centuries, an era that was affected by significant social, ecclesiastical, cultural, intellectual, and spiritual changes.[56] Another important Victorine canon was Thomas Gallus (d. 1246), who was educated at the Abbey of St. Victor and later became abbot at the Victorine abbey in Vercelli, Italy. These notable Victorines enriched medieval theology and spirituality and bridged two different intellectual strands within the monastic tradition—one that focused more on the spiritual development of monks, and another that stressed the Scholastic tradition with its strong emphasis on speculative and theoretical discourses.

Bonaventure was one of many medieval theologians and mystics who embraced both of these strands. In doing so, he was greatly influenced by the Victorine canons. He was particularly influenced by Hugh of St. Victor and Thomas Gallus with regard to his affective apophaticism, which emerges in the last chapter of the *Itinerarium*. The following two sections will explore the development of affective Dionysianism focusing on the two Victorine masters—Hugh and Gallus. This will help locate Bonaventure's mysticism and apophaticism within a wider context and facilitate a better understanding of the *Itinerarium*.

Hugh of St. Victor

The Abbey of St. Victor was founded by William of Champeaux (ca. 1070–1121) in Paris. William originally intended to retire from his ecclesiastical and educational position in 1108. However, he was persuaded to continue teaching in the new compound of the abbey, and eventually established the School of St. Victor. It was not long after the foundation of the school that the Victorines gained a great scholarly reputation, fueled by the intellectual prowess and leadership of Hugh of St. Victor (d. 1142). Hugh was a master of great erudition and a prolific writer who greatly contributed to medieval developments in theology, philosophy, biblical exegesis, and spiritual contemplation, leaving indelible imprints on medieval Dionysianism. Hugh of St. Victor embraced certain Dionysian themes and was keenly interested in his *Celestial Hierarchy* and its themes of knowledge and negation.

However, the Hugonian adaptation of Dionysianism was not without its own peculiar emphasis. According to Dionysian mystical theology, during the final stage of the anagogical journey to God, the contemplative must renounce all knowing so as to plunge into the darkness of unknowing. While Dionysius only suggests the abandonment of intellectual activities at this threshold of unknowing, Hugh insists that in place of intellect the contemplative needs love in order to be united with God.[57] Hugh draws this conclusion from Dionysius's etymological interpretation of the angelic hierarchy. In the *Celestial Hierarchy*, Dionysius explicates the meanings of the Hebrew words for "seraphim" and "cherubim": "Those with a knowledge of Hebrew are aware of the fact that the holy name 'seraphim' means 'fire-makers,' that is to say, 'carriers of warmth.' The name 'cherubim' means 'fullness of knowledge' or 'outpouring of wisdom.'"[58] Here, Dionysius relates "seraphim" to fire; however, he never describes the seraphic fire as the fire of love—that connection was made by the translator Eriugena. Although Eriugena did not explicitly associate fire with charity or love in his translation of the seventh chapter of the *Celestial Hierarchy*, in his commentary on the same text, he metaphorically connected the attributes of fire with those of love.[59]

Hugh of St. Victor adopted this identification of the seraphic fire with the fire of love, but added an additional innovation. Eriugena, who linked the seraphim to love, never explicitly ranked seraphim/love and cherubim/knowledge. It was Hugh that insisted on the superiority of love over knowledge, drawing on the hierarchy of angels, wherein the seraphim is the highest rank. Hugh concludes: "Love [*dilectio*] surpasses knowledge, and is greater than intelligence. He [the beloved of the *Song*[60]] is loved more than understood, and love enters and approaches where knowledge stays outside."[61] Hugh's take on love involves not only the Dionysian angelic hierarchy, but also the metaphor of the affectionate union of lovers in the bridal chamber as described in the Song of Songs: a lover leaves his knowledge outside when he enters the bridal chamber. Although Hugh himself rarely showed interest in Dionysian apophaticism, the Hugonian union is apophatic in that the "bridal chamber" is a realm beyond knowing. In Hugh's apophaticism, the bridal chamber of love replaces the unknown darkness of Mount Sinai. This is important in that union with the unknown God through love is the governing principle of Bonaventure's mysticism. Indeed, Rorem stresses that Hugh "opened the way for this influential turn of the Dionysian apophatic toward the Franciscan affective."[62]

Thomas Gallus

Hugh's appropriation of Dionysian apophaticism was inherited and advanced by his successor Richard of St. Victor, and passed on to abbot Thomas Gallus

(d. 1246), who in his turn developed the final form of the Victorine mysticism, making it available to the Franciscans.[63] Gallus (i.e., "the Frenchman") was born in France in the late twelfth century and joined the Abbey of St. Victor as a canon. At the Abbey, he was immersed in the tradition of the Victorines that flourished under Hugh and Richard. In addition, the canon was also well trained in the Scholastic tradition that was rapidly developing in Paris. In 1219, he moved to the Abbey of St. Andrew in Vercelli, Italy, and in 1226 became abbot there.[64] His educational background prepared him well for his role in systematizing Victorine Dionysianism.

Bernard McGinn divides the medieval adaptation of Dionysianism into two periods, roughly before and after the thirteenth century. Thinkers of the old Dionysianism (before 1200) such as John Scotus Eriugena and Hugh and Richard of St. Victor drew on the Dionysian corpus selectively for their own purposes, motivated primarily by the apostolic authority of Dionysius. Thinkers of the new Dionysianism, in contrast, approached the Dionysian corpus in a systematic and comprehensive way. This new Dionysianism would unfold in two broad streams. One would be distinguished by its emphasis on knowledge and another by its emphasis on love in the spiritual ascent to God. The emphasis on knowledge lies at the center of the speculative or intellectual Dionysianism advocated by Albert the Great (ca. 1200–1280) and continued by Meister Eckhart (ca. 1260–1327). In contrast, affective Dionysianism, presented systematically by Thomas Gallus and adapted by the Franciscans—in particular Bonaventure, as well as by the author of *The Cloud of Unknowing*—emphasizes the superiority of love over knowledge.[65]

The discussion above presented Hugh of St. Victor's attempt to combine the mystical interpretation of the Song of Songs with his adaptation of Dionysian mysticism and briefly explored the roles of and relationship between knowledge and love within the anagogical journey. Gallus was more systematic and detailed in this synthesizing attempt. Well-versed in both the Dionysian corpus and the Song of Songs, Gallus created "an extended dialogue" between the two texts. He saw that both texts deal with different aspects of the knowledge of God: Dionysius's *Mystical Theology* treats the theoretical, whereas the Song of Songs unfolds the practical aspect of mystical theology.[66]

This dialogue between the Dionysian corpus and the Song of Songs resulted in Gallus's reinterpretation of the Dionysian apophatic ascent. In the *Mystical Theology*, Dionysius writes, "Here, being neither oneself nor someone else, one is supremely united to the completely unknown by an inactivity of all knowledge, and knows beyond the mind by knowing nothing."[67] This intellectualized apophatic statement was "paraphrased" by Gallus as follows:

Separated from all things and from oneself, as it were, one is united to the intellectually unknown God *through a uniting of love which effects true knowledge* by means of a knowledge much better than intellectual knowledge, and, because intellectual knowledge is left behind, one knows God above intellect and mind.[68]

The phrase in italics clearly manifests Gallus's "interpolation"[69] of the affective reading of the Song of Songs into his reinterpretation of Dionysius's mystical theology.[70]

Though Gallus's thought is in line with his predecessors' emphasis on *affectus*, he is distinctive in his systematic formulation of medieval Dionysianism and in his effort to bring the Song of Songs into dialogue with Dionysian writings. In addition, McGinn argues, Gallus went further in his understanding of the superiority of love over knowledge. Hugh and Richard understood that love subsumes knowledge, but this idea still acknowledges the role of knowledge in the unitive ascent to God. However, Gallus broke the link between love and knowledge at the final step in the divine union, understanding that union in solely affective terms. McGinn writes:

Gallus's understanding of the relation of knowledge to the higher uniting of love differs from this[71] by emphasizing a separation, or cutting off, of all knowing before the flight into the amorous *unitio deificans*. In other words, love no longer *subsumes* preparatory forms of knowing, however necessary, but *discards* or *rejects* them.[72]

While agreeing with McGinn on Gallus's role in the development of affective Dionysianism, Rorem suggests that the Carthusian Hugh of Balma (d. 1304) played a more significant role in drawing a sharp line between knowledge and love:

Whereas for Gallus and his predecessors, love was the true, higher form of knowledge, for Hugh of Balma there was little or no continuity at all between the lower, intellectual process and the higher union of love. Although Hugh's work is not well known today, it was the source of the "anti-intellectualism" often noted in *The Cloud of Unknowing.*[73]

Whether Gallus argued for the need for a total break between love and knowledge or whether he left room for some relationship between them, there is no doubt that he saw love as predominant over knowledge, emphasizing its role in the apophatic flight to union with God. As will be seen, this would greatly influence Bonaventure's mystical theology.

THE BONAVENTURIAN DIALECTIC
OF CATAPHASIS AND APOPHASIS

Bonaventure and Dionysius

For Bonaventure, all religious practices—whether intellectual study, prayer, or the practice of virtue—ultimately aim at union with God. In his explanation of the threefold spiritual reading of the scriptures in *On the Reduction of the Arts to Theology*, Bonaventure asserts that the allegorical reading of scriptures teaches the doctrines of divinity and humanity that arise from faith; the moral reading teaches one how to live morally, and the anagogical reading teaches the mystical union of the soul with God.[74] He identifies union with God as "the ultimate goal" of all three readings, which he learned from distinguished teachers: "The first is taught chiefly by Augustine; the second, by Gregory; the third, by Dionysius."[75] Although Augustine's and Gregory's contributions should not be underestimated, Bonaventure was greatly indebted to Dionysius for his mystical theology. Further, he reveals that he learned a great deal about Dionysius from the Victorines—Hugh and Richard of St. Victor—in his brief genealogy of the three ancient masters: "Anselm follows Augustine; Bernard follows Gregory; Richard follows Dionysius. For Anselm excels in reasoning; Bernard, in preaching; Richard, in contemplation. But Hugh excels in all three."[76] Rorem summarizes the Victorine influence on Bonaventure: "[Bonaventure's] creative work is the culmination of the Victorines' integration of Dionysian darkness into the Western legacy of love for Christ crucified."[77]

Rorem presents the threefold influence of Dionysian *anagogia* (ascent spirituality) in the West: the Neoplatonic framework of procession and return,[78] the elevation of contemplation from perceptible to conceptual things, and the renunciation of intellectual activity and knowledge at the entrance to the darkness of silence.[79] All of these Dionysian elements prevail in the Bonaventurian ascent to God, particularly in the *Itinerarium*.

Among the multifaceted Dionysian influences on the Bonaventurian *anagogia*, the remainder of this chapter will focus on the apophatic union with God that prevails at the last stage of the ascent. Bonaventure's exploration of the anagogical movement in the *Itinerarium* will provide some insights into the Bonaventurian adaptation of the mystical theology of Dionysius. The focused study of mystical union with God will also help address the dynamic relationship between cataphasis and apophasis and provide some keys for understanding the tension between them, and also the tension between the intellectual and spiritual life. Both of these tensions will be discussed later in the chapter.

Bonaventurian Apophaticism

In the final chapter of the *Itinerarium*, Bonaventure repeats Dionysius's prayer invoking the triune God to guide the soul to the mystical knowledge of the divine. In addition, he quotes Dionysius's advice to his friend Timothy to leave behind everything—perceptible and conceptual things, and even one-self—so that the soul will be lifted up to the divine darkness.[80] Bonaventure's description of the end of the anagogical journey to God, which follows his six steps of cataphatic contemplation, is similar to what Dionysius describes in the *Mystical Theology*.

In the *Itinerarium*, Bonaventure contemplates God by reading the Book of Creation, in which the creator manifests Himself in His shadows, vestiges, images, and similitudes. Each of these created things is analogically related as *verbum divinum* to its creator, the *Verbum Dei*. Any *verbum divinum* created by God can be part of a cataphatic discourse because it bears some similarity to its creator. At the same time, it should be noted that all *verba divina* are inherently dissimilar to the *Verbum Dei* because of God's transcendent nature.[81] This inherent dissimilarity is what leads eventually to apophatic silence. In other words, the analogical discourse of *verbum divinum* is ultimately deficient for conveying the truth of *Verbum Dei*. As Timothy Johnson writes, "*The Journey of the Soul into God* discloses in this interplay between the kataphatic and apophatic, the inability of the Book of Creation to impart more than a captivating glimpse of the Author."[82] Bonaventure never explicitly explained the dialectic of dissimilarity in the *Itinerarium*; however, Johnson argues that this apophatic strand is woven into the texture of the cataphatic discourse of the six-step ascent to God.[83]

This dynamic between similar and dissimilar that leads theological discourses from the cataphatic to apophatic prevails in the Dionysian corpus.[84] Denys Turner explains the Dionysian dialectic of dissimilarity on two levels. First, it would be a paradox to say that a thing can be similar and dissimilar at one and the same time. Second, the discourse of similarity and dissimilarity presupposes a common ground for a comparison between different things, but there is an unbridgeable abyss between the creature and the creator. Therefore the comparative notion of dissimilarity itself fails, which entails the failure of any theological discourse on which it is grounded.

The dialectic of dissimilarity can also be understood as the dialectic of affirmation and negation, which eventually leads to the apophatic renunciation of both modes of speaking of God. First, there is the similarity of a created thing to its creator, which allows affirmative discourse. Then, there is the negation of this discourse due to the inherent dissimilarity of the thing and its creator. Finally, there is the failure of the very notion of dissimilarity or difference, which entails the negation of both affirmation and negation.

This dialectic of affirmation and negation is the principle that dominates the metaphysical contemplations of chapters 5 and 6 of the *Itinerarium*. While the contemplations of God in the first four chapters are mediated by metaphors, vestiges, images, and the restored similitude, in chapters 5 and 6 the dialectic of dissimilarity dominates. These chapters contemplate God in a direct and abstract way, speculating on the two highest attributes of God, Being and Goodness.

First, contemplating God in His Being, Bonaventure enlists the essential attributes of divine Being: that God is "the first, the eternal, the most simple, the most actual, the most perfect, and the supremely one being."[85] While each of these attributes implies the others,[86] it also simultaneously connotes its opposite: "Being itself is both first and last, eternal and most present, most simple and greatest, most actual and unchangeable, most perfect and immense, supremely one and all-embracing."[87] The two divine attributes of each pair are seemingly contradictory yet simultaneously implicative of the other, which arouses admiration in the mind of the contemplative, who remains at a loss for how to express this mystical paradox.[88] Thus, the paradoxical pairs of divine attributes usher the contemplative into apophatic silence through the threefold process of affirmation, negation, and negation of both affirmation and negation.[89]

The same apophatic dialectic is at work as an underlying principle in chapter 6 in which Bonaventure is concerned with the properties of the trinitarian Persons in contemplating the Divine Goodness. Reflecting God as supreme goodness leads the contemplative to the realization of the six characteristics of the interrelationship between the Three Persons of the Trinity: supreme communicability, supreme consubstantiality, supreme conformability, supreme coequality, supreme coeternity, and supreme mutual intimacy.[90] A further contemplation of these six characteristics results in recognizing another set of contradictory but at the same time mutually embracing pairs: "The highest communicability together with the property of the persons, highest consubstantiality together with the plurality of hypostases, highest conformability together with discrete personality, highest co-equality together with order, highest co-eternity together with emanation, the highest intimacy together with mission."[91] The contemplation of these incomprehensible pairs leads to the same apophatic wonder shown above in the analysis of chapter 5.[92]

Bonaventure next turns to Jesus Christ, in whom divinity and humanity are united in a most profound way, with all the infinite, divine attributes joined to the finite, human attributes.[93] The human soul will be enabled to consider the invisible divine attributes by beholding Jesus Christ, the Son of God, the perfect image of God. Meditating on Jesus Christ, the soul transcends all visible and knowable things to reach the invisible and unknowable

God. Denys Turner explains that while the soul finds all the affirmations of God in Christ, it is also led to the Father, who is hidden.[94] That is to say, Christ is the ladder through which one climbs from the cataphatic to the apophatic contemplation of God. In this consideration of the union of divinity and humanity in Christ, the soul perfects its intellectual contemplation, and there is nothing left for the human mind except to rest "in the dazzling darkness of a silence."[95] The last chapter of the *Itinerarium* focuses on the soul's ecstatic rise to this apophatic silence.

Thus, the Dionysian dialectics of similarity and dissimilarity, cataphasis and apophasis, and affirmation and negation are the dynamic principles of the anagogical movement that dominate the *Itinerarium*—but not without a Bonaventurian transformation. There are three distinctive elements in Bonaventure's adaptation of Dionysianism or Dionysian mysticism that he inherited from his medieval predecessors: the prevalence of affectivity, the essential place of Christ, and the significant role of Francis as a concrete model of the spiritual journey to union with God. The following three sections will consider these distinctive themes of the *Itinerarium*.

Affectivity: Union with God in Love

The Prevalence of Affection in Bonaventurian Dionysianism

As shown in the brief survey of the medieval development of Dionysianism above, the most noticeable shifts were the emphasis of love over knowledge and the change in the nature of love (or eros) from cosmic, cognitive eros to a more affective intersubjective eros. These shifts in understanding the nature and supremacy of love are reflected in Bonaventure's description of the soul's final flight to mystical union with God. In the *Itinerarium*, however, the role of affectivity is not confined to the final stage of union with God; rather, it prevails throughout the anagogical journey.[96]

In the prologue of the *Itinerarium*, Bonaventure rejects the idea that the spiritual journey is solely intellectual and affirms the necessity of affectivity. Bonaventure insists that those who set out on the six-step journey are, in the first place, to be disposed to affectivity. He dedicates his treatise not just to anyone but

> to those who are already disposed by divine grace—to the humble and pious; to those who are devout and sorrowful for their sins; to those anointed with the oil of gladness; to those who are lovers of divine wisdom and are inflamed with desire for it; and to those who wish to give themselves to glorifying, admiring, and even savoring God.[97]

Here, while the preparatory requirements of humility, devotion, repentance, and gladness all confirm the necessity of affectivity in the soul's journey, there is a further requirement that demands closer attention: the desire for the Divine Wisdom. The desire for wisdom is ambivalent in the context of the present discussion because it bears on both affective desire and intellectual knowledge. A close study of the desire for wisdom will facilitate an understanding of Bonaventure's integrative accommodation of affectivity and intellect, which can be distinguished from Dionysius's more intellectual theology.

First of all, according to Dionysius, the desire for wisdom can be understood as an intellectual aspiration to know. Denys Turner interprets eros in the Dionysian corpus as the yearning for knowledge in an intellectual sense.

> The ascent of the *mind* . . . is therefore the *eros* of knowing, the passion and yearning for the vision of the One, which projects the mind up the scale; it is the dialectics of knowing and unknowing which govern that progress, and it is not in the traditional metaphors of affectivity, touch, taste and smell, but in the visual metaphors of light and dark, seeing and unseeing, that that progress is described.[98]

As Turner insists, whereas the ultimate object one desires to achieve in Dionysian mystical theology can be considered to be purely intellectual in nature, the object desired in Bonaventure's spiritual ascent is not exclusively intellectual, but rather includes both affectivity and intellectuality; Bonaventure understands that wisdom embraces both knowledge and affection. This Bonaventurian understanding of wisdom also reveals the Franciscan master's concern that those engaged in theoretical and speculative activities maintain a balance between the intellectual and spiritual life.

The reflections Bonaventure presents in the *Itinerarium* illumine the divine truths or transcendental attributes of God so that his readers will glorify, admire, and savor God, who ought to be glorified, admired, and savored.[99] Among these three activities, admiration is noteworthy for its central role in the spiritual journey. Philotheus Boehner explains that, in Bonaventure's thought, these three activities are distinct from one another: "The first step of the *Itinerarium* leads only to praise or glorify God (cf. 1.15). To admire God is more; it is the step that leads to mystical peace. To savor God means to actually experience the deep joy of the mystical union. This, of course, is the ultimate goal of the *Itinerarium*, described in Chapter VII."[100] As Boehner points out, while the early stages of reflection would lead the contemplative to praising or glorifying God, in the later stages of reflection (discussed in chapters 3–6) he will be lifted up in admiration, recognizing God's unfathomable splendor and encountering Him in His incomprehensible divine reality.[101]

This admiration results from Bonaventure's six-step reflection on the universe, the human mind, and the divine attributes. In his description of these speculative stages of the *Itinerarium*, Bonaventure employs the metaphor of light: "The soul becomes like the dawn, the moon, and the sun corresponding to the steps of illumination that lift up the soul in wonder at the Bridegroom."[102] The higher one climbs the ladder to God, the more brightly his soul will be illumined, and the deep contemplation guided by the suggested steps will most assuredly lead the contemplative to wonder. Then, in great amazement the soul will rise up to the union with the Bridegroom wherein it experiences or "savors" God in the ecstatic union of love. As such, admiration is a natural consequence of intellectual contemplation as well as a transformative activity leading to a more affective and experiential state of union; and the soul shows the involvement of both intellect and affectivity in Bonaventure's description of the spiritual journey toward union with God.[103]

Bonaventure's concern for the integration of intellect and affectivity is clearly stated in the prologue of the *Itinerarium*, quoted in chapter 1 but worth repeating here, in a discussion of Bonaventure's integration of intellect and spirituality, where he admonishes the reader:

> Do not think that reading is sufficient without unction, speculation without devotion, investigation without admiration, circumspection without exultation, industry without piety, knowledge without charity, intelligence without humility, study without divine grace, the mirror without the inspiration of divine wisdom.[104]

As Ewert Cousins rightly puts it, in the *Itinerarium*, "philosophical speculation is joined with mystical affectivity."[105]

While both intellect and affectivity are central components in the spiritual journey as described by Bonaventure, they are clearly ranked according to importance. In the *Itinerarium*, a highly intellectual treatise, affectivity takes supremacy over intellect, a disposition Bonaventure inherited from the Victorines. Just before he sets out to unfold his speculative reflections, Bonaventure instructs the reader to give more attention "to the stimulation of affect than to the instruction of the intellect."[106] When the soul is prepared to enter the chamber of the Bridegroom, the encounter with the beloved consists more in "the experience of affections than in rational considerations."[107] Again, in chapter 7, Bonaventure stresses the supremacy of affectivity as he asserts that the soul's passing over[108] to God through the crucified Christ is possible when all intellectual activities are renounced and one's total affection is directed to God.[109]

The Dominance of Affectivity at the Final Stage of the Journey

To better understand the dominant role of affectivity in Bonaventure's final stage, as distinguished from the preeminence of the intellect at most of the stages of the *Itinerarium*, attention must be paid to Bonaventure's understanding of the various powers of the soul. In chapter 1, Bonaventure presents six levels of the powers of the soul by which one can ascend to union with God.[110] The six powers of the soul, corresponding to the six steps of the ascent, are "sense, imagination, reason, understanding, intelligence, and the highest point of the mind or the spark of conscience [*sensus, imaginatio, ratio, intellectus, intelligentia et apex mentis seu synderesis scintilla*]."[111] Etienne Gilson stresses that these six powers do not represent six separate faculties of the soul, but "six different aspects of the same faculty . . . considered as it turns successively to different objects."[112] That is to say, the six powers of the soul are all different aspects of the same intellect.[113] However, distinguished from the other five aspects, which are primarily functions of the intellect, the highest or the *apex mentis* is not associated with the intellect only but also the will. Bonaventure equates *apex mentis* with *synderesis scintilla*, or the spark of conscience.[114] According to Bonaventure, *synderesis* is that which "stimulates one toward the good."[115] He sees this natural tendency toward or desire for goodness as an affective power, distinguishing it from *conscientia*, or conscience, which is an intellectual disposition of the soul.[116]

Scholarly schemes that associate the six powers of the soul with the six stages of the *Itinerarium* bring about a mismatch between the affective sixth power and the intellectual contemplation of the sixth chapter. McGinn provides a solution. In an original diagram, he shows the seven chapters of the *Itinerarium* and the six powers of the soul side by side. Rather than relating each of the six steps of the mystical ascent to each of the six powers of the soul one by one, McGinn rearranges the relationship between the two categories by associating chapters 5 and 6 taken together with *intelligentia* and chapter 7 with *apex mentis*.[117] In doing so, he embraces two arguments: one, that as the highest activity of the soul, the *apex mentis* must be associated with the final stage of the soul's ascent to God; and two, that the affectivity of the *apex mentis* accords with the affective ecstasy involved in the final union of the soul with God.

Ecstasis and Excessus unto God

In the *Itinerarium*, Bonaventure uses the Greek word *ecstasis* and the Latin word *excessus* without distinction.[118] The etymological meaning of the Greek *ecstasis* is "standing outside the self" and the Latin *excessus* means "departure or death"; the definitions of both imply the idea of breaking out from a previous state. He employs these terms twenty-three times altogether—*ecstasis* three times, *excessus* twenty times—to describe the dynamic status of the soul primarily at the final stage of the mystical ascent. Boehner uses *mentalis excessus* as simply "another term for the mystical union."[119] However, these terms are not only used to describe the ultimate state of the mystical union itself. *Excessus* also implies means, path, transition, or uplifting to reach a higher level.[120] Therefore, in the *Itinerarium* the dynamic terms *ecstasis* and *excessus* indicate either the transitional stage in one's spiritual progress or the final state of the same process.

Though there can be different understandings regarding whether the terms *ecstasis* and *excessus* imply the final state of union or the process leading to it, there is no doubt that the terms are affective in nature. Not only are *ecstasis* and *excessus* themselves affective in nature, but they also imply other affective activities. According to Bonaventure, the soul becomes disposed to *ecstasis* through devotion, admiration, and exultation, all of which involve affection.[121] While affection plays a crucial role, *ecstasis* also has other results at the transitional moment of one's spiritual leap to God: "When [with] love the soul embraces the incarnate Word, receiving delight from him and passing over to him [through] ecstatic love, it receives its sense of taste and touch."[122] This ecstatic love enables the soul to stand outside itself and transition to union with God. In the transition to and experience of union, the soul should abandon the activities of intellect, and only affection should be at work.[123]

The Relationship between the Ecstatic Love and Intellectual Activity

There is no doubt that the Bonaventurian ascent involves both affectivity and intellect, unlike Dionysius's predominantly intellectual ascent. In addition, the supremacy of love over knowledge is apparent at the final stage of the *Itinerarium*. Bonaventure is clear in his opinion that in the soul's passing over to union with God, all intellectual activities and knowledge should be abandoned in favor of the utmost in affection.[124] This renunciation of intellect at the final stage of ecstatic union, however, does not depreciate the significant role of intellect in the rest of the anagogical journey. Whereas the *ecstasis* or *excessus mentis* is predominantly affective, the path that leads to the stage of *ecstasis* is both intellectual and affective. In the beginning of the *Itinerarium*, as noted earlier, Bonaventure instructs his readers to balance intellectual activities with affective virtues and devotional practices.

To better understand how intellectual contemplation leads to the rise of the affections, there is a need to return to chapters 5 and 6, in which, at the height of the speculative contemplation of the divine attributes, the soul comes to a place of admiration in its encounter with incomprehensible divine realities.[125]

Furthermore, it is amazed as it contemplates Jesus Christ, which leads eventually to *excessus mentis* or *excessus contemplationis*.[126] All the illuminative stages of the *Itinerarium* are directed toward this encounter with Jesus Christ, the contemplation of whom silences all intellectual activities, and at the same time, ironically, perfects the intellectual journey. Bonaventure writes, "Here, with God the mind reaches the perfection of its illumination on the sixth step, as on the sixth day. Nothing further remains but the day of rest when in an ecstatic insight the discerning power of the human mind *rests from all the work that it has done*."[127] At the summit of all its intellectual contemplations, the soul comes face to face with mysteries beyond its intellectual capacity, which entails renunciation of the intellect and requires the highest form of affection. Thus, the realization of unknowing which leads the soul into ecstasy and darkness is *ignorantia docta* or "learned ignorance."[128] Bernard McGinn rightly states the relationship of knowledge to ecstatic love: although the *apex affectus* is not an intellectual power, it

> still bears some kind of relation to knowledge and to what can be expressed in language, both because it draws up into itself all the preparatory cognitive operations that are part of the journey into God just at the moment it leaps beyond them, and also because although what is received is incommunicable, the person who receives it is transformed by this contact in a way that enables him or her to be a better channel of divine illumination.[129]

While he weighs in on the apophatic and affective experience of union with God, Bonaventure acknowledges the effect and necessity of intellectual efforts to reach the final goal of union in love and in the silencing of all knowledge. In *On the Reduction of the Arts to Theology*, Bonaventure concludes with a summary of the relationship between knowledge, theology, and charity.

> And so it is evident how the *manifold wisdom* of God, which is clearly revealed in sacred Scripture, lies hidden in all knowledge and in all nature. It is clear also how all divisions of knowledge are servants of theology, and it is for this reason that theology makes use of illustrations and terms pertaining to every branch of knowledge. It is likewise clear how wide the illuminative way may be, and how the divine reality itself lies hidden within everything which is perceived or known. And this is the fruit of all sciences, that in all, faith may be strengthened, God *may be honored*, character may be formed, and consolation may be derived from union of the Spouse with the beloved, a union which takes place through charity: a charity in which the whole purpose of sacred Scripture, and thus of illumination descending from above, comes to rest—a charity without which all knowledge is vain because no one comes to the Son except through the Holy Spirit who teaches us *all the truth, who is blessed forever. Amen.*[130]

For Bonaventure, all sorts of knowledge serve theology so that one can be illuminated to the essential teaching of the whole of scriptures, which is charity. Scientific knowledge helps the human mind see the manifestation of the divine in all things created by God. Nevertheless, what leads to union with God in the end is charity. As charity is "the fruit of all sciences," Bonaventure maintains that all intellectual activities and knowledge aim at charity or *ecstasis*,[131] and he acknowledges the contribution of intellectual activity to this ultimate end.

Christ, the Way, and the Door to the Apophatic Union with God

Along with Bonaventure's strong pairing of affection with intellect in the soul's return to God, Denys Turner notes another way in which Bonaventure radically transforms Dionysian apophaticism: his Christocentrism.[132] Bonaventure's theology and spirituality always put Christ at the center. The Son of God is for him the central Person of the Trinity, as he is the total expression of the Father's boundless love, a love that is associated with the divine nature of fruitfulness and self-communicative goodness. The Son also participates with the Father in the procession of the Third Person, the Holy Spirit. This procession is the result of the loving bond between the Father and the Son. The centrality of the Second Person is manifested beyond the triune relationship in his active involvement in creation as the exemplar, and in his decisive participation in salvation history through his Incarnation and Passion, all of which reveal God's love to the universe.[133] Bonaventurian Christocentism is closely associated with divine love within and outside the Trinity. The Franciscan master's metaphysical Christocentricism and his affective mystical theology are also grounded in the mystical spirituality of Francis, who experienced God as good and loving through the crucified Christ.

Christ the Center in the Itinerarium

Christocentrism is a central principle in Bonaventure's work, particularly in the later part of chapter 6 of the *Itinerarium*. As seen above, the soul's speculative contemplation of God culminates in the person of Christ, in whom God and humanity, and also seemingly opposed divine characteristics, are joined. For Bonaventure, the soul's contemplations of God's Being and Goodness result in wonder, a wonder arising from its consideration of the unity in the opposites of God's transcendental attributes. The contemplation of Jesus Christ astonishes even more as the soul considers the unity of the opposites of finite and infinite, immanence and transcendence, in the person of Christ.[134]

The contemplation of this mystical union of God and humanity surpasses the human intellect.[135]

For Bonaventure, the unity of the finite and the infinite in Christ can be compared to the meeting of the cataphatic and the apophatic in Christ. The two ways of knowing God meet in "the Way" (Jn 14:6). As the Word of God, Christ is the invisible Book of Creation or Principle of Creation through which the universe was made, and it is only in Christ, with his spiritual senses restored, that the contemplative can properly read the Book of Creation.[136] Most cataphatic discourses are associated in one way or another with this Book of Creation—they speak of God through the vestige, image, and similitude of God in created things, as shown in the writings of Dionysius and in Bonaventure's *Itinerarium*. In this regard, as Turner rightly puts it, Christ is "the résumé of the cataphatic," and all the affirmative contemplations of God in the creature lead to Christ who is the true image of God.[137] In Christ, the contemplative reads not only the Book without, but also the Book within; that is to say, both the creature and the creator,[138] for in Christ the creature and the creator are united. Furthermore, in Christ the contemplative transcends the creature and the cataphatic to reach the creator and the apophatic, for Christ who is the Son leads us to his Father, the invisible God. In this transition from the contemplation of the immanent God in which cataphatic theology dominates, to contemplation of the transcendent God in which apophatic theology dominates, the contemplative is required to silence his words and his intellect. Thus, in the Christology of Bonaventure, Christ is the key that unlocks the dialectic of cataphasis and apophasis.

Closely related to this, the crucified Christ holds a significant place in Bonaventure's Christology. While metaphysical Christocentrism primarily involves intellect and speculative discourse, the crucified Christ, who was central in Francis's spirituality and mystical experience, is closely associated with affective contemplation and plays a decisive role in the movement towards an apophatic union with God.

The Crucified Christ in the Itinerarium

For Bonaventure, Christ is "the way and the door" through which the contemplative transcends all perceptible and conceptual things and passes over to union with God. At the end of the six-step intellectual journey, the soul reaches the most profound mysteries, which defy intellectual comprehension and therefore demand the renunciation of the intellect.[139] The soul's journey of ascent to God does not end there, however. Anyone who contemplates the Mercy Seat or the union of God and humanity in the person of Christ "with faith, hope, and love, devotion, admiration, joy, appreciation, praise, and rejoicing" now beholds Christ on the cross.[140] While intellectual contemplation of the person of Christ led the contemplative to incomprehensible mysteries, now "the most burning love of the Crucified"[141] lifts up his eyes and soul so that the soul may be united with Christ on the cross. Here, there is a paradox—the mystical journey is at one and the same time ascending and descending: the anagogical movement toward union is bound downward for the tomb where the soul rests with Christ.

This passing over to death is possible only through one's inflamed desire to transform himself into his lover, even unto death on the cross. Bonaventure insists that only this love of the Crucified can lead one to God in ecstatic love.[142] Although affection for the Crucified is essential for union with God, Bonaventure does not discount the preparatory stage of purification involving prayers and the six stages of illuminative contemplation; rather, he sees these as means of enhancing a burning love of the crucified Christ: "Desires can be inflamed in us in two ways, namely through the cry of prayer which makes us cry aloud with groaning of the heart, and through the brightness of contemplation by which the mind turns most directly and intently to the rays of light."[143] Aided by these measures, the contemplation of the crucified Christ is still the only way to ecstatic union with God.

While both chapters 6 and 7 contemplate Christ, there is a notable difference between them. Chapter 6 contemplates the person of Christ, who is the union of God and humanity, whereas chapter 7 focuses on the crucified Christ and his Passion. Contemplation of the Incarnate Word is primarily intellectual in nature, whereas contemplation of the crucified Christ is primarily a matter of affection and burning love. This fervent affection toward the crucified Christ carries the contemplative out of himself and moves him into God.[144] Finally, the spiritual journey in the pursuit of peace through the illumination of the soul[145] ends with one's entrance with Christ into darkness through death, which is impossible except through total renunciation.

> Only one who loves this death can see God, for it is absolutely true that *no one can see me and live.* Let us die, then, and enter into this darkness. Let us silence all our cares, desires, and imaginations. Let us pass over with the crucified Christ *from this world to the Father*, so that when the Father has been shown to us, we may say with Philip: *It is enough for us.*[146]

Thus, Christ is not only "the point of juncture of the cataphatic and the apophatic,"[147] but He is also the meeting point of the two different gazes—the intellectual and the affective. Christ is the way leading the soul through the six-step intellectual journey, the door through which the soul can breach the impassable wall separating the creator and the creature in the self-denying love of the crucified Christ, and the destination of the spiritual journey, at the end of which the soul is finally united with God and rests in peace.

Francis, the Guide for the Spiritual Journey to God

Francis and the Crucified Christ

Bonaventure acknowledges at the outset of the *Itinerarium* that the centrality of the crucified Christ in the treatise was inspired by St. Francis of Assisi, especially Francis's vision of the crucified seraph.

Bonaventure writes that love of the crucified Christ "so absorbed" the spirit of Francis that it left the physical marks of the Passion on the body of the saint.[148] In the prologue, Bonaventure begins his description of the multistep spiritual journey to God by referring to Francis as an inspirational model, and in chapter 7 he ends by presenting the saint as a witness who completed the mystical journey.

> All this was shown also to blessed Francis when, in a rapture of contemplation on the top of the mountain where I reflected on the things I have written here, a six-winged Seraph fastened to a cross appeared to him. . . . Here he was carried out of himself in contemplation and passed over into God. And he has been set forth as the example of perfect contemplation just as he had earlier been known as the example of action, like another Jacob transformed into Israel. So it is that God invites all truly spiritual persons through Francis to this sort of passing over, more by example than by words.[149]

Although Bonaventure begins and ends his treatise of spiritual ascent with Francis and his mystical experience at Mount Alverna, in between he rarely mentions the saint. However, Bernard McGinn argues that despite no explicit reference to him in the middle chapters of the *Itinerarium*, Francis is still serving as Bonaventure's model: "Bonaventure's treatment of the stages of contemplative ascent . . . is nothing more than a laying out of what had taken place in the soul of Francis as a model for all ecstatics."[150] McGinn asserts that Francis, "as the ideal expression of the crucified Jesus, is the exemplar of our journey, or reduction, back into God."[151]

Bonaventure's understanding of Francis as "the exemplar of the crucified Christ"[152] is fully unfolded in his biography of the saint, the *Major Legend of St. Francis*. Bonaventure is amazed that Francis's desire for the crucified Christ was acknowledged by God granting him seven visions of the cross of Christ, from the first vision in which he saw a palace full of military weapons with the insignia of Christ's cross to the vision of the seraph in the form of the crucified Christ at Mount Alverna.[153] After enumerating the seven visions, Bonaventure explicates their meaning in a conversation with Francis, as it were.

> Behold, you have arrived with seven apparitions of the cross of Christ wondrously apparent and visible in you or about you following an order of time, like six steps leading to the seventh where you finally found rest. For the cross of Christ, both offered to and taken on by you at the beginning of your conversion and carried continuously from that moment throughout the course of your most proven life and giving example to others, shows with such clarity of certitude that you have finally reached the summit of Gospel perfection that no truly devout person can reject this proof of Christian wisdom ploughed into the dust of your flesh. No truly believing person can attack it, no truly humble person can belittle it, since it is truly divinely expressed and *worthy of complete acceptance*.[154]

The essential role of the crucified Christ in the *Itinerarium* is most certainly a product of Bonaventure's profound reflection on the life of the founder of his order, in particular the saint's mystical experience at Alverna. Bonaventure's recurring references to the vision of the cross indicates his view of how much Francis's life and spirituality revolved around Christ. McGinn argues that the seven visions of the cross "mark the stages in an itinerary of deepening understanding of the meaning of the cross," the perfection of which was manifested in the reception of the stigmata on the saint's body.[155]

Furthermore, as McGinn points out, Bonaventure links the seven visions of the cross in the *Major Legend* with the seven stages of the *Itinerarium*,[156] drawing on his own words in the *Major Legend*: "Behold, you have arrived with seven apparitions of the cross of Christ wondrously apparent and visible in you or about you following an order of time, like six steps leading to the seventh where you finally found rest."[157] This parallel confirms again Bonaventure's understanding that Francis's life and spirituality are centered on the crucified Christ.

Francis, the Model for the Bonaventurian Dialectic of Cataphasis and Apophasis

Of course, Bonaventure had admired Francis long before composing the *Itinerarium* and his hagiography, and McGinn asserts that Francis provided Bonaventure with constant inspiration that enabled him not just to summarize and synthesize the Christian tradition, but to transform them.[158] Nevertheless, it seems clear that Bonaventure came to contemplate the life of the saint more deeply after his election as minister general of the Franciscan Order, a position that required him to appeal to the broader audience of his Franciscan brothers and sisters, as well as the ordinary faithful. Joshua Benson suggests that the marked prevalence of the mystery of the crucified Christ in the later writings, including the *Itinerarium*, the *Major Legend,* and the *Collations on the Gifts of the Holy Spirit* is a manifestation of Bonaventure's deeper understanding of Francis's spirituality, centered on Christ and His Passion.[159]

The influence of Francis on Bonaventure's adaptation of Dionysianism is not limited to the saint's love of the crucified Christ. Just as Christ is the mediator between transcendence and immanence, Francis also played a significant role in bridging the gap between the mystical realm of the divine and the concrete life of humanity. Timothy Johnson argues that for Bonaventure the mystical pilgrimage to transcendence requires a particular place where the divine can reveal itself, and the life of Francis was such a place. That is to say, Francis was a *"locus theologicus,"*[160] not only for Bonaventure, but also for all spiritual persons desiring to pass over to God in conformity with the crucified Christ.[161]

For Johnson, the presence of Francis in Bonaventure's mystical treatise represents a notable shift in the historical development of Christian mysticism. Distinguished from previous mystical writings which drew mostly on biblical figures like Moses, Benjamin, or Rachel, Johnson insists that Bonaventure was inspired to present Francis to the reader as "a tangible touchstone of transcendence,"[162] the concrete model of a spiritual seeker. Walking with him, the seeker can move from the splendor of the creation to its creator, from intellect to affectivity, from speculation to spiritual experience, and from cataphatic discourse to apophatic peace.

In chapter 11 of the *Major Legend,* after briefly praising the depth of Francis's understanding of the scriptures, Bonaventure expresses his admiration for the saint's penetrating insight into the divine mysteries, in which intellect gives way to affection:[163] "For his genius, pure and unstained, penetrated *hidden mysteries,* and where the knowledge of teachers stands outside, the passion of the lover entered."[164] Thus described by Bonaventure, Francis appears as the embodiment of a long mystical tradition that began with Dionysius, whose works were transformed by affective monasticism.

It is easy to recognize that Bonaventure's understanding of the saint's life and experiences represents a uniquely medieval appropriation of Dionysian mysticism. As this chapter has argued, this can be seen in the dominance of affectivity and the centrality of Christ, prevalent themes in Bonaventure's mysticism as manifested in the *Itinerarium.* On the one hand, Christ who is the manifestation of the mystery of God the Father, and Francis of Assisi whose mystical experience was highly visual, concrete, and affirmative, support cataphasis. However, on the other, these two figures play decisive roles in the apophatic ascent to God as they are the mediators between cataphasis and apophasis. The love manifested in the Crucifixion and Francis's love for the crucified Christ are essential in the spiritual ascent to the union with God, which is an apophatic experience.

SUMMARY

Chapter 3 explored the development of Christian mysticism, in particular focusing on the development of Dionysianism in the medieval West and the crucial influence of medieval Dionysianism on Bonaventure's mysticism, which is a central feature of the latter part of the *Itinerarium*.

Early Dionysianism was explored in regard to the Dionysian categories of theology, the relationship between those categories—in particular between cataphatic and apophatic theologies—and the nature of the apophatic union with God. In his sophisticated description of the spiritual ascent to God, Dionysius tries to reconcile the contrasting doctrines of the divine: the divine manifestation of God in creation and the transcendence of God. While Dionysius stresses the unknowability of the transcendent One, he does not repudiate the affirmative elements of Christianity—moral purification, sacraments, and the scriptures—to which the cataphatic theological discourses have their primary recourse. He acknowledges that the creature's existential purpose is to praise and glorify God through affirmation, as well as the necessity of affirmation along the path of becoming enlightened as to the transcendence of God.

When it comes to the nature of the ultimate goal of Dionysian ascent, scholars like Turner and Rorem argue that it is primarily intellectual because the union with the divine ends in apophatic knowing. However, there still seems to be room for other interpretations, such as the affective and experiential interpretation of Louth, not to mention the development of these themes in the Middle Ages.

The mystical theology of Dionysius appealed to the minds and hearts of medieval Christians, providing them with valuable resources for elaborate articulations of the intellectual and spiritual life of Christians. However, Christian intellectuals and mystics did not simply adopt early Dionysianism, but instead developed it so that affectivity assumed a crucial place in the anagogical journey to God.

Bonaventure inherited Dionysianism as adapted by earlier medieval thinkers. This is manifest in the *Itinerarium*, his spiritual treatise of a mystical journey to God. The seemingly contradictory yet at the same time complementary relationship between Dionysian cataphasis and apophasis can be seen throughout the *Itinerarium*. The six-step contemplation of God through His vestiges, images, similitudes, and attributes certainly involves affirmative speculation, but Bonaventure is well aware of the ineffability of God, and the Dionysian dialectic of affirmation and negation and the related principle of dissimilarity play a crucial role as the journey moves upward to the unknowable God. Finally, Dionysius's apophatic theology dominates and love for the crucified Christ decisively raises the soul to union with God in silence. The emphasis on love and the significant role of Christ, in particular in the form of the Crucified, were obviously drawn from the affective adaptation or the medieval bent of Dionysianism, which holds that the love for the Crucified enables one to leave oneself so as to be united with God and rest in unitive love. This affective medieval adaptation is distinguished from the early Dionysianism, in which the union with God is considered to be apophatic knowing. This Bonaventurian adaptation of Dionysian mysticism was also, as Bonaventure himself witnesses, inspired by the mystical experience of Francis.

Bonaventure's description of a spiritual journey to a mystical union with God employs the dialectic of affirmation (cataphatic theology) and negation (apophatic theology). Though at the final unitive stage, all intellectual activity should be abandoned in recognition of the ineffability of the mystical state, this does not imply the futility of cataphatic discourse and intellectual contemplation. For Bonaventure, all forms of speculative contemplation on the creature, the soul, and the divine attributes comprise a spiritual staircase that leads a Christian soul to union with God in silence.

NOTES

1. *Itinerarium mentis in Deum* (hereafter cited as *Itin.*) 7.1, in *Itinerarium Mentis in Deum*, trans. Zachary Hayes, introduction and "Notes & Commentary" by Philotheus Boehner, vol. 2 of *WSB*, rev. ed. (St. Bonaventure, NY: Franciscan Institute, 2002), 133 (hereafter cited as *WSB*).

2. *Itin.* 7.3–4, in *WSB*, 2:135–37.

3. He is also referred to as simply "Dionysius," or as "Pseudo-Denys."

4. The surviving Dionysian corpus includes four treatises and ten letters: *The Divine Names* (hereafter cited as *DN*); *The Mystical Theology* (hereafter cited as *MT*); *The Celestial Hierarchy* (hereafter cited as *CH*); *The Ecclesiastical Hierarchy*; and *Letters* I–X. Quotations from the Dionysian texts are taken from the English translation by Colm Luibheid, in collaboration with Paul Rorem. See Pseudo-Dionysius, *Pseudo-Dionysius: The Complete Works*, trans. Colm Luibheid, with introductions by Jaroslav Pelikan, Jean Leclercq, and Karlfried Froehlich (Mahwah, NJ: Paulist Press, 1987). Luibheid's translation is based on the Greek text of the Migne edition. Jacques Paul Migne, ed., *Patrologia Cursus Completus, Series Graeca*, vol. 3 (Paris, 1857).

5. Besides cataphatic and apophatic theologies, Dionysius also mentions symbolic theology and mystical theology. However, he never provides definitive meanings of these terms, and this has given rise to various categorizations of Dionysian theologies

by modern scholars. Nevertheless, all four theologies can be merged into the categories of cataphatic and apophatic. Symbolic theology, which primarily concerns analogies of God, involves an affirmative discourse, and can therefore be categorized as cataphasis. Mystical theology focuses on the union with God in silence with all affirmative discourses and thoughts about God relinquished. It primarily employs negative discourse, and it can therefore be categorized as apophasis. Deirdre Carabine views these four theologies not as separate, but rather interwoven in a continuous movement leading to the transcendent God.

> Kataphatic theology, which can be said to culminate in symbolic theology, is concerned with the manifestation of God and how he can be named through his effects. Apophatic theology, which uses affirmations as a springboard from which to proceed to negation, culminates in mystical theology and is concerned with the nature of God as he is in himself, apart from his effects. (Deirdre Carabine, *The Unknown God: Negative Theology in the Platonic Tradition: Plato to Eriugena* [Louvain: Peeters Press, 1995], 287)

6. *CH* 2.3, in *Pseudo-Dionysius: The Complete Works*, 149.

7. *DN* 1.1, in *Pseudo-Dionysius: The Complete Works*, 49–50.

8. *DN* 1.2, in *Pseudo-Dionysius: The Complete Works*, 50 (bracketed insertion mine). Here, the Good refers to God who is the Good.

9. *DN* 1.1, in *Pseudo-Dionysius: The Complete Works*, 49.

10. *DN* 1.1, in *Pseudo-Dionysius: The Complete Works*, 49.

11. *DN* 1.2 (Rom 11:33), in *Pseudo-Dionysius: The Complete Works*, 50.

12. *DN* 1.2, in *Pseudo-Dionysius: The Complete Works*, 50.

13. *DN* 1.3, in *Pseudo-Dionysius: The Complete Works*, 50–51.

14. *MT* 2, in *Pseudo-Dionysius: The Complete Works*, 138; see also *DN* 1.5, in *Pseudo-Dionysius: The Complete Works*, 54. For a discussion of praising God in the Dionysian theology, see Andrew Louth, *The Origins of the Christian Mystical Tradition: From Plato to Denys*, second ed. (Oxford: Oxford University Press, 2007), 160–61; Paul Rorem, *Pseudo-Dionysius: A Commentary on the Texts and an Introduction to Their Influence* (Oxford: Oxford University Press, 1993), 193.

15. *MT* 2, in *Pseudo-Dionysius: The Complete Works*, 138.

16. *DN* 1.4–7, in *Pseudo-Dionysius: The Complete Works*, 51–56.

17. *MT* 1.2, in *Pseudo-Dionysius: The Complete Works*, 136.

18. Denys Turner, *The Darkness of God: Negativity in Christian Mysticism* (Cambridge: Cambridge University Press, 1995), 45.

19. Rorem, *Pseudo-Dionysius: A Commentary*, 166: See also Janet Williams, "The Apophatic Theology of Dionysius the Pseudo-Areopagite-I," *Downside Review* 117, no. 408 (1999): 158.

20. Louth, *The Origins of the Christian Mystical Tradition*, 163.

21. Denys Turner argues that the Western Christian employment of the metaphors of light and darkness, ascent and descent, resulted from a Christian merger of the Greek and Hebraic intellectual and religious cultures, represented, respectively, by the "Allegory of the Cave" in Book 7 of Plato's *Republic* and the story in Exodus of Moses's encounter with Yahweh on Mount Sinai. See Turner, *The Darkness of God*, 11–18.

22. *MT* 1.3 (Ex 19), in *Pseudo-Dionysius: The Complete Works*, 136–37.

23. *MT* 1.3, in *Pseudo-Dionysius: The Complete Works*, 137.

24. *MT* 1.3, in *Pseudo-Dionysius: The Complete Works*, 137.

25. Kevin Corrigan and L. Michael Harrington, "Pseudo-Dionysius the Areopagite," *The Stanford Encyclopedia of Philosophy* (Summer 2018 edition), ed. Edward N. Zalta, https://plato.stanford.edu/archives/sum2018/entries/pseudo-dionysius-areopagite/ (accessed March 9, 2019). In addition to these two interpretations of the final stage of divine union, Louis Bouyer suggests a third, that it is "ontological," arguing that union with God ends in the contemplative's divinization, the fruit of an ontological transformation. See Louis Bouyer, *The Spirituality of the New Testament and the Fathers* (London: Burns & Oates, 1960), 416–20.

26. Turner, *The Darkness of God*, 47.

27. Turner, *The Darkness of God*, 4.

28. Turner, *The Darkness of God*, 47.

29. See Turner, *The Darkness of God*, 29, and Dionysius's articulation of love and yearning in *DN* 4.10–16, in *Pseudo-Dionysius: The Complete Works*, 78–83.

30. *DN* 4.10, in *Pseudo-Dionysius: The Complete Works*, 79–80.

31. Turner, *The Darkness of God*, 47.

32. *MT* 1.3, in *Pseudo-Dionysius: The Complete Works*, 137. See also *CH* 2.4, in *Pseudo-Dionysius: The Complete Works*, 151:

Now when we apply dissimilar similarities to intelligent beings, we say of them that they experience desire, but this has to be interpreted as a divine yearning for that immaterial reality which is beyond all reason and all intelligence. It is a strong and sure desire for the clear and impassible contemplation of the transcendent. It is a hunger for an unending, conceptual, and true communion with the spotless and sublime light, of clear and splendid beauty.

33. *DN* 4.12–13, in *Pseudo-Dionysius: The Complete Works*, 81–83.

34. *DN* 4.12, in *Pseudo-Dionysius: The Complete Works*, 81 (bracketed insertion mine).

35. *DN* 4.12–13, in *Pseudo-Dionysius: The Complete Works*, 81–83.

36. Louth, *The Origins of the Christian Mystical Tradition*, 175. See also *DN* 4.13, in *Pseudo-Dionysius: The Complete Works*, 82. In the Dionysian corpus, the Greek term *ekstasis* means to "be taken wholly out of oneself." For the meaning of "ecstasy" in Dionysius, see Rorem, *Pseudo-Dionysius: A Commentary*, 147, 165, and *Pseudo-Dionysius: The Complete Works*, 130n266.

37. Jan Vanneste points out the total absence of both the terms "eros" and "agape" in the *Mystical Theology*. See Jan Vanneste, "Is the Mysticism of Pseudo-Dionysius Genuine?" *International Philosophical Quarterly* 3, no. 2 (1963): 286–306.

38. Rorem, *Pseudo-Dionysius: A Commentary*, 165.

39. Paul Rorem, *Biblical and Liturgical Symbols within the Pseudo-Dionysian Synthesis* (Toronto: Pontifical Institute of Mediaeval Studies, 1984), 137. This discussion of the nature of ecstasy is closely related to the discussion of the definition of mysticism. While modern readers tend to associate mysticism with mystical rapture entailed by an affective experience of God, an understanding that has developed

since the medieval period, the ancient Greek definition and the early Christian under-standing of mysticism was not emotional and experiential. Jan Vanneste has studied Dionysian mystical theology from the perspective of the medieval and modern under-standing of mysticism, and naturally concludes that "there is no authentic supernatu-ral mysticism expressed in the text of Pseudo-Dionysius if we interpret it in a strictly objective way." Vanneste, "Is the Mysticism of Pseudo-Dionysius Genuine?" 305. Rorem warns that readers and scholars of the Dionysian corpus should be cautious not to read it through a "medieval, affective overlay." Rorem, *Pseudo-Dionysius: A Commentary*, 230n28.

40. Rorem, *Pseudo-Dionysius: A Commentary*, 230n28; also 184. Colm Luibheid translates a sentence that includes the word *ekstasis* in *MT* 1.1 as follows: "By an undivided and absolute abandonment of yourself and everything, shedding all and freed from all, you will be uplifted to the ray of the divine shadow which is above everything that is." See *Pseudo-Dionysius: The Complete Works,* 135. Unlike Louth's translation, the term "ecstasy" has been omitted. It is possible that Luibheid inten-tionally omitted the term so that there would be no allusion to the emotional and ex-periential implications of "ecstasy" and "mysticism" with which modern readers are familiar. It is noteworthy that Paul Rorem collaborated with Luibheid on the English translation appearing in the *The Complete Works*.

41. Turner criticizes the affective interpretation of the medieval mystics as an "anti-mysticism" because it runs contrary to the Dionysian understanding of mysti-cism focused on intellectual hiddenness. Turner, *The Darkness of God*, 4.

42. Turner, *The Darkness of God*, 47.

43. Rorem, *Pseudo-Dionysius: A Commentary*, 238.

44. Hilduin also wrote a hagiographical account of the life of Saint Denis, in which Pseudo-Dionysius was identified with the apostolic Dionysius the Areopagite referred to in the book of Acts and with the first bishop of Paris and martyr, Saint Denis. See Jaroslav Pelikan, introduction to *Pseudo-Dionysius: The Complete Works*, 22, and Jean Leclercq, introduction to *Pseudo-Dionysius: The Complete Works*, 26; Rorem, *Pseudo-Dionysius: A Commentary*, 15–16.

45. Jean Leclercq, introduction to *Pseudo-Dionysius: The Complete Works*, 26–27; Rorem, *Pseudo-Dionysius: A Commentary*, 16.

46. Rorem, *Pseudo-Dionysius: A Commentary*, 237. In his survey of medieval influences on each Dionysian work, Paul Rorem repeatedly draws attention to the tendency of medieval writers to interpret Dionysius's words or ideas in accordance with their own theology or arguments.

47. Bernard McGinn, *The Foundations of Mysticism: Origins to the Fifth Century* (New York: Crossroad, 1991), 182.

48. The six "bends," or changes in emphasis, presented by Rorem are as follows:

First, the Areopagite's original local hierarchy of clergy and laity was stretched into a uni-versal pyramid of ultimate authority. Second, the author's vague comment about scriptural symbols was bent into a hoary warrant for excluding biblical allegory from theological argumentation. Third, the format of a liturgical commentary was stretched and bent so as to multiply allegories and typologies. Fourth, Neoplatonism's timeless procession and re-turn was given a chronological and eschatological bent and transformed into Christianity's salvation history of creation, incarnation, and final salvation. Fifth, the ascent to unknowing was considered as preparatory to a final union of love as medieval Dionysians added Christ and love to *The Mystical Theology*. Furthermore, even though the three ways were originally all phases or levels of thought in Dionysius, they were later shaped into moral purification, intellectual illumination, and a unitive perfection through love, although this material was not among the subjects chosen for direct presentation in this commentary. (Rorem, *Pseudo-Dionysius: A Commentary*, 238–39)

49. Paul Rorem, "The Uplifting Spirituality of Pseudo-Dionysius," in *Christian Spirituality: Origins to the Twelfth Century*, ed. Bernard McGinn, John Meyendorff, and Jean Leclercq (New York: Crossroad, 1985), 144.

50. Rorem, "The Uplifting Spirituality," 144.

51. For the Dionysian influence on medieval aesthetics, in particular regarding Abbot Suger's (1081–1151) appropriation of *The Celestial Hierarchy* to provide a theoretical articulation of Gothic architecture, see Rorem, *Pseudo-Dionysius: A Commentary*, 78–83.

52. Rorem summarizes the whole Dionysian corpus as a series of theological descriptions of "the epistemological uplifting"—first transiting from perceptible symbols to the conceptual realms through negating dissimilar images then proceeding to the ineffable transcendence of the divine through the negation of all symbols and concepts. Rorem, "The Uplifting Spirituality," 142, 132–51.

53. McGinn, *The Foundations of Mysticism*, 182.

54. McGinn, *The Foundations of Mysticism*, 182.

55. Paul Rorem's historical survey of the misrepresentation and reinterpretation of the Dionysian dialectic of knowing and unknowing provides the reader of the *Itinerarium* general knowledge of the medieval adjustments to Dionysian mysticism. See Rorem, *Pseudo-Dionysius: A Commentary*, 214–25.

56. The Victorines were regular canons who were clerics living in a religious community following the Augustinian Rule. For a brief introduction to the Victorines, see Grover A. Zinn, "The Regular Canons," in *Christian Spirituality*, 218–28; Bernard McGinn, "The Victorine Ordering of Mysticism," in *The Growth of Mysticism: Gregory the Great Through the 12th Century* (New York: Herder and Herder Book, 1994), 363–418. For a brief study primarily concerning the relationship between Dionysianism and the Victorines, see Rorem, *Pseudo-Dionysius: A Commentary*, 216–19.

57. Rorem briefly explains how the Victorines, under the significant influence of Eriugena, came to place love above knowledge. Paul Rorem, *Hugh of Saint Victor* (Oxford: Oxford University Press, 2009), 172–76; see also Rorem, *Pseudo-Dionysius: A Commentary*, 216–19.

58. *CH* 7.1, in *Pseudo-Dionysius: The Complete Works*, 161.

59. See John Scotus Eriugena, chap. 7, lines 139–43 of *Expositiones in Ierarchiam Coelestem*, ed. Jeanne Barbet, vol. 31 of *Corpus Christianorum Continuatio Mediaevalis* (Turnholt: Brepols, 1975), 95. The reference to Eriugena's commentary on this text is indebted to Rorem, *Hugh of Saint Victor*, 173.

60. Refers to the Song of Songs in the Old Testament.

61. Jacques Paul Migne, ed., *Patrologia Cursus Completus, Series Latina*, vol. 175 (Paris, 1854), 1038D, quoted in Rorem, *Hugh of Saint Victor*, 175.

62. Rorem, *Hugh of Saint Victor*, 175.

63. Rorem, *Pseudo-Dionysius: A Commentary*, 217–18.

64. For a brief introduction to the life of Thomas Gallus, see Bernard McGinn, *The Flowering of Mysticism: Men and Women in the New Mysticism (1200–1350)*, vol. 3 of *The Presence of God: A History of Western Christian Mysticism* (New York: Crossroad, 1998), 78–79.

65. Bernard McGinn, "Thomas Gallus and Dionysian Mysticism," *Studies in Spirituality* 8 (1998): 83–84; McGinn, *The Flowering of Mysticism*, 78–79. For a historical survey of the development of the two streams of medieval Dionysianism, see Rorem, *Pseudo-Dionysius: A Commentary*, 214–25.

66. McGinn, *The Flowering of Mysticism*, 80.

67. *MT* 1.3, in *Pseudo-Dionysius: The Complete Works*, 137.

68. Thomas Gallus, *Extractio*, in *MT* 1, in Philippe Chevalier, ed., *Dionysiaca*, vol. 1 (Paris: Desclée, 1937), 710n578, quoted in McGinn, *The Flowering of Mysticism*, 81. Gallus's *Extractio* both translated and paraphrased the Dionysian treatises for ordinary readers. See McGinn, "Thomas Gallus and Dionysian Mysticism," 84n11.

69. Rorem, *Pseudo-Dionysius: A Commentary*, 219.

70. Gallus's synthesizing attempt was not limited to his interpretation of Dionysian texts. Gallus brought the account of eros/agape in the fourth chapter of the *Divine Names* into his commentary on the Song of Songs "in order to justify his inserting the affective erotic language of the Song into the vision of cosmic eros described by Dionysius." McGinn, *The Flowering of Mysticism*, 81; see also 360n49.

71. That is, love subsuming knowledge.

72. McGinn, *The Flowering of Mysticism*, 82.

73. Rorem, *Pseudo-Dionysius: A Commentary*, 221. In order to support his argument about the separation between knowledge and love originating with Gallus, McGinn quotes some phrases from Gallus's corpus to the effect that the supraintellectual journey to a union with God or to the divine light requires leaving behind all intellectual effort. This is obviously Gallus's interpretation of Dionysius's *Mystical Theology*, but McGinn's argument that Gallus was the first thinker to assert the need for a complete abandonment of knowledge is not persuasive. For example, Hugh of St. Victor's well-known phrase—"love enters and approaches where knowledge stays outside" (*Patrologia Latina* 175:1038D)—may have anticipated Gallus's position. It is also worth noting that Gallus's paraphrase of the text of *Mystical Theology* implies to a certain extent the idea of "love subsuming knowledge," rather than the total cessation of intellectual processes. McGinn's argument would benefit from a clearer explanation of the difference between Hugh's and Gallus's positions with respect to the relationship between knowledge and love on the journey of ascent.

74. Bonaventure, *On the Reduction of the Arts to Theology*, trans., with introduction, Zachary Hayes, vol. 1 of *WSB* (St. Bonaventure, NY: Franciscan Institute, 1996), in *WSB*, 1:43–45.

75. *On the Reduction of the Arts to Theology*, in *WSB*, 1:45.

76. *On the Reduction of the Arts to Theology*, in *WSB*, 1:45.

77. Rorem, *Pseudo-Dionysius: A Commentary*, 220.

78. The dialectic of procession and return is dominant in the *Itinerarium*. For example, *Itin.* prol. 1, in *WSB*, 2:35: "In the beginning I call upon that First Beginning from whom all illumination flows as from the *God of lights*, and from whom comes *every good and perfect gift*," and prol. 2, in *WSB*, 2:37: "I was there reflecting on certain ways in which the mind might ascend to God." Ewert Cousins compares the metaphorical movements of procession and return—downward and upward—in the *Itinerarium* to the architectural structure of the Gothic cathedral: "The movement of the stone as it reaches up toward heaven reflects the ascent through creation which Bonaventure describes in *The Soul's Journey*, and the light streaming through the stained glass windows reflects the downward movement of God expressing himself in the variety of creatures and in his gifts of grace." Ewert H. Cousins, introduction to *Bonaventure: The Soul's Journey into God·The Tree of Life·The Life of St. Francis*, trans. and ed., with introduction and annotations, Ewert H. Cousins (New York: Paulist Press, 1978), 16–17.

79. Rorem, "The Uplifting Spirituality of Pseudo-Dionysius," 147.

80. *MT* 1.1, in *Pseudo-Dionysius: The Complete Works*, 135; *Itin.* 7.5, in *WSB*, 2:137–39.

81. For the dialectic of similarity and dissimilarity between the creature and the creator in Bonaventure, see Timothy Johnson, "Reading Between Lines: Apophatic Knowledge and Naming the Divine in Bonaventure's Book of Creation," *Franciscan Studies* 60 (2002): 139–58.

82. Johnson, "Reading Between Lines," 149.

83. Johnson, "Reading Between Lines," 158.

84. See Turner, *The Darkness of God*, 19–46, esp. 40–46.

85. *Itin.* 5.5, in *WSB*, 2:117.

86. *Itin.* 5.6, in *WSB*, 2:117.

87. *Itin.* 5.7, in *WSB*, 2:119.

88. Turner, *The Darkness of God*, 128.

89. Turner, *The Darkness of God*, 129.

90. *Itin.* 6.2, in *WSB*, 2:125.

91. *Itin.* 6.3, in *WSB*, 2:127.

92. Turner, *The Darkness of God*, 129.

93. *Itin.* 6.4–6, in *WSB*, 2:129–31.

94. Turner, *The Darkness of God*, 131.

95. *Itin.* 6.7, in *WSB*, 2:131; see also *Itin.* 7.5, in *WSB*, 2:139.

96. For a detailed study of the role of affectivity in the *Itinerarium*, see Elizabeth Dreyer, "Affectus in St. Bonaventure's Description of the Journey of the Soul to God" (PhD diss., Marquette University, 1982). See also Elizabeth Dreyer, "Bonaventure the Franciscan: An Affective Spirituality," in *Spiritualities of the Heart: Approaches to Personal Wholeness in Christian Tradition*, ed. Annice Callahan (New York: Paulist Press, 1990), 33–44; Elizabeth Dreyer, "Affectus in St. Bonaventure's Theology," *Franciscan Studies* 42 (1982): 5–20.

97. *Itin.* prol. 4, in *WSB*, 2:39–41.

98. Turner, *The Darkness of God*, 47. In the *Itinerarium*, "the traditional metaphors of affectivity, touch, taste and smell" are prevalent.

99. See *Itin.* prol. 4, in *WSB*, 2:38–40.

100. Philotheus Boehner, "Notes & Commentary" on *Itinerarium*, *WSB*, 2:151. For "admiration" in the *Itinerarium*, see also Dreyer, "Affectus in St. Bonaventure's Description of the Journey," 127, 135.

101. See *Itin.* 3.7, in *WSB*, 2:93; 4.3 (99–101); 5.7 (119); 6.3 (125–29). For example, *Itin.* 6.3 (125–27):

> But as you contemplate these matters, beware that you do not think that you have come to comprehend the incomprehensible. For you still have something to consider in these six characteristics that will lead the eye of our mind with great strength to a stupor of admiration. For here we find the highest communicability together with the property of the persons. . . . Who would not be rapt in wonder at the thought of such marvels [*Quis ad tantorum mirabilium aspectum non consurgat in admirationem*]?

102. *Itin.* 4.3, in *WSB*, 2:101.

103. Admiration is also associated with the emotion of fear that arises at the soul's overwhelming realization of the unknowability of God. See Boehner, "Notes & Commentary" on *Itinerarium*, in *WSB*, 2:151–52. McGinn points out that in chapters 5 and 6 it is not Bonaventure's intent to demonstrate something regarding the divine attributes, but rather to arouse admiration. See McGinn, *The Flowering of Mysticism*, 108.

104. *Itin.* prol. 4, in *WSB*, 2:39.

105. Cousins, introduction to *Bonaventure*, 22.

106. *Itin.* prol. 5, in *WSB*, 2:41.

107. *Itin.* 4.3, in *WSB*, 2:101.

108. "*Transitus*" in Latin.

109. *Itin.* 7.4, in *WSB*, 2:137.

110. *Itin.* 1.6, in *WSB*, 2:49–51.

111. *Itin.* 1.6, in *WSB*, 2:50–51. McGinn surveys the historical development of the scheme of the multiple powers of the soul that was later adapted by Bonaventure. He shows that the Bonaventurian sixfold scheme is an extension of a fourfold and later a fivefold scheme, to the latter of which Bonaventure added the *apex mentis*. See Bernard McGinn, "Ascension and Introversion in the *Itinerarium Mentis in Deum*," in *S. Bonaventura 1274–1974*, ed. Jacques-Guy Bougerol and Etienne Gilson (Rome: Collegio S. Bonaventura, 1974), 3:547–48. However, elsewhere, McGinn shows that prior to Bonaventure, Thomas Gallus had added the "high point of the power of attraction" or the "spark of the *synderesis*" (*apex affectionsis/scintilla synderesis*) to the upper level of the various powers of the soul in an attempt to merge the affective eros of the Song of Songs and the cosmic eros of the *Divine Names*. This is further confirmation of Gallus's influence on Bonaventure. See McGinn, *The Flowering of Mysticism*, 81–82, 106.

112. Etienne Gilson, *The Philosophy of St. Bonaventure*, trans. Dom Illtyd Trehowan and Frank J. Sheed (Paterson, NJ: St. Anthony Guild, 1965), 483n31; see also 329. This reference comes from McGinn, "Ascension and Introversion," 538. Bonaventure distinguishes four faculties of the soul: the vegetative, the sensitive, the intellect, and the will in the rational soul. See Gilson, *The Philosophy of St. Bonaventure*, 343.

113. See Gilson, *The Philosophy of St. Bonaventure*, 343.

114. For a detailed note about *apex mentis* or *synderesis*, see Boehner, "Notes & Commentary" on *Itinerarium*, 163n11.

115. *II Commentarius in quatuor libros Sententiarum Petri Lombardi*, d. 39, a. 2, q. 1, in *Doctoris seraphici S. Bonaventurae Opera omnia*, 2:910, quoted in Boehner, "Notes & Commentary" on *Itinerarium*, in *WSB*, 2:163n11.

116. "For conscience dictates and *synderesis* either desires or flees from. . . . And so in order that we may speak properly, *synderesis* names the affective power in as far as it is naturally fit for the good and tends toward the good; conscience, on the other hand, names the disposition of the practical intellect." *II Commentarius in quatuor libros Sententiarum Petri Lombardi*, d. 39, a. 2, q. 1, in *Opera omnia*, 2:914, 917 quoted in Boehner, "Notes & Commentary" on *Itinerarium*, in *WSB*, 2:163n11. Both Boehner and Cousins translate *synderesis* as conscience, which results in some confusion in light of the fact that Bonaventure distinguishes *synderesis* and *conscientia*. See Cousins, introduction to *Bonaventure*, 62.

117. See McGinn, *The Flowering of Mysticism*, 107.

118. Bonaventure also uses other terms to describe the final stages of the unitive ascent, such as *unitio amoris* and *sapientia vera*. See George H. Tavard, *Transiency and Permanence: The Nature of Theology According to St. Bonaventure* (St. Bonaventure, NY: Franciscan Institute, 1954), 241. For a detailed discussion of the Bonaventurian ecstasy or excess (*excessus*), see Tavard, *Transiency and Permanence*, 240–47; McGinn, *The Flowering of Mysticism*, 106–12; Karl Rahner, "The Doctrine of the Spiritual Senses in the Middle Ages," in *Theological Investigations* (New York: Crossroad, 1979), 16:117–28.

119. Boehner, "Notes & Commentary" on *Itinerarium*, in *WSB,* 2:147. In his own translation of the *Itinerarium*, Boehner frequently employs "transport" for *excessus*. See Bonaventure, *Itinerarium Mentis in Deum*, vol. 2 of *The Works of Saint Bonaventure*, trans. Philotheus Boehner and F. Laughlin (St. Bonaventure, NY: Franciscan Institute, 1956). See also Dreyer, "Affectus in St. Bonaventure's Description," 121–22.

120. For example: "Ut transeat ad pacem per ecstaticos excessus sapientiae christianae" (*Itin.* prol. 3, in *WSB*, 2:36); "Ut transiens in illud per ecstaticum amorem" (*Itin.* 4.3, in *WSB*, 2:100); "Per . . . suspensiones excessuum" (*Itin.* 4.4, in *WSB*, 2:100–102); "De excessu mentali et mystico, in quo requies datur intellectui, affectu totaliter in deum per excessum transeunte" (*Itin.* 7.1, in *WSB*, 2:132); "Ubi in Deum transiit per contemplationis excessum" (*Itin.* 7.3, in *WSB*, 2:134); "Etenim te ipso et omnibus immensurabili et absoluto purae mentis excessu, ad superessentialem divinarum tenebrarum radium omnia deserens et ab omnibus absolutus ascendes" (*Itin.* 7.5, in *WSB*, 2:138). While *excessus* mostly implies a transitional stage, there are cases in which *ecstasis/excessus* is associated with the state of the ultimate goal; for example, "ad ecstaticam pacem," *Itin.* prol. 1, in *WSB*, 2:34, in which *ecstasis* is descriptive of the final goal of peace.

121. *Itin.* 4.3, in *WSB*, 2:101. The exultation that one experiences at the point of union with God is obviously an affective feeling; admiration involves the will (an affective aspect of the soul) and devotion is "an affective feeling toward God and Christ." For a detailed explanation, see Dreyer, "An Affective Spirituality," 41.

122. *Itin.* 4.3, in *WSB*, 2:98–101: "Dum caritate complectitur Verbum incarnatum, ut suscipiens ab ipso delectationem et ut transiens in illud per ecstaticum amorem recuperat gustum et tactum." The English version is quoted from Zachary Hayes's translation except the two words in brackets. I employed different prepositions than those in Hayes to stress the implication of transition and means.

123. See, *Itin.* 7.4, 7.6, in *WSB*, 2:137, 139.

124. *Itin.* 7.4, in *WSB*, 2:137.

125. *Itin.* 5.7, 6.3, in *WSB*, 2:119, 125–29.

126. *Itin.* 6.4, 6.6–7, 7.2, in *WSB*, 2:129, 131, 135. Ewert Cousins argues that the coincidence of opposites is prevalent in Bonaventure's writings. Particularly the last three chapters of the *Itinerarium* show how reflecting on the coincidence of opposites in the divine attributes of God, in the personal attributes of the Trinity, and in the person of Christ leads the soul to ecstatic union with God. See Ewert Cousins, "The Coincidence of Opposites in the Christology of Saint Bonaventure," *Franciscan Studies* 28 (1968): 27–45; Ewert Cousins, "Itinerarium Mentis in Deum," chap. 3 in *Bonaventure and the Coincidence of Opposites* (Chicago: Franciscan Herald Press, 1978), 69–96.

127. *Itin.* 6.7, in *WSB*, 2:131.

128. Bonaventure, *Breviloquium* 5.6.8, in *Breviloquium*, trans., with introduction and notes, Dominic V. Monti, vol. 9 of *WSB* (St. Bonaventure, NY: Franciscan Institute, 2005), 196.

129. McGinn, *The Flowering of Mysticism*, 111.

130. *On the Reduction of the Arts to Theology*, in *WSB*, 1:61. See also *On the Reduction of the Arts to Theology*, in *WSB*, 1:45.

131. McGinn, *The Flowering of Mysticism*, 376n216. On Bonaventure's emphasis on the affective power of love in the soul's rising up to God in his other writings, see Timothy Johnson, *The Soul in Ascent: Bonaventure on Poverty, Prayer, and Union with God*, rev. ed. (St. Bonaventure, NY: Franciscan Institute, 2012), 179–84. Following Bonaventure's threefold way to the ecstatic peace of contemplation proposed in his *Commentary on the Gospel of Luke*, Timothy Johnson articulates the anagogical journey of the soul, drawing on Bonaventure's various texts. The threefold way consists of the way of James, the way of Peter, and the way of John, which, respectively, correspond to the ways of purification, illumination, and union. These two threefold categories again are reflected in the structure of the *Itinerarium*, in which, although not explicitly confirmed by Johnson, each way corresponds to first the prologue, then chapters 1 through 6, and finally chapter 7. Johnson's articulation of the triple way leading to ecstatic peace helps locate the dense text of the *Itinerarium*, heavily laden with philosophical, theological, spiritual, and historical implications, within the development of Bonaventure's theology and spirituality. See Johnson, *The Soul in Ascent*, 149–93.

132. Turner, *The Darkness of God*, 131–32. There are different opinions concerning the role of Christ in Dionysian mysticism. Without doubt, Dionysius brings Christ into his writings, but Bernard McGinn notes that "the Areopagite's remarks on Christ are scattered and to some extent unassimilated into his more systematic works." McGinn, *The Foundations of Mysticism*, 180.

133. On Bonaventurian Christocentrism, see Zachary Hayes, *The Hidden Center: Spirituality and Speculative Christology in St. Bonaventure* (1981; repr., St. Bonaventure, NY: Franciscan Institute, 2000); Zachary Hayes, "Christ the Center," in *Bonaventure: Mystical Writings* (New York: Crossroad, 1999), 114–27; Zachary Hayes, "Christology and Metaphysics in the Thought of Bonaventure," in "Celebrating the Medieval Heritage: A Colloquy on the Thought of Aquinas and Bonaventure," Supplement, *The Journal of Religion* 58 (1978): S82–S96; Ilia Delio, "Theology, Metaphysics, and the Centrality of Christ," *Theological Studies* 68 (2007): 254–73.

134. *Itin.* 6.4–7, in *WSB*, 2:129–31.

135. *Itin.* 7.1, in *WSB*, 2:133.

136. *Itin.* 4.2, 4.3, in *WSB*, 2:97–99, 99–101. In the description of the soul's transformation, Bonaventure explains how in contemplating three aspects of Christ (the uncreated Word, the inspired Word, and the Incarnate Word), the three theological virtues—faith, hope, and charity—purify, illuminate, and perfect the soul. He asserts that the soul embraces the Incarnate Word in love and passes over to Christ in ecstatic love.

137. Turner, *The Darkness of God*, 130–31.

138. *Itin.* 6.7, in *WSB*, 2:131.

139. *Itin.* 7.1, in *WSB*, 2:133.

140. *Itin.* 7.2, in *WSB*, 2:135.

141. *Itin.* prol. 3, in *WSB*, 2:37.

142. *Itin.* prol. 3, in *WSB*, 2:37–39.

143. *Itin.* prol. 3, in *WSB*, 2:39.

144. *Itin.* 7.4, 7.6, in *WSB*, 2:137, 139. Bonaventure uses the allegories of light and fire to represent the intellectual and affective aspects of the spiritual journey, respectively.

145. *Itin.* prol. 1, 3, in *WSB*, 2:35, 37.

146. *Itin.* 7.6, in *WSB*, 2:139. Biblical references to the italicized phrases come from, in order, Ex 33:20, Jn 13:1, and Jn 14:8.

147. Turner, *The Darkness of God*, 132.

148. *Itin.* prol. 3, in *WSB*, 2:37.

149. *Itin.* 7.3, in *WSB*, 2:135.

150. McGinn, *The Flowering of Mysticism*, 94.

151. McGinn, *The Flowering of Mysticism*, 93.

152. McGinn, *The Flowering of Mysticism*, 93.

153. The seven visions of the cross, revealed either to Francis himself or to others, are recorded by Bonaventure in *Major Legend* 1.3, 1.5, 2.1, 3.5, 4.9, 4.10, and chapter 13, in *FA:ED*, 2:532–33, 534, 536, 544–45, 556, 557, and 630–39. McGinn, *The Flowering of Mysticism*, 96; Ewert Cousins, "The Image of St. Francis in Bonaventure's *Legenda Major*," in *Bonaventuriana: Miscellanea in Onore di Jacques Guy Bougerol OFM*, ed. Francisco de Asís Chavero Blanco (Rome: Edizioni Antonianum, 1988), 317, 320.

154. *Major Legend*, 13.10, in *FA:ED*, 2:638–39.

155. McGinn, *The Flowering of Mysticism*, 96.

156. McGinn, *The Flowering of Mysticism*, 96

157. *Major Legend*, 13.10, in *FA:ED*, 2:638–39. See also *Itin*. prol. 3, 1.1–7, 7.1, in *WSB*, 2:37–39, 45–51, 133–35. The reference in the *Itinerarium* to the quotation from the *Major Legend* comes from Cousins, annotation to *The Life of St. Francis*, in *Bonaventure*, 314n45.

158. McGinn, *The Flowering of Mysticism*, 93.

159. Joshua Benson, "The Christology of the *Breviloquium*," in *A Companion to Bonaventure*, ed. Jay M. Hammond, J. A. Wayne Hellmann, and Jared Goff (Leiden: Brill, 2014), 284–87.

160. Timothy Johnson, "Place, Analogy, and Transcendence: Bonaventure and Bacon on the Franciscan Relationship to the World," in *Innovationen durch Deuten und Gestalten: Klöster im Mittelalter zwischen Jenseits und Welt*, ed. Gert Melville, Bernd Schneidmüller, and Stefan Weinfurter (Regensburg: Schnell & Steiner, 2014), 86. On Francis as the embodiment of a narrative or map of the spiritual pilgrimage to the divine and facilitator of a participative reading of the *Itinerarium*, see Timothy Johnson, "Dream Bodies and Peripatetic Prayer: Reading Bonaventure's *Itinerarium* with Certeau," *Modern Theology* 21, no. 3 (July 2005): 413–27; Timothy Johnson, "Prologue as Pilgrimage: Bonaventure as Spiritual Cartographer," *Miscellanea Francescana* 106–107 (2006–2007): 445–64.

161. See *Itin.* 7.3, in *WSB*, 2:135.

162. Johnson, "Place, Analogy, and Transcendence," 87. See also Johnson, "Dream Bodies and Peripatetic Prayer," 418–19.

163. See Dreyer, "An Affective Spirituality," 40–41.

164. *Major Legend* 11.1, in *FA:ED*, 2:612. See also *Itin.* 7.4, 7.6, in *WSB*, 2:137, 139.

Chapter Four

The Tension between Moderate and Radical Subitism

Chinul's Integration of Sŏn and Kyo and Advocacy of Kanhwa Sŏn

Chapter 2 examined Chinul's accommodating approach to Hwaŏn scriptural and philosophical studies and his efforts to integrate them into Sŏn meditation. Chinul wanted to bring together the two competing schools of Kyo and Sŏn for the benefit of Buddhist practitioners because he was convinced that intellectual learning could benefit Sŏn practitioners by providing them a theoretical understanding of the Buddhist soteriological path and goal. Chinul's conviction regarding the complementary relationship between the teachings of Kyo and Sŏn was grounded on his own personal experience, which seemed to confirm that relationship. Chapter 2 explored Chinul's *Treatise on the Complete and Sudden Attainment of Buddhahood*, a treatise which drew heavily on Li Tongxuan's exposition on the *Huayan jing*. On the one hand, Chinul was intent on demonstrating the theoretical and practical common ground between Sŏn and the doctrinal teachings of Hwaŏm, which were grounded in the Hwaŏm scriptures. On the other, he was also concerned to assert the superiority of Sŏn over Kyo by stressing the value of nonintellectual forms of meditation.

In *Complete and Sudden Attainment*, Chinul maintains an ambivalent attitude toward the efforts of the intellect—he advocates for a moderate accommodation to theoretical learning and intellectual meditation while at the same time radically renouncing them. This ambivalent approach prevails in another of Chinul's works, *Excerpts from the Dharma Collection and Special Practice Record with Personal Notes*.[1] *Excerpts* also acknowledges the complementarity between Kyo and Sŏn and the merit of intellectual studies, but asserts the superiority of nonintellectual meditation—it expounds *kanhwa* Sŏn, a radical form of Sŏn meditation that had recently been introduced into the Korean Buddhist community and that rejects any conceptual understandings.

Excerpts only briefly introduces the new meditation technique, but Chinul expounds it in detail in *Treatise on Resolving Doubts about Observing the Keyword*. In this posthumously published work, Chinul actively advocates *kanhwa* meditation, seeming to downplay the role of the intellect. In *Resolving Doubts*, Chinul's soteriological approach moves from a moderate accommodation of intellectual religious practices to a radical rejection of them.[2]

The tension between these two approaches had already been present in Chan as it had developed in China. David J. Kalupahana argues that the Chinese Chan tradition developed through a syncretization of two distinct schools of Mahāyāna Buddhist philosophy—Madhyamaka and Yogācāra—which originated in India in the second and fourth century, respectively. These two schools were introduced into China and then were strongly influenced by Taoism, the indigenous Chinese transcendental philosophy. That the transcendental or apophatic approach of the Madhyamaka school, an approach that attacks Scholastic theories by means of dialectical negations, was incorporated into Chan, can be seen in the dismissive attitude of Chan practitioners toward doctrinal study and Scholastic philosophy. At the same time, the Chan school adopted the the Yogācāra school's emphasis on meditation.[3] Chan would further combine Yogācārin thought with buddha-nature thought, and this synthesis would contribute to the preeminence in the Chan school of investigating the mind and the theoretical verification of optimistic and positive language.

This chapter will first explore the development of Chan in China, highlighting the inherent tension between cataphasis and apophasis in Chan thought. This tension will be further discussed with regard to two seemingly contrasting Buddhist schools, the Madhyamaka and Buddha-Nature schools. The chapter will proceed to an investigation of Chinul's writings, in particular *Excerpts* and *Resolving Doubts*, in order to show the consistent tension between his moderate accommodation of scriptures and doctrines, which involves a cataphatic approach, and his renunciation of words and concepts, an apophatic approach. This tension between cataphasis and apophasis was addressed in chapter 2, which primarily explored Chinul's integration of doctrinal studies with Sŏn practice. This chapter will further investigate the tension between these two approaches, particularly in light of other tensions deriving from various modes of meditation and various doctrinal understandings of ultimate reality.

BUDDHIST APOPHASIS AND CATAPHASIS

Negative Discourse and Expressive Discourse

As noted in the chapters on Bonaventure, the *terms* "cataphasis" and "apophasis" are rooted in the Christian theological tradition. They were coined by Pseudo-Dionysius, a late fifth-, early sixth-century Christian writer of Syrian origin, and have been incorporated into theological discourses throughout Christian history with great enthusiasm. However, Christianity does not have a monopoly on the *concepts* of cataphasis and apophasis, which can be understood as referring to "positive discourse" and "negative discourse," respectively. Buddhist thinkers too have developed these concepts. Robert M. Gimello introduces the Buddhist counterparts of the Christian terms "expressive" (or cataphatic) discourse (C. *zhequan*, K. *ch'ajŏn* 遮詮) and "negative" (or apophatic) discourse (C. *biaoquan*, K. *p'yojŏn* 表詮). These terms were described by Guifeng Zongmi 圭峰宗密 (780–841), a patriarch of both Huayan and Chan, as one of ten differences between the Emptiness school (C. Kongzong, K. Kongjong 空宗) and the (Buddha) Nature school (C. Xingzong, K. Sŏngjong 性宗). Zongmi's explanation of these terms is as follows:

> The two lineages differ from one another as regards their use of negative (i.e. apophatic) discourse (*che-ch'üan*) and expressive (i.e. kataphatic) discourse (*piao-chüan*). "Negative" means rejecting what is not the case. "Expressive" means manifesting what is the case. That is to say, negation is the denial of all things other than the real. Consider for example the scriptures' exposition of the true and marvelous principle of Buddha-nature. All the scriptures say that neither is it born nor does it perish, that is neither soiled nor pure, that it is without either cause or effect, that it is neither characterizable nor conditioned, that is neither common nor noble, that it is neither essential nor accidental, etc. This is all negative discourse. In the scriptures and authoritative treatises the phrase "is not" (*fei*) is used to negate all existents. It may appear as many as thirty to fifty times in a single passage. The same is true of the phrases "not have" and "no" (*wu, pu*). Thus does one speak of the "hundredfold negation." But when the scriptures speak of "the illumination of insight and enlightenment," of "the mirror-like radiance of the spirit," of "brilliant refulgence," of "universal repose," etc., then they are using expressive discourse.
>
> Now, if there were not such substantial realities as "insight," what could be revealed as the Buddha-nature, what could be said "neither to be born nor to perish" and so forth? One must recognize that understanding in the very perception of what is presently at hand is precisely the Buddha-nature of the mind. Then can one say that such understanding "neither was born in the past nor will perish in the future," etc. It is like speaking of salt. To say that it is not sweet is negation, whereas to say that it is brackish is expression. Or, in the case of water,

to say that it is not dry is negation, but to say that it is wet is expression. The "hundred negations" mentioned in all the doctrinal systems of Buddhism are all negative locutions, but the direct manifestation of the one truth is accomplished by expressive discourse.

The discourses of the emptiness lineage are exclusively negative, but the discourse of the nature lineage partakes of both negation and expression. Exclusive negation is incomplete [i.e. its meanings are not explicit, not fully realized—*neyārtha*], but the combination of negation with expression hits the mark exactly. Men of these days [i.e. ninth-century China] all regard negative discourse as profound and expressive discourse as shallow. Thus they set store only by such phrases as "neither mind nor Buddha," "neither conditioned nor characterizable," and finally "all is ineffable." This is all due to their mistaking purely negative discourse for profundity and to their failure to aspire after an intimate personal realization of the substance of the truth.[4]

Here, Zongmi defends cataphatic discourse against what he saw as a preference for apophasis in the Chan community of his time. He felt that this preference was pretentious and often masked a lack of real understanding—a kind of fake profundity—and he argued for the superiority of the buddha-nature teaching over the emptiness teaching.

As Zongmi explains, the Emptiness school and Buddha-Nature school can be distinguished by the way in which they employ negative and expressive discourse. He points out that the Emptiness school employs exclusively negative discourse, while the Buddha-Nature school employs both. Since cataphasis alone is insufficient, Zongmi's own philosophical discourse uses a combination of expressive and negative discourse. As explained by Zongmi, the two modes of discourse and the doctrine of the two schools are interconnected: the distinctive teachings of each school provide theoretical grounds for their choice of discourse, and the negative or expressive discourse they use in turn enhances their doctrinal positions.

Chan's Incorporation of the Two Discourses and Two Schools

The Teaching of Emptiness and Apophasis

The Chan school of meditation is usually deemed to be within the broad Mahāyāna tradition of Buddhism, especially the Madhyamaka school, which ardently advocates the doctrine of emptiness. This Mahāyāna doctrine of emptiness (S. śūnyatā) is expounded in the early Mahāyāna scriptures, including the *Prajñāpāramitā sūtras* (the "Perfection of Wisdom" sūtras).[5] These scriptures declare that wisdom (S. *prajñā*) is a penetrating insight into the true nature of all things in the universe. The true nature of things that wisdom discovers is the emptiness of all things; that is, that there is no inherent substantial nature (S. *svabhāva*). Wisdom sees that all things are, as they are, ultimately "empty," lacking any form, quality, or existence; emptiness is for this reason called "thusness" or "suchness" (*tathatā*). In addition, since all things are empty, they are all the same without distinction, so emptiness is also denoted by the term "sameness" (*samatā*). This emptiness is ineffable, transcending all concepts and words. Although wisdom in this school is understood as a nondual awareness of things as empty, implying the absence of linguistic or intellectual activity, in the Indo-Tibetan tradition this nondual, nondiscriminative insight was believed to be the result of an intellectual analysis. The philosophers of India and Tibet thought that attaining perfect nondual and nonconceptual wisdom involves conceptual activities employed in the process leading to enlightenment.[6]

The Madhyamaka school (also known as the "Middle Way") grounded its philosophical system on the Perfection of Wisdom sūtras. This philosophical school, founded by Nāgārjuna, who is believed to have lived in South India during the second century, advocated the doctrine of emptiness. The Indian philosopher is well known for his use of the method of didactic negation, through which he refutes all philosophical arguments favoring the concept of intrinsic nature or inherent existence.[7] Based on Nāgārjuna's thought, the Madhyamaka school seeks to disprove the ontological claim that things can exist independently and permanently. However, it does not reject the existence of phenomena that arise as a result of causes and conditions, and the school identifies emptiness with dependent origination (S. *pratīyasamutpāda*, C. *yuanqi*, K. *yŏn'gi* 緣起). Thus, it takes the "middle way," avoiding the two extremes of, on the one hand, belief in intrinsic nature (or intrinsic being, S. *svabhāva* 自性), and, on the other, nihilism.

For Nāgārjuna emptiness is not a "doctrine" to be propounded or explicated. Rather it is a method, a way of thinking, in which "doctrines" presented in cataphatic language (i.e., what the Buddhist calls "views"=*dṛṣṭi*) are refuted by being deconstructed and thus made null and void. He engages in logical debates that reveal the absurdity of conclusions derived from affirmative statements. This is called the "*prasangika*" method ("reductio ad absurdum" in Western logic). Nāgārjuna uses negative, not positive, discourse when he discusses the ultimate reality of things. Thus, Nāgārjuna's Buddhist discourse can be compared in general to the negative or apophatic theology of the Christian tradition.[8]

The Emptiness school's preference for negation is not just a strategic choice for refuting opponents in debate, but is a practical outworking of the doctrine of emptiness itself. The apophasis of this school first draws on its view of language, which asserts that words and associated concepts do not actually refer to real things because all things are without any substance. Any positive locution would generate delusion and attachment to things as if they positively existed. Emptiness, by contrast, teaches that there are no permanent substances, but that all things arise and disappear according to the principle of dependent origination. Therefore, as it was put by Gimello, emptiness is "the very principle of denial of determinacy"[9] within the apophatic system of the Mahāyāna discourse. In this regard, through its denial of "referential capacity,"[10] Madhyamaka claims the invalidity of any predication or ascription, even one related to the teaching of emptiness itself.[11] These considerations reveal a distinction between two categories of Buddhist apophasis: the rhetoric of negative expressions and the negation of any form of discourse.

Views of language and the doctrinal premises that undergirded them would also have a significant influence on practice. Most importantly, a mistrust of language and conceptual discourse would cause some practitioners to favor meditation over textual and doctrinal studies. Chan is the best example of this with its favoring of apophatic language and stress on meditation. However, the relationship between the two modes of discourse and meditation is more complicated than just a simple correlation between apophasis and meditation—this is because there are various methods of meditation that differ from each other in a manner analogous to the way in which apophasis and cataphasis differ from each other.

Mistrust in language based on the intrinsic limitations of verbal expression in regard to describing ultimate reality not only encourages meditative practice in general, but also raises suspicions about "intellectual" meditation practices relying on words and concepts. For those who mistrust words and concepts, while meditation may entail profound intellectual understanding, it is ultimately bound to fail in its efforts to grasp reality. Indeed, for those practitioners, the involvement of the conceptualization process in meditation is believed to hinder the meditator from a direct, unmediated realization of reality by generating attachment to concepts. Thus, intellectual meditation is closely connected with cataphasis and its related linguistic and doctrinal understandings, and nonintellectual meditation avoids conceptualization because of an apophatic distrust of language and concepts.

In summary, the apophasis that is closely related to the Emptiness school may be understood from three perspectives. First, it refers to negative expressions, which explicitly use "not," "no," or other words of negative meaning. It may also refer to any verbal expression which does not involve explicit negation, but which is still intended to break down usual linguistic rules. Second, this kind of apophatic discourse derives from a strong mistrust of language and is theoretically related to the indescribability of ultimate truth. And third, all of this promotes nondiscursive meditation, as in forms of Chan meditation in which the object of meditation is a paradoxical, senseless phrase.[12]

The doctrine of emptiness and its favored mode of discourse, apophasis, would come to be embraced by Chan adepts who read and studied the texts of the Emptiness school. Out of the many Perfection of Wisdom sūtras that expound the doctrine of emptiness, the *Diamond Sūtra* (S. *Vajracchedikā Prajñāpāramitā Sūtra*, C. *Jingang bore jing*, K. *Kŭmgang panya kyŏng* 金剛 般若經) is especially noteworthy for its immense popularity and influence on the development of Chan. The rhetoric of paradox in this scripture must have appealed to Chan adepts.[13] This sūtra would have a great influence on Huineng 慧能 (638–713), the sixth patriarch of Chan, so much so that the scripture is considered to be one of two "twin pillars," along with the *Nirvāṇa Sūtra* (S. *Mahāparinirvāṇa sūtra*, C. *Niepan jing*, K. *Yŏlban kyŏng* 涅槃經) of Huineng's Chan. Huineng derived his negative rhetoric and ideas of emptiness from the *Diamond Sūtra* and the affirmative idea of the buddha-nature from the *Nirvāṇa Sūtra* and *Laṅkāvatārasūtra*.[14]

The Teaching of Buddha-Nature and Cataphasis

Inevitably, the tenet of emptiness elicited criticism because of its nihilistic characteristics. Its relentless criticism of affirmative statements, refusal to establish any confirmed view of its own, dominant rhetoric of negation and paradox, and the term śūnyatā, "emptiness" itself, were altogether more than enough fodder for critics.[15]

Contrary to the prevalent use of negative language in the doctrine of emptiness, the rhetoric of the buddha-nature (C. *foxing*, K. *pulsŏng* 佛性) doctrine is affirmative. This is manifested in the term "buddha-nature" itself, which suggests an optimistic view of human nature and Buddhist soteriology. The doctrine of buddha-nature claims that all sentient beings not only possess the potential to realize buddhahood but also that they are all already endowed with the attributes of a buddha. In this regard, buddha-nature connotes the cause and fruition of buddhahood. It will be recalled that this idea was the primary theme expounded by Chinul in *Complete and Sudden Attainment*. This double meaning is also implied in the Sanskrit term *tathāgatagarbha* (C. *rulai zang*, K. *yŏrae jang* 如來藏). "*Tathāgata*" means "thus come" or "thus gone," and "*garbha*" means either "embryo" or "womb." Considering that "*tathāgata*" is an epithet for Śākyamuni Buddha, the compound word *tathāgatagarbha* can mean either the potentiality to become a buddha or the state of a fully developed buddha in a womb. When the term is understood as the fruition of buddhahood, it is associated with other positive terms like *dharmakāya*, nirvāṇa, perfect wisdom, and realization.[16]

Tathāgatagarbha is also identified with the mind,[17] *dharmadhātu*, and "suchness." All these terms, which refer to a metaphysical grounding, seem "substantialist,"[18] a position that was vigorously refuted by the Madhyamaka school. Sallie B. King, however, asserts that despite its substantialist implications, those who advocated these positive descriptions of absoluteness did not intend to negate the doctrine of emptiness but rather aimed at the "experiential fulfillment of emptiness."[19] King argues that these descriptions were promoted as an antidote to the negativity of Madhyamaka language that advocates of buddha-nature were concerned would frighten and discourage people.[20] Though King attempts to reconcile the contradictory positions of the Buddha-Nature and Emptiness schools by treating the buddha-nature as subservient to the emptiness doctrine, the *Tathāgatagarbha* tradition's claim of buddha-nature was not merely rhetorical or pedagogical, but rather substantive, as *tathāgatagarbha* signified "the original pristine pure ontological Buddha-ness intrinsic in all things."[21] In the *Tathāgatagarbha* tradition, emptiness refers to the emptiness of everything except buddha-nature. This contradicts the teaching of the Emptiness school, which refutes any substantial nature. This tension between the doctrines of buddha-nature and emptiness would be left unresolved in Chan texts.

Integration of the Teachings of Emptiness and Buddha-Nature in Chan

An attempt to integrate the seemingly contradictory teachings of emptiness and *tathāgatagarbha* is made in the *Awakening of Faith in Mahāyāna* (C. *Dasheng qisin lun*, K. *Taesŭng kisinnon* 大乘起信論).[22] This text is regarded as the pinnacle of the development of *tathāgatagarbha* thought[23] in East Asian Buddhism owing to the significant influence it had on its development, including on Chan and Huayan. It identifies the mind as the common essence of both saṃsara and nirvāṇa and explains that the mind has two aspects: the absolute reality called suchness or thusness and the relative reality of phenomena. The absolute aspect of the mind involves two further, distinct subaspects—empty and nonempty. The mind is empty (śūnya) insofar as it has never been defiled by deluded thoughts and insofar as it is devoid of any permanence or independence. The mind, in short, is ineffable and indescribable beyond any word or concept. At the same time, the mind is nonempty (aśūnya) in that it is eternal, permanent, immutable, pure, self-sufficient, and endowed with undefiled, excellent qualities.[24] Since the essential nature of the mind transcends all predications and conceptualizations, any discourse or thought about the mind is "of" the mind, and identifying the mind with a term like "suchness" is a limited way of explaining it.[25] Thus, the term suchness involves both negative and affirmative approaches in that it implies the transcendence of the nature of the mind, and at the same time it attempts "to establish some sort of communication," even in a limited manner.[26]

This synthesis of emptiness and buddha-nature is incorporated in the *Platform Sūtra of the Sixth Patriarch* (C. *Liuzu tanjing*, K. *Yukcho tan'gyŏng* 六祖壇經), the quintessential text of Chan, and one of the most significant texts for understanding Chinul's Sŏn.[27] As a purported record of a sermon by Huineng, the text focuses on persuading its audience to concentrate on seeing their own nature. William Porter,[28] a translator of and commentator on the text, justly summarizes the sixth patriarch's teaching as follows: "This is the teaching of Huineng: See your nature and become a buddha. The rest is simply an attempt at deconstruction, the deconstruction of the walls that imprison us in our dungeons of delusion—including the delusions that arise in the course of studying and practicing the teachings of the Buddha."[29] Huineng emphasizes the originally pure nature of the human mind, that is the buddha-nature, and encourages Buddhist practitioners to meditate on their own minds. While affirmative terms like buddha-nature 佛性, one's own nature 自性, dharma-nature 法性, dharma-body 法身, original nature 本性, and pure and calm mind 清淨心 prevail in the text, the text also draws on some of the negative rhetoric and ideas in the *Diamond Sūtra*, which, as Huineng himself states, played a pivotal role in his spiritual advancement and pedagogy.[30]

Negative ideas and expressions from the *Diamond Sūtra* are clearly incorporated in Huineng's explanation of "no-thought" (C. *wunian*, K. *munyŏm* 無念), a crucial principle of Chan practice.[31] Huineng synthesizes the doctrines of buddha-nature and emptiness by correlating the seeing of one's own true nature with the practice of no-thought:

> If, standing upon your own nature and mind, you illuminate with wisdom and make inside and outside clear, you will know your own original mind. If you know your original mind, this then is deliverance. Once you have attained deliverance this then is the *prajñā samādhi*. If you have awakened to the *prajñā samādhi*, this then is no-thought. What is no-thought? The Dharma of no-thought means: even though you see all things, you do not attach to them, but, always keeping your own nature pure, cause the six thieves to exit through the six gates. . . . If you awaken to the Dharma of no-thought, you will penetrate into all things thoroughly, and will see the realm of the Buddha. If you awaken to the sudden doctrine of no-thought, you will have reached the status of the Buddha.[32]

Huineng employs the term "emptiness" itself in his identification of the nature of the mind as emptiness.[33] However, considering what the idea of emptiness is intended to connote in the *Platform Sūtra*, the emptiness that Huineng mentions does not seem compatible with the emptiness of the *Diamond Sūtra*. First, whereas in the Perfection of Wisdom scripture emptiness is employed as a sword to cut off any kind of affirmation, whether emptiness takes the form of explicit negation, paradoxical absurdity, or ontological negation,[34] Huineng uses the idea of emptiness to explain the boundless capacity of the mind, which can contain many things and even opposite things simultaneously. Second, whereas the intention of the negative and paradoxical expression of the Emptiness school lies only in refuting affirmative views, the negative discourse of the *Platform Sūtra* aims beyond mere deconstruction of ideas or concepts. In being freed from any thoughts, one's mind can be cleared so that the person can see his own nature, which is identified as buddha-nature.[35] Therefore, it can be said that the *Platform Sūtra* deliberately vacillates between the doctrines of emptiness and buddha-nature—when it comes to the nature of ultimate reality it embraces positive formulations of buddha-nature thought, while at the same time employing the negative rhetoric and logic of emptiness thought.

It was inevitable that conflicts would arise among Chan adepts as Chan tried to reconcile the contending teachings of emptiness and buddha-nature. An emphasis on emptiness entailed the advocacy of a radical approach that refutes affirmative teachings, but taking the affirmative approach exposed the school to the risk of approving inherent nature or existence. The tensions inherent in any effort to synthesize the two schools into one theoretical and practical religious system involved, in short, competing attitudes toward the use of words and concepts. Based on this overview of the doctrinal positions of the two Mahāyāna schools and their distinctive attitudes to language, the following section will discuss in detail Chan approaches to verbal discourse.

CATAPHASIS AND APOPHASIS IN THE DEVELOPMENT OF CHAN

Chan is well known for its avowed antitextual, anti-intellectual stance, and for its focus on meditation. Nevertheless, this meditative Buddhist tradition has never excluded verbal discourses altogether. Therefore, before becoming immersed in Chan approaches to apophasis and cataphasis, there is a need to address the popular perception that Chan rejects language and conceptualization. The following pages will examine the historical development of various Chan approaches to texts and studies.

The Chan Attitude to Scriptural and Doctrinal Studies

Most people, whether scholars of Buddhism or not, can easily see that the four principles of Chan—"separate transmission of the dharma outside of doctrinal teaching" 教外別傳, "no establishment of words and letters" 不立文字, "direct pointing to the mind of man" 直指人心, and "seeing into nature and becoming a buddha" 見性成佛—evidence its anti-intellectual and anti-textual stance. Among the four principles, the first two disparage practices grounded on the scriptural, philosophical, and exegetical traditions produced over the thousands of years of Buddhist history. The latter two stress the essential impact of intuitive meditation on the human mind and on human nature on the path to enlightenment. These principles summarize Chan's unique identity—an identity characterized by the special mind-to-mind transmission of its teachings from master to disciple. Here, "special transmission" does not mean the conveyance of any substantial dharma but rather the approval by an enlightened master of the authenticity of his student's experience of the ineffable.

The varied Chan texts produced throughout its history—in particular the biographical collections of eminent Chan masters, the records of their exchanges with students, and the collections of *gong'an*—have been used to bolster Chan orthodoxy. Some explicitly note the origin of the four principles, tracing them back to Bodhidharma or even to the prototypical anecdote of the esoteric communication between Śākyamuni and his disciple Mahākāśyapa.[36] Contrary to the belief that the four principles were well known and well established by the end of the Tang period in China (618–907), it is, rather, most likely that they came to be confirmed as "normative," identifying elements of the Chan tradition near the beginning of the Song period (960–1278).[37]

Up to that point, the Chan community in general had had a friendly attitude toward Buddhist scriptural and doctrinal traditions, acknowledging their legitimacy and efficacy for practice. Since the introduction of Buddhism into China, the Buddhist scriptures had been regarded as the legitimate and authoritative vehicle for the transmission of the authentic teachings of the Buddha. Although the emerging indigenous movement of Chan might have challenged the conventional Scholastic traditions, it did not yet imply a total rejection of long-established soteriological paths. For example, the enlightenment story of Huineng 慧能, who, as noted in chapter 2, has been seen as the emblematic figure of Chan orthodoxy, may shed light on the the early Chan community's actual approach to the Buddhist scriptures. The *Platform Sūtra of the Sixth Patriarch* provides the detailed story of the transmission of the dharma from the fifth patriarch Hongren 弘忍 (602–675) to the sixth patriarch Huineng 慧能. According to this text, after learning of Huineng's spiritual capabilities, Hongren secretly summoned him.

At midnight the Fifth Patriarch called me into the hall and expounded the *Diamond Sūtra* to me. Hearing it but once, I was immediately awakened, and that night I received the dharma. None of the others knew anything about it. Then he transmitted to me the dharma of Sudden Enlightenment and the robe, saying: "I make you the Sixth Patriarch. The robe is proof and is to be handed down from generation to generation. My dharma must be transmitted from mind to mind. You must make people awaken to themselves."[38]

Unfortunately, almost nothing about the historical figure of Huineng can be confirmed because of a lack of firm evidence. Indeed, the depiction of him in the *Platform Sūtra* consists of both "creative realities and historical fictions."[39] Whether this Chinese scripture, one of the most significant texts of the Chan school, conveys accurate historical information or not, one note-worthy point which underlines Chan's renunciation of words and its embrace of esoteric mind-to-mind transmission is that the text portrays the unlettered Huineng being immediately awakened upon listening to Hongren's exposition of the *Diamond Sūtra*. Obviously, in this awakening event, the *Diamond Sūtra* itself played a pivotal—if not decisive—role as catalyst, and it seems there was no resistance to or reluctance in expounding and listening to the revered scripture.[40]

In fact, an accommodating attitude toward and even close relationship with the traditional Buddhist scriptures prevails in the *Platform Sūtra*—it derives many ideas, terms, and phrases from various scriptures.[41] In addition, the *Platform Sūtra* itself is primarily concerned with recording Huineng's sermons, as the autobiographical narration states, "so that they might become known to later generations and be of benefit to students of the Way, in order that they might receive the pivot of the teaching and transmit it among themselves, taking these words as their authority."[42] The author was well aware of the benefit of transmitting essential Buddhist teachings in the form of text. Therefore, contrary to the rhetoric of the later Chan tradition, it is hard to conclude that Huineng and the scripture itself intended to promote a hostile attitude toward scriptural studies and the use of words and letters. Even when it comes to Huineng's illiteracy,[43] a personal trait that would be emphasized in the later Chan tradition with the goal of supporting the practice of mind-to-mind transmission, Philip Yampolsky contends that the compiler of the early version of the sūtra was not much concerned with it, but rather highlighted Huineng's ability to understand and teach the dharma.[44]

It is clear that the emerging Chan movement during the Tang period did not insist on the total rejection of scriptures, doctrines, words, or letters. Rather, Chan adepts maintained an open attitude toward conventional Buddhist approaches and endeavored to integrate Chan with doctrinal teachings.[45] Zongmi's claim regarding the compatibility between Chan and Jiao was a fitting example of this attitude.[46] Even when the fourth statement, "separate transmission outside the doctrinal teachings," began to appeal to a broad circle within the Chan community in the early Song period, one prominent Chan school, Fayan zong 法眼宗, carried on the integrative approach toward doctrinal teachings, grounding its ideas on Buddhist Scholasticism.[47] Yongming Yanshou 永明延壽 (904–975), who had a significant influence on Chinul, was a renowned Chan master of this school.

Those who attempted to integrate the Buddhist teachings conveyed through texts into their articulations of Chan principles, however, were well aware of the pervasive cautions that were issued against the dangers of the mere study of Buddhist texts and doctrines. Nevertheless, they contended that the Chan patriarchs only warned Chan students of blind and vain attachment to teachings learned through words and letters and were not urging their total abandonment. Furthermore, the supposed renunciation of words seems to go against the fact that the Chan masters left an enormous amount of written materials that recorded the events of "separate transmission," enlightenment poems verbalizing the experience of the ineffable, and prolix commentaries on those very Chan texts.[48] Albert Welter understands that for the early Chan patriarchs and those masters who embraced textual and doctrinal teachings, the principle of "do not establish words and letters" was taken "not as a denial of the recorded words of the Buddha or the doctrinal elaborations by learned monks, but as a warning to those who had become confused about the relationship between Buddhist teaching as a guide to the truth and mistook it for the truth itself."[49]

Even those Chan masters who advocated separate transmission and no establishment of words and letters did not totally renounce scriptures nor cease literary activities. For example, Dahui Zonggao, who had a great impact on Chinul and postulated the meditation technique of *huatou* (K. *hwadu*) investigation, was very cautious about the intellectual obstacles generated by reading scriptures and engaging in philosophical debates. He opposed the idea that the Buddhist scriptures transmit the true dharma of the Buddha. Nevertheless, when preaching or writing letters, he often referred to Buddhist scriptures and to the words of renowned Chan masters and *gong'an*s. On the one hand, Dahui reproached Chan students for attempting to investigate *gong'an* intellectually, and intentionally burned the copies and even the printer's block of *Biyan lu* 碧岩錄—his master Yuanwu Keqin's 圓悟克勤 collection of *gong'an*s—because of his concern about his students' attachment to the text. On the other hand, he expounded *kanhua* (K. *kanhwa*) Chan, which, despite fostering intuitive investigation, utilized the device of written *gong'an*.[50] Thus, Dahui's interpretation of "no establishment of words and letters" and "separate transmission"—despite his relatively radical stance in comparison with the Tang period Chan monks or some Song period monks—did not mean a total rejection of words and scriptures, but rather showed his conviction that the dharma of the Buddha cannot be fully conveyed nor grasped through conceptual processes relying on words and intellectual activities.[51]

In the early stage of its development, the Chan movement needed to establish its legitimacy and authority in order to distinguish itself from established Buddhist schools in China. Since it neither elaborated or postulated an original doctrinal system nor had its own scriptures attributed to the Buddha, the early Chinese Chan patriarchs created a pedigree that involved the dharma of the Buddha being transmitted from master to disciple. This was done in order to show the orthodoxy of the Chan movement. The life stories of the patriarchs, their enlightenment experiences, and their exchanges with other monks were documented in order to establish the authenticity of the Chan tradition.

There was also a pedagogical purpose in compiling the stories and words of Chan masters in the light of older Buddhist traditions. The emerging Chan movement told the stories of the Chan masters and their exchanges with other Chan masters and students so as to instruct others in the way of Chan. Thus, the Chan tradition began to collect the stories of early Chan patriarchs and their riddle-like exchanges or *gong'an*s, and the collections continued to expand over time. Each individual record of question-and-response is *gong'an*, and the collections of these *gong'an*s became a textbook to which a Chan master could refer in order to teach his students and examine their spiritual advancement. The *gong'an*s were also used as topics for meditation.[52] While a *gong'an* was adopted primarily for its instructive benefits during the Tang period, in the Song period, meditating on the *gong'an* became a primary Chan practice, which evolved into full-blown *gong'an* Chan 公案禪.

Gong'an Chan—Wenzi Chan and Kanhua Chan

Gong'an Chan would develop into two different and competing strands—*wenzi* Chan and *kanhua* Chan.[53] While both strands make extensive use of *gong'an*s, they have different approaches to the Buddhist scriptures and to the employment of various literary genres. *Wenzi* Chan (K. *munja* Sŏn 文字禪) literally means "lettered Chan,"[54] and reflects the social, cultural, and religious environment in which the Confucian literati and educated aristocrats held a prominent place. In this context, the adepts of *wenzi* Chan pursued literary activities in order to obtain the patronage of influential laymen and to adapt Chan to the broader Chinese intellectual context. It was in this context that *wenzi* Chan monks understood the importance of literary prowess, which would become an essential feature of Chan intellectuals. These Chan monks sought to make Chan appealing to the literati by expressing their religious experiences in mystical, poetic verses. They avoided the anti-intellectual and antitextual propensities of the broader Chan community and advocated incorporating the efforts of the various intellectual traditions into conventional Buddhist practices. They were concerned about laziness and iconoclastic behavior in the Buddhist community, problems which they believed were influenced by the hagiographical depiction of Chan masters and partly attributable to a failure to properly understand Chan soteriology. Thus, *wenzi* Chan promoted a harmonious relationship between Chan and Jiao in the course of establishing the identity of Chan during the Tang period.[55]

The harmonious, integrative stance of *wenzi* Chan continued into the early Northern Song period 北宋 (960–1127),[56] in which numerous *gong'an* collections were compiled by Chan adepts. It was during this period that Juefan Huihong 覺範慧洪 (1071–1128), a Chan master of the Huanglong 黃龍 collateral branch of the Linji 臨濟 lineage of Northern Song Chan, coined the term *wenzi* Chan 文字禪 to describe this integrative stance, which produced a vast number of Chan texts. Those who supported this inclusivist Chan approach participated in Buddhist practices involving the use of language and conceptualization. Although they agreed with the four principles of Chan, which had been accepted as normative principles by this time, their interpretations of them were moderated by the acceptance and use of words and letters. These practitioners held that "no establishment of words and letters" (C. *buli wenzi* 不立文字) meant simply no *attachment* to scriptures and doctrines. Therefore, as long as they were cautious about the dangers of the intellect, there was no need to completely renounce words and letters (C. *buli wenzi* 不離文字).

Wenzi Chan and *kanhua* Chan were sometimes rivals, but neither rejected every aspect of the teachings and practices of the other. For example, Huihong did not denigrate the emphasis on meditation in *kanhua* Chan, and Dahui did not insist on a total renunciation of literary discourses or compositions, although he was concerned about the danger of practitioners being trapped in words and letters. George A. Keyworth III concludes his research on the historical development of *wenzi* Chan, which culminated in Huilong's articulation of it, with the following comparison of it to Dahui's *kanhua* Chan: "Dahui's legacy of *kanhua* Chan represents perhaps the flowering of Song dynasty Linji Chan praxis, while literary Chan signifies Huihong's advocacy for erudition within the mature Chan institution."[57] Keyworth even suspects that Dahui's harsh words criticizing Huihong's *wenzi* Chan might have been a fabrication of later generations.

The competitive relationship between *wenzi* Chan and *kanhua* Chan is not an exceptional phenomenon in the history of Chan Buddhism. Robert M. Gimello sees the history of Chan development as the record of a persistent tension between resistance against and compliance with particular paths (S. *mārga*) or systematic soteriological schemes which, it was claimed, if faithfully followed would guide practitioners to the goal of liberation.[58] The meditation-oriented tradition of Chan originated in a resistance to conventional Buddhist practices that relied heavily on theoretical studies. However, as has been discussed, there was diversity in the Chan tradition: some adepts radically rejected doctrinal and scriptural discourses, but some interpreted the antiliterary claims of Chan more moderately, as a mere warning against attachment to texts and learning. What Gimello calls "lettered Chan" belongs to this moderate position, which endeavored to integrate conventional Buddhist paths into a reformed soteriological approach.[59]

However, this moderate, syncretic approach would generate the expression of concerns and criticism from some radically minded monks. Dahui was one of these, and he came to expound *kanhua* Chan, a movement intent on minimizing or eradicating what he saw as the problems resulting from this moderate approach. Again, even within this method of *huatou* (K. *hwadu* 話頭) investigation, tensions arose between radical and moderate investigations, a distinction that corresponded to the two kinds of *huatou*—dead word (*sagu* 死句) and live word (*hwalgu* 活句)—and the two kinds of *huatou* meditation—investigation of meaning (*ch'amŭi* 參意) and investigation of the word, (*ch'amgu* 參句)—both of which will be explored in detail later.

Chinul's Moderate and Radical Sŏn Approaches

Chinul's thought was in part a product of this persistent tension between moderate and radical approaches. His approach to Sŏn practice was located within the broader context of East Asian Chan, and he embraced within himself the dialectical development of Chan that was the result of the contentious interaction between the moderate and radical approaches.[60] In general, Chinul agreed with subitism, the radical approach in Sŏn that asserts the existence of sudden awakening rather than gradual development leading to awakening; however, subitism itself was divided into the two subcategories of moderate and radical. Moderate subitism, which Chinul ardently supported throughout his life, advocates sequential or gradual cultivation following one's sudden awakening, whereas radical subitism asserts that one's sudden awakening, if authentic, does not require further gradual cultivation since cultivation is completed at the moment of the sudden awakening. The soteriological scheme of sudden awakening with gradual cultivation corresponds to moderate subitism, whereas *kanhwa* (C. *kanhua*) practice corresponds to radical subitism.

Recalling chapter 2, it can be seen that Chinul's soteriological approach transitioned from moderate to radical. However, Buswell argues that even when Chinul was promoting the radical approach of *kanhwa* Sŏn, he had "not entirely abandoned his interest in incorporating *kanhwa* Sŏn into the moderate subitism of sudden awakening/gradual cultivation."[61] In distinguishing two types of investigation—investigation of the meaning and of the word— and recommending these two distinctive practices to people with different abilities, he effectively joined moderate subitism to the radical subitism of *kanhwa* Sŏn.[62]

In-gyŏng, a Korean scholar and Buddhist monk, asserts that, as in China, Korean Buddhism witnessed persistent conflicts between the moderate approach of harmonizing Sŏn and Kyo and the radical approach of separate transmission, conflicts which strongly informed Chinul's Sŏn theory and practice. In-gyŏng describes the difficulty of reconciling these apparently contradictory approaches, but argues that sustaining both approaches promotes the healthy development of Buddhism as they challenge and complement each other.[63]

It is undeniable that Chinul never fully resolved the tensions between Kyo and Sŏn. Although he attempted to integrate Kyo into Sŏn, advocating for Kyo's instructive and preparatory function in Sŏn practice, he always claimed the superiority of the Sŏn approach—whether it be the Sŏn of his early writings or more specifically *kanhwa* Sŏn in his later writings. The inherent tensions between the inclusive and exclusive approaches to Sŏn practice generated many debates and critical observations from advocates of both. However, In-gyŏng argues that this contentious interaction was constructive rather than destructive for the development of Sŏn.

This section has explored the historical development of different Chan approaches to texts, doctrines, and words. In contrast to the monochromatic image of Chan held by some modern people, the meditative Buddhist tradition has advocated for and adopted a number of different positions on the issues raised. The early Chan school was relatively accommodating and sympathetic toward scriptures, doctrines, and words and this position continued throughout Chan history, at least among some practitioners. However, the emphasis on meditation and mistrust of language that is inherent in the theory and practice of Chan would inevitably result in the adoption of a more radical approach to texts and studies by some. These two tendencies have contributed to the dialectical development of Chan over time. This tension has never been fully resolved, but rather, theoretical and soteriological emphases have shifted at different times from one side to the other. The same tension prevails in Chinul's Sŏn, which inherited the broad spectrum of Chan theory and practice. While exploring how this tension unfolds in Chinul, the next section will consider Chinul's related approach to apophasis and cataphasis.

CATAPHATIC AND APOPHATIC DISCOURSES
AND MEDITATION FOR CHINUL

Radical Rejection and Radical Acceptance

Chapter 2 explored the two approaches of radical rejection and radical acceptance, originally employed by Zongmi, the Chinese master. Chinul adapted
these categories, however, with a different intention. He was attempting
to prove the correspondence between Hwaŏm and Sŏn, whereas it was the
Chinese master's intention to present a comprehensive framework for the
vast array of doctrinal, philosophical, and scriptural traditions that had been
transmitted to and developed in China.

Chinul insisted on the ultimate correspondence of those two Buddhist traditions. Nevertheless, he also acknowledged that Hwaŏm and Sŏn disproportion-
ately employ one approach over the other: radical rejection is a prominent characteristic of Sŏn discourse, whereas Hwaŏm primarily employs the approach of
radical acceptance. The emphasis on radical rejection and radical acceptance in
Sŏn and Hwaŏm, respectively, is related to their distinctive stances regarding
intellectual studies and conceptual meditation. Hwaŏm is characterized by its
approval of cataphatic discourse and theoretical learning, whereas Sŏn is well
known for its apophatic discourse and practical focus on meditation. The two
contrasting approaches of radical rejection and radical acceptance which are
dominant in Sŏn and Hwaŏm, respectively, can be compared to cataphasis and
apophasis. To see this more clearly, it is necessary to revisit Chinul's adaptation
of these two approaches—already explored in chapter 2—this time from the
perspective of his attitude toward apophasis and cataphasis.

*The Relationship between the Mind as Void, Calm, and Numinous
Awareness, the Two Doctrinal Teachings (Emptiness vs. Buddha-Nature),
and the Two Modes of Discourse (Apophasis vs. Cataphasis)*

One's predilection for the exclusivity of radical rejection or the inclusivity of
radical acceptance seems to be related to one's understanding of the nature of
the mind, or all dharmas. According to Chinul:

> This mind-essence, which is the ineffable object of awakening, is the nature of
> all dharmas; it subsumes all wonders and transcends words and speech. Since it
> transcends words and speech, it incorporates the approach of sudden realization
> in which the mind is forgotten. Since it subsumes all wonders, it includes the
> aspect that supports the flourishing of attribute and function.[64]

This explanation of the mind draws on the Heze school's view of mind
in its essence as the mind of void and calm (*kongjŏk sim* 空寂心) and in its

function as numinous awareness (*yǒngji* 靈智),[65] and also its understanding of dharma as inherently possessing two aspects, immutability and adaptability.[66] The mind is inherently immutable as it is unproduced, unextinguished, unconditioned, and signless due to its void and calm nature. At the same time, its numinous function that adapts to everything can be aware of all phenomena in the universe and all operations of the mind.[67]

Chinul's definition of the mind as void, calm, and numinous awareness, as influenced by the Heze school, is closely related to the two doctrinal teachings (emptiness and buddha-nature) and the two modes of discourse (apophatic and cataphatic). The relationship between the understanding of the mind, the two doctrinal teachings, and the two modes of discourse can be seen in Zongmi's writings, cited by Chinul in *Excerpts*. In this citation, Zongmi, in a discourse about the true nature of the mind, answers a question on the necessity of affirmative terms in addition to the negative expressions common in many Mahāyāna scriptures:

Question: The explanations of the ideal nature given throughout the Mahāyāna sūtras, in the teachings of every past and present school of Sǒn, and even in the Heze school, all say the same thing: [the ideal nature] is unproduced and unextinguished, unconditioned and signless; neither profane nor sacred, neither right nor wrong; ineffable and unascertainable. It is enough now just to rely on this [perspective]. What need is there to bring up the idea of numinous awareness?

Answer: These are all examples of apophatic discourse; they are not yet capable of exposing the essence of the mind. If we do not point out that the clear, constant awareness that is present now, never interrupted and never dark, is your own mind, then what do we speak of as being unconditioned (*asaṃskṛta*), signless (*alakṣaṇa*), and so forth? For this reason, you must understand that all the various teachings simply explain that it is this awareness that is unproduced (*anutpāda, anutpanna*) and unextinguished (*aniruddha, anirodha*), and so forth. Consequently, Heze pointed out the knowledge and vision present within that void and signless state so that people would acknowledge it and comprehend that their own minds pass from one lifetime to another, generation after generation, interminably, until eventually they achieve buddhahood. Furthermore, Heze was able to refer to various terms like unconditioned, unabiding, even ineffable, and so forth, by simply referring to them all as the void and quiescent awareness in which everything is subsumed. Voidness (*śūnyatā*) means that it is devoid of all signs; it is still an apophatic term. Quiescence (*śānti*) is the immutable attribute of the real nature; it is not the same as empty nothingness. Awareness refers to the attribute that exposes the thing itself; it is not the same as conceptual discrimination (*vikalpa*). Only this, then, is the innate essence of the true mind. Therefore, from the initial arousal of the aspiration for enlightenment (*bodhicitta*) up through the attainment of buddhahood, there is only quiescence and only awareness, immutable and uninterrupted. It is only according to the respective stage [along the bodhisattva path] that the designations and attributes [of quiescence and awareness] are slightly different.[68]

Zongmi points out that the term "numinous awareness" exposes the mind-essence whereas all those negative expressions such as "unproduced and unextinguished," "neither profane nor sacred," and "ineffable and unascertainable" are not capable of doing so. However, Zongmi argues that although negative expressions do not expose the mind-essence, they nevertheless point to the mind itself; otherwise, there would be no value in this kind of discourse. For Zongmi, negative expressions refer to the essence of the mind in a hidden way, whereas affirmative terms like "awareness" express it in a positive way. Here, he does not insist that any expressive words, including "awareness," can fully ascertain the true nature of the mind or buddha-nature, but rather he admits that they are only attributes that point to the mind-essence. For Zongmi, this is the proper understanding of Buddhist cataphasis.[69]

It is obvious, therefore, that the two doctrinal teachings of emptiness and buddha-nature are integrated into Zongmi's understanding of mind-essence. Moreover, the dialectics of apophasis and cataphasis or of emptiness and buddha-nature that are imbedded in the Heze phrase, "The mind of void and calm awareness," can be further explored by considering Zongmi's elaboration of this phrase in the quotation above: "Voidness (śūnyatā) means that it is devoid of all signs; it is still an apophatic term. Quiescence (śānti) is the immutable attribute of the real nature; it is not the same as empty nothingness. Awareness refers to the attribute that exposes the thing itself; it is not the same as conceptual discrimination (*vikalpa*)."[70] With this statement, Zongmi explicitly recognizes the empty nature of the mind. However, he is prudent enough to exclude a nihilistic understanding of the emptiness teaching by interpreting "quiescence" as an attribute revealing the nature of the mind.

Here, Zongmi's definition of "quiescence" is ambivalent insofar as it implies both the empty nature of the mind and the nature of the mind as buddha-nature. On the one hand, when Zongmi states that quiescence is "not the same as empty nothingness," he implies the term's connection to the emptiness teaching while at the same time desiring to dissociate it from nihilistic nothingness. On the other hand, his definition of it as an attribute of the real nature of the mind is a reference to the buddha-nature teaching. In this regard, the term "quiescence" is presented by Zongmi as a bridge over which one can move from the apophatic term "voidness" to the cataphatic term "awareness." However, distinguishing the term from "conceptual discrimination" (C. *fenbie*, K. *punbyŏl* 分別), Zongmi is cautious not to present a false idea of mind-essence by employing expressive (or cataphatic) terms. Zongmi's careful employment of expressive discourses could be called "disciplined cataphasis."[71]

The close connection between the two teachings and the two modes of discourse is clearly asserted in another passage by Zongmi.

> To sum up, the teachings involve the two approaches of apophasis [the school that teaches absolute annihilation] and kataphasis [the school of direct revelation], and if we try to ascertain their real import they refer respectively to true voidness (*chin'gong/zhenkong* 真空) and sublime existence (*myoyu/miaoyou* 妙有). If we probe the original mind, we find that it subsumes both essence and function. Now, the Hongzhou and Oxhead schools presume that wiping all traces away is the be all and end all (*chigŭk/zhiji* 至極); this involves only the apophatic teachings and the attribute of true voidness. Although they may master essence, they overlook function, for their approach is deficient regarding the kataphatic teachings and the attribute of sublime existence.[72]

Here, Zongmi uses two terms 遣 (C. *qian*, K. *kyŏn*) and 顯 (C. *xian*, K. *hyŏn*), which can be translated as "negation" 遣 (or apophasis) and "revelation" 顯 (or cataphasis), respectively, as alternatives for "apophatic discourse" (K. *cha'jŏn*, C. *zhequan* 遮詮) and "cataphatic discourse" (K. *p'yojŏn*, C. *biaoquan* 表詮).[73] While both apophatic discourse and cataphatic discourse refer to the same ineffable reality, Zongmi asserts that the former is closely related to the teaching of true voidness (or emptiness), which primarily concerns the essence of the mind, whereas the latter implies the teaching of buddha-nature and pertains to the function of the mind. Here, Zongmi uses the phrase "sublime (or mysterious) existence," which obviously refers to the mind or the buddha-nature. However, by adding the adjective "sublime (or mysterious)," he intends to avoid the mistake of concluding that the mind-nature is an inherent "existence" of nature. In this regard, the term "sublime existence" could be seen as another example of Zongmi's "disciplined cataphasis." As a whole, the Heze understanding and definition of the mind embrace both elements of two seemingly contrasting pairs: emptiness and buddha-nature, and apophasis and cataphasis. Chan itself is the product of the theoretical integration of these two doctrinal teachings and two modes of discourse.

Besides the two pairs of Buddhist terms—negative/expressive discourse and negation/revelation—discussed above, there is one more pair, radical rejection and radical acceptance, that must be examined more closely. The following section will explore these two terms, particularly as presented by Zongmi and later adopted by Chinul. This investigation will further elucidate the distinction between Buddhist apophasis and cataphasis and their correlation with Buddhist doctrinal teachings, and also their correlation to the distinction between Sŏn and Kyo.

Radical Rejection and Radical Acceptance for Zongmi and Chinul

The terms radical rejection (K. *chŏn'gan*, C. *quanjian* 全揀) and radical acceptance (K. *chŏnsu*, C. *quanshou* 全收), were examined already in chapter 2 in terms of Zongmi's integration of different doctrinal teachings and Chinul's discussion of the compatibility between Sŏn and Kyo. These two terms are closely related to the two pairs of terms introduced above—negative discourse/expressive discourse (C. *zhequan/biaoquan*, K. *ch'ajŏn/p'yojŏn* 遮詮/表詮), and negation/revelation (C. *qian/xian*, K. *kyŏn/hyŏn* 遣/顯). Although all of the schemes presented thus far can generally be divided into the two categories of apophasis and cataphasis, it should be noted that the pair radical rejection/radical acceptance (全揀/全收) is distinguished from the other two pairs in that radical rejection/radical acceptance concern primarily two different approaches to characteristics of the mind, whereas negative discourse/expressive discourse and negation/revelation merely describe modes of discourse. Here is Zongmi's explanation of radical rejection/radical acceptance:

"Radical rejection" means just to expose the essence by directly pointing out that the numinous awareness is in fact the nature of the mind and that everything else is spurious. Consequently, [the *Avataṃsakasūtra*] says, "[The profound realm of the tathāgatas] is not something that can be apprehended by consciousness, / It is also not a mental object," and so forth; it also is neither nature nor characteristics, neither Buddha nor sentient being. It leaves far behind the tetralemma [*catuṣkoṭi*; viz. is, is not, both is and is not, neither is nor is not] and is free from the hundred negations (*paekpi/baifei* 百非). "Radical acceptance" means that [there][74] are none of the tainted and pure dharmas that are not the mind. Because the mind has become deluded, it spuriously gives rise to deluded actions, which ultimately lead to the four modes of birth [*yoni*, viz., oviparous, viviparous, moistureborn, and metamorphic] within the six rebirth destinies in this worldly realm with all its different types of filth. Because the mind awakens, functioning is generated from its essence and there are none of [those functions, from] the four boundless states (*apramāṇa*), the six perfections (*pāramitā*), up to the four analytical knowledge (*pratisaṃvid*), the ten powers (*bala*), the sublime body, and the pure [buddha-]realm that are not made manifest. Since it is this mind that manifests all dharmas, each and every one of those dharmas is in fact the true mind.[75]

Zongmi connects the two categories of radical rejection and radical acceptance, respectively, to the second "teaching of cryptic meaning that eradicates characteristics to reveal the dharma nature" (C. *miyi poxiang xianxing jiao* 密意破相顯性教), and to the first "teaching of cryptic meaning that relies on [dharma] nature to speak of characteristics" (C. *miyi yixing shuoxiang jiao* 密意依性説相教), the latter of which focuses on the immanence of the truth in phenomena. Consequently, the second teaching involves negative discourse that refutes all characteristics or phenomena on the premise that they are all unreal or untrue, and advocates an approach that points directly to the true nature of the mind. On the other hand, the first teaching involves expressive discourse on the premise that all characteristics or phenomena expose the true nature of the mind. Zongmi insists that the third "teaching of directly revealing that the mind is the nature" (C. *xianshi zhenxin jixing jiao* 顯示眞心即性 教) embraces the other two teachings.[76]

Taking into consideration all that has been discussed so far, it is possible to draw the following conclusions: on the one hand, apophatic discourse is closely related to an emphasis on the void, calm, and immutable essence of the mind, which is grounded on the doctrinal teaching of emptiness. On the other, cataphatic discourse is related to an emphasis on an understanding of the mind's actual function—its perception of all internal and external phenomena—which the enlightened mind would perceive as revelation of the true nature of the mind.

While Chinul generally followed Zongmi, his use of the terms "radical rejection" and "radical acceptance" can be differentiated from Zongmi's in two respects. First, Chinul uses these terms to verify the compatibility between Sŏn and Hwaŏm (or Kyo); and second, his discussion primarily concerns the cultivation of the mind, which is related not only to verbal discourse but also meditation. Chinul writes: "This mind-nature operates in two different modes: radical rejection (*chŏn'gan/quanjian* 全揀) and radical acceptance (*chŏnsu/quanshou* 全收). Those of you who are cultivating the mind should consider [these two modes] carefully."[77] Since Chinul's first use of the terms was explained in detail in chapter 2, the following discussion will concentrate on Chinul's presentation of the two terms and their relationship to sudden awakening.

Significantly, Chinul considers sudden awakening to be the prerequisite for the balanced practice of both radical rejection and radical acceptance. He is concerned that without sudden awakening, both approaches are imperfect, and that practitioners will come to a deficient realization of the true nature of the mind. Chinul explains:

> It should now be clear that, if you do not have a sudden awakening to the nature of the one true mind and in [that benighted state] you just reject everything, then you will succumb to an understanding derived from ineffability. But if you just accept everything, then you will succumb to an understanding derived from consummate interfusion (*wŏnyung/yuanrong* 圓融). In both cases, you will fall into intellectual understanding, which will make it difficult to reach the access to awakening. If you want acceptance and rejection to function freely and nature and characteristics to be unimpeded, you must have a sudden awakening to the

one mind. If you want a sudden awakening, it is absolutely imperative not to succumb to intellectual understanding.[78]

Here, Chinul clearly asserts that both radical rejection and radical acceptance can be employed in religious practices only on the basis of sudden awakening.[79] This condition prevents one from attaining mere intellectual understanding—the risk of both approaches. Despite this potential danger, both approaches are indispensable elements of religious practice. However, although Chinul urges the balanced adoption of both radical rejection and radical acceptance, he values the former approach over the latter for it is the primary approach to be employed at the moment of awakening.[80] In addition, Chinul also asserts the superior efficacy of Sŏn by contending that Sŏn, which primarily involves the approach of radical rejection, leads to "an immediate crossing-over to liberation," whereas Kyo intends to serve "as the support for tens of thousands of generations."[81]

As discussed in chapter 2, Chinul adopts an integrative attitude, acknowledging the efficacy of doctrinal, philosophical discourses. However, he also insists on the superiority of Sŏn, and urges others to abandon Kyo approaches and adopt Sŏn approaches that involve the apophatic approach of radical rejection.

> Although both schools [Sŏn and Kyo] employ these two modes, they each have their own emphases, so neither can be criticized. [The instructions of the Sŏn patriarchs] involve an immediate crossing-over to liberation; they are a concise approach. Therefore, although [Sŏn] cites the teachings, it does so to shed light on the source; it is not pure doctrine. Those who do not understand the implications of this try to use the profound and superficial tenets of Kyo to evaluate the basic premise of Sŏn and end up indulging in baseless slander. Great is their mistake! If weighty people will lay down the tenets of Kyo, simply take up "the one-thought present right now" in their own minds, and in this wise probe the basic premise of Sŏn, then they will have some attainment. A person of faith should consider these words closely.[82]

Chinul's preference for Sŏn over Kyo is manifest in this quotation. For Chinul, Kyo is subservient to Sŏn, helping Sŏn practitioners attain a better intellectual understanding of Sŏn teachings.[83] In addition, Chinul draws attention to the limitations of Kyo and intellectual discourses in general: "Today, we see that people who are cultivating the mind initially employ this term 'numinous awareness' to develop an understanding of distinctions and to contemplate their own mind. This is just the approach of the exoteric transmission that uses words and speech to resolve doubts; it does not entail a personal realization of the essence."[84] The discourses about the nature of the mind and the path of mind cultivation are intended to encourage students "to develop the efficacy of tracing back the radiance [of the mind] by drawing on the description of the void and quiescent numinous awareness; and due to the efficacy of looking back on that radiance, they will gain the ineffable essence of mind."[85] Thus, Chinul presents a soteriological framework that consists of intellectual practice involving cataphatic discourses, along with more contemplative practices that are more closely related to apophatic discourses.

The Transition from Cataphasis to Apophasis

The shift in Chinul's orientation away from words and studies is noticeable in *Excerpts* as the exposition nears its conclusion. Chinul first restates the intention and essential points of his theoretical exposition: "The approach to dharma I have discussed so far has been designed for students who can generate the access to the understanding-awakening while relying on words; it has offered a detailed assessment of the two aspects of dharma—adaptability and immutability—and the two approaches concerning person—sudden awakening and gradual cultivation."[86] Then, however, Chinul states that cultivation, which relies on words and intellectual understanding, should be overcome and replaced so that one can achieve an experiential realization of the absolute reality. He introduces the shortcut approach of *kanhwa* investigation as a way of surmounting the obstacle of intellectual understanding by leaving words and concepts behind, enabling a sudden realization of the ineffable essence of the mind. In his discussion of this shortcut approach, Chinul cites to a significant number of apophatic quotations and anecdotes offered by eminent monks, mostly Sŏn masters. These are intended to assert the weakness of language for enabling an experiential realization of the ultimate truth, with the aim of prompting students to go beyond the theoretical meaning of Buddhist teachings.

The transition from cataphasis to apophasis is well represented in Dahui's words quoted by Chinul:

> Guifeng called it "numinous awareness." Heze said in regard to it, "The one word 'awareness' is the gateway to all wonders." Huanglong Sixin Sou said that "the one word 'awareness' is the gateway to all calamities." It is easy to get what Guifeng and Heze meant, but hard to get Sixin's intent. Right here, you must be endowed with eyes that transcend this world. You cannot explain it to anyone; you cannot transmit it to anyone. For this reason, Yunmen said, "The great majority of statements are like brandishing a sword before a doorway. But beneath that one word [the live word of the *hwadu*] there will certainly be a road that leads to salvation. If this were not the case, you would die beneath that word."[87]

Zongmi characterized the phrase "numinous awareness" as an essential description of the true nature of the mind, helping practitioners "determine what is primary and what subsidiary in regard to awakening and cultivation."[88] The phrase was also described as "the gateway to all wonders" [K. *chungmyo chimun* 衆妙之門]. However, contrary to this affirmative interpretation, the same phrase also can be "the gateway to all calamities" [K. *chunghwa chimun* 衆禍之門]. What can be deemed beneficial in the path to enlightenment can also be an obstacle preventing practitioners from progressing on "a road that leads to salvation." Chinul declares that what "numinous awareness" refers to is inexpressible and unascertainable and that even the term "buddha-nature" cannot fully grasp the true nature of the mind.[89] Therefore, as pedagogically efficient as the employment of intellectual discourse could be for religious practitioners of inferior faculties, as long as they remain in descriptive and explanatory teachings, they are prevented from spiritually advancing toward a direct realization of the nature of the mind. Attachment to the words employed in doctrinal discourses leads students to an impasse that they need to overcome.

However, although it is possible that the employment of words may result in the malady of mere intellectual understanding, there are also words that can help practitioners surmount this hurdle by challenging them to abandon intellectual activity altogether. Chinul draws a distinction between these two kinds of words.

> You must know that people who are cultivating the path in this present degenerate age of the dharma should first, via intellectual understanding that accords with reality, discern clearly their own mind's authentic and deceptive aspects, its production and cessation, and its essential and secondary features. Next, through a word that splits nails and cuts through iron, you should probe closely and carefully until a place appears where you can find salvation.[90]

Those with inferior faculties can at least attain a proper understanding of the dharma. However, once a student acquires intellectual understanding, he should free himself from the restraint of that understanding so as to gain a direct realization of it. Chinul asserts that this process of cleansing knowledge and vision can be done through words and phrases when they are properly chosen and meditated on. The words which are involved in intellectual understanding and the words which are intended to break intellectual understanding are, respectively, identified as "dead words" (*sagu* 死句) and "live words" (*hwalgu* 活句), which roughly correspond to cataphasis and apophasis, respectively. Chinul's choice of terms and his introduction of the shortcut approach of *kanhwa* Sŏn shows that, by the end of *Excerpts*, Chinul seems to have become more suspicious of cataphatic approaches than ever before.

This section explored two types of Buddhist discourse—cataphasis and apophasis—and Chinul's thoughts about both as manifested primarily in *Ex-*

cerpts. In this work, Chinul asserted the compatibility of Kyo and Sŏn, while at the same promoting Sŏn by urging his readers to move beyond the intellectual practices of Kyo to the meditative practices of Sŏn. Chinul briefly introduced *kanhwa* Sŏn as a way of helping practitioners take this step, mentioning dead words and live words and three mysterious gates. While Chinul's shift to and preference for *kanhwa* Sŏn appears primarily in the final section of *Excerpts*, further evidence of this shift appears in *Resolving Doubts*. In this work, Chinul's tone is much more apophatic, presenting in greater detail *kanhwa* Sŏn, the distinction between dead words and live words, and the three mysterious gates. The following section will explore *Resolving Doubts* with a focus on these three themes.

The Meditative Practice of *Kanhwa* Sŏn

The Shortcut Approach of Kanhwa *Sŏn in Chinul's Treatise "Resolving Doubts about Observing the Keyword"*

In *Excerpts*, as discussed above, Chinul stresses that although acquiring intellectual understanding via words and concepts is beneficial to both Sŏn adepts of inferior capacity and students of Kyo, eventually they all need to overcome the affliction of intellectual understanding to access true realization. This process is advocated not only by the Sŏn school but also by the Kyo school, as Li Tongxuan states: "Initially, enter in faith through acquired understanding; subsequently, unite [with the unimpeded *dharmadhātu*] through nonconceptualization."[91] However, Chinul insists that the soteriological process is not necessarily sequential, starting from the attainment of intellectual understanding regarding dharma and person, then moving on to a realization of the ultimate reality free of words and concepts. Those with superior capacity or advanced Sŏn students can skip straight to the stage of religious practice not involving verbal or conceptual approaches. Chinul writes:

> Those in the Sŏn school who have gained access through the shortcut remain unaffected from the beginning by acquired understanding in regard to both dharmas and their attributes. Straight off, they take up a tasteless *hwadu* and are concerned only with raising it to their attention and focusing on it. . . . In a moment, they unexpectedly activate one instant of realization concerning the *hwadu*, and as discussed previously, the *dharmadhātu* of the one mind becomes utterly perfect and radiant.[92]

Chinul asserts that the shortcut approach of *kanhwa* meditation[93] helps practitioners avoid the dangers of intellectual understanding that result from the employment of words and concepts. At the moment of sudden awakening, the wonder of the *dharmadhātu* will reveal itself to them. Chinul persistently claims that the realization of the *dharmadhātu*, which is the ultimate goal of the Hwaŏm school, is also the telos to which Sŏn students aspire. In this regard, he understands that Sŏn and Hwaŏm share a common soteriological aim. Nevertheless, there are important differences.

> Consequently, if we compare contemplation practice in the complete teachings with this one moment of realization in the Sŏn approach, then "inside the teachings" [Kyo] and "outside the teachings" [Sŏn] are quite different, and, therefore, the relative slowness or rapidity over time [for their respective practices to be completed] is not the same: this is something we can easily recognize. As it is said, "The separate transmission outside the teachings far excels the vehicle of the teachings. It is not something with which those of shallow intelligence can cope."[94]

There are different capacities not only as between Kyo and Sŏn students, but also among Sŏn students. Therefore, there are some who will have difficulty in properly employing the Sŏn approaches without encountering obstacles like being trapped in intellectual understanding.[95]

The varying degrees of capacity among Sŏn adepts necessitate differentiated approaches to religious practice that accord with the spiritual capacities of individual students. Chinul introduces various Sŏn approaches that can be employed in accordance with the faculties of each, including the three mysterious gates (*samhyŏn mun* 三玄文)—the mystery in the essence (*ch'ejung hyŏn* 體中玄), the mystery in the words (*kujung hyŏn* 句中玄), and the mystery in the mystery (*hyŏnjung hyŏn* 玄中玄); two kinds of words—dead words (*sagu* 死句) and live words (*hwalgu* 活句); and two types of *hwadu* investigation—investigation of the meaning of *hwadu* (*ch'amŭi* 參意) and investigation of the word or critical phrase itself (*ch'amgu* 參句). Chinul discusses all these schemes in his explanation of *kanhwa* Sŏn in order to elucidate the new meditation technique. The following pages will explore Chinul's explanations of *kanhwa* Sŏn and these various approaches with the tension between cataphasis and apophasis in mind.

Kanhwa *Sŏn*

As explained previously, *kanhwa* Sŏn (C. *kanhua* Chan 看話禪) is an efficacious meditation technique. The term for this technique literally indicates that one observes or investigates a keyword identified as *hwadu* 話頭 (C. *huatou*, lit., "head of speech"). A *hwadu* is derived from a *kongan* (C. *gong'an* 公案, lit., "public text-case"), a recorded anecdote derived from a Sŏn master's instruction to his students. The *hwadu* is a phrase or keyword that condenses or represents an exchange between a master and a student. Chinul discusses the *Mu hwadu* 無話頭 *kongan*, drawing on an anecdote involving Dahui.

The following is Dahui's introduction of the *Mu hwadu*, along with a brief explanation of *hwadu* practice:

> As long as the affective consciousnesses[96] have not been eliminated, the fire in the heart will continue to rage. At exactly such a time, keep your attention on the *hwadu* on which [you have generated a] doubt. For example, a monk asked Zhaozhou, "Does a dog have the buddha-nature, or not?" Zhaozhou replied, "No [*mu*]!" You should only be concerned about keeping [this question] before you and your attention always focused.[97]

Here, the entire record of conversation that occurred between a monk and Zhaozhou is *kongan*, and the simple response of "no" ("*mu*")[98] is *hwadu*. Dahui instructs Sŏn adepts to always keep focused on this one word "*mu*," or whatever keyword they choose, without interruption or distraction and without any intellectual engagement.[99] Chinul further elucidates:

> Because [Dahui] confers the *hwadu* along with this sort of explanation, students should then do nothing more than simply raise it to their attention and investigate it throughout the twelve time-periods of the day and in all four postures [*īryāpatha*, viz., walking, standing, sitting, lying down]. They should not presume that their mind-natures are either separate from words or free of signs; nor should they have any understanding that conditioned origination is unimpeded. If there is even one thought left of conceptual understanding regarding the Buddhadharma, they will remain immersed in these ten maladies of understanding. Therefore they should lay them down, one by one, while avoiding any deliberations about whether or not to lay them down or whether or not they are immersed in a malady. They unexpectedly activate one instant of realization in regard to the tasteless, elusive *hwadu*, and the *dharmadhātu* of the one mind becomes utterly evident and clear.[100]

Immersing himself in the investigation of the *hwadu*, a meditator must abandon any emotional, linguistic, conceptual, or even volitional activities, as Chinul insists that the direct realization of the Buddhadharma or the *dharmadhātu* should be pursued "without seeking them."[101] In seeking a direct experience of the ultimate reality through investigating the *hwadu*, one must not only "remain free of ratiocination via mind or consciousness along the road of speech or the road of meaning," but also "stay clear of any idea of a temporal sequence in which views, learning, understanding, or conduct are to be developed."[102] This should be done while avoiding even the desire to abandon all mental activities[103] and without any discriminative consciousness of subject and object.[104]

Obviously, *kanhwa* Sŏn is a mental activity involving a word or phrase, and therefore it seems natural that the human mind operates intellectually with a given *hwadu*. However, Dahui identifies this intellectual operation as malady and warns the meditator not to fall prey to it. He lists ten maladies of knowledge and conceptual understanding (*sipchong chihae chi pyŏng* 十種知解之病) that can arise when meditating on the *hwadu* "*mu.*"

[1] You should not understand it to mean yes or no. [2] You should not presume it is the no of the true nonexistence. [3] You should not try to understand it doctrinally. [4] You should not ponder over it logically at the mind-consciousness base. [5] You should not assume that the master [is explaining the *hwadu*] when he raises his eyebrows or twinkles his eyes. [6] You should not devise stratagems [for resolving the *hwadu*] through the way of words. [7] You should not hide yourself inside a shell of unconcern. [8] You should not consider [the *hwadu*] at the place where you raise it to your attention. [9] You should not look for evidence in the wording. [10] You should not grasp at a deluded state, simply waiting for awakening. There is absolutely no need to use the mind in any way. Once the mind is without any abiding place, do not fear falling into emptiness, for that is certain to be a good place. As soon as a rat enters the ox horn [trap], [wrong] views (*dṛṣṭi*) and the inversions (*viparyāsa*) are then both eradicated.[105]

Here, the reference of a rat trapped in an ox horn, associated with an ancient custom of southern China, metaphorically describes what happens in *kanhwa* meditation. When a rat enters an ox horn to get the oil, it wedges itself in and cannot escape. The metaphor implies that the practitioner of *hwadu* meditation reaches the point at which intellectual activities are no longer possible and they therefore must be abandoned.[106]

The strategy of pushing a meditator into an unresolvable deadlock is implied by the term *hwadu* (話頭). As has been mentioned, the word literally means "head of speech," or metaphorically, "apex of speech." According to Buswell's interpretation, speech is indicative of the discriminative tendency of the human mind—linguistic, logical, conceptual, imaginative, affective, etc.—and investigation of the *hwadu* pushes speech and all other mental activities to the point where they cannot proceed further. At that point, mental activities halt and all conceptualization is relinquished. The driving force in this process is doubt, which is generated while maintaining focus on the *hwadu*.[107]

According to Chinul, following Dahui, doubt (*ŭijŏng* 疑情) is a mental state of puzzlement and frustration that arises when confronting intellectual challenges. It pushes the meditator to intellectual and emotional unease, described as "gnawing on an iron rod," until the intellect must cease operating.[108] Dahui advises meditators to put all their energy into investigating the *hwadu*, and to immerse themselves in doubt to the point where all conceptual, affective, and sensory discrimination is eradicated and they ultimately reach the direct experience of the *dharmadhātu*.[109] The main purpose of *hwadu* is to build up to an extreme the uneasy sensation of doubt and insecurity produced by the meditator's inability to resolve the problem that is the subject of the meditation through ordinary ratiocinative processes.[110]

Investigating the Meaning and the Word

The disintegration of doubt, which plays a crucial role in the awakening of the mind, can be pursued through the two different types of *hwadu* meditation—investigating the meaning (*ch'amŭi* 參意) and investigating the word (*ch'amgu* 參句).[111] Those engaging in contemplative practice through investigating the meaning of the *hwadu* dispel doubt by gaining right understanding, which leads to a certain kind of awakening. However, this awakening may retain traces of the maladies of understanding, and may not be that much different from the intellectual understanding attained by scholar-monks relying on words and letters. The intellectual awakening achieved through the investigation of the meaning of *hwadu* corresponds to the understanding-awakening at the first level of ten faiths in the soteriological framework of Hwaŏm.[112] On the other hand, those engaging in the investigation of the word gain a personal realization of the one mind, then display *prajñā* and spread the Buddhadharma by instructing students according to their capacities. This kind of awakening is a realization-awakening.[113]

The *mu hwadu* 無話頭 recommended by Dahui can be investigated according to these two types of *hwadu* meditation. First, those investigating the meaning of the *hwadu* look into the intent of the master Zhaozhou. They endeavor to find out why the master answered that a dog does not have the buddha-nature, and also explore the meaning of the answer in light of Buddhist teachings. This approach to *hwadu* meditation suits the Sŏn students whose capacity is not sufficiently advanced to immerse themselves in contemplation without engaging in any intellectual activities. This way of *hwadu* meditation parallels cataphatic discourse insofar as it is intended to identify the intelligible affirmative teachings of Buddhism associated with the *hwadu*.

On the other hand, advanced students of Sŏn are encouraged to engage directly in an investigation of the word *mu* 無 itself, setting aside all mental activity. Here, the *hwadu* is metaphorically described as not having any taste or as "tasteless"[114] (*mumi* 無味, or *molchami* 沒滋味[115]). When a meditator attempts to investigate the meaning of *mu*, all of the intellectual processes associated with words and concepts—logic, grammar, discrimination of subject and object—operate. However, the tasteless *hwadu* hinders the mind from engaging in intellectual activities that may generate a discriminative meaning. It functions as a broom constantly sweeping away intervening intellectual processes.[116] This way of meditation parallels apophatic discourse, which stresses the inefficacy of language and associated conceptual process in the search for ultimate truth.

Dead Words and Live Words

Obviously, the generation of concepts involves the use of words, either written or spoken. Chinul introduces the Sŏn distinction between two kinds of words: dead words and live words. "Dead words" (*sagu* 死句) refer to phrases, whether they be detailed explanations or brief statements, that facilitate intellectual understanding but are prone to obstruct the realization of ineffable reality, whereas "live words" (*hwalgu* 活句) relate to the nondiscriminative *hwadu*s of the shortcut approach.[117]

This distinction parallels the distinction between investigations of the meaning and the word. In general, dead words refer to prolix explanations or short doctrinal statements; however, even one word can be a dead word if it arouses discriminative knowledge. Chinul refers to Huineng's warning: "Even when I call it 'one thing,' that still isn't correct. How dare you call it 'original fount' or 'buddha-nature'?"[118] Chinul and Huineng are concerned that not only descriptions of ultimate reality involving phrases with explicit definitions or meanings, but also calling ultimate reality "one thing," which does not imply any doctrinal or philosophical connotation, can jeopardize the goal of practitioners by provoking their engagement in intellectual activities. In the same vein, the single word "awareness" (*chi* 知), the essential word summarizing Zongmi's teachings, can be considered "the gateway to all calamities."[119] Therefore, designation of a phrase or word as "dead" or "live" depends not only on its length and implied philosophical meaning but also on how it functions in meditation. While one can acquire an intellectual understanding of Buddhist teachings via dead words, the investigation of live words leads to an experiential realization of the true nature of the reality.[120]

It seems somewhat contradictory that the Sŏn tradition, which advocates the principle of "no establishment of words and letters" (C. *buli wenzi*, K. *pullip munja* 不立文字), should develop a meditation practice that employs words. Nevertheless, taking into consideration its efficacy as a soteriological expedient, *hwadu* can be "conceived of as a form of spiritual homeopathy, using a minimal, but potent, dosage of the poison of words to cure the malady of conceptualization."[121]

The Three Mysterious Gates

What has been explored thus far—*kanhwa* meditation, investigation of meaning and words, and dead and live words—all concern specific practices or specific aspects of Sŏn. The threefold classification of the mysterious gates is a more comprehensive scheme presenting various Sŏn approaches to practice. The three mysterious gates (*samhyŏn mun* 三玄門), introduced in the earlier part of *Resolving Doubts*, are repeatedly discussed by Chinul when he is considering different types of religious practices, especially when he is comparing religious practices involving intellectual understanding with those intent on overcoming that understanding. Chinul explains the three mysterious gates as follows:

> In the Sŏn school, there also are slight differences in the many access gates designed for people of varying capacities. Some rely on the principles of mind-only or consciousness-only and thus access the mystery in the essence (*ch'ejung hyŏn* 體中玄). This first mysterious gate involves explanations like the complete teachings' unimpeded interpenetration between all phenomena. Nevertheless, since such people continue to hold onto views and opinions about the Buddhadharma, they cannot gain liberated purification. Others rely on the cleansing knowledge and vision exhibited by way of response to the fundamental matter (*ponbunsa* 本分事) and access the mystery in the word (*kujung hyŏn* 句中玄), which destroys that knowledge and understanding of the Buddhadharma that is still present at the level of the first mysterious gate. This mystery includes such *hwadu*s of the shortcut school as "the cypress tree in front of the courtyard" and "three catties of flax." Nevertheless, setting up these mysterious gates was the idea of the Sŏn masters of old. They used the words of the *hwadu*s as responses to the fundamental matter in order to eliminate the maladies [of conceptual understanding]. Thus, they established this second mystery [viz., the mystery in the word]. But as long as students do not eliminate these words of cleansing knowledge and vision, they will not be able to be self-reliant in the realm of birth and death. Therefore, they established the third [mystery]: the mystery in the mystery (*hyŏnjung hyŏn* 玄中玄). This [mystery] was intended to destroy the previous cleansing knowledge and vision through such activities as pausing, keeping silence, striking, or shouting.[122]

The scheme of the three mysterious gates was first employed by Linji Yixuan 臨濟義玄 (d. 866), and was adopted and developed by several Chan masters before Chinul. The distinction between the three mysteries as adopted by Chinul was formulated by the Yunmen 雲門 master Jianfu Chenggu 薦福承古 (d. 1045),[123] and later cited by Chinul in *Resolving Doubts, Complete and Sudden Attainment*, and *Excerpts*.[124]

Clearly, this threefold scheme is a Sŏn classification that systematizes various Sŏn approaches to contemplation and which parallels the doctrinal classification of Kyo.[125] Here, Chinul categorizes conceptual and intellectual contemplation as the incipient stage of Sŏn practice, the "mystery in the essence." Obviously, Kyo monks also engage in this kind of contemplation. However, the Sŏn master valorizes Sŏn over Kyo for its immediate efficacy—whereas the teachings of Kyo are generally explanatory and prolix, intent on inducing intellectual understanding in "tens of thousands of generations," the purpose of Sŏn teachings and practices is to facilitate "the immediate crossing-over liberation" or "mysterious penetration" into the principles of advanced students by use of terse statements.[126]

According to Chinul, those who employ this gate of the mystery in the essence, whether they be Kyo monks or Sŏn adepts, acquire proper intellectual understanding "that accords with reality, [and they] discern clearly their own minds' authentic and deceptive aspects, its production and cessation, and its essential and secondary features."[127] The first gate, the mystery in the essence, is a necessary approach to practice for people of inferior abilities, who can be easily deluded by experiences in the sense-sphere.

However, those employing this approach are subject to the risk of holding on to intellectually formed views. They therefore need another approach that can cleanse them of intellectual knowledge and vision. This brings Chinul to the second gate, which enables students to access the "mystery in the word." This approach also employs words, but words intended to break intellectual understanding rather than induce it. Chinul assigns the shortcut approach of *hwadu* (C. *huatou* 話頭) meditation (or Dahui's *kanhwa Sŏn*) to this second category.

Although the second mysterious gate, the mystery in the word, aims at eliminating the maladies of conceptual understanding, this approach still involves words. Therefore, it is necessary to employ the third approach—the "mystery in the mystery," which involves pauses, gestures, and nonverbal expressions devoid of any conceptualization. The iconoclastic images associated with Sŏn are closely related to this third approach.

This threefold soteriological scheme progresses from contemplation of cataphatic statements to more apophatic phrases intended to eliminate conceptualization. It finally employs nonverbal expressions as catalysts to a sudden awakening to the ineffable truth.[128]

A Comprehensive View of Kanhwa Sŏn and Associated Categories

The discussion up to this point has introduced various distinctions related to *kanhwa* meditation employed by Chinul. It will be noticed that these distinctions are closely connected with each other. When a Sŏn meditator examines the meaning of a given *hwadu*, this helps him acquire the right understanding of the word or phrase in light of the Buddhist teachings, but he only accesses understanding-awakening with traces of understanding still remaining, which obstruct a direct personal experience of true reality, unmediated by any conceptualization process. In this *hwadu* meditation, the word of *hwadu* becomes a dead word, and the meditative practice belongs to the first of the threefold gates, the mystery in the essence. This level of Sŏn practice suitable for beginners corresponds to most Kyo meditation practices, which are heavily grounded in detailed explanations of Buddhist doctrines.

On the other hand, investigating the word itself without engaging in intellectual activity leads to a direct realization of the true nature of reality or the *dharmadhātu*, which is considered to be the realization-awakening. Here, the keyword or *hwadu* functions as a live word that leads to salvation. Although Chinul identifies this *hwadu* meditation with the second mysterious gate, the mystery in the word,[129] a further reading of *Resolving Doubts* reveals a contradictory interpretation of *kanhwa* Sŏn in terms of its relationship with the threefold mysterious gates.[130] Chinul points out that the second mysterious gate still retains some intellectual traces—although these may be very subtle—that should be eliminated through the mystery in the mystery.[131] However, in contrast to the characteristics of the second mystery, *kanhwa* Sŏn, when it is properly practiced, does not involve any conceptualization process, so that elimination of intellectual maladies, which is a crucial purpose of the third gate, is not required at all.[132] Theoretically, a Sŏn adept with superior abilities would engage in *hwadu* meditation without the involvement of any discriminative mental activity from the beginning; nevertheless, from a practical perspective, *kanhwa* meditation can serve as a bridge for practitioners who need to eliminate the impediment of conceptualization during the gradual development of their religious practice.

The idea that ideal practice of *hwadu* meditation is not obstructed by conceptualization is based on Sŏn's ontological and epistemological principle regarding the true nature of the mind. Chinul explains:

> According to the authentic, definitive teaching, then, deluded thoughts are originally void with nothing further that can be left behind, and all the uncontaminated factors (*anāsravadharma*) are originally the true nature. The operation of their sublime functioning, which adapts to conditions, remains forever uninterrupted. There is, furthermore, no need to eliminate them. It was solely for those sentient beings who grasp at false names and signs and find it difficult to achieve the mysterious awakening that the Buddha moreover did not distinguish wholesome from unwholesome, defiled from pure, or mundane from supramundane, but instead eliminated everything. For this reason, those who bear this [sudden] teaching are able to remain in accord with the undifferentiated, signless principle and understand that there is neither a subject nor an object of speech, neither a subject nor an object of thought. Subsequently, they can leave behind this understanding and this thought and gain access to the gate of true suchness. Therefore, this is simply called the buddhahood that is achieved through realization of the principle.[133]

Since everything is originally void, there is actually nothing to eliminate. Even the volitional effort to abandon all discrimination arises from one's deluded views on mind and existence.

Thus, in *Resolving Doubts*, Chinul promotes the investigation of the word of the *hwadu* with all conceptualization processes abandoned from the beginning. His emphasis on nonconceptualization naturally entails the promotion of non-intellectual religious practices along with apophatic discourses that are intended to prevent practitioners from falling into attachment to positive statements.

It can thus be seen that Chinul's writing takes a markedly more favorable tone toward apophatic practices in *Resolving Doubts* as compared to his earlier writings, which is manifested in his zealous promotion of *kanhwa* Sŏn.[134] Although in this treatise Chinul does not definitively rebut the inclusive approach to scriptural and doctrinal studies and intellectual meditation that he advocated in most of his writings (discussed in chapter 2),[135] his confidence in Sŏn and his emphasis on nonintellectual meditation, specifically *kanhwa* Sŏn, is striking. Overall, his earlier writings tend to demonstrate a "liberal attitude toward Kyo and [a] restrained discussion of Sŏn,"[136] whereas his later writings show a more critical attitude toward Kyo and a focus on the nonintellectual aspect of Sŏn practice, which culminates in his promotion of *kanhwa* technique.

SUMMARY

This chapter has explored the Buddhist counterparts of the Christian terms apophasis and cataphasis by investigating Buddhist discourses and their connection to the primary Chan Buddhist doctrines and meditative practices and more specifically to Chinul's Sŏn theory and practice. When it comes to apophasis and cataphasis in Chan, three features are noteworthy.

First, the tension between apophasis and cataphasis was already inherent in Chinese Chan, which developed as a synthesis of the doctrinal teachings of two distinct schools—the Emptiness school and the Buddha-Nature school, the latter of which combined mind-only and buddha-nature teachings. The former is characterized by apophatic discourse and a negative view of language, whereas the latter is marked by cataphatic discourse and a positive view of language. The prevalence of negative and paradoxical expressions in Chan can be largely attributed to the apophatic approach of the Emptiness school. On the other hand, the affirmative predications and explanations found in Chan draw on the cataphatic approach of the Buddha-Nature school.

Chan (or Sŏn) embraced both of these seemingly contrasting ways of discourse, and it developed distinctive features as the result of its attempt to compromise between them. In general, Chan rhetoric is less nihilistic than that of the Madhyamaka school. While Chan acknowledges the ineffability of the ultimate truth, it does not focus on denying all affirmative views and statements, but rather offers some soteriological paths that employ words and concepts. It has been shown already that some Chan masters interpreted the Chan principle "no establishment of the dharma relying on words and speech" not to imply a total renunciation of language, but rather only a caution about attachment to concepts. It is undeniable that Chan utilizes language and concepts. However, Chan is differentiated from the other doctrinal schools in that its verbal discourse is much more terse. It should be noted that although Chan discourse in general is not as prolix or elaborate as that of the cataphatic doctrinal schools, it still embraces affirmative words and concepts like mind, buddha-nature, and other categorical terms. As for Chinul, he adopted a significant number of Hwaŏm terms and concepts in his discussion of Sŏn theories and practices.

Second, the Chan school has developed two competing approaches to the use of language: one is the exclusive approach of radically renouncing words and concepts and instead employing iconoclastic and nonverbal alternatives, and a second is the inclusive approach of accommodating words and concepts with caution. Clearly, the former attitude resonates with that of adherents of the Emptiness school. On the other hand, the latter attitude is related to the teaching of buddha-nature, and could be described as "disciplined" in that its supporters acknowledge the limitations of verbal expression and carefully choose words in order to enhance spiritual practices despite their inherent limitations and risks.

Third, the distinction between cataphasis and apophasis in Chan is connected with its different styles of meditation. Contemplative practice is characteristic of Chan and distinguishes it from other Buddhist schools, especially those that center on texts and doctrinal, philosophical studies (e.g., Jiao/Kyo 教). In this regard, Chan is generally sympathetic to the negative view of language that underlies apophatic discourse. However, in looking at the specific features of its different meditative practices, it becomes clear that Chan meditation involves some elements of both cataphasis and apophasis: Chan meditation employs different approaches to conceptualization, including radical rejection and its disciplined employment—which parallel apophasis and cataphasis, respectively.

Finally, it is appropriate to summarize Chinul's Sŏn thought, taking into consideration the relationship between Buddhist teachings, modes of discourse, and styles of meditation. First, as the Chan writings do, Chinul's work contains both apophasis and cataphasis. On the one hand, negative and paradoxical rhetoric is prevalent in his writings, which are employed for the purpose of asserting the ineffability of the truth. His early writings emphasized the importance of Sŏn practice, but his later writings shifted their emphasis to nonintellectual meditation. On the other hand, Chinul's writings are also full of affirmative and explanatory statements intended to persuade Kyo monks to concentrate on the cultivation of their minds and to encourage Sŏn adepts by providing them with a theoretical foundation for their meditative practices. With this purpose in mind, Chinul integrates Huayan terms and doctrines into his scheme, as can be seen in *Complete and Sudden Attainment* and other writings.

Second, when it comes to the usage of words and concepts in religious practice, Chinul took an inclusive cataphatic stance for most of his life. In this, he seemed to follow *wenzi* Chan (or lettered Chan). Chinul persistently promoted the benefits of language and concepts in the development of spiritual practices. This accommodating approach is directly related to his advocacy of learning and studies even for Sŏn adepts, which, he was convinced, would help them be equipped with a proper intellectual understanding of the truth and a proper soteriological path and guide their spiritual practices in the right direction. However, in his later life, Chinul appears to have taken a more radical, apophatic approach as manifested in *Resolving Doubts*. In this work, Chinul emphasizes the maladies of intellectual understanding. Although he still recognizes the efficacy of learning for the benefit of those with inferior spiritual capacities, his attitude toward the cataphatic approach appears to be increasingly dismissive over time. Thus, his view of language and concepts shifted from cataphatic appreciation to apophatic refutation. This change can be clearly seen in his advocacy of *kanhwa* Sŏn.

Third, the relationship between the apophasis/cataphasis distinction and meditation in Chinul's Sŏn thought can be examined from the perspective of the relationship between two other distinctions: Kyo/Sŏn and intellectual/ nonintellectual meditation. Sympathetic as he might have been with textual and doctrinal studies, as a Sŏn adept himself, Chinul's main concern was the promotion of meditation. In fact, he composed most of his treatises in order to foster Sŏn meditation within the Buddhist community. Although meditation itself is in general closely related to apophasis in its great caution with respect to language and concepts, the various ways of actually conducting meditative practices can be divided into a radical rejection of words and conceptualization and a disciplined accommodation of them. Chinul understood that the doctrinal schools also stipulate methods of contemplation, and that their methods are sympathetic with cataphasis in that they engage in intellectual meditation drawing on the affirmative teachings of the respective schools. In contrast to the Kyo meditation, he stresses that Sŏn meditation proposes the attainment of direct realization without words and concepts.

In the same vein, Chinul's writings promoting and explicating Sŏn meditation emphasize the ineffability of the truth, and *kongan*s and *hwadu*s employed in that meditation are intended to break logical thought and the grammar of language. This intention of Sŏn rhetoric corresponds to apophasis. Of course, meditation associated with apophasis is not meant for everyone, not even for all Sŏn adepts—Chinul admits that only those with superior faculties are capable of engaging in this kind of meditation. Although Chinul promotes nonconceptual Sŏn meditation throughout his writings, it is in his later writings that he emphasizes this way of meditation more ardently, in particular by introducing and expounding the *kanhwa* meditation technique. Overall, the marked change in Chinul's view of language and concepts parallels the shift of his view of meditation from sympathy toward intellectual meditation to active advocacy of nonconceptual meditation.

Thus, Chinul's Sŏn theory and practice is a tapestry woven with both the fabric of cataphasis and the fabric of apophasis. In his later life, as he was claiming the superiority of Sŏn and promoting *kanhwa* meditation, the apophatic preference became preeminent. Nevertheless, his Sŏn never became entirely apophatic—just as a tapestry needs different kinds of fabric, so Chinul's formulation of Sŏn is a complex combination of various Buddhist theoretical and practical traditions incorporating both cataphasis and apophasis.

NOTES

1. *Excerpts from the Dharma Collection and Special Practice Record with Personal Notes*, in Chinul, *Numinous Awareness Is Never Dark*.

2. On the tension between moderate and radical formulations in Chinul's soteriological thought, see Robert E. Buswell Jr., "Pojo Chinul and Kanhwa Sŏn: Reconciling the Language of Moderate and Radical Subitism," in *Zen Buddhist Rhetoric in China, Korea, and Japan*, ed. Christoph Anderl (Leiden: Brill, 2012), 345–61; Robert E. Buswell Jr., "Chinul's Ambivalent Critique of Radical Subitism in Korean Sŏn Buddhism," *The Journal of the International Association of Buddhist Studies* 12, no. 2 (1989): 20–44.

3. See David J. Kalupahana, *Buddhist Philosophy: A Historical Analysis* (Honolulu: University of Hawaii Press, 1976), 163–76. For a brief introduction to the Madhyamaka and Yogācāra schools, see Damien Keown, *A Dictionary of Buddhism* (Oxford: Oxford University Press, 2003), s.vv. "Madhyamaka," "Yogācāra." Kindle edition.

4. This is Robert M. Gimello's translation of a passage from Zongmi's *Prolegomenon to the Collection of Expressions of the Chan Source* (hereafter cited

as *Chan Prolegomenon*) (C. *Chanyuan zhuquan ji duxu* 禪源諸詮集都序) *Taishō shinshū daizōkyō* 大正新修大藏經. 48.0406b17–c04 (hereafter cited as "T"): 六遮詮表詮異者。遮謂遣其所非。表謂顯其所是。又遮者揀却諸餘。表者直示當體。如諸經所說真妙理性。每云。不生不滅。不垢不淨。無因無果。無相無為。非凡非聖。非性非相等。皆是遮詮(諸經論中。每以非字非却諸法。動即有三十五十箇非字也。不字無字亦爾。故云絕百非)若云知見覺。照靈鑒光明。朗朗昭昭。惺惺寂寂等。皆是表詮。若無知見等體。顯何法為性。說何法不生滅等。必須認得見今了然。而知即是心性。方說此知不生不滅等。如說鹽云不淡是遮。云鹹是表。說水云不乾是遮。云濕是表。諸教每云絕百非者。皆是遮詞直顯一真。方為表語。空宗之言但是遮詮。性宗之言有遮有表。但遮者未了。兼表者乃的。今時學人皆謂。遮言為深。表言為淺。故唯重非心非佛。無為無相。乃至一切不可得之言。良由但以遮非之詞為妙。不欲親自證認法體。 Bracketed insertions in original. Gimello's translation is quoted from Robert M. Gimello, "Mysticism in Its Contexts," in *Mysticism and Religious Traditions*, ed. Steven T. Katz (New York: Oxford University Press, 1983), 76–77. For another English version, see Jeffrey Lyle Broughton, *Zongmi on Chan* (New York: Columbia University Press, 2009), 144–45.

5. For a brief introduction to the doctrine of emptiness and the Perfection of Wisdom sūtras, see Paul Williams, *Mahāyāna Buddhism: The Doctrinal Foundations*, second ed. (London: Routledge, 2009), 45–62. See also Heinrich Dumoulin, *Zen Buddhism: A History—India and China*, trans. James W. Heisig and Paul Knitter (New York: Macmillan Publishing, 1994), 41–45.

6. As will be seen, many Chan adepts argued against any interconnectedness between intellectual analysis and the realization of the perfect wisdom, insisting instead on abandoning any form of conceptual process. See Williams, *Mahāyāna Buddhism*, 49–51.

7. For the Mādhyamaka school and Nāgārjuna, see Williams, *Mahāyāna Buddhism*, 63–83. For a brief introduction to Nāgārjuna and his philosophy, see also *The Princeton Dictionary of Buddhism*, s.v. "Nāgārjuna." Kindle edition.

8. Dumoulin, *Zen Buddhism: A History*, 44.

9. Robert M. Gimello, "Apophatic and Kataphatic Discourse in Mahāyāna," *Philosophy East and West* 26, no. 2 (1976): 120.

10. Gimello, "Apophatic and Kataphatic Discourse in Mahāyāna," 131. Gimello explains:

> Just as particular material forms lack ontological own-being, so all predications lack the linguistic equivalent of own-being—to wit, referential meaning. The Buddhist ultimate truth of emptiness is ineffable, then, but in a special sense—not because our words fall short of describing some transcendent absolute reality called "emptiness," but because all words are such that they lack referential content or are "empty" of substantive meaning (*artha-śūnya-śabda*). (Gimello, "Apophatic and Kataphatic Discourse in Mahāyāna," 120)

11. Gimello, "Apophatic and Kataphatic Discourse in Mahāyāna," 120.

12. Gimello, "Mysticism in Its Contexts," 78.

13. Dumoulin, *Zen Buddhism: A History*, 44–45. The paradoxical logic stating that A is A because it is not A is repeatedly employed in the *Diamond Sūtra*. This can be illustrated by two quotations. "Because the Tathagata spoke of the 'heap of merit' as a non-heap. That is how the Tathagata speaks of 'heap of merit.'" (8) "The Lord said: If any Bodhisattva would say, 'I will create harmonious Buddhafields,' he would speak falsely. And Why? 'The harmonies of Buddhafields, the harmonies of Buddhafields,' Subhuti, as no-harmonies have they been taught by the Tathagata. Therefore he spoke of 'harmonious Buddhafields.'" (10b) Using this logic, the sūtra refutes both affirmation and negation, both of which derive from discriminative perception of something. Therefore, whether it be affirmative statement or negative statement, one should not hold on to it. The sūtra denies even the teachings of the Buddha, stating: "From the Dharma should one see the Buddhas, From the Dharmabodies comes their guidance. Yet Dharma's true nature cannot be discerned, And no one can be conscious of it as an object." (26b) Dharma is ineffable, and indescribable, therefore, one should not hold on to any statement as it contains any intelligible truth. The Buddha warns Subhuti, saying, "Subhuti, that 'seizing on a material object' is a matter of linguistic convention, a verbal expression without factual content. It is not a dharma nor a no-dharma. And yet the foolish common people have seized upon it." (30b) For these quotations from the *Diamond Sūtra*, see *Buddhist Wisdom Books: The Diamond and the Heart Sutra*, trans. Edward Conze, rev. ed. (London: Unwin Paperbacks, 1988). The numbers in parenthesis indicate chapter numbers.

14. Dumoulin, *Zen Buddhism: A History*, 142.

15. Sallie B. King, *Buddha Nature* (Albany, NY: State University of New York Press, 1991), 7. King asserts:

> Mādhyamika is not nihilistic and is negative only in the form of its language and dialectic; strictly speaking, its philosophical standpoint is not negative, because negativity is dualistic and śūnyatā is the emptying of all dualisms. Thus, regardless of the philosophical status of Yogācāra, Mādhyamika itself cannot occupy a negative pole in any typology of philosophical positions.

16. For an analysis of the term "*tathāgatagarbha*," see King, *Buddha Nature*, 4.

17. Identification of *tathāgatagarbha* with the mind is the result of a conflation of the teachings of Yogācāra and those of *tathāgatagarbha*. The Yogācāra school, whose source is largely attributed to two brothers, Asaṅga and Vasubandhu, who lived in the fourth and fifth centuries, emphasizes meditation, and is well known for its doctrines of mind-only (*cittamātra*) and consciousness-only (*vijñaptimātra*), which claim that all experiences of external objects are not real because they are constructions of the mind and only the mind is real. This idea of mind-only would be combined with the ideas of buddha-nature and *dharmadhātu*, and the mind would come to be seen as the pure, eternal, ontological ground of reality (*dharmadhātu*), from which all phenomena arise. See King, *Buddha Nature*, 1–28; Williams, *Mahāyāna Buddhism*, 84–148; *The Princeton Dictionary of Buddhism*, s.v. "Yogācāra."

18. Dan Lusthaus, "Buddhist Philosophy, Chinese," in *Routledge Encyclopedia of Philosophy* (London: Routledge, 1998), https://www.rep.routledge.com/articles/

overview/buddhist-philosophy-chinese/v-1/sections/the-awakening-of-faith-in
-mahayana (accessed March 12, 2019).

19. King, *Buddha Nature*, 11.

20. Robert M. Gimello too points out that the various alternatives to the teachings and radical apophatic discourses of the Madhyamaka school were intended to "assert the salvific value of kataphasis, the spiritual utility of positive and affirmative language." These alternatives acknowledged the caution about cataphatic language that characterized the Madhyamaka school, but they chose cataphatic language over "the unremitting distrust of positive language" for soteriological purposes. See Gimello, "Apophatic and Kataphatic Discourse in Mahāyāna," 119.

21. Lusthaus, "Buddhist Philosophy, Chinese."

22. This scripture is commonly attributed to the Indian monk Aśvaghoṣa (first or second century), and was first translated into Chinese by Paramārtha (499–569). However, it is now generally accepted to be of Chinese origin. For an introduction and English translation of the text with commentary, see Yoshito S. Hakeda, trans., *The Awakening of Faith*, with introduction and commentary (New York: Columbia University Press, 1967). See also Williams, *Mahāyāna Buddhism*, 115–19.

23. Hakeda, introduction to *The Awakening of Faith*, 15.

24. *The Awakening of Faith*, 31–36.

25. *The Awakening of Faith*, 33.

26. Hakeda, commentary to *The Awakening of Faith*, 34.

27. See Robert E. Buswell Jr., introduction to *Chinul: Selected Works*, trans. with introduction and annotations, Robert E. Buswell Jr., vol. 2 of *Collected Works of Korean Buddhism* (Seoul: Jogye Order of Korean Buddhism, 2012), 17 (hereafter cited as *CSW*).

28. Porter is also known by his pen-name, Red Pine.

29. Red Pine, trans., introduction to *The Platform Sutra: The Zen Teaching of Hui-neng* (Berkeley: Counterpoint Press, 2006), 61. John R. McRae also points out the primacy of the buddha-nature and the significance of seeing one's own nature in Huineng's teachings. See John R. McRae, trans., *The Platform Sutra of the Sixth Patriarch*, BDK English Tripiṭaka Series (Berkeley: Numata Center for Buddhist Translation and Research, 2000), xiii.

30. For a discussion of the synthesis of the buddha-nature and no-thought in the *Platform Sūtra*, see Dumoulin, *Zen Buddhism: A History*, 142–48.

31. Huineng presents the core of his teachings through three negations:

> Good friends, in this teaching of mind, from ancient times up to the present, all have set up no-thought as the main doctrine, non-form as the substance, and non-abiding as the basis. Non-form is to be separated from form even when associated with form. No-thought is not to think even when involved in thought. Non-abiding is the original nature of man. (*The Platform Sūtra* 17, in Philip B. Yampolsky, trans., *The Platform Sutra of the Sixth Patriarch* [1967; repr., New York: Columbia University Press, 2012], 137–38)

These three negations are paraphrases of words from the *Diamond Sūtra*, which are based on the idea of emptiness. See Red Pine, commentary on *The Platform Sutra*, 141–42.

32. *The Platform Sūtra* 31, in Yampolsky, *The Platform Sutra of the Sixth Patriarch*, 153.

33. *The Platform Sūtra* 24, in Yampolsky, *The Platform Sutra of the Sixth Patriarch*, 146.

34. Huineng advises his disciples to employ the paradoxical rhetoric that prevails in the *Diamond Sūtra*:

> As things rise and sink, you must separate from dualism. When you explain all things, do not stand apart from nature and form. Should someone ask you about the Dharma, what you say should all be symmetrical and you must draw parallels for everything. Since they originate each from the other, if in the end dualisms are all completely cast aside, there will be no place for them to exist. (*The Platform Sūtra* 45, in Yampolsky, *The Platform Sutra of the Sixth Patriarch*, 170–71)

35. Red Pine, introduction to *The Platform Sutra*, 61.

36. During his lecture to an assembly of Buddhists on Vulture Peak, the Buddha held up a flower, and while all remained in silence, Mahākāśyapa broke into a smile, in which the Buddha identified the secret transmission of the dharma to his disciple. Albert Welter contends that this story developed and was promoted in such a way as to bolster Chan orthodoxy, in particular the self-affirming statement of "separate transmission outside the doctrinal teachings." Albert Welter, "Mahākāśyapa's Smile: Silent Transmission and the Kung-an (Kōan) Tradition," in *The Kōan: Texts and Contexts in Zen Buddhism*, ed. Steven Heine and Dale S. Wright (Oxford: Oxford University Press, 2000), 75–109.

37. Welter, "Mahākāśyapa's Smile," 75–109. Welter's research focuses on the historical development and establishment of the principle "separate transmission of the dharma outside of doctrinal teaching." For further studies of the development of "separate transmission outside of doctrinal teaching," see T. Griffith Foulk, "Sung Controversies Concerning the 'Separate Transmission' of Ch'an," in *Buddhism in the Sung*, ed. Peter N. Gregory and Daniel A. Getz Jr. (Honolulu: University of Hawaii Press, 1999), 220–94. See also *The Princeton Dictionary of Buddhism*, s.vv. "*zhizhi renxin*," "*jianxing chengfo*," "*buli wenzi*," "*jiaowai biechuan*." While three of the four principles—"no establishment of words and letters," "direct pointing to the mind of man," and "seeing into nature and becoming a buddha"—were well established as normative statements of the Chan school by the beginning of the Song period and were attributed to Bodhidharma, it was not until the mid-tenth century that the fourth principle, "separate transmission of the dharma outside of doctrinal teaching," first appeared in *Zutang ji* 祖堂集 (K. *Chodang chip*, "Collection of the Patriarch's Hall"), compiled in 952. It later appeared in *Tiansheng guangdeng lu* 天聖廣燈錄 (K. *Ch'ŏnsŏng kwangdŭngnok*, "Tiansheng Era Expanded Lamp Record"), compiled in 1036. The latter is the primary text that contributed to the official acceptance of the principle in the Chan tradition. The four statements would appear altogether in *Zuting shinyuan* 祖庭事苑 (K. *Chojŏng sawŏn*, "Garden of Matters from the Patriarchs' Hall"), compiled in 1108.

38. *The Platform Sūtra* 9, in Yampolsky, *The Platform Sutra of the Sixth Patriarch*, 133.

39. McRae, introduction to *The Platform Sutra*, xiv. It is thought that Heze Shenhui 荷澤神會 (684–758), the putative disciple of Huineng, was involved in the establishment of the legend of Huineng. For the shaping of the legend of and the composition of the *Platform Sūtra*, see Yampolsky, introduction to *The Platform Sutra*, 1–121. See also John R. McRae, *The Northern School and the Formation of Early Ch'an Buddhism* (Honolulu: University of Hawaii Press, 1986), 1–4.

40. Yampolsky, introduction to *The Platform Sutra*, 112.

41. Yampolsky, introduction to *The Platform Sutra*, 114–16.

42. *The Platform Sūtra* 1, in Yampolsky, *The Platform Sutra of the Sixth Patriarch*, 126.

43. The sūtra mentions Huineng's illiteracy twice. In section eight, Huineng asks someone to read verses written on the wall and to write some verses for him. In section forty-two, Huineng admits his inability to read. See *The Platform Sūtra* 8, 42, in Yampolsky, *The Platform Sutra of the Sixth Patriarch*, 132, 165.

44. Yampolsky, introduction to *The Platform Sutra*, 112.

45. Welter, "Mahākāśyapa's Smile," 86.

46. "The sutras are buddha word, while Chan is the intention of the buddhas. The mouth and mind of the buddhas cannot possibly be contradictory." Zongmi, *Chan Prolegomenon*, in Broughton, *Zongmi on Chan*, 109.

47. Welter, "Mahākāśyapa's Smile," 86–91. Welter understands the rise of Fayan zong in the context of the stability and continuation of the refined Buddhist tradition of the Tang period.

48. For example, Chan adepts developed a complex genre of literature known as the *gong'an*s, or Chan cases. A case in *Biyan lu* 碧巖錄 (K. *Pyŏgam nok*, "Blue Cliff Record"), one of the most famous *gong'an* collections, which was compiled by Yuanwu Keqin 圓悟克勤 (1062–1135) with an elaborate commentary on Xuedou Chongxian's 雪竇重顯 (980–1052) anthology *Xuedou heshang baice songgu* 雪竇百則頌古, consisted of several components:

> A typical case in the *Biyan lu* begins with a "pointer" by Yuanwu to direct the student toward the important issue raised in the *gong'an*; this is followed by the *gong'an* itself, with Yuanwu's interlinear annotation, Yuanwu's exposition of the *gong'an*, explanatory verses by Xuedou with Yuanwu's interlinear notes, and a concluding commentary to the verses, also by Yuanwu. (Robert E. Buswell Jr., "The 'Short-Cut' Approach of *K'an-hua* Meditation: The Evolution of a Practical Subitism in Chinese Ch'an Buddhism," in *Sudden and Gradual: Approaches to Enlightenment in Chinese Thought*, ed. Peter N. Gregory [Honolulu: University of Hawaii Press, 1987], 345)

See also *The Princeton Dictionary of Buddhism*, s.v. "Biyan lu."

49. Welter, "Mahākāśyapa's Smile," 94.

50. Miriam Levering explores Dahui Zonggao's relationship with Juefan Huihong (1071–1128), the well-known Chan literatus, and she asserts that Dahui's literary projects and in general his literary prowess must have benefited from the interaction. See Miriam Levering, "A Monk's Literary Education: Dahui's Friendship with Juefan Huihong," *Chung-Hwa Buddhist Journal* 13, no. 2 (May 2000): 369–84.

51. Hee-uk Pyŏn, "Kyohak ihu, kyowoe pyŏljŏn ihu: kyowoe pyŏljŏn ŭi haesŏkhak," *Ch'ŏlhak sasang* 55 (2015): 45–48.

52. Buswell, "The Short-Cut Approach of K'an-hua Meditation," 344.

53. The discussion of *wenzi* Chan is indebted to George A. Keyworth III, "Transmitting the Lamp of Learning in Classical Chan Buddhism: Juefan Huihong (1071–1128) and Literary Chan" (PhD diss., University of California Los Angeles, 2001), 281–324.

54. Robert M. Gimello translates the Chinese phrase "*wenzi* Chan" 文字禪 as "lettered Chan" instead of the often-used translation "literary Chan." He argues that the English phrase "literary Chan" conveys a derogatory meaning, implying "a merely literary imitation of true Chan," a meaning that has in fact been held by many within the Chan community. This meaning was different from Huihong's original articulation, which was intended to advocate for the integration of literacy and learning into Chan spiritual life. Gimello asserts that the English translation of "*wenzi*" as "lettered" gives the term a more positive connotation. See Robert M. Gimello, "Mārga and Culture: Learning, Letters, and Liberation in Northern Sung Ch'an," in *Paths to Liberation: The Mārga and its Transformations in Buddhist Thought*, ed. Robert M. Gimello and Robert E. Buswell Jr. (Honolulu: University of Hawaii Press, 1992), 381, 415n17.

55. Keyworth, "Transmitting the Lamp of Learning," 285–86. See also Gimello, "Mārga and Culture," 381.

56. The Song dynasty is divided into two periods: the Northern Song period, during which the dynasty governed most of eastern China with its capital located in Bianjing 汴京 (now, Kaifeng 開封) in the northern part of the empire, and the Southern Song period (1127–1276), during which the dynasty was forced to retreat to the southern part of China after losing its northern territory to the emerging Jin dynasty 金朝 (1115–1234) and relocating its capital to Lin'an 臨安 (now, Hangzhou 杭州).

57. Keyworth, "Transmitting the Lamp of Learning," 317.

58. Gimello, "Mārga and Culture," 371–84.

59. Gimello articulates the affective motivations of *wenzi* Chan as follows:

> Throughout Ch'an history there have been periods in which committed Ch'an practitioners—some recoiling from real or perceived spasms of Ch'an antinomianism, others moved by impatience with the recurrent stagnation of Ch'an quietism, still others distressed by attacks on Ch'an from non-Buddhist quarters—have reasserted the claim that Ch'an, for all its singularity, is nonetheless Buddhist. (Gimello, "Mārga and Culture," 377)

In general, Chan practitioners who advocated "lettered Chan" promoted the orthodoxy of Chan tradition, while at the same time interacting with and incorporating the cultural products of their time. Gimello, "Mārga and Culture," 377.

60. See Robert M. Gimello, "Sudden Enlightenment and Gradual Practice: A Problematic Theme in the Sŏn Buddhism of Pojo Chinul in the Ch'an Buddhism of Sung China," *Pojo sasang* 4 (1990): 163–203; Buswell, "Pojo Chinul and Kanhwa Sŏn," 345–61.

61. Buswell, "Pojo Chinul and Kanhwa Sŏn," 356.

62. Buswell, "Pojo Chinul and Kanhwa Sŏn," 356–60.

63. In-gyŏng, *Hwaŏm kyohak kwa kanhwa Sŏn ŭi mannam—Pojo ŭi 'Wŏndon sŏngbullon' kwa 'Kanhwa kyŏrŭiron' yŏn'gu* (Seoul: Myŏngsang sangdam yŏn'guwŏn, 2006), 191–95.

64. *Excerpts*, in *Numinous Awareness*, 167: 然此所悟離念心體 即諸法之性 包含眾妙 亦超言詞超言詞故 合忘心頓證之門 含眾妙故 有相用繁興之義。*Han'guk Pŭlgyo chŏnsŏ* 韓國佛教全書 [*Complete books of Korean Buddhism*] H 4.759a16–19 (hereafter cited as "H").

65. See *Excerpts*, in *Numinous Awareness*, 99, 111–13.

66. See *Excerpts*, in *Numinous Awareness*, 107–9.

67. The inseparable relationship between *samādhi* and *prajñā* consists in the idea that *samādhi*, the calm and absolute aspect of the mind, is the essence of *prajñā*, and *prajñā*, the dynamic and analytical aspect of the mind, is the function of *samādhi*. This is closely related to the twofold understanding of the mind. See Buswell, introduction to *CSW*, 46.

68. *Excerpts*, in *Numinous Awareness*, 112–13: 問據諸大乘經及古今諸宗禪門 乃至荷澤所說理性 皆同云無生無滅 無為無相 無凡無聖 無是無非 不可說不可證 今但依此即是 何必要須說靈知耶 /答此並是遮過之辭 未爲現示心體 若不指示現今 了了常知 不斷不昧 是自心者 說何無爲無相等耶 是知諸教 只說此知無生無滅等也 故荷澤於空無相處 指示知見 令人認得 便覺自心 經生越世 永無間斷 乃至成佛也 又荷澤收束無爲無住 乃至不可說等種種之言 但云空寂知 一切攝盡 空者空却諸相 猶是遮遣之言 寂是實性不變動義 不同空無也 知是當體表現義 不同分別也 唯此方爲眞心本體 故始自發心 乃至成佛 唯寂唯知 不變不斷 但隨地位 名義稍殊。H 4.745a17–b10 (bracketed insertions in original). As regards the phrase 遮過之辭 (*ch'agŏ chi pyŏn*, "apophatic discourse"), Buswell in his English translation replaces 遮過 (*ch'agŏ*, meaning "to cover up mistakes") with 遮遣 (*ch'agyŏn*, meaning "to negate" or "to deny"), taking into consideration a Ch'osŏn dynasty xylograph. See Buswell, annotation to *Excerpts*, in *Numinous Awareness*, 231n61.

69. See *Excerpts*, in *Numinous Awareness*, 113–14. Zongmi elucidates the function and limitation of expressive terms in his answer to the question concerning the difference between the ideas of numinous awareness from the Heze school and numinous attention from the Hongzhou school. On the premise that there could be many different expressive terms, since one essence could be revealed through many different attributes, Zongmi explains:

> Although Hongzhou referred to numinous attention, it was just to indicate that sentient beings have this [quality]. It is like inferring they all have the buddha-nature but without directly pointing it out. For them, pointing it out means simply to infer that it is that which is capable of speech and so forth. But if they try to ascertain exactly what [mind-nature, buddha-nature, and so forth] are, all they will be able to say is that "these are all provisional names, not conclusive dharmas. (*Excerpts*, in *Numinous Awareness*, 113–14): 洪州雖云靈覺但是 標衆生有之 如云皆有佛性之言 非的指示 指示則但云能語言等 若細詰之 即云一切假名 無有定法。H 4.745b19–22 (bracketed insertions in original).

70. *Excerpts*, in *Numinous Awareness*, 113.

71. Gimello, "Apophatic and Kataphatic Discourse in Mahāyāna," 119; see also 132.

72. This passage from Zongmi is quoted by Chinul in *Excerpts*, in *Numinous Awareness*, 114: H4.745b22–c3 且統論敎有遣顯二門 推其實義 有眞空妙有 究其本心 具體具用今洪州牛頭 以拂迹爲至極 但得遣敎之意 眞空之義雖成其體 失於顯敎之意 妙有之義闕其用也. Bracketed insertions in original. Zongmi is criticizing the unbalanced use of an apophatic approach by two Chan schools. However, his words here seem to contradict his categorization of the Oxhead school as *minjue wuji zong* 泯絕無寄宗 that teaches total annihilation and the Hongzhou school, along with the Heze school, as *zhixian xinxing zong* 直顯心性宗 that emphasizes the revelation of the mind-nature in all phenomena. *Excerpts*, 105. A detailed discussion of Zongmi's classifications is beyond the scope of this book. For a brief explanation of apophasis and cataphasis as used in *Excerpts*, see Buswell, *Excerpts*, in *Numinous Awareness*, 233n67, 231n61.

73. Rather than explicating them in detail once again here, what follows is Robert Buswell's concise definition:

"Apophatic discourse" (K. *ch'ajŏn*, C. *zhequan* 遮詮): *lucus a non lucendo* explanations that describe an object exclusively in negative terms, explaining what it is not, until by a process of elimination some sense of what the object actually is comes to be conveyed. It is the opposite of kataphatic discourse (K. *p'yojŏn*, C. *biaoquan* 表詮), which involves positive descriptions of an object's qualities and attributes. Ideally, descriptions of practice and the states developed thereby should include both aspects. (*Resolving Doubts*, in *CSW*, 351n65)

74. Bracketed insertion mine.

75. Quoted from Zongmi's *Chan Prolegomenon* by Chinul in *Excerpts*, in *Numinous Awareness*, 167–68: 全揀者 但剋體 直指靈知 卽是心性 餘皆虛妄 故云非識所識 亦非心境等 乃至非性非相 非佛非衆生 離四句絶百非也 全收者 染淨諸法無不是心 心迷故 妄起惑業 乃至四生六道 雜穢國界心悟故 從體起用 四等六度乃至四辯十力妙身淨刹 無所不現 旣是此心現起諸法故 法法全卽眞心。 With the exception of the insertion referenced in note 74, all bracketed insertions in original. H 4. 759b22–c6. For Zongmi's original words, see Broughton, *Zongmi on Chan*, 140–41; T 2015:48.0405c6–22.

76. See *Chan Prolegomenon*, in *Zongmi on Chan*, 120–41; T 2015:48.0402b15–405c29.

77. *Excerpts*, in *Numinous Awareness*, 167 (bracketed insertion in original).

78. *Excerpts*, in *Numinous Awareness*, 168–69: 以是當知 若不頓悟一眞心性 但於中揀一切則滯在離言之解 收一切則又滯圓融之解 皆落意解 難爲悟入矣 若欲收揀自在性相無碍 則須頓悟一心 若欲頓悟 切須不滯意解。 H 4.759b21–c2 (bracketed insertion in original). See also *Complete and Sudden Attainment*, in *CSW*, 284.

79. Once one has a sudden awakening freed from intellectual understanding, he perceives both transcendent and expressive aspects of the mind without contradiction or obstruction. Chinul describes that state as follows:

If we can free ourselves from intellectual understanding and thereby awaken suddenly to the one mind, we then will know that the mind contains all wonders and transcends all words and speech, and our application of radical acceptance and radical rejection will be free and unimpeded. Therefore, we know that the mind of numinous awareness, which is the object of awakening, is the unadulterated and authentic nature that is as vast as the sea. Although it cannot be spoken of, it can adapt itself to conditions and manifest the four modes of birth, the six rebirth destinies, a sublime body, a pure [buddha] land, and all other kinds of tainted and pure dharmas; this is therefore called conditioned origination (*pratīyasamutpāda*). But since this origination is actually unoriginated, it is called the inconceivable origination. Hence, [just above, Zongmi] says that "each and every one of those dharmas is in fact the true mind.... Each and every one of those images is the mirror itself." In this wise, then, after awakening to the mind, we establish [the salutary] and clear away [the unsalutary]; so, what obstruction can there be? (*Excerpts*, in *Numinous Awareness*, 169): 若透脫意解 頓悟一心 則方知此心 包含衆妙 亦超言詞 全收全揀 自在無碍矣 故知所悟靈知之心 即純眞性海 當不可說 而能隨緣 現起四生六道 及妙身淨刹等 染淨諸法 故名緣起 起即無起 名不思議起 故云法法全即眞心 如影影皆鏡等 如是則悟心之後 建立掃蕩 有何妨碍。H 4.759b21–c2 (bracketed insertions in original).

80. For this reason, if you end up succumbing [to intellectual understanding], then even though both your acceptance and rejection may be imperfect, at the very moment that you reach the gateway to awakening and bring an end to all expedient stratagems, you will be extremely close to radical rejection alone. Exposing the essence by pointing directly to the numinous awareness is the role of radical rejection. Consequently, we should know that the disciplined approach to awakening of the eminent masters of our school also considers the abandonment of numinous awareness to be the greatest of wonders. (*Excerpts*, in *Numinous Awareness*, 169): 以故滯則雖收揀 俱非 當於悟門 勸絶方便 唯全揀切近 故剗體 直指靈知 在全揀門也 故知本分宗師 鍛鍊悟門 亦遣靈知最爲妙矣。H 4.759c2–6 (bracketed insertion in original).

81. *Excerpts*, in *Numinous Awareness*, 171.

82. *Excerpts*, in *Numinous Awareness*, 171–72: 雖兩家皆有二門 然各有所長 不可相非 既在即時度脫 攝略爲門故 雖有引教皆爲明宗 非純教也 不知此意者 但將教義深淺 度量禪旨 徒興謗讟 所失多矣 若大量人 放下教義 但將自心現前一念 叅詳禪旨 則必有所得 如有信士 傾鑑此言。H 4.760b3–10 (bracketed insertions in original).

83. *Excerpts*, in *Numinous Awareness*, 97. Chinul also states: "Initially, enter in faith through acquired understanding, subsequently, unite [with the unimpeded *dharmadhātu*] through nonconceptualization." *Resolving Doubts*, in *CSW*, 323–24 (bracketed insertion in original).

84. *Excerpts*, in *Numinous Awareness*, 185: 今見修心人 先以靈知之言 生解分別觀察者心故 只是顯傳門言說除疑 非是親證其體。H 4.763c12–15.

85. *Excerpts*, in *Numinous Awareness*, 186: 當知吾所謂悟心之士者 非但言說除疑 直是將空寂靈知之言 有返照之功 因返照功 得離念心體者也。H 4.763c21–764a2 (bracketed insertion in original).

86. *Excerpts*, in *Numinous Awareness*, 186: 然上來所擧法門 並是爲依言生解悟入者 委辨法有隨緣不變二義 人有頓悟漸修兩門 (以二義 知一藏經論之指歸 是自心之性相 以兩門 見一切賢聖之軌轍 是自行之始終如是揀辨本末了然 令人不迷 遷權就實 速證菩提)。H 4.764a3–9.

87. *Excerpts*, in *Numinous Awareness*, 187: 圭峰謂之靈知 荷澤謂之知之一字 衆妙之門 黃龍死心叟云 知之一字 衆禍之門 要見圭峰荷澤則易 要見死心則難 到這裏(第六八張) 須是具超方眼 說似人不得 傳與人不得也 是以雲門云 大凡 下語 如當門按劒 一句之下須有出身之路 若不如是 死在句下。H 4.764a17–b1 (bracketed insertion in original).

88. *Excerpts*, in *Numinous Awareness*, 97, 186.

89. See *Excerpts*, in *Numinous Awareness*, 187. Chinul quotes Huineng from the *Platform Sūtra*: "The patriarch said, 'Even when I call it one thing [K. *ilmul* 一物], that still isn't correct. How dare you call it 'original fount' [K. *ponwŏn* 本源] or 'buddha-nature' [K. *pulsŏng* 佛性]?" *Excerpts*, 187 (bracketed insertions mine): 祖 曰我喚作一物尚自不中 那堪喚作本源佛性。H 4.764b5–6.

90. *Excerpts*, in *Numinous Awareness*, 192–93: 須知而今末法修道之人 先以如 實知解 決擇自心眞妄生死本末了然 次以斬釘截鐵之言 密密地字細柔詳 而有出 身之處。H 4.766a1–4.

91. Quoted in *Resolving Doubts*, in *CSW*, 346: 先以聞解信入 後以無思契 同。Bracketed insertion in original.

92. *Resolving Doubts*, in *CSW*, 346–47: 禪門徑截得入者 初無法義聞解當情 直 以無滋味話頭 但提撕擧覺而已。(故無語路義路 心識思惟之處 亦無見聞解行 生等 時分前後。) 忽然 話頭噴地一發 則如前所論 一心法界 洞然圓明。

93. For a brief introduction to Chinul's *kanhwa* Sŏn, see Buswell, introduction to *CSW*, 75–88. Buswell also surveys the development of uniquely Chinese meditation techniques, and reckons that *kanhwa* meditation is the result of the sinification of Buddhism. Buswell, "The 'Short-Cut' Approach of *K'an-hua* Meditation," 321–77. See particularly 343–56 for the development of *kanhwa* meditation from the *kongan* tradition and an explanation of this meditative technique derived from Dahui,.

94. *Resolving Doubts*, in *CSW*, 346–47: 故 與圓教觀行者 比於禪門一發者 教內 教外 迥然不同故 時分遲速亦不同 居然可知矣。故云「教外別傳 迥出教乘 非淺 識者 所能堪任。」Bracketed insertions in original.

95. Chinul explains in detail the danger of being trapped in intellectual understanding by citing Dahui in *Resolving Doubts* as follows:

In the Sŏn approach too there are those of average and inferior capacities who find it hard to cope with this secret transmission. Some of them may try to sequester their minds and access the principle by leaving behind words and cutting off thought, but they cannot penetrate through the conditionally originated phenomenal dharmas right in front of their eyes. Master Dahui of Jingshan rebuked them: "Those who force themselves to pacify and calm their minds are people who seek to develop understanding while guarding their amnesia and embracing void-calmness." Others assume that the normal mind used every day by ordinary people is the ultimate path; but they do not seek the sublime awakening and say, "Let's take it easy and stay natural; there's no need to worry about whether mental states arise or thoughts are stirred, for the arising and ceasing of thoughts is originally without any real essence." Sŏn Master Dahui also rebuked them: "These are people who try to develop understanding by presuming that guarding the natural essence is the ultimate dharma." (*Resolving Doubts*, in *CSW*, 347): 禪門 亦有密付難堪 中下之流。或以 離言絕慮 冥心入理 而於目前 緣起事法 未能透得。故徑山大慧禪師 訶曰「硬休去 歇去者 此是守忘懷空寂 而生解者也。」 或認凡夫 日用平常心 以爲至道 不求妙悟

曰 「但放曠 任其自在 莫管生心動念。 念起念滅 本無實體。」 故大慧禪師 亦訶曰
「這介 又是守自然體 爲究竟法 而生解者也。」

This phrase could be considered a commentary on the following sentence from
Excerpts: "It should now be clear that, if you do not have a sudden awakening to the
nature of the one true mind and in [that benighted state] you just reject everything,
then you will succumb to an understanding derived from ineffability." *Excerpts*, in
Numinous Awareness, 168–69: 以是當知 若不頓悟一眞心性 但於中揀一切則滯在
離言之解。 H 4.759b21–c2 (bracketed insertion in original).

  96. Buswell translates *chŏngsik* 情識 literally as "the affective consciousnesses,"
which refer to the deluded capacity for discrimination, feelings, or any mental function of deluded people. See *Digital Dictionary of Buddhism*, s.v. "*chŏngsik* 情識."

  97. Quoted in *Resolving Doubts*, in *CSW*, 334–35: 情識未破 則心火熠熠地 正
當恁麼時 但只以所疑底話頭提撕。 如僧問趙州 「狗子還有佛性也無」 州云
「無」 只管提撕舉覺。 Bracketed insertions in original. Investigation of the *Mu
hwadu* is also discussed by Chinul in *Excerpts*. See *Excerpts*, in *Numinous Awareness*, 191–92; H 4.765b18–c18.

  98. *Mu* 無 literally means "not to be" or "not to have"; therefore, here, the response means that a dog does not have the buddha-nature.

  99. This discussion of *hwadu* Sŏn is indebted to Buswell, introduction to *CSW*,
75–80.

  100. *Resolving Doubts*, in *CSW*, 335–36: 如是下注脚 給話頭故 學者 於十二時
中 四威儀內 但提撕舉覺而已。 其於心性道理 都無離名絶相之解 亦無緣起無
碍之解。 才有一念佛法知解 便滯在十種知解之病。 故一一放下 亦無放下不放
下 滯病不滯病之量 忽然於沒滋味 無摸索底話頭上 噴地一發 則一心法界 洞然
明白。 Bracketed insertions in original.

  101. *Resolving Doubts*, in *CSW*, 336. See also Dahui's words, quoted in *Excerpts*:

Zhaozhou's topic [*hwa/hua* 話, viz., the *hwadu*], "a dog doesn't have the buddha-nature,"
must be kept raised before you regardless of whether you are happy or mad, calm or dis-
turbed. First, don't set your mind on expecting an awakening; if you do, you are saying
to yourself, "I am now deluded." If you cling to your delusion and just wait for awakening to come, then even though you pass through kalpas as numerous as dust motes, you
will never get it. When you raise the *hwadu*, you just have to rouse yourself and inquire,
"What does this mean?" (*Excerpts*, in *Numinous Awareness*, 192, bracketed insersion in
original): 又云趙州狗子無佛性話 喜怒靜鬧亦須提撕 第一不得用意等悟 若用意等悟
則自謂我卽今迷 執迷待悟 縱經塵劫 亦不能得 但舉話頭時 略科撒精神 看是箇甚麼
道理。 H 4.765c14–16.

See also *Excerpts*, in *Numinous Awareness*, 191–92; *Resolving Doubts*, in *CSW*,
320.

  102. *Resolving Doubts*, in *CSW*, 346.
  103. *Resolving Doubts*, in *CSW*, 336.
  104. *Resolving Doubts*, in *CSW*, 328.
  105. *Resolving Doubts*, in *CSW*, 334–35: 不得作有無會。 不得作眞無之無卜
度。 不得作道理會。 不得向意根下思量卜 度。 不得向揚眉瞬目處揉根。 不

得向語路上作活計。 不得颺在無事甲裏。 不得向舉起處承當。 不得文字中引
證。 不得將迷待悟。 直須無所用心 心無所之時 莫怕落空。 這裏却是好處。
驀然 老鼠入牛角 便見倒斷也。 Bracketed insertions in original. These ten maladies are also listed in *Excerpts,* in *Numinous Awareness*, 191–92 (H 4.765c1–13),
but Chinul rearranges the list in *Resolving Doubts*. For Buswell's paraphrasing, see
annotation to *Excerpts*, in *Numinous Awareness*, 275n304.

106. Buswell, annotation to *Resolving* Doubts, in *CSW*, 335n38.

107. *Resolving Doubts*, in *CSW*, 334.

108. Buswell, introduction to *CSW*, 83.

109. *Excerpts*, in *Numinous Awareness*, 189.

110. Dahui viewed the daily life of ordinary people as the ideal setting for the
hwadu meditation. He argued that the mental stress and unresolved problems generated in daily life and the discrepancy between a conventional awareness of one's
nature conceived in great defilements and one's true nature, which is identical to the
nature of the buddha, amplify perplexity and frustration. See Buswell, "The 'Short-
Cut' Approach of *K'an-hua* Meditation," 51–56. As the definition of doubt (*ŭijŏng*
疑情) discussed above indicates, the characteristics and soteriological role of doubt
in *kanhwa* Sŏn have an affective dimension. However, in the Indian Buddhist tradition, the primary dimension of doubt (S. *vicikitsā*, C. *yi*, K. *ŭi* 疑) seems to have been
intellectual—it was viewed as intellectual uncertainty and was categorized as one of
the five hindrances to mental absorption (S. *nīvaraṅa*, C. *gai*, K. *kae* 蓋), along with
sensual desire, ill will, sloth and torpor, and restlessness and worry. For the historical
transformation of the meaning of doubt, see Robert E. Buswell Jr., "Kanhwa Sŏn e
issŏsŏ ŭijŏng ŭi chŏnhwan: The Transformation of Doubt in Kanhwa Sŏn," *Pojo sasang* 41 (2014): 1–16; Robert E. Buswell Jr., "The Transformation of Doubt (Ŭijŏng
疑情) in Chinese Meditation," in *Love and Emotions in Traditional Chinese Literature*, ed. Halvor Eifring (Leiden: Brill, 2004), 225–36.

111. See *Resolving Doubts*, in *CSW*, 352–54. See also Buswell, introduction to
CSW, 83. While Dahui's *hwadu* investigation was primarily the investigation of the
word, Buswell argues that Chinul accepted all levels of students into the practice of
hwadu meditation and "graft[ing] *kanhwa* practice onto a sudden awakening/gradual
cultivation soteriological schema." See Robert E. Buswell Jr., "Chinul's Systemiza-
tion of Chinese Meditative Techniques in Korean Sŏn Buddhism," in *Traditions
of Meditation in Chinese Buddhism*, ed. Peter N. Gregory (Honolulu: University
of Hawaii Press, 1986), 220, and Buswell, "The Short-Cut' Approach of *K'an-hua*
Meditation," 370n106. It is conventional to translate the term 參 (C. *can*, K. *ch'am*)
as "investigate." However, deliberation or investigation is a derivative meaning of the
term. It originally means "to join" or "to enter." While *chamŭi* 參意 means "investigation of meaning," *ch'amgu* 參句 can be translated as "joining with" or "confronting" the *hwadu* word.

112. Buswell, introduction to *CSW*, 83.

113. Buswell, annotation to *Resolving Doubts*, in *CSW*, 352–53n69.

114. Buswell, annotation to *Resolving Doubts*, in *CSW*, 352–53n69.

115. *Excerpts*, in *Numinous Awareness*, 189; H 4.764c21.

116. In-gyŏng, "*Kanhwa kyŏrŭiron* ŭi Hwaŏm kyohak pip'an," *Pojo sasang* 15 (2001): 60. In-gyŏng explains that *kanhwa* Sŏn defies the conventional system of epistemology that is part of Kyo, and in particular, the doctrinal teachings of Hwaŏn. He argues that all linguistic systems are based on the foundational principle of discriminative signifier and signified (*ŭiri punje* 義理分齊). A word has a meaning that signifies its object, but is not necessarily identical to its object. The mind understands the external and internal realms through a logical and conceptual system but this intellectual understanding is different from a direct experience of these realms. *Kanhwa* Sŏn refutes the linguistic system of dualistic discrimination, and aims at breaking it and achieving a direct and immediate experience of reality, eschewing indirect perception resulting from conceptualization. See In-gyŏng, "*Kanhwa kyŏrŭiron* ŭi Hwaŏm kyohak pip'an," 56–63; In-gyŏng, *Hwaŏm kyohak kwa Kanhwa Sŏn ŭi man-nam*, 158–72.

117. "In the Sŏn school, all these true teachings derived from the faith and understanding of the complete and sudden school, which are as numerous as the sands of the Ganges, are called dead words (*sagu* 死句) because they induce people to generate the obstacle of understanding. But they also may help neophytes who are not yet able to investigate the live word (*hwalgu* 活句) of the shortcut approach by instructing them in complete descriptions that accord with the nature in order to ensure that their faith and understanding will not retrogress." (*Resolving Doubts*, in *CSW*, 319): 禪門中 此等圓頓信解 如實言敎 如河沙數謂之死句 以令人生解碍故。 並是爲初心學者 於徑截門活句 未能 參詳故 示以稱性圓談 令其信解 不退轉故。

The distinction between dead words and live words is traditionally attributed to Yunmen Wenyan's 雲門文偃 (864–949) disciple Dongshan Shouchu 洞山守初 (?–990). See Buswell, introduction to *CSW*, 81.

118. *Excerpts*, in *Numinous Awareness*, 187: 祖曰我喚作一物尙自不中 那堪喚作本源佛性。 H 4.764b5–6.

119. *Excerpts*, in *Numinous Awareness*, 187; H 4.764a17–b1.

120. *Resolving Doubts*, in *CSW*, 320.

121. Buswell, "The Short-Cut Approach of K'an-hua Meditation," 347–48.

122. *Resolving Doubts*, in *CSW*, 329–32: 禪門 亦有多種根機 入門稍異。 或有依唯心唯識道理 入體中玄 此初玄門 有圓教事事無碍之詮也。 然此人 長有佛法知見在心 不得脫洒。 或有依本分事 祇對洒落知見 入句中玄 破初玄門 佛法知見。 此玄 有徑截門 庭前栢樹子 麻三斤等話頭。 然立此三玄門 古禪師之意 以本分事 祇對話頭 爲破病之語故 置於第二玄。 然未亡洒落知見言句 猶於生死界 不得自在故 立第三玄中玄 良久黙然棒喝作用等 破前洒落知見。 Bracketed insertions in original.

123. See Buswell, introduction to *CSW*, 84n142. For the historical development of the interpretation of the threefold scheme, see also Yŏng-sik Chŏng, "Ch'ŏnbok Sŭnggo, Kakbŏm Hyehong kŭrigo Pojo Chinul ŭi samhyŏnmun haesŏk," *Han'guk Pulgyohak* 54 (2009): 5–34; Migyŏng Ha, "Sŏn ŏrok ŭl t'onghan Imje samgu ŭi chŏn'gae wa kŭ t'ŭkching," *Han'guk Sŏnhak* 29 (2011): 127–67.

124. The scheme of the three mysterious gates is discussed in *Complete and Sudden Attainment*, exposition 4, in *CSW*, 286–87 and *Excerpts*, in *Numinous Awareness*,

193–94. Chinul elucidates the three mysterious gates in *Resolving Doubts* in a much more detailed manner than in these two writings.

125. See Buswell, introduction to *CSW*, 88.

126. *Resolving Doubts*, in *CSW*, 348.

127. *Excerpts*, in *Numinous Awareness*, 193 (bracketed insertion is mine).

128. Buswell, introduction to *CSW*, 87–88.

129. *Resolving Doubts*, in *CSW*, 330.

130. There are two additional points that need to be explained in Chinul's discussion of the three mysterious gates. First, he asserts that *kanhwa* Sŏn by itself is a sufficient expedient for leading its practitioner to enlightenment, and that there is no need for another approach to address possible traces of intellectual understanding. And second, according to the brief discussion of the three mysterious gates as it appears in *Excerpts* at 193, the third mystery can be understood as the ultimate goal of the path of the mystery in the word, rather than itself being a separate, advanced path to enlightenment. Chinul wrote *Resolving Doubts* with the clear purpose of advocating the new Sŏn meditation technique and claiming the superiority of Sŏn over Kyo. Therefore, even though he introduces the threefold scheme of Sŏn approaches and identifies *kanhwa* Sŏn with the second, the overall discussion of *kanhwa* Sŏn is not strictly confined to the framework of the threefold scheme. Chinul freely adapts the system with or without comment for the purpose of bolstering his arguments.

131. *Resolving Doubts*, in *CSW*, 330–31.

132. *Resolving Doubts*, in *CSW*, 346–47.

133. *Resolving Doubts*, in *CSW*, 328–29: 據眞實了義 則妄念本空 更無可離 無漏諸法 本是眞性 隨緣妙用 永不斷絕 又不應破。 但爲一類衆生 執虛妄名相 難得玄悟故 佛且不揀善惡染淨世出世間 一切俱破。 是故 聞此敎者 隨順平等無相之理 作無能說可說能念可念之解 然後 離此解此念 得入眞如門故 但名證理成佛。 Bracketed insertion in original.

134. See Buswell, introduction to *CSW*, 78. Buswell notes the radical shift of Chinul's soteriological approach from Sŏn practice influenced by Zongmi's theory to his advocacy of Dahui's *kanhwa* Sŏn, even to the point that the newly introduced meditation technique overshadows all other Sŏn practices developed before Dahui. Although Buswell admits that Hyesim, Chinul's disciple, might have intervened in the editorial process of *Resolving Doubts*, Buswell believes that Hyesim's exclusive promotion of *kanhwa* Sŏn is a continuation of the radical crystalization of Chinul's thought around *kanhwa* Sŏn in the latter part of his life. Buswell, "Pojo Chinul and Kanhwa Sŏn," 359.

135. In his research on the relationship between the three paths 三門 of Chinul that was the basis of Kim Kun-su's systematization of Chinul's thought, Ch'oe Yŏn-sik asserts the complementary relationship between the three paths articulated by Kim Kun-su. He insists that the third path of the shortcut approach of *kanhwa* complements the other two paths, the path of the concurrent cultivation of *samādhi* and *prajñā* and the path of faith and understanding according to the complete and sudden teaching. Despite his understanding of the superiority of the path of shortcut approach of *kanhwa*, rather than exclusively advocating this path, Chinul takes an inclusive attitude toward the other two paths. Ch'oe also argues that the shortcut path synthesizes

the process of the sudden awakening and subsequent cultivation. Sudden awakening and gradual cultivation correspond, respectively, to the path of faith and understanding according to the complete and sudden teaching and the path of the concurrent cultivation of *samādhi* and *prajñā*. The shortcut path embraces the other two paths, for through the *kanhwa* Sŏn a practitioner comes to a realization-awakening (sudden awakening) and at the same time can sustain the ultimate wisdom attained through that enlightenment without further obstruction (cultivation). In this regard, Ch'oe sees the shortcut approach of *kanhwa* as the culmination of Chinul's Sŏn thought. See Yŏn-sik Ch'oe, "Chinul Sŏn sasang ŭi sasangsajŏk kŏmt'o," *Tongbang hakchi* 144 (2008): 145–67.

136. Buswell, introduction to *CSW*, 79. For another discussion on the harmonic and complementary relationship of the three paths and the critical role of the path of the shortcut approach of *kanhwa*, see Sŏk-am Kim, "Pojo Chinul ŭi kanhwa kyŏngjŏl e taehayŏ," *Han'guk Sŏnhak* 5 (2003): 101–22.

Conclusion

This book is a comparative study of two medieval religious leaders, the Christian Bonaventure of Bagnoregio (ca. 1217–1274) and the Buddhist Pojo Chinul of Korea (1158–1210). Both attempted to reconcile two competing models of religious life—one based on intellectual pursuits and the other on spiritual development—by demonstrating how scriptural study and theological study do not impede meditative and spiritual growth. These two masters saw that both the intellectual and the prayerful dimensions of monastic and religious life are not only compatible with one another, but in fact are both essential aspects of these modes of life. In the course of investigating these integrative endeavors by both masters, this book has also concerned itself with the contrasts highlighted by and possible reconciliation of various theological tensions, such as cataphasis vs. apophasis and immanence vs. transcendence.

In order to address these issues, this book has presented an analysis of the writings and respective religious traditions of these medieval masters. This conclusion briefly presents the views of both Bonaventure and Chinul on these issues and discuss the similarities and dissimilarities between each of their conceptions of religious life.

BONAVENTURE'S INTEGRATION OF SCHOLASTICISM AND FRANCISCAN SPIRITUALITY

Concerning Bonaventure, it must be kept in mind that the Order of Friars Minor was founded by St. Francis, a humble man from Assisi, and was a religious movement charged with a zeal for living a simple life according to the gospel. Though in its early days, Francis's movement was full of evangelical enthusiasm and little emphasis was placed on the life of the mind, the intellectual aspects of its religious life became increasingly prominent. As the order grew from a band of simple men to a well-organized religious order with educated clerics and simple brothers coexisting, tensions began to surface. Some feared that intellectualization and clericalization were robbing the order of its pristine character.

Bonaventure of Bagnoregio led this fast-growing order at the dawn of this period of internal conflict. Bonaventure himself, who studied and taught at the University of Paris, was one of the most celebrated intellectuals of his time, and he did not consider intellectual learning to be at odds with the spiritual life. He rather insisted that study and learning are conducive to the development of Christian virtues and are integral to the spiritual quest for union with God. But at the same time, Bonaventure inherited Francis's zeal for the simple religious life, and he had a profound understanding of Francis's spiritual and mystical insights, which he considered to be divine gifts bestowed on the simple man of Assisi. This integrative attitude toward the spiritual and intellectual life is manifested throughout his writings, but is nowhere more pronounced than in his spiritual masterpiece, the *Itinerarium mentis in Deum* or *The Soul's Journey into God*. Although on the one hand, this is a spiritual treatise through which the author leads the reader to the attainment of the spiritual goal of mystical union with God, on the other, it is also an intellectual essay laden with highly sophisticated, difficult-to-understand philosophical and theological concepts. In this work, Bonaventure integrated his intellectual knowledge of various academic disciplines with his spiritual insights in order to present a road map intended to lead Christians to a mystical experience of God.

In the *Itinerarium*, Bonaventure integrates not only intellectual learning and spiritual practice, but also cataphatic and apophatic theologies. This Dionysian distinction between two kinds of theology is closely related to the doctrine of God as both immanent and transcendent. While the manifestation of God in creation and in the Incarnation permits positive or cataphatic theological discourse, along with meditation on God through His vestiges, images, and similitudes as articulated in the first six-step speculations of the *Itinerarium*, the transcendence of God demands negative or apophatic theological discourse, as shown in the description of the soul's mystical union with God in the last part of the text. At the stage of this mystical union, the soul's intellectual reflections about creatures and God yield to an affective gaze at Christ on the cross that extends beyond all knowing.

Despite his belief in the ineffability of God and the higher order (truth) of apophasis, Bonaventure nevertheless considers cataphatic discourse and intellectual meditation on God through perceptual and conceptual things to be useful. Indeed, he sees them as steps leading to mystical union with God. Thus, cataphasis and apophasis are intricately intertwined in the text of the *Itinerarium*. Not only cataphasis and apophasis, but in Bonaventure's road map to union with God, the various aspects of the religious life—intellectual/ spiritual, cataphasis/apophasis, and immanence/transcendence—are dynamically integrated.

CHINUL'S INCORPORATION OF DOCTRINAL STUDIES INTO SŎN PRACTICE

Pojo Chinul, the Sŏn master of medieval Korea, was required by historical circumstances to address monastic and philosophical issues comparable to those faced by Bonaventure. There existed in the Korea of his day long-standing tensions between Buddhist monks engaged principally in learning and those engaged principally in the meditative practices of Sŏn. The former, known as the Kyo monks, focused on scriptural and doctrinal learning, whereas the latter, the partisans of Sŏn, emphasized meditation, especially nonconceptual meditation. Scholarly monks held Sŏn adepts in low esteem for their limited knowledge of Buddhist scriptures and doctrines, and Sŏn adepts dismissed Kyo monks as comprehending only conventional truth (*smvṛti-satya*), not ultimate truth (*paramārtha-satya*). They asserted that ultimate truth could only be realized through a kind of meditation that does not rely on words and concepts.

Concerned with the futility of this conflict, Chinul strove to integrate both kinds of Buddhism into his religious practice. Although he was a committed Sŏn practitioner, he was also well versed in the textual and doctrinal traditions of Buddhism. On the basis of his own experiences, he asserted that what one can achieve through vigorous Sŏn meditation cannot contradict what the Buddhist scriptures teach. As he said, "The mouth of the Buddha and the minds of the patriarchs can certainly not be in contradiction to one another."[1] This integrative attitude toward Sŏn and Kyo is prevalent throughout Chinul's writings. He attempts to demonstrate the correspondence between Sŏn principles and Kyo doctrines and addresses the positive role of study for the advancement of Sŏn practice.

The different emphases of Sŏn and Kyo on meditation and learning, respectively, is closely related to differences between their dominant modes of discourse. Although both Sŏn and Kyo insist on the ineffability of ultimate truth or true reality, Kyo tends to employ positive discourses to a greater degree than one finds in Sŏn texts, whereas apophatic discourses that include negation and paradox, are characteristic of Son rhetoric.

The two schools differ similarly in their preferred approaches to meditation. Whereas scholarly monks practice discursive meditation, Sŏn adepts, in particular those believed to be possessed of what Buddhists call "superior faculties," are encouraged to employ intuitive meditative techniques, such as *kanhwa* Sŏn, a technique that investigates a critical phrase or word so as to thwart, and thereby transcend, mere intellectual understanding. *Kanhwa* Sŏn, a kind of apophasis in practice, places great weight on the ineffability of ultimate reality. Chinul incorporated both cataphasis and apophasis in his writings as he strove to synthesize Huayan doctrinal teachings and Sŏn theory. At the same time, there is a noticeable transition from cataphasis to apophasis later in his life, as the focus of his writings moves from a demonstration of the compatibility between Sŏn and Kyo toward the practice of Sŏn meditation.

These correlations between different emphases on learning and meditation and different modes of discourse are also related to two important Mahāyāna doctrines—emptiness and buddha-nature. Apophasis is closely related to the doctrine of emptiness, which the Madhyamaka school advocated through the devices of negative dialectic and paradox. Cataphasis is, on the other hand, related to the doctrine of buddha-nature. Sŏn Buddhism embraced both of these Buddhist teachings, but in terms of rhetorical style, Sŏn favored emptiness discourse and employed the positive rhetoric of buddha-nature chiefly for the purpose of encouraging Sŏn adepts to have confidence in the possibility of attaining buddhahood. Efforts to synthesize the doctrines of emptiness and buddha-nature, which were often considered contradictory, resulted in internal tensions within Sŏn Buddhism. Those strands of Sŏn that emphasized the doctrine of buddha-nature were often criticized as being substantialist and therefore heterodox. Chinul described these theoretical conflicts and adopted a moderate stance with respect to cataphasis and intellectual meditation, which drew criticism from Sŏn adepts, who favored emptiness teaching and nonconceptual meditation. In Chinul's development of Sŏn theory and practice, various aspects of the religious life—study/meditation, cataphasis/apophasis, and emptiness/buddha-nature—are dynamically integrated, but not without some tensions still remaining.

BONAVENTURE AND CHINUL

Having presented summaries of Bonaventure's and Chinul's individual approaches to the question of the relationship between the religious life and doctrinal discourse, it is useful to highlight any notable similarities and differences between them on this topic.

First, convinced as they were of the compatibility between learning and spiritual life, both Bonaventure and Chinul acknowledge the utility of intellectual studies for the spiritual advancement of a religious practitioner, especially because it helped develop a life of discipline and virtue. Chinul regarded scriptural, doctrinal learning and study as essential to Buddhist practice and complementary to Sŏn meditation, an integrative stance that can be distinguished from the radical dismissal of study and meditation among some in the Sŏn community of his time. Just as Chinul endeavored to reconcile the competing Buddhist schools and incorporate the study of scriptures and doctrines into Sŏn theory and practice, so also Bonaventure played a prominent role as a mediator between similar tensions within and outside the Franciscan Order. Within the order, Bonaventure avoided extreme stances that either overemphasized the dangers of intellectualism or prioritized learning and study over spiritual life. Against outside critics challenging the legitimacy of the Franciscan way of life, he also demonstrated that study and learning can contribute to a holy life, and at the same time defended Franciscan poverty, drawing on the scriptures and church teachings. This is analogous to Chinul's attempt to demonstrate the compatibility between Sŏn and Kyo.

Second, while both Bonaventure and Chinul employed a combination of cataphasis and apophasis in their theologies, for both, apophasis came to assume pride of place. Bonaventure's explanation of the mystical journey to God in the *Itinerarium* moves from cataphatic discourse involving philosophical and theological concepts toward an apophatic discourse that calls the practitioner to renounce all intellectual activities, enabling a leap into the mystery of God. However, there is a notable difference between Bonaventure and Chinul related to the use of cataphasis and apophasis. Chinul took the position that cataphasis and apophasis should be employed by Buddhist practitioners according to each practitioner's spiritual capacity. He believed that instructive and explanatory statements and intellectual meditation are suitable for those with inferior faculties, whereas negative or paradoxical statements and nonratiocinative meditation are fitting for those with superior faculties. In contrast, Bonaventure, though presenting a step-by-step spiritual journey, did not insist that one should proceed through each step in accordance with one's capacities. Bonaventure's *Itinerarium* implies the idea of gradual spiritual progress—as a spiritual pilgrim advances in his mystical journey, the primary modes of discourse and theology move from cataphasis to apophasis, but Bonaventure did not classify those seeking union with God according to their innate spiritual faculties and did not prescribe or proscribe certain steps according to the spiritual seeker's capacities. For Bonaventure, even if a seeker does not follow his intellectually sophisticated description of the first six stages of the *Itinerarium*, that person still can reach mystical union with God through virtuous living and love of Christ, as could be seen in the life of Francis.

Chinul's distinction between different spiritual faculties is related to the Buddhist doctrine of rebirth, a doctrine that also explains the Sŏn belief in the sudden awakening of some practitioners without prior cultivation. According to this doctrine, although it would seem that one suddenly awakens to the ultimate reality, in fact, the practitioner who thus awakens had already undergone rigorous spiritual exercises throughout multiple lifetimes. By contrast, Bonaventure's Christian theology sees the spiritual achievement of a simple, unlearned man like Francis—and following from his example, the possibility of any believer's advancement to the highest spiritual achievements—to be the result of divine grace.

Chinul's understanding of a practitioner's advancement from cataphasis to apophasis, whether in this life or over multiple lifetimes, parallels his own transition in later life toward an emphasis on nonintellectual meditation. This book did not examine whether there was a similar chronological transition from cataphasis to apophasis in Bonaventure's writings. However, considering that over the course of his career Bonaventure moved from being an academic to a religious leader with pastoral responsibilities and that his own mystical spirituality might have been deepened in the way that he described in the *Itinerarium*, it is possible that his writings might have become more apophatic over time—if not in his method of theological and spiritual discourse, then in the weight he assigned to mystical experience and God's transcendence. Investigation of this possible transition should be taken up in future studies.

Third, for both Bonaventure and Chinul, the relative importance of cataphasis and apophasis is related to underlying doctrinal tensions in their respective traditions. In Christianity, cataphatic and apophatic discourses and practices are associated, respectively, with the immanence and the transcendence of God. In Buddhism, the "expressive" and the "negative" and the meditative practices associated with each are closely related, respectively, to the Buddhist teachings of buddha-nature and emptiness. This similarity does not mean, however, that immanence in Christianity is the same thing as buddha-nature in Buddhism, nor does it mean that the transcendence of God in Christianity is the same thing as emptiness in Buddhism.

In Christianity, the manifestation of God in his creatures is still imperfect, and the human perception of God through creatures is limited due to the ontological chasm between creator and creatures, which is the result of human sin. On the other hand, Buddhism, in particular Chinul's Sŏn theory, has a seemingly more optimistic view of phenomena and of the human capacity for enlightenment, as the buddha-nature doctrine emphasizes the identity of the nature of phenomena and principle and the potentiality that all sentient beings can attain buddhahood.

Fourth, for both Bonaventure and Chinul, the distinction between cataphasis and apophasis is comparable to two different modes of religious practice—"meditation" and "contemplation." The scholar of religious studies Frederic B. Underwood concisely defines and distinguishes meditation and contemplation as follows: "Meditation is usually rumination on a particular religious subject, while contemplation is a direct intuitive seeing, using spiritual faculties beyond discursive thought and ratiocination."[2] This distinction between meditation and contemplation is helpful for understanding Bonaventure's two modes of meditation (or contemplation), as well as for understanding Chinul's two meditative approaches.

Following this distinction, it could perhaps be said that Bonaventure's spiritual journey, in particular his *Itinerarium*, consists of meditation leading to contemplation. The first six steps in this well-planned, multistage guide are conducive to speculative meditation on God, while the last step eschews intellectual meditation and demands affective engagement, which should be understood as "contemplation." Bonaventure himself rarely uses the term "meditation" (*meditatio*) in the *Itinerarium*,[3] and neither does he provide a clear explanation of the term that corresponds to the above definition. Rather, he employs the term "contemplation" (*contemplatio*) to refer to both speculative meditation and intuitive contemplation. Nevertheless, when Bonaventure uses the term meditation as distinguished from contemplation in the first chapter of the *Itinerarium*, the distinction corresponds to that of Underwood's definition of both terms:

> These powers [the natural powers of the soul] must also be brought to that knowledge which illuminates, and this happens in meditation. And they must be brought to the wisdom that perfects, and this takes place in contemplation. For just as no one arrives at wisdom except through grace, justice, and knowledge, so no one arrives at contemplation except by means of penetrating meditation, a holy life-style, and devout prayer.[4]

In the *Itinerarium*, instead of meditation, Bonaventure frequently employs the term "speculation" (or *speculatio*), whose meaning in fact implies meditation as defined by Underwood.[5] All of the first six chapters of the *Itinerarium* are "speculations" on God through and in the created world, through and in the human mind, and through and in the divine attributes, eventually leading to "the mystical transport of the mind in which rest is given to the intellect and through ecstasy our affection passes over totally into God."[6]

This distinction in Bonaventure finds a parallel in Chinul. As chapter 4 demonstrated, the Sŏn master distinguishes between two kinds of meditation: one involving words and concepts and another renouncing them; however, along with this similarity, two differences between Bonaventure and Chinul with regard to their views on meditation must be noted.

First, Bonaventure's two kinds of contemplation, that is, intellectual contemplation and sapiential contemplation,[7] or meditation (speculation) and contemplation, are more organically related than Chinul's two modes of meditation. Bonaventure views intellectual contemplation as a preparatory and necessary path leading to sapiential contemplation. Although he suggests that knowledge attained through intellectual meditation must eventually be renounced, he never adopts a dismissive tone toward speculation or intellectual knowledge about God. On the other hand, Chinul, though he acknowledges its efficacy, especially for monks with inferior faculties, emphasizes the dangers of intellectual meditation over its benefits. Chinul especially urges practitioners of superior faculties not to be engaged at all in meditation that relies on words and concepts.

Second, the role of affection distinguishes Bonaventure's sapiential contemplation from Chinul's *kanhwa* meditation. This difference is related to their divergent views of the ultimate goal of the spiritual/intellectual journey. In the *Itinerarium*, Bonaventure points the way toward attaining union with a personal God. The way to perceive and encounter God in Christianity is personal, and affection is an essential element in any personal relationship. While the ultimate goal of the spiritual journey for a Christian is union with God, the ontological chasm between the creator and the created hinders him or her from reaching this union on the epistemological and ontological level. Affection or charity helps him or her bridge this gulf in order to attain it.[8] In contrast, in Buddhism, especially Mahāyāna Buddhism, compassion, considered to be one of the two essential elements of Buddhist practice along with wisdom, plays a significant role in Buddhist spiritual exercise *at the initial stage*. The compassionate resolve of the bodhisattvas—who exert themselves to attain enlightenment so that they can lead all sentient beings to enlightenment—encourages them on their spiritual journey. Although compassion may motivate and empower a spiritual practitioner, and an enlightened one would act to spread the buddha-dharma for the sake of all sentient beings out of immense compassion, it is not a crucial element at the final step to enlightenment. Thus, although compassion is a crucial element of Buddhist practice in Chinul's writings, its role is not as prominent as is affective love for Christ in the thought of Bonaventure. Chinul's apophasis seems similar to the intellectual apophasis of early Dionysianism rather than the affective apophasis of medieval Dionysianism.

EPILOGUE

The ascent to intimate union with God in Christianity and the awakening to the true nature of reality in Buddhism are the ultimate religious experiences of these two religions. These final aims of each religion's spiritual quest are inconceivable and ineffable, beyond intellect and words, and most practitioners of the two religions have not reached this ultimate state. The ideas that God is transcendent and beyond our reach, and that the nature of absolute reality cannot be grasped due to its empty nature, may give rise to pessimism in Christians and Buddhists in that their vigorous intellectual efforts to understand God and absolute reality may ultimately be in vain. What would be the use of studying and intellectual meditation if it is necessarily to no avail? An answer to this despairing question could be that the transcendence of God and the emptiness of absolute reality are not the last word—practitioners must try to be encouraged by the doctrine of the immanence of God and the teaching of buddha-nature with their affirmative views of the accessibility of God and the potential for enlightenment.

The historical development of the Christian and Buddhist traditions demonstrate that these two seemingly contradictory points of doctrine have led in both traditions to varying levels of emphasis on the different modes of theological discourse (cataphasis and apophasis) and different forms of religious practice (spiritual and intellectual). Both Bonaventure and Chinul inherited these divergent discourses and practices and then incorporated the tensions they imply into their own spiritual and intellectual development. They both recognize and stress the efficacy of study and intellectual meditation, but also the importance of spiritual life and nonintellectual meditation.

It is easy for religious practitioners who are heavily engaged in the academic study of religion or in intellectual tasks to be caught up in this particular aspect of religious practice, and they may risk neglecting other aspects. Bonaventure and Chinul could be wise guides for these practitioners by encouraging them through the example of their lives and their writings to balance their intellectual and spiritual lives, and by reminding them that the ultimate goal of their studies is not mere intellectual satisfaction, but rather spiritual fulfillment. Furthermore, the fact that the doctrine of transcendence and the apophatic attitude are incorporated in the intellectual and spiritual life of these two figures might remind intellectuals to be humble, but not discouraged, in the course of their work.

Comparative studies of religions always lead to a recognition of similarities and differences. These recognitions have the potential to positively impact one's attitude toward other religions, and even toward one's own. As discussed in this book, the tension between the intellectual and spiritual life and endeavors to integrate them are found in both Christianity and Buddhism. The study of this tension leads to other related tensions, such as seemingly contradictory understandings of God or the ultimate reality and the tension between the use of affirmative language in religious discourse and an acknowledgment of the limitations of employing human words and concepts to understand God or the ultimate reality. The similarities highlighted here may first of all encourage people of these two religious traditions to reach out to each other, and the differences highlighted here may provide adherents of both religions an opportunity to not only gain a better understanding of the other religion, but also of their own: the significant aspects of their own traditions might stand out as never before when compared to another tradition.

NOTES

1. *Preface and Conclusion from Condensation of the Exposition of the Avataṃsakasūtra*, in *Chinul: Selected Works*, trans. with introduction and annotations, Robert E. Buswell Jr., vol. 2 of *Collected Works of Korean Buddhism* (Seoul: Jogye Order of Korean Buddhism, 2012), 358 (in *Preface from the Condensation*).

2. Frederic B. Underwood, s.v. "meditation," in *Encyclopedia of Religion*, ed. Lindsay Jones, second ed. (Detroit: Macmillan Reference, 2005), 9:5816–22, at 5816.

3. He uses the term *meditatio* only twice in the *Itinerarium*. See *Itinerarium mentis in Deum* (hereafter cited as *Itin.*) 1.8, in Bonaventure, *Itinerarium Mentis in Deum*, trans. Zachary Hayes, introduction and "Notes & Commentary" by Philotheus Boehner, vol. 2 of *Works of St. Bonaventure*, rev. ed. (St. Bonaventure, NY: Franciscan Institute, 1994), 53 (hereafter cited as *WSB*).

4. *Itin.* 1.8, in *WSB*, 2:53.

5. In the *Breviloquium*, Bonaventure expounds the process of speculation as follows:

> In other righteous people it occurs in the manner of speculation, which begins with the senses and from there reaches the imagination, from the imagination proceeds to the reason, from the reason to the understanding, from the understanding to the intelligence, and from the intelligence to wisdom or even to an ecstatic knowledge, which begins in this life to reach fulfillment in eternal glory. (Bonaventure, *Breviloquium* 5.6.7, in *Breviloquium*, trans. with introduction and notes, Dominic V. Monti, vol. 9 of *WSB* [St. Bonaventure, NY: Franciscan Institute, 2005], 195)

See also Boehner, "Notes & Commentary" on *Itinerarium*, in *WSB*, 2:148–49. Bonaventure also employs the term contemplation (*contemplatio*) for both speculative meditation and intuitive contemplation. Bonaventure, *Collations on the Hexaemeron* (*Collations on the Six Days*) 5.24, in *Collations on the Hexaemeron: Conferences on the Six Days of Creation*, trans. with introduction and notes, Jay M. Hammond, vol. 18 of *WSB* (St. Bonaventure, NY: Franciscan Institute, 2018), 152–53. In addition, scholars distinguish intellectual contemplation and sapiential contemplation. For example, Maurizio Malaguti presents this Bonaventurian distinction as follows:

> There are two forms of contemplation: a) intellectual contemplation is the fruit of the gift of intelligence and leads to quiet through the possession of truth. The gift of intellect is, in fact, rational contemplation of the Creator and the spiritual creatures; b) sapiential contemplation is the gift of taste and love for truth (*sapientia*) and leads to peace and enjoyment of the supreme Good. (Maurizio Malaguti, s.v. "contemplation," in *Dizionario Bonaventuriano: Filosofia, Teologia, Spiritualità,* ed. Ernesto Caroli [Padova, Italia: Editrici Francescane, 2008], 264–71, at 265)

See also Ephrem Longpré, s.v. "Bonaventure (Saint)," in *Dictionaire de Spiritualité: Ascétique et Mystique Doctrine et Histoire,* ed. Marcel Viller, Charles Baumgartner, and André Rayez, vol. 1 (Paris: G. Beauchesne et ses fils, 1937), 1819–43.

6. This quotation is the title of chapter 7 of the *Itinerarium,* see *WSB,* 2:133.

7. See Malaguti, s.v. "contemplation," in *Dizionario Bonaventuriano,* 265.

8. See *Itin.* 7.5, in *WSB,* 2:137–39.

Appendix

Further Reading

Buswell, Robert E. Jr., ed. *Currents and Countercurrents: Korean Influences on the East Asian Buddhist Tradition*. Honolulu: University of Hawaii Press, 2005.

——, ed. *Tong Asia sok Hankuk Pulgyo sasangga*. Seoul: Tongguk taehakkyo ch'ulp'anbu, 2014.

——, *The Zen Monastic Experience: Buddhist Practice in Contemporary Korea*. Princeton, NJ: Princeton University Press, 1992.

Ch'oe, Chong-su. "Pojo Chinul ŭi Sŏn sasang e taehan chaegoch'al." In *Han'guk Pulgyo munhwa sasangsa*, vol. 1, 917–34. Seoul: Sŏul Kasan Pulgyo munhwa chinhŭngwon, 1992.

Ch'oe, Sŏng-nyŏl. "*Wŏndon Sŏngbullon* ŭi sipsin e taehayŏ." *Pulgyo hakpo* 29 (1992): 471–94.

Ch'u, Man-ho. *Namal yŏch'o Sŏn chong sasangsa yŏn'gu*. Seoul: Iron kwa silch'ŏn, 1992.

Gernet, Jacques. *Buddhism in Chinese Society: An Economic History from the Fifth to the Tenth Centuries*. Translated by Franciscus Verellen. New York: Columbia University Press, 1995.

Geumgang Center for Buddhist Studies, Geumgang University. *Korean Buddhism in East Asian Perspectives*. Seoul: Jimoondang, 2007.

Gimello, Robert M., and Peter N. Gregory, eds. *Studies in Ch'an and Hua-yen*. Honolulu: University of Hawaii Press, 1983.

Gimello, Robert M., Koh Seung-hak, Richard D. McBride II, Robert E. Buswell Jr., Hwansoo Ilmee Kim, and Yong-tae Kim. *The State, Religion, and Thinkers in Korean Buddhism*. Seoul: Dongguk University Press, 2014.

Gregory, Peter N. "Sudden Enlightenment Followed by Gradual Cultivation: Tsung-mi's Analysis of Mind." In *Sudden and Gradual: Approaches to Enlightenment in Chinese Thought*, edited by Peter N. Gregory, 279–320. Honolulu: University of Hawaii Press, 1987.

Hubbard, Jamie, and Paul L. Swanson, eds. *Pruning the Bodhi Tree: The Storm Over Critical Buddhism*. Honolulu: University of Hawaii Press, 1997.

In-gyŏng. "Pojo ŭi Hwaŏm kyohak ŭi suyong kwa pip'an: yŏn'gi mun kwa sŏnggi mun e taehan haesŏk ŭl chungsim ŭro." *Pojo sasang* 20 (2003): 9–33.

Kang, Mun-sŏn. "Tangdae Sŏn esŏ Songdae Sŏn ŭiroŭi yudongjŏk yŏnbyŏn ŭi kwajŏng: Taehye Chonggo ijŏn ŭl chungsim ŭro." *Pulgyo hakpo* 59 (2011): 7–30.

Kim, Chi-gyŏn. "Chinul esŏŭi Sŏn kwa Hwaŏm ŭi sangŭi." *Pojo sasang* 1 (1987): 123–33.

Kim, Chong-ik. "Han'guk Pulgyo che chongp'a sŏngnip ŭi yŏksajŏk koch'al." *Pulgyo hakpo* 16 (1979): 29–58.

Kim, Ing-sŏk. *Hwaŏmhak kaeron*. Seoul: Pŏmnyunsa, 1974.

Koh, Seung-Hak (Ko, Sŭng-hak). "Chinul's Hwaŏm Thought in the *Hwaŏmnon Chŏryo*." *Acta Koreana* 17, no. 1 (June 2014): 163–91.

Kye-hwan. "Hwaŏm ŭi pŏpkye yŏn'gi." *Pojo sasang* 17 (2002): 399–424.

Lancaster, Lewis R., and Chai Shin Yu, eds. *Introduction of Buddhism to Korea: New Cultural Patterns*. Berkeley: Asian Humanities Press, 1989.

Lee, Yŏng-ho (Jin Wol). "Sip-il segi Han'guk Pulgyogye ŭi Sŏn chong sanghwang kwa t'ŭkching." *Pulgyo hakpo* 56 (2010): 85–110.

Park, Kŏn-ju. "*Chŏryo sagi* wa *Kanhwa kyŏrŭiron* esŏŭi kanhwa Sŏn pŏpmun kwa kŭ munjejŏm." *Chindan hakpo* 116 (2012): 1–26.

Pyŏn, Hee-uk. "Kanhwa Sŏn esŏ am kwa alji motam ŭi ŭimi." *Ch'ŏlhak sasang* 37 (2010): 1–24.

———. "Taehye ŭi munja kongbu pip'an kwa ŏnŏ chungdo." *Pulgyo hak yŏn'gu* 10 (2005): 61–92.

Shim, Jae-ryong. *Chinul yŏn'gu: Pojo Sŏn kwa Han'guk Pulgyo*. Seoul: Sŏul taehakkyo cu'ulp'anbu, 2004.

———. *Koryŏ sidae ŭi Pulgyo sasang*. Seoul: Sŏul taehakkyo ch'ulp'anbu, 2006.

———. "Pojo kuksa Chinul ŭi *Wŏndon sŏngbullon* sangyŏk: kŭ ŭi Sŏn Kyo ilch'I ch'egye rŭl chungsim ŭro." *Pojo sasang* 13 (2000): 117–49.

Sŏ, Tae-won. "Ŏnŭi chi pyŏn kwa kyooe pyŏljŏn." *Pojo sasang* 18 (2002): 215–46.

Yi, Chong-ik. "Chinul ŭi Hwaŏm sasang." In *Sungsan Pak Kil-chin paksa hoegap kinyŏm: Han'guk Pulgyo sasang sa*, edited by Ki-du Han, 515–50. Seoul: Sungsan Pak Kil-chin Paksa Hoegap kinyŏm saŏphoe, 1975.

———. "Pojo kuksa ŭi Sŏn-Kyo kwan." *Pulgyo hakpo* 9 (1972): 67–97.

Yi, Tŏk-chin. "Chinul ŭi sŏnggisŏl e taehan ilgoch'al." *Pojo sasang* 13 (2000): 389–422.

Bibliography

Armstrong, Regis J. "Francis of Assisi and the Prisms of Theologizing." *Greyfriars Review* 10, no. 2 (1994): 179–206.

Armstrong, Regis J., OFM Cap., J. A. Wayne Hellmann, OFM Conv., and William J. Short, OFM, eds. *Francis of Assisi—The Saint.* Vol. 1 of *Francis of Assisi: Early Documents.* New York: New City Press, 1999.

———. *Francis of Assisi—The Founder.* Vol. 2 of *Francis of Assisi: Early Documents.* New York: New City Press, 2000.

Arnald of Sarrant, *Chronicle of the Twenty-Four Generals of the Order of Friars Minor.* Translated by Noel Muscat, OFM. Malta: Tau Franciscan Communications, 2010.

Barbet, Jeanne. *Corpus Christianorum Continuatio Mediaevalis.* Vol. 31. Turnholt: Brepols, 1975.

Benson, Joshua. "Bonaventure's *De reductione artium ad theologiam* and Its Early Reception as an Inaugural Sermon." *American Catholic Philosophical Quarterly* 85 (2011): 7–24.

———. "The Christology of the *Breviloquium.*" In *A Companion to Bonaventure,* edited by Jay M. Hammond, J. A. Wayne Hellmann, and Jared Goff, 247–87. Leiden: Brill, 2014.

———. "Identifying the Literary Genre of the *De reductione artium ad theologiam*: Bonaventure's Inaugural Lecture at Paris." *Franciscan Studies* 69 (2009): 149–78.

Blastic, Michael W., OFM, Jay M. Hammond, and J. A. Wayne Hellmann, OFM Conv., eds. *The Writings of Francis of Assisi: Letters and Prayers.* Vol. 1 of *Studies in Early Franciscan Sources.* St. Bonaventure, NY: Franciscan Institute, 2011.

Bonaventure. *Bonaventure: The Soul's Journey into God·The Tree of Life·The Life of St. Francis.* Translated with introduction by Ewert H. Cousins. New York: Paulist Press, 1978.

———. *Breviloquium.* Translated with introduction and notes by Dominic V. Monti. Vol. 9 of *Works of St. Bonaventure.* St. Bonaventure, NY: Franciscan Institute, 2005.

————. *Bringing Forth Christ: Five Feasts of the Child Jesus*. Translated by Eric Doyle. Oxford: Sisters of the Love of God Press, 1988.

————. *Collations on the Hexaemeron: Conferences on the Six Days of Creation*. Translated with introduction and notes by Jay M. Hammond. Vol. 18 of *Works of Bonaventure*. St. Bonaventure, NY: Franciscan Institute, 2018.

————. *Collations on the Seven Gifts of the Holy Spirit*. Translated with introduction by Zachary Hayes. Notes by Robert J. Karris. Vol. 14 of *Works of St. Bonaventure*. St. Bonaventure, NY: Franciscan Institute, 2008.

————. *Collations on the Ten Commandments*. Translated with introduction by Paul J. Spaeth. Vol. 6 of *Works of St. Bonaventure*. St. Bonaventure, NY: Franciscan Institute, 1995.

————. *Commentary on the Sentences: Philosophy of God*. Translated with introduction and notes by R. E. Houser and Timothy B. Noone. Vol. 16 of *Works of St. Bonaventure*. St. Bonaventure, NY: Franciscan Institute, 2013.

————. *Disputed Questions on the Mystery of the Trinity*. Translated with introduction by Zachary Hayes. Vol. 3 of *Works of St. Bonaventure*. 1979. Reprint, St. Bonaventure, NY: Franciscan Institute, 2000.

————. *Doctoris seraphici S. Bonaventurae opera omnia*. 10 vols. Edited by the Fathers of the Collegium S. Bonaventurae. Ad Claras Aquas (Quaracchi): Ex typographia Collegii S. Bonaventurae, 1882–1902.

————. *Itinerarium Mentis in Deum*. Translated by Zachary Hayes. Introduction and "Notes & Commentary" by Philotheus Boehner. Vol. 2 of *Works of St. Bonaventure*. Rev. ed. St. Bonaventure, NY: Franciscan Institute, 2002.

————. *Itinerarium Mentis in Deum*. Translated by Philotheus Boehner and F. Laughlin. Vol. 2 of *The Works of Bonaventure*. St. Bonaventure, NY: Franciscan Institute, 1956.

————. *On the Reduction of the Arts to Theology*. Translated with introduction by Zachary Hayes. Vol. 1 of *Works of St. Bonaventure*. St. Bonaventure, NY: Franciscan Institute, 1996.

————. *St. Bonaventure's Writings Concerning the Franciscan Order*. Translated with introduction by Dominic V. Monti. Vol. 5 of *Works of St. Bonaventure*. St. Bonaventure, NY: Franciscan Institute, 1994.

Bougerol, J. Guy. *Introduction to the Works of Bonaventure*. Translated by José de Vinck. Paterson, NJ: St. Anthony Guild, 1964.

Bouyer, Louis. *The Spirituality of the New Testament and the Fathers*. London: Burns & Oates, 1960.

Bowman, Leonard J. "Bonaventure's 'Contuition' and Heidegger's 'Thinking': Some Parallels." *Franciscan Studies* 37 (1977): 18–31.

Brewer, J. S., ed. *Monumenta franciscana*. London: Longman, 1858.

Brooke, Rosalind B. *Early Franciscan Government: Elias to Bonaventure*. Cambridge: Cambridge University Press, 1959.

————, trans. and ed. *Scripta Leonis, Rufini et Angeli Sociorum S. Francisci: The Writings of Leo, Rufino and Angelo, Companions of St. Francis*. Oxford: Oxford University Press, 1970.

Broughton, Jeffrey Lyle. *Zongmi on Chan.* New York: Columbia University Press, 2009.

Burr, David. *The Spiritual Franciscans: From Protest to Persecution in the Century after Saint Francis.* University Park, PA: Pennsylvania State University, 2001.

Buswell, Robert E. Jr. "Chinul's Ambivalent Critique of Radical Subitism in Korean Sŏn Buddhism." *The Journal of the International Association of Buddhist Studies* 12, no. 2 (1989): 20–44.

————. "Chinul's Systematization of Chinese Meditative Techniques in Korean Buddhism." In *Traditions of Meditation in Chinese Buddhism*, edited by Peter N. Gregory, 199–242. Honolulu: University of Hawaii Press, 1986.

————. "The Identity of the *Popchip pyŏrhaeng nok* [*Dharma Collection and Special Practice Record*]." *Korean Studies* 6 (1982): 1–16.

————. "Kanhwa Sŏn e issŏsŏ ŭijŏng ŭi chŏnhwan: The Transformation of Doubt in Kanhwa Sŏn." *Pojo sasang* 41 (2014): 1–16.

————. "Pojo Chinul and Kanhwa Sŏn: Reconciling the Language of Moderate and Radical Subitism." In *Zen Buddhist Rhetoric in China, Korea, and Japan*, edited by Christoph Anderl, 345–61. Leiden: Brill, 2012.

————. "The 'Short-cut' Approach of *K'an-hua* Meditation: The Evolution of a Practical Subitism in Chinese Ch'an Buddhism." In *Sudden and Gradual: Approaches to Enlightenment in Chinese Thought*, edited by Peter N. Gregory, 321–77. Honolulu: University of Hawaii Press, 1987.

————. *Tracing Back the Radiance: Chinul's Korean Way of Zen.* Honolulu: University of Hawaii Press, 1991.

————. "The Transformation of Doubt (Ŭijŏng 疑情) in Chinese Meditation." In *Love and Emotions in Traditional Chinese Literature*, edited by Halvor Eifring, 225–36. Leiden: Brill, 2004.

Buswell, Robert E. Jr., and Donald S. Lopez Jr. *The Princeton Dictionary of Buddhism.* Princeton: Princeton University Press, 2013. Kindle edition.

Carabine, Deirdre. *The Unknown God: Negative Theology in the Platonic Tradition: Plato to Eriugena.* Louvain: Peeters Press, 1995.

Caroli, Ernesto, ed. *Dizionario Bonaventuriano: Filosofia·Teologia·Spiritualità.* Padova, Italy: Editrici Francescane, 2008.

Carpenter, Charles. *Theology as the Road to Holiness in St. Bonaventure.* New York: Paulist Press, 1999.

Ch'en, Kenneth K. S. *Buddhism in China.* Princeton, NJ: Princeton University Press, 1964.

Ch'oe, Sŏng-nyŏl. "Pojo Chinul ŭi *Wondon Sŏngbullon* punsŏk." *Pŏmhan ch'ŏrhak* 24 (Autumn 2001): 131–45.

Ch'oe, Yŏn-sik (Choe, Yeonshik). "*Chinsim chiksŏl* ŭi chŏja e taehan saeroun ihae." *Chindan hakpo* 94 (2002): 77–101.

————. "Chinul Sŏn sasang ŭi sasangsajŏk kŏmt'o." *Tongbang hakchi* 144 (2008): 145–67.

————. "*Pŏpchip pyŏrhaeng nok chŏryo pyŏngip sagi* rŭl t'onghae pon Pojo sammun ŭi sŏnggyŏk." *Pojo sasang* 12 (1999): 113–46.

Chevalier, Philippe, ed. *Dionysiaca*. Vol. 1. Paris: Desclée, 1937.

Chinul, Pojo. *Chinul: Selected Works*. Translated with introduction and annotations by Robert E. Buswell Jr. Vol. 2 of *Collected Works of Korean Buddhism*. Seoul: Jogye Order of Korean Buddhism, 2012.

———. *Chŏngsŏn Chinul*. Vol. 2 of *Han'guk chŏnt'ong sasang ch'ongsŏ Pulgyo p'yŏn*. Seoul: Taehan Pulgyo Chogye chong Han'guk chŏnt'ong sasangsŏ kanhaeng wuiwŏnhoe ch'ulp'anbu, 2009.

———. *The Korean Approach to Zen: The Collected Works of Chinul*. Translated with preface and introduction by Robert E. Buswell Jr. Honolulu: University of Hawaii Press, 1983.

———. *Numinous Awareness Is Never Dark: The Korean Buddhist Master Chinul's Excerpts on Zen Practice*. Translated with introduction and annotations by Robert E. Buswell Jr. Honolulu: University of Hawaii Press, 2016.

———. *Pojo chŏnsŏ*. Seoul: Pojo sasang yŏn'guwŏn, 1989.

———. *Pojo Kuksa chip*. Seoul: Dongguk yŏkkyŏngwŏn, 1995.

———. *Pojo pŏbŏ* 普照法語. Translated by T'an-hŏ Kim. Edited by Han-am Pang. Rev. ed. Seoul: T'anhŏ Pulgyo munhwa chaedan, 2006.

Chŏng, Hŭi-kyŏng. "Pojo Chinul ŭi Sŏn Kyo ilch'i e taehan chaegoch'al." *Pojo sasang* 39 (2013): 114–47.

Chŏng, Yŏng-sik. "Ch'ŏnbok Sŭnggo, Kakpŏm Hyehong kŭrigo Pojo Chinul ŭi samhyŏn mun haesŏk." *Han'guk Pulgyohak* 54 (2009): 5–34.

Chung, Byung-jo. *History of Korean Buddhism*. Seoul: Jimoondang, 2007.

Conze, Edward, trans. *Buddhist Wisdom Books: The Diamond and the Heart Sutra*. Rev. ed. London: Unwin Paperbacks, 1988.

Corrigan, Kevin, and L. Michael Harrington. "Pseudo-Dionysius the Areopagite." *The Stanford Encyclopedia of Philosophy*. Edited by Edward N. Zalta. Summer 2018 ed. https://plato.stanford.edu/archives/sum2018/entries/pseudo-dionysius -areopagite/.

Coulter, Dale. "The Victorine Sub-structure of Bonaventure's Thought." *Franciscan Studies* 70 (2012): 399–410.

Cousins, Ewert H. *Bonaventure and the Coincidence of Opposites*. Chicago: Franciscan Herald Press, 1978.

———. "The Coincidence of Opposites in the Christology of Saint Bonaventure." *Franciscan Studies* 28 (1968): 27–45.

———. "The Image of St. Francis in Bonaventure's *Legenda Major*." In *Bonaventuriana: Miscellanea in Onore di Jacques Guy Bougerol ofm*, edited by Francisco de Asís Chavero Blanco, 311–21. Rome: Edizioni Antonianum, 1988.

Crowley, Von Theodore. "St. Bonaventure Chronology Reappraisal." *Franziskanische Studien* 56, no. 2 (1974): 310–22.

Cullen, Christopher M. *Bonaventure*. Oxford: Oxford University Press, 2006.

Delio, Ilia. *Simply Bonaventure*. Hyde Park, NY: New City Press, 2001.

———. "Theology, Metaphysics, and the Centrality of Christ." *Theological Studies* 68 (2007): 254–73.

Desbonnets, Théophile. *From Intuition to Institution: the Franciscans*. Translated by Paul Duggan and Jerry Du Charme. Chicago: Franciscan Herald, 1988.

Doyle, Eric. *The Disciple and the Master: St. Bonaventure's Sermons on St. Francis of Assisi*. Chicago: Franciscan Herald Press, 1984.

Dreyer, Elizabeth. "Affectus in St. Bonaventure's Description of the Journey of the Soul to God." PhD diss., Marquette University, 1982.

———. "Affectus in St. Bonaventure's Theology." *Franciscan Studies* 42 (1982): 5–20.

———. "Bonaventure the Franciscan: An Affective Spirituality." In *Spiritualities of the Heart: Approaches to Personal Wholeness in Christian Tradition*, edited by Annice Callahan, 33–44. New York: Paulist Press, 1990.

Dumoulin, Heinrich. *Zen Buddhism: A History—India and China*. Translated by James W. Heisig and Paul Knitter. New York: Macmillan Publishing, 1994.

Foulk, T. Griffith. "Sung Controversies Concerning the 'Separate Transmission' of Ch'an." In *Buddhism in the Sung*, edited by Peter N. Gregory and Daniel A. Getz Jr., 220–94. Honolulu: University of Hawaii Press, 1999.

Gamboso, Vergilio, ed. *Fonti agiografiche antoniane*. Padua: Edizioni Messaggero, 1985.

Gilson, Etienne. *The Philosophy of St. Bonaventure*. Translated by Dom Illtyd Trehowan and Frank J. Sheed. Paterson, NJ: St. Anthony Guild Press, 1965.

Gimello, Robert M. "Apophatic and Kataphatic Discourse in Mahāyāna: A Chinese View." *Philosophy East and West* 26, no. 2 (1976): 117–36.

———. "Mārga and Culture: Learning, Letters, and Liberation in Northern Sung Ch'an." In *Paths to Liberation: The Mārga and Its Transformations in Buddhist Thought*, edited by Robert M. Gimello and Robert E. Buswell Jr., 371–437. Honolulu: University of Hawaii Press, 1992.

———. "Mysticism in Its Contexts." In *Mysticism and Religious Traditions*, edited by Steven T. Katz, 61–88. New York: Oxford University Press, 1983.

———. "Sudden Enlightenment and Gradual Practice: A Problematic Theme in the Sŏn Buddhism of Pojo Chinul and in the Ch'an Buddhism of Sung China." *Pojo sasang* 4 (1990): 163–203.

Grayson, James Huntley. *Korea—A Religious History*. Rev. ed. New York: RoutledgeCurzon, 2002.

Gregory, Peter N. "Bridging the Gap: Zongmi's Strategies for Reconciliating Textual Study and Meditative Practice." *Journal of Chinese Buddhist Studies* 30 (2017): 89–124.

———. "The Integration of Ch'an/Sŏn and The Teachings (*Chiao/Kyo*) in Tsung-mi and Chinul." *The Journal of the International Association of Buddhist Studies* 12, no. 2 (1989): 7–19.

———. *Tsung-mi and the Sinification of Buddhism*. 1991. Paperback ed. Honolulu: University of Hawaii Press, 2002.

Grendler, Paul F. *The Universities of the Italian Renaissance*. Baltimore: Johns Hopkins University, 2002.

Ha, Mi-gyŏng. "Sŏn ŏrok ŭl t'onghan Imje samgu ŭi chŏn'gae wa kŭ t'ŭkching." *Han'guk Sŏnhak* 29 (2011): 127–67.

Hakeda, Yoshito S., trans., with introduction and commentary. *The Awakening of Faith*. New York: Columbia University Press, 1967.

Hammond, Jay M. "Bonaventure's Itinerarium: A Respondeo." *Franciscan Studies* 67 (2009): 301–21.

———. "Dating Bonaventure's Inception as Regent Master." *Franciscan Studies* 67 (2009): 179–226.

———. "Order in the *Itinerarium.*" In *Divine and Created Order in Bonaventure's Theology*, by J. A. Wayne Hellmann, translated and edited with an appendix by Jay M. Hammond, 191–271. St. Bonaventure, NY: Franciscan Institute, 2001.

Hayes, Zachary. *Bonaventure: Mystical Writings*. New York: Crossroad, 1999.

———. "Christ, Word of God and Exemplar of Humanity: The Roots of Franciscan Christocentrism and Its Implications for Today." *The Cord* 41, no. 1 (1996): 3–17.

———. "Christology and Metaphysics in the Thought of Bonaventure." In "Celebrating the Medieval Heritage: A Colloquy on the Thought of Aquinas and Bonaventure." Supplement, *The Journal of Religion* 58 (1978): S82–S96.

———. *The Hidden Center: Spirituality and Speculative Christology in St. Bonaventure*. 1981. Reprint, St. Bonaventure, NY: Franciscan Institute, 2000.

Hŏ, Hŭng-sik. *Koryŏ Pulgyosa Yŏn'gu*. Seoul: Iljogak, 1986.

———. "Koryŏ sidae ŭi kuksa·wangsa chaedo wa kŭ kinŭng." *Yŭksa hakpo* 67 (1975): 1–44.

———. "Koryŏ sidae ŭi sŭngkwa chedo wa kŭ kinŭng." *Yŏksa kyoyuk* 19 (1976): 103–38.

Im, Yŏng-suk. "Chinul ŭi ch'ansul Sŏnsŏ wa kŭ soŭikyŏngjŏn e kwanhan yŏn'gu." *Sŏjihak yŏn'gu* 1 (1986): 251–67.

In-gyŏng. *Hwaŏm kyohak kwa kanhwa Sŏn ŭi mannam—Pojo ŭi Wŏndon sŏngbullon kwa Kanhwa kyŏrŭiron yŏn'gu*. Seoul: Myŏngsang sangdam yŏn'guwŏn, 2006.

———. "*Kanwha kyŏrŭiron* ŭi Hwaŏm kyohak pip'an." *Pojo sasang* 15 (2001): 50–72.

Johnson, Timothy, ed. *Bonaventure: Mystic of God's Word*. Hyde Park, NY: New City Press, 1999.

———. "Dream Bodies and Peripatetic Prayer: Reading Bonaventure's *Itinerarium* with Certeau." *Modern Theology* 21, no. 3 (July 2005): 413–27.

———. "Place, Analogy, and Transcendence: Bonaventure and Bacon on the Franciscan Relationship to the World." In *Innovationen durch Deuten und Gestalten: Klöster im Mittelalter zwischen Jenseits und Welt*, edited by Gert Melville, Bernd Schneidmüller, and Stefan Weinfurter, 83–95. Regensburg: Schnell & Steiner, 2014.

———. "Prologue as Pilgrimage: Bonaventure as Spiritual Cartographer." *Miscellanea Francescana* 106–107 (2006–2007): 445–64.

———. "Reading Between Lines: Apophatic Knowledge and Naming the Divine in Bonaventure's Book of Creation." *Franciscan Studies* 60 (2002): 139–58.

———. *The Soul in Ascent: Bonaventure on Poverty, Prayer, and Union with God*. Rev. ed. St. Bonaventure, NY: Franciscan Institute, 2012.

Jones, Lindsay, ed. *Encyclopedia of Religion*. Second ed. Detroit: Macmillan Reference, 2005.

Kalupahana, David J. *Buddhist Philosophy: A Historical Analysis.* Honolulu: University of Hawaii Press, 1976.

———. *A History of Buddhist Philosophy: Continuities and Discontinuities.* Honolulu: University of Hawaii Press, 1992.

Kang, Kŏn-gi. *Ch'ammaŭm iyagi: Chinsim chiksŏl kangŭi.* Seoul: Puril ch'ulpansa, 2004.

———. *Chŏnghye kyŏlsamun kangŭi.* Seoul: Puril ch'ulpansa, 2006.

———. *Maŭm tangnŭn kil: Susim kyŏl kangŭi.* Second ed. Seoul: Puril ch'ulpansa, 2008.

———. *Moguja Chinul yŏn'gu.* Chŏnju, Korea: Puch'ŏnim sesang, 2001.

———. *"Susim kyŏl* ŭi ch'egye wa sasang." *Pojo sasang* 12 (1999): 9–47.

Keel, Hee-Sung. *Chinul: The Founder of the Korean Sŏn Tradition.* 1984. Reprint, Fremont, CA: Jain Publishing, 2012.

———. *"Pŏpchip pyŏrhaengnok chŏryo pyŏngip sagi* wa Chinul Sŏn sasang ŭi kusŏng [*Pŏpchip pyŏrhaengnok chŏryo pyŏngip sagi* and the Structure of Chinul's Sŏn Thought]." *Pojo sasang* 17 (2002): 379–98.

Keown, Damien. *A Dictionary of Buddhism.* Oxford: Oxford University Press, 2003. Kindle edition.

Keyworth, George A., III. "Transmitting the Lamp of Learning in Classical Chan Buddhism: Juefan Huihong (1071–1128) and Literary Chan." PhD diss., University of California Los Angeles, 2001.

Kim, Chong-myŏng. "Chinul ŭi *Pŏpchip pyŏrhaengnok chŏryo pyŏngip sagi* e mich'in ch'ogi Sŏnjongsŏ ŭi sasangjŏk yŏnghyang: Kyubong Chongmil ŭi chŏnsul ŭl chungsim ŭro." *Pojo sasang* 11 (1998): 135–90.

Kim, Jinwung. *A History of Korea: From "Land of the Morning Calm" to States in Conflict.* Bloomington, IN: Indiana University Press, 2012.

Kim, Pang-nyong. "*Chinsim chiksŏl* ŭi chŏja e taehan koch'al." *Pojo sasang* 15 (2001): 73–118.

Kim, Sŏk-am. "Pojo Chinul ŭi kanhwa kyŏngjŏl e teahayŏ." *Han'guk Sŏnhak* 5 (2003): 101–22.

Kim, Yong-tae. *Global History of Korean Buddhism.* Seoul: Dongguk University Press, 2014.

King, Sallie B. *Buddha Nature.* Albany, NY: State University of New York Press, 1991.

Ko, Ik-chin. *Han'guk kodae Pulgyo sasangsa.* Seoul: Tongguktae ch'lp'anbu, 1989.

Ko, Yŏng-sŏp. "Pojo Chinul ŭi sasang hyŏngsŏng e yŏnghyang ŭl kkich'in kosŭng: *Pojo chŏnsŏ* anp'ak ŭi kosŭngdŭl ŭl chungsim ŭro." *Pojo sasang* 42 (2014): 13–53.

Kwŏn, Ki-jong. "*Kye ch'osim hagin mun* ŭi yŏn'gu." *Pojo sasang* 12 (1999): 55–70.

Lai, Whalen. "Chinese Buddhist Causation Theories: An Analysis of the Sinitic Mahayana Understanding of Pratityasamutpada." *Philosophy East and West* 27, no. 3 (July 1977): 241–64.

Lambert, Malcolm. *Franciscan Poverty.* St. Bonaventure, NY: Franciscan Institute, 1998.

LaNave, Gregory F. "Bonaventure's Theological Method." In *A Companion to Bonaventure,* edited by Jay M. Hammond, J. A. Wayne Hellmann, and Jared Goff, 81–120. Leiden: Brill, 2014.

————. "Knowing God through and in All Things: A Proposal for Reading Bonaventure's *Itinerarium mentis in Deum*." *Franciscan Studies* 67 (2009): 267–99.

————. "The Place of Holiness in the Task of Theology according to Saint Bonaventure." PhD diss., Catholic University of America, 2002.

————. *Through Holiness to Wisdom: The Nature of Theology According to Bonaventure*. Rome: Istituto storico dei Cappuccini, 2005.

Landini, Laurentio C. "The Causes of the Clericalization of the Order of Friars Minor: 1209–1260 in the Light of Early Franciscan Sources." PhD diss., Pontificia Universitas Gregoriana, Facultas Historiae Ecclesiasticae, 1968.

Laughlin, M. F. "Joachim of Fiore," 876–77. In *New Catholic Encyclopedia*. Vol. 7. Second ed. Detroit: Gale, 2003.

Leclercq, Jean. "The Renewal of Theology." In *Renaissance and Renewal in the Twelfth Century*, edited by Robert Benson, 68–87. Toronto: University of Toronto, 1991.

Lee, Yŏng-ho (Jin Wol). "Sip-i segi ch'ogi ŭi Han'guk Sŏn chong kwa Chogye chong sŏngnip sigi sogo." *Pulgyo hakpo* 59 (2011): 129–52.

Levering, Miriam. "A Monk's Literary Education: Dahui's Friendship with Juefan Huihong." *Chung-Hwa Buddhist Journal* 13, no. 2 (May 2000): 369–84.

Longpré, Ephrem. "Bonaventure (saint)." In *Dictionnaire de Spiritualité Ascétique et Mystique, Doctrine et Histoire*. Vol. 1, edited by Marcel Viller, cols. 1773–76. Paris: G. Beauchesne et Ses Fils, 1932–1995.

Louth, Andrew. *The Origins of the Christian Mystical Tradition: From Plato to Denys*. Second ed. Oxford: Oxford University Press, 2007.

Lusthaus, Dan. "Buddhist Philosophy, Chinese." In *Routledge Encyclopedia of Philosophy*. London: Routledge, 1998. https://www.rep.routledge.com/articles/overview/buddhist-philosophy-chinese/v-1/sections/the-awakening-of-faith-in-mahayana.

Mäkinen, Virpi. *Poverty Rights in the Late Medieval Discussion on Franciscan Poverty*. Leuven: Peeters, 2001.

McGinn, Bernard. "Ascension and Introversion in the *Itinerarium Mentis in Deum*." In *S. Bonaventura 1274–1974*. Vol. 3, edited by Jacques-Guy Bougerol and Etienne Gilson, 535–52. Rome: Collegio S. Bonaventura, 1974.

————. *The Flowering of Mysticism: Men and Women in the New Mysticism (1200–1350)*. Vol. 3 of *The Presence of God: A History of Western Christian Mysticism*. New York: Crossroad, 1998.

————. *The Foundations of Mysticism: Origins to the Fifth Century*. New York: Crossroad, 1991.

————. "Thomas Gallus and Dionysian Mysticism." *Studies in Spirituality* 8 (1998): 81–96.

————. "The Victorine Ordering of Mysticism." In *The Growth of Mysticism: Gregory the Great Through the 12th Century*, 363–418. New York: Herder and Herder Book, 1994.

McRae, John R. *The Northern School and the Formation of Early Ch'an Buddhism*. Honolulu: University of Hawaii Press, 1986.

————, trans. *The Platform Sutra of the Sixth Patriarch*. BDK English Tripiṭaka Series. Berkeley: Numata Center for Buddhist Translation and Research, 2000.

Menesto, Enrico, and Stefano Brufani, eds. *Fontes Franciscani*. Assisi: Edizioni Porziuncola, 1995.

Miccoli, Giovanni. "The Writings of Francis as Sources for the History of Franciscan Origins." Translated by Edward Hagman. *Greyfriars Review* 18, no. 1 (2004): 1–21.

Migne, Jacques Paul, ed. *Patrologia Cursus Completus: Series Graeca*. Vol. 3. Paris, 1857.

————, ed. *Patrologia Cursus Completus: Series Latina*. Vol. 175. Paris, 1854.

Moorman, John. *A History of the Franciscan Order: From its Origins to the Year 1517*. Oxford: Clarendon Press, 1968.

Nimmo, Duncan. *Reform and Division in the Franciscan Order: From Saint Francis to the Foundation of the Capuchins*. Rome: Capuchin Historical Institute, 1987.

Noone, Timothy, and R. E. Houser. "Saint Bonaventure." In *The Stanford Encyclopedia of Philosophy*. Edited by Edward N. Zalta. Winter 2014 ed. http://plato.stanford.edu/archives/win2014/entries/bonaventure/.

Osborne, Kenan. *The Franciscan Intellectual Tradition: Tracing Its Origins and Identifying Its Central Components*. St. Bonaventure, NY: The Franciscan Institute, 2003.

Park, Yun-jin. "Koryŏ Chŏn'gi wangsa kuksa ŭi immyŭng kwa kŭ kinŭng." *Han'guk hakpo* 116 (2004): 139–74.

————. "Koryŏ Ch'ŏnt'ae chong ŭi chongpa munjae: Chosŏn ch'o Ch'ŏnt'ae chong ŭi Sŏn chong kwuisok ŭi yŏksajŏk paegyŭng." *Han'guksa hakpo* 40 (2010): 413–45.

————. "Koryŏ hugi wangsa·kuksa ŭi sare wa kinŭng ŭi pyŏnhwa." *Han'guk chungsesa yŏn'gu* 19 (2005): 63–116.

————. "Koryŏ sidae wansa·kuksa e taehan taeu." *Yŏksa hakpo* 190 (2006): 1–32.

Pou y Marti, José M, ed. *Bullarium Franciscanum*. Vol. 3 (1471–1484). Ad Claras Aquas (Quaracchi): Collegium S. Bonaventurae, 1949.

Pseudo-Dionysius. *Pseudo-Dionysius: The Complete Works*. Translated by Colm Luibheid. Introduction by Jaroslav Pelikan, Jean Leclercq, and Karlfried Froehlich. Mahwah, NJ: Paulist Press, 1987.

Pyŏn, Hee-uk. "Kyohak ihu, kyowoe pyŏljŏn ihu: kyowoe pyŏljŏn ŭi haesŏkhak." *Ch'ŏlhak sasang* 55 (2015): 33–59.

Quinn, John F. "Chronology of St. Bonaventure (1217–1257)." *Franciscan Studies* 32 (1972): 168–86.

Rahner, Karl. "The Doctrine of the Spiritual Senses in the Middle Ages." In *Theological Investigations*. Vol. 16. Translated by David Morland, 117–28. New York: Crossroad, 1979.

Red Pine [William Porter], trans., with introduction. *The Platform Sutra: The Zen Teaching of Hui-neng*. Berkeley: Counterpoint Point, 2006.

Reeves, Marjorie. *The Influence of Prophecy in the Later Middle Ages: A Study in Joachimism*. Oxford: Clarendon, 1969.

Roest, Bert. *Franciscan Learning, Preaching and Mission c. 1220–1650*. Vol. 10 of *The Medieval Franciscans*. Boston: Brill, 2014.

———. *A History of Franciscan Education c. 1210–1517*. Leiden: Brill, 2000.

Rorem, Paul. *Biblical and Liturgical Symbols within the Pseudo-Dionysian Synthesis*. Toronto: Pontifical Institute of Mediaeval Studies, 1984.

———. *Hugh of Saint Victor*. Oxford: Oxford University Press, 2009.

———. *Pseudo-Dionysius: A Commentary on the Texts and an Introduction to Their Influence*. Oxford: Oxford University Press, 1993.

———. "The Uplifting Spirituality of Pseudo-Dionysius." In *Christian Spirituality: Origins to the Twelfth Century*, edited by Bernard McGinn, John Meyendorff, and Jean Leclercq, 132–51. New York: Crossroad, 1985.

Rout, Paul. *Francis and Bonaventure*. Liguori, MO: Triumph, 1996.

Sabatier, Paul. *The Life of St. Francis of Assisi*. Translated by Louise S. Houghton. London: Hodder and Stoughton, 1902.

Sauer, Joseph. "Alexander of Hales." In *The Catholic Encyclopedia*. Vol. 5. New York: Robert Appleton, 1909. http://www.newadvent.org/cathen/01298a.htm.

Schlütter, Morten. *How Zen Became Zen: The Dispute over Enlightenment and the Formation of Chan Buddhism in Song-Dynasty China*. Honolulu: University of Hawaii Press, 2008.

Schmucki, Oktavian, OFM Cap. "St. Francis's Level of Education." Translated by Paul Barrett OFM. *Greyfriars Review* 10, no. 2 (1996): 153–70.

Schumacher, Lydia. "Bonaventure's Journey of the Mind into God: A Traditional Augustinian Ascent?" *Medioevo: Rivista di Storia della Filosofia Medievale* 37 (2012): 201–29.

Şenocak, Neslihan. *The Poor and the Perfect: The Rise of Learning in the Franciscan Order, 1209–1310*. Ithaca, NY: Cornell University Press, 2012.

Seth, Michael J. *A History of Korea: From Antiquity to the Present*. Lanham, MD: Rowman & Littlefield Publishers, 2011.

Sheldrake, Philip. *Spirituality and Theology: Christian Living and the Doctrine of God*. London: Darton, Longman & Todd, 1998.

Shim, Jae-ryong. *Korean Buddhism: Tradition and Transformation*. Seoul: Jimoon-dang, 1999.

———. "The Philosophical Foundation of Korean Zen Buddhism: The Integration of Sŏn and Kyo by Chinul (1158–1210)." PhD diss., University of Hawaii, 1979.

———. *Tongyang ŭi chihye wa Sŏn*. Seoul: Segyesa, 2005.

Sixtus IV. *Superna caelestis*. In http://www.franciscan-archive.org/bullarium/supern-e.html.

Sixtus V. *Triumphantis Hierusalem*. In http://www.franciscan-archive.org/bullarium/triumphe.html.

Taehan Pulgyo Chogye chong p'ogyowŏn. *Han'guk Pulgyosa: Chogye chong sa rŭl chungsim ŭro*. Seoul: Chogye chong Press, 2011.

Tavard, George H. *Transiency and Permanence: The Nature of Theology According to St Bonaventure*. St. Bonaventure, NY: Franciscan Institute, 1954.

Turner, Denys. *The Darkness of God: Negativity in Christian Mysticism.* Cambridge: Cambridge University Press, 1995.

Van Fleteren, Frederick. "The Ascent of the Soul in the Augustinian Tradition." In *Paradigms in Medieval Thought Applications in Medieval Disciplines,* edited by Nancy van Deusen and Alvin E. Ford, 93–110. Lewiston, NY: Edwin Mellen Press, 1990.

Vanneste, Jan. "Is the Mysticism of Pseudo-Dionysius Genuine?" *International Philosophical Quarterly* 3, no. 2 (1963): 286–306.

Vermeersch, Sem. *The Power of the Buddhas: The Politics of Buddhism During the Koryŏ Dynasty (918–1392).* Cambridge, MA: Harvard University Asia Center, 2008.

Viller, Marcel, Charles Baumgartner, and André Rayez, eds. *Dictionaire de Spiritualité: Ascétique et Mystique Doctrine et Histoire.* Vol. 1. Paris: G. Beauchesne et ses fils, 1937.

Wei, Ian P. *Intellectual Culture in Medieval Paris: Theologians and the University c. 1100–1330.* Cambridge: Cambridge University Press, 2012.

Welter, Albert. "Mahākāśyapa's Smile: Silent Transmission and the Kung-an (Kōan) Tradition." In *The Kōan: Texts and Contexts in Zen Buddhism,* edited by Steven Heine and Dale S. Wright, 75–109. Oxford: Oxford University Press, 2000.

Williams, Janet. "The Apophatic Theology of Dionysius the Pseudo-Areopagite-1." *Downside Review* 117, no. 408 (1999): 157–72.

Williams, Paul. *Mahāyāna Buddhism: The Doctrinal Foundations.* Second ed. London: Routledge, 2009.

Wulf, Maurice de. *The History of Medieval Philosophy.* Translated by P. Coffey. London: Longmans, Green, and Company, 1909.

Yampolsky, Philip B., trans., with introduction. *The Platform Sutra of the Sixth Patriarch.* 1967. Reprint, New York: Columbia University Press, 2012.

Yi, Pyŏng-uk. "Chongmil kwa Pojo ŭi sŏn'gyogwan pigyo." *Pojo sasang* 12 (1999): 77–112.

——. "Pojo Chinul ŭi Sŏn-Kyo t'onghap ŭi yŏrŏ yuhyŏng." *Pojo sasang* 14 (2000): 100–123.

Yoshihide, Yoshizu. *Kegonzen no shiōshi-teki kenkyū.* Tokyo: Daitō shuppansha, 1985.

Zinn, Grover A. "Book and Word. The Victorine Background of Bonaventure's Use of Symbols." In *S. Bonaventura, 1274–1974,* vol. 2, 143–69. Roma, Grottaferrata: Collegio S. Bonaventura, 1973.

——. "The Regular Canons." In *Christian Spirituality: Origins to the Twelfth Century,* edited by Bernard McGinn, John Meyendorff, and Jean Leclercq, 218–28. New York: Crossroad, 1985.

Index

admiration, 35, 167, 169–70, 172, 188n101, 188n103, 189n121
Admonitions (Francis of Assisi), 10
Admonitions to Neophytes (Chinul), 89–90
affection, 33–34; to God, 170, 254
affective consciousness (K. *chŏngsik*), 242n96
affectivity: Cousins on, 170; intellect and, 170; *Itinerarium mentis in Deum* theme, 168–71; at journey's final stage, 171
affirmation and negation dialectic, 1, 166–68, 181, 233n13
agape, 158, 183n37, 186n70
Albert of Pisa, 13
Albert the Great, 158, 163
Alexander IV (pope), 23, 24
Alexander of Hales, 7, 20–21, 58n87
Amitābha Buddha, 74, 94
anagogia (ascent spirituality), 165
Anthony of Padua: humility of, 15, 28, 53n17; poverty and, 15; simplicity of, 28
anti-intellectualism, 164
apex mentis, 171, 188n111
Apology of the Poor (Bonaventure), 23

apophaticism. *See* Buddhist cataphasis and apophasis; cataphaticism and apophaticism
Aquinas, Thomas, 60n100, 159
Aristotelianism, 23, 28; four causes in, 29; at University of Paris, 19
ascent into God: Gallus on, 164; in *Itinerarium mentis in Deum*, 38–39, 45, 160; unitive ascent, 164, 189n118
ascent spirituality (*anagogia*), 165
Augustine, 28, 31, 36, 49, 161, 165; Bonaventure influenced by, 43–44, 48, 66n197; on soul, 38
Augustinians, 7, 43
Avataṃsaka school, 73. *See also* Huayan school; Hwaŏm school
Avataṃsakasūtra, 85–86, 91, 114, 116
Awakening of Faith in Mahāyāna, 200
awakenings: of Chinul, 84–88, 142n114; to *prajñā*, 104; to *samādhi*, 104; to true reality, 255–56. *See also* realization-awakening; sudden awakening; understanding-awakening
awareness, 80; introspective, 85; Zongmi and, 224. *See also* numinous awareness

About the Author

Yongho Francis Lee is assistant professor of systematic theology at the Pontifical University Antonianum in Rome. His research focuses on the intellectual and spiritual dialogue between East and West, in particular between Buddhism and Christianity (with focus on the Franciscan tradition). His scholarly interests also include the study of ecology from an interreligious perspective and comparative theology within the Asian context.